P9-DFI-342

Encyclopedia of North American
REPTILES AND AMPHIBIANS

Encyclopedia of North American
REPTILES AND
AMPHIBIANS

CHRIS MATTISON

Thunder Bay
P·R·E·S·S
San Diego, California

597.9097
4 mat

THUNDER BAY
P · R · E · S · S

Thunder Bay Press

An imprint of the Advantage Publishers Group
5880 Oberlin Drive, San Diego, CA 92121-4794
www.thunderbaybooks.com

The Brown Reference Group plc
(incorporating Andromeda Oxford Ltd)
8 Chapel Place
Rivington Street
London EC2A 3DQ
England

ISBN 1-59223-427-5

Library of Congress Cataloging-in-Publication Data
available upon request.

Project Directors: Graham Bateman, Lindsey Lowe

Editors: Virginia Carter, Angela Davies

Art Editor and Designer: Steve McCurdy

Picture Researcher: Alison Floyd

Main Artists: Denys Ovenden, Philip Hood, Myke Taylor,
Ken Oliver

Maps: Steve McCurdy, Tim Williams

Production: Alastair Gourlay, Maggie Copeland

Printed in Singapore
1 2 3 4 5 09 08 07 06 05

Title page: **American alligator**
Half title: **Red-eyed
leaf frog**

*Pacific giant
salamander*

Contents

*American
green treefrog*

Western banded gecko

Corn snake

Common snapping turtle

Text by Val Davies

Introduction

REPTILES AND AMPHIBIANS form not one but two distinct classes of animals; in fact, it may come as a surprise to some readers to learn that reptiles are more closely related to birds than they are to amphibians. Amphibians made the transition from the totally aquatic life of fish to life on land about 365 million years ago during the Devonian Period. Reptiles evolved from amphibians some 340 million years ago, a significant development in their evolution being the laying of amniotic eggs (shelled eggs in which the embryo is surrounded by three special membranes: the amnion, chorion, and allantois). By 310 million years ago these early land-dwelling animals that laid amniotic eggs split into two branches, one that would eventually lead to the mammals and the other to today's reptiles and birds.

It is convenient, however, to study reptiles and amphibians as a single unit because both groups both contain animals that are often secretive and hard to observe without some effort (unlike birds, for example, which tend to be easy to find and watch). People who study reptiles and amphibians—herpetologists—are usually interested in both groups even though they often specialize in one or the other.

Reptiles and amphibians share one important characteristic: Unlike birds and mammals (including ourselves), reptiles and amphibians do not generate their own body heat by metabolizing food. Instead, they rely on outside sources for heat (ultimately the sun in one form or another), making these animals "ectotherms" (meaning "heat from outside"). Far from being a drawback, this method of temperature regulation gives certain advantages to reptiles and amphibians. In particular, because they do not rely on food to generate heat, they require far less food than "warm-blooded" creatures need and can therefore survive in places where there is often little to eat. That is why reptiles are often the dominant group of animals in deserts, where heat is plentiful but food is in short supply. There they can raise their body temperature easily by basking and are able to manage on about one-twelfth of the amount of food that a bird or a mammal of equivalent size would need. During periods of inactivity reptiles can last for many days, weeks, or even months with no food at all.

Dependence on external sources of heat also has a bearing on the behavior and distribution of reptiles and amphibians. They tend to be more numerous in warmer parts of the world than in cooler ones. Where they do live in cool places, they are active in the day and bask in the sun but hibernate during the winter. In warmer places they often do the opposite: They become nocturnal, keep to the shade during the day, and (if they come from very hot dry places) they may take shelter during the hottest months of the year to avoid overheating or dehydration, a process termed "estivation." Generally reptiles require higher temperatures than amphibians.

North American Diversity

BECAUSE NORTH AMERICA has such a wide range of climatic regions and habitats it has a rich and varied herpetofauna. Altogether there are about 300 species

Image of animal in typical pose

Common name	Western diamondback rattlesnake

Name and scientific classification of animal

Scientific name	*Crotalus atrox*
Subfamily	Crotalinae
Family	Viperidae
Suborder	Serpentes
Order	Squamata
Length	From 30 in (76 cm) to 7 ft (2.1 m)

Sizes given in imperial units followed by metric equivalent

Key features	Body has large diamond-shaped markings along the back, each outlined with lighter scales; background color gray to brown, may be reddish brown or pink; head large and rounded with a wide dark stripe from the eye to the angle of the jaws; tail conspicuously banded in black and white, ending in a large rattle (series of horny segments made of keratin)
Habits	Nocturnal in summer but active in late afternoon and early morning in the spring and fall; terrestrial
Breeding	Live-bearer with litters of 4–25
Diet	Small mammals up to the size of young prairie dogs and rabbits
Habitat	Desert, semidesert, arid scrub, and dry grassland
Distribution	North America almost from coast to coast; ranges from southeastern California and the Gulf of California to the Gulf Coast of Texas and south into Mexico
Status	Very common in places
Similar species	The Mojave rattlesnake, *C. scutulatus*, is very similar, and its range overlaps in places
Venom	A potent hemotoxin leading to severe symptoms and possibly death unless treated

Basic description of animal, its life, its distribution, and conservation status (see Glossary)

Locator maps showing each animal's normal range

⊕ *Summary panel presents key facts and figures for each animal.*

of reptiles and 200 species of amphibians, ranging from the huge alligators of the southern swamps to tiny frogs no bigger than a fingernail and burrowing snakes as thin as shoelaces. The continent is especially rich in salamanders; there are more species and families (128 species in 9 families) than anywhere else in the world.

The warmer southern states are home to more reptile species than the cooler northern ones, whereas the climate in the northern parts is more suitable for amphibians. The other effect of climate is to limit the occurrence of large species, whose bodies take a long time to warm up, to warmer regions. So the southern states, as well as having more species, also tend to have the largest ones. The American alligator, for example, is only found in the Southeast. Also, all the largest snakes and lizards are southern; many of them are found in the deserts of the Southwest, which is a haven for reptiles.

All these factors obviously affect the ease with which reptiles and amphibians can be found and studied. Under warm conditions it may be necessary to search for them at night or by looking under stones, logs, and trash during the day, when they are hiding. In northern states searching for them during the winter is fruitless, although they may be present in large numbers in the spring. This is especially true of many amphibians, which are explosive breeders with many hundreds of individuals migrating to breeding ponds within a few days of each other. Searching for salamanders in the Pacific Northwest can be extremely rewarding but requires sharp eyes and the willingness to face damp, cool weather.

Among other important groups the iguanid lizards, such as fence lizards, collared lizards, and chuckwallas are numerous in drier regions. It is possible to watch them easily with a pair of close-focusing binoculars if you sit quietly. Many of the world's rattlesnake species live in the desert regions of the United States, notably in Arizona, which has more species than any other state. They tend to be particularly active at night, although some may also be seen during the day.

The rattlesnakes and a few related pit vipers, such as the cottonmouth and the copperhead, are the only reasonably common dangerous snakes in North America; even so, the number of people killed by snakes is minuscule—less than 10 per year—compared with the number of snakes killed by people, especially in cars. Many snakes, including harmless species, are also killed deliberately and unnecessarily out of prejudice.

Encyclopedia of North American Reptiles and Amphibians

IN THIS ENCYCLOPEDIA there are detailed articles of 82 species and groups of related reptiles and amphibians, all occurring in Central and North America, with most in the United States. Two introductory articles (What is an Amphibian? and What is a Reptile?) describe the body structure, biology, and natural history of amphibians and reptiles respectively. The articles that follow have been selected to give the broadest range of animals found in these areas. For each animal there is a detailed summary panel (see left) that gives key facts and figures. Then the main article describes the animal's most interesting features. Throughout there are detailed artwork portrayals and dynamic photographs of the animals in the wild.

An interest in reptiles and amphibians will soon lead to the realization that these animals are affected by human activities almost more than any others. Unlike birds and mammals, reptiles and amphibians are not very mobile; many individuals live out their whole lives in a few square yards, while some entire species have ranges that can be measured in acres. This makes reptiles and amphibians especially vulnerable since, once wiped out, a population is unlikely to recover through recolonization.

Pollution and habitat destruction are the worst enemies of reptiles and amphibians, although the reasons for the rapid disappearance of many amphibians are not clear. Many species that were common just a generation ago are now hard to find, and some will never be seen again. Many scientists predict that one-third of the world's frogs will be extinct within a decade. Amphibians have been likened to the canaries that miners used to carry—they are sensitive to changes and their decline is an indicator that all is not right with the environment. The challenge for future generations will be to find a way to arrest these declines or reverse them.

WHAT IS AN AMPHIBIAN?

Amphibians are vertebrates that evolved from fish about 350 to 400 million years ago. They share some characteristics with fish, and most of them return to the water for the most important event in their life—reproduction. All amphibians have certain characteristics in common with each other, including an aquatic larval stage (known as tadpoles), although some do not need water to lay their eggs—instead, they develop inside the egg capsule or, in a few cases, inside the body of one of their parents.

While the body shape of amphibians can vary, they are all covered with skin through which they can breathe. In order to do this, the skin has to be kept moist with secretions produced by glands just below the surface, so many amphibians are slightly moist or slimy to the touch. Most of them live in damp places to avoid drying out. However, some species rely more on skin breathing (cutaneous respiration) than others, and a few can even survive in deserts because they have evolved physical and behavioral adaptations to that hostile environment.

As a very rough guide, amphibians with dry skin, such as typical toads in the genus *Bufo*, tend to use their lungs more and their skin less than those with moist skin, such as most typical frogs in the genus *Rana*. At the opposite extreme a number of amphibians—especially newts and salamanders, but also a few frogs and caecilians—are totally aquatic and never voluntarily leave the water, even after they have transformed into adults.

Amphibians are divided into three groups, or orders. They are the Caudata (formerly Urodela), which includes the newts and salamanders, the Anura (frogs and toads), and the Gymnophiona (caecilians).

Caecilians

The Gymnophiona contains about 159 species and is not very well known. Its members are elongated amphibians that are mostly restricted to tropical countries. They have a series of annuli, or rings, around their bodies, and they resemble earthworms. Caecilians have internal fertilization; some species lay eggs, but others give birth to live young. Some spend their whole lives in water, whereas others leave the water after they have metamorphosed and live in burrows in damp soil and leaf litter.

Definitions and Exceptions

The word amphibian comes from the Greek *amphi* and *bios*, literally meaning "two lives," and amphibians are often described as vertebrates that have an aquatic larval stage and an adult stage that lives on land. There are many exceptions to that description, however, including some species that do not have an aquatic larval stage as well as others that do not have a terrestrial adult stage.

Nevertheless, all amphibians (with the possible exception of the caecilians) are easily recognizable for what they are: They are animals with smooth, moist skins; they are more or less tied to damp habitats, and they nearly always require a body of fresh water in which to breed.

CLASS AMPHIBIA—3 orders, 44 families, over 5,359 species

Order Gymnophiona—caecilians: 6 families, about 36 genera, 159 species

Order Caudata (Urodela)—salamanders and newts: 10 families, 58 genera, over 400 species

Order Anura—frogs and toads: 28 families, about 346 genera, over 4,800 species

⊕ Likely to be mistaken for large earthworms, caecilians are long-bodied, limbless amphibians with virtually no tail. This is an Asiatic yellow-striped caecilian, Ichthyophis species.

There are many gaps in our knowledge of them because they are so difficult to find and observe, and it is likely that many more species await discovery.

Newts and Salamanders

The other two groups are more familiar. Newts and salamanders, of which there are just over 400 species, typically have roughly cylindrical bodies with a tail and four legs (although some have only two legs). Many of them return to water at some stage, often in the spring, to lay their eggs. Some develop enlarged fins and brighter colors at this time. Others breed on land.

Newts and salamanders are found mostly in the Northern Hemisphere in Europe, Asia, and in North, Central, and South America, but a few species reach

⊖ Frogs come in many sizes and colors. Some, like Rhacophorus arboreus, the Japanese treefrog, live in trees and build foam nests around their eggs.

⊙ Typical salamanders have an elongated body, a long tail, and two pairs of legs, as in Rhyacotriton cascadae, the cascade torrent salamander.

extreme northern Africa. They shun the light and live in dark, damp places, rarely appearing on the surface in the daytime except during rain. Some species live in caves, and others live in underground streams; several of them do not metamorphose, living their entire lives as larvae and breeding in that condition.

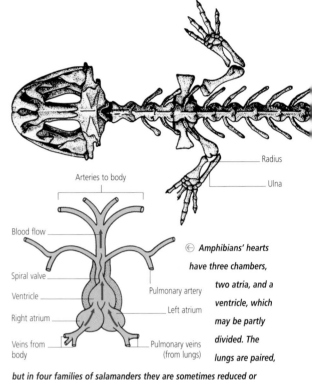

⊕ *Fertilized eggs of amphibians have gelatinous envelopes but lack the protective membrane found in all higher vertebrates. Amphibian eggs also lack shells and therefore must be laid in fresh water or in moist places to avoid drying out. Larvae possess external gills, and in frog tadpoles they become enclosed in a chamber by a flap of skin (the operculum). Metamorphosis from larva to adult stage is often abrupt, and the two forms may differ markedly in structure.*

Unfertilized egg

Unswollen gelatinous envelope (jelly)

Vitelline membrane

Fertilized egg

Inner jelly capsule

Outer gelatinous envelope (jelly)

Arteries to body

Blood flow

Spiral valve

Ventricle

Right atrium

Veins from body

Pulmonary artery

Left atrium

Pulmonary veins (from lungs)

Radius

Ulna

⊖ *Amphibians' hearts have three chambers, two atria, and a ventricle, which may be partly divided. The lungs are paired, but in four families of salamanders they are sometimes reduced or completely absent; in caecilians the left lung is greatly reduced.*

Amphibian Fertilization

Fertilization in amphibians can be internal or external. Nearly all frogs have external fertilization: The male fertilizes the eggs by releasing his sperm over them as they emerge from the female's body. This is usually done while he is clasping her in a hold known as "amplexus." Amplexus helps align the male and female cloacae so that the eggs have the best chance of being fertilized.

Most salamanders, however, have internal fertilization: The male's sperm fertilizes the female's eggs while they are still in her body. Internal fertilization is less wasteful than external fertilization, which can be a hit-and-miss affair, with sperm being washed away before it reaches some of the eggs. Internal fertilization also allows salamanders to mate on the land, whereas most frogs have to mate in the water—not always the safest or most convenient place. The only salamanders that have external fertilization are species

that are thought to have evolved early on, many of which live in water, such as the hellbenders. All caecilians have internal fertilization.

With internal fertilization the male deposits a package of sperm (a spermatophore) after courtship that can include amplexus or after a visual display with little or no contact. The female immediately picks up the spermatophore with her cloaca and transfers it to a spermatheca—a small chamber near the end of her reproductive tract. The spermatophore stays there until the eggs move down the oviduct, past the spermatheca, at which point they are fertilized. Some species can store sperm in the spermatheca for many months or even years, while others can store it only for a few days or weeks. In live-bearing species the sperm fertilizes the eggs while they are still high up inside the oviduct, where they continue their development.

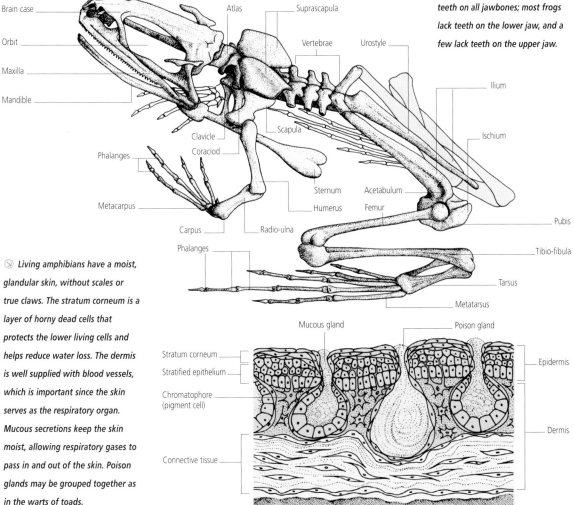

Fibula

Tibia

Tail vertebrae

Femur

Maxillary bone

Pedicle

Socket

Crown

Joint

↑ ↓ The skeletons of salamanders and frogs reveal many of the ways in which the two groups have evolved independently. Salamanders have a long, flexible body and a long tail supported by many vertebrae, whereas frogs have no tail and a short, rigid backbone consisting of a greatly reduced number of vertebrae. The fore- and hind limbs of salamanders are of roughly equal size; but the hind limbs of most frogs have become greatly lengthened, enabling them to leap large distances, and they are supported by a massive, strong pelvic girdle. Frogs have much larger heads relative to their body size, and both groups have very wide mouths, enabling them to take large prey. Their skulls provide plenty of space for their well-developed eyes.

↑ Amphibians have pedicellate teeth, with the crown attached to a narrow pedicel (or base) by uncalcified fibrous tissue, allowing the tooth to bend inward. Salamanders and caecilians have teeth on all jawbones; most frogs lack teeth on the lower jaw, and a few lack teeth on the upper jaw.

Brain case

Atlas

Suprascapula

Vertebrae

Urostyle

Orbit

Maxilla

Mandible

Ilium

Ischium

Clavicle

Scapula

Phalanges

Coraciod

Metacarpus

Sternum

Acetabulum

Humerus

Femur

Carpus

Radio-ulna

Pubis

Phalanges

Tibio-fibula

Tarsus

Metatarsus

↘ Living amphibians have a moist, glandular skin, without scales or true claws. The stratum corneum is a layer of horny dead cells that protects the lower living cells and helps reduce water loss. The dermis is well supplied with blood vessels, which is important since the skin serves as the respiratory organ. Mucous secretions keep the skin moist, allowing respiratory gases to pass in and out of the skin. Poison glands may be grouped together as in the warts of toads.

Mucous gland

Poison gland

Stratum corneum

Stratified epithelium

Epidermis

Chromatophore (pigment cell)

Dermis

Connective tissue

Most newts and salamanders are rather dull in color to match the background against which they live, but several have brightly colored undersides. Others have bold warning colors to signal that they have poison glands in their skin. Many cave-dwelling species are pale, and their internal organs are sometimes visible through their skin.

Adult newts and salamanders eat invertebrates such as earthworms and grubs, and large species may also eat other amphibians and small vertebrates such as mice. Their larvae are carnivorous and eat small aquatic invertebrates such as crustaceans, which are often abundant in the rich waters in which they develop.

Most salamanders have internal fertilization and lay eggs that they attach to stones or water plants. However, a few primitive species have external fertilization. A few

Cutaneous Respiration

Aquatic salamanders, caecilians, and frogs may absorb all (or nearly all) the oxygen they need through their skin. In this way they avoid having to come to the surface to breathe at regular intervals. Members of the salamander family Plethodontidae have done away with lungs altogether and are commonly called lungless salamanders.

Because of the surface-area-to-body-mass ratio most of the "skin breathers" are small; but some larger species also breathe through their skin, using anatomical and behavioral "tricks" to increase the amount of oxygen they can take in.

Aquatic skin breathers need to live in waters that are rich in oxygen, which usually means cool, fast-flowing streams with turbulence. Wide mountain rivers and streams that run over gravel and rocks, forming riffles, are ideal and are the home of species such as the hellbender, *Cryptobranchus alleganiensis*, and aquatic frogs such as the Lake Titicaca frog, *Telmatobius culeus*. These amphibians may enhance their oxygen uptake even more by developing highly vascular skin—frilly folds of skin along their flanks that increase their surface area—or by shaking periodically to prevent oxygen-depleted water from forming a "jacket" around them.

give birth to well-developed larvae, and a couple of species retain the larvae in their oviducts until they are fully developed, at which point they are born on land.

Frogs and Toads

Frogs and toads are the most successful group of amphibians, with about 4,800 species found throughout most of the world except Antarctica. They are most numerous in tropical regions, where over 50 species may live side by side in a small area of forest. They can coexist because they have diversified into many different lifestyles, or "niches." For example, there may be species living in the forest canopy, in tree holes, in leaf litter, or in burrows, all within a small area of forest. There are also variations in body size, in the prey they eat, the methods by which they find it, and their breeding places.

Frogs and toads may be active by day or by night, they may rely on camouflage for defense against predators, or they may be brightly colored to warn of potent toxins in their skin. All these variations limit the amount of competition between species.

Frogs and toads are carnivorous, and their prey includes animals as diverse as small soil-dwelling invertebrates that are almost invisible to the human eye up to mice, rats, and snakes, depending on the size of the frog. Many species also eat smaller frogs and toads, and some eat the young of their own species. They may actively search for prey, or they may wait in ambush for it. Many species' tadpoles, however, are herbivorous, feeding on the layers of algae and bacteria that accumulate on rocks, plants, and other underwater debris. They feed by rasping away at these surfaces, using several rows of teeth positioned above and below the mouth.

Frogs and toads have a remarkably varied repertoire of breeding habits. With just a handful of exceptions they have external fertilization—the male releases sperm over the eggs as the female lays them. Males of most species find mates by calling. Frogs are among the most vocal of animals, with several hundred males sometimes coming together to form breeding choruses that can be heard for several miles. Most North American and European species lay their eggs in ponds and rivers. The eggs hatch into

⊙ *A frog fossil from France,* Rana aquensis, *dates from the Oligocene epoch, beginning 37 million years ago. It is believed that all three groups of modern amphibians shared a common ancestor.*

tadpoles that subsequently develop legs, then lungs, and finally absorb their tails before emerging onto land as small replicas of their parents.

In other parts of the world, however, breeding does not always follow the same pattern. There are species that lay their eggs out of the water, sometimes on leaves overhanging ponds, for example, so that the tadpoles can drip into the water as they hatch. Sometimes they lay their eggs in damp moss, where the whole of their development takes place inside the egg, and they hatch as froglets. In other species the parents carry the eggs, and sometimes also the tadpoles, to protect them during the early part of their development and to ensure that they get a good start.

Amphibian Ancestors

The earliest amphibian fossils have been found in Australia and Greenland. They were formed in the Devonian Period (410 to 325 million years ago), when the continents were joined into a single landmass (known as Pangaea), and Greenland lay over the equator. Most scientists think that amphibians sprang from a group of fish whose members are extinct now. They are known as the crossopterygians, and they had lungs and bony frames to their fins.

→ *From fish to amphibian. Crossopterygian fish,* Eusthenopteron *(1);* Ichthyostega, *one of the earliest amphibians, c. 300 million years ago (2).*

→ *Giant amphibians from the Triassic, 225–190 million years ago.* Mastodonsaurus *(3) measured 13 feet (4 m) from snout to tip of tail;* Diadectes *(4) was 10 feet (3 m) long; and* Eryops *(5) was smaller, at 5 feet (1.5 m) in length.*

13

The fins evolved eventually into four limbs, allowing the early ancestors of amphibians to crawl out of the water and support themselves on the land. The reason they left the water is anybody's guess, but it may have been to avoid competition, find new sources of food, or colonize new bodies of water when their pools started to dry out or became too crowded. Most of these early amphibians had already died out by the Jurassic Period, 220 million years ago.

The origins of the three living orders of amphibians and their relationships to each other are a mystery. The oldest fossil amphibian to bear any resemblance to species alive today was a primitive frog called *Triadobatrachus* that lived about 250 million years ago. It had more vertebrae than modern frogs and a short tail. Fossil salamanders have also been found, including one from China dating from about 150 million years ago. It differs little from the surviving species of hellbenders and giant salamanders. There are no fossils showing the links between the fishlike ancestors and modern salamanders and caecilians. This gives us no clue to the appearance of the ancestors of either of these groups or to when they may have started to follow different evolutionary paths. We will have to wait until older fossil amphibians are discovered before we can fill in some of the gaps.

Conservation

Reading about amphibians and their problems in a modern world can be a sobering and, at times, depressing experience. Time and time again the phrases "diminishing populations," "threatened with extinction," and "possibly extinct" crop up.

Species at risk range from the frail-looking olm, *Proteus anguinus*, in Italy and Slovenia (whose cave-system habitat is being slowly poisoned by chemicals seeping down through the limestone) to the pugnacious and seemingly indestructible giant salamanders of the Pacific Northwest, whose crystal-clear mountain streams

⊝ *Now probably extinct, the Costa Rican golden toad,* Bufo periglenes, *was discovered in the 1960s. Over 1,000 were seen at a breeding site in 1987; but only 11 were present in 1990, and none have been seen since.*

are becoming silted up through clear-cutting of forests. This causes silt to accumulate on the riverbeds, filling in the spaces between the gravel in which the larvae live, clogging up their gills, and making it difficult for them to find food. The unique and rare tailed frog, *Ascaphus truei*, which lives in these streams, is also facing an uncertain future.

Problems exist on a small scale at a local level and on a large scale globally. Local pressures include deforestation in rain forests and elsewhere, draining of wetlands, and small-scale pollution such as runoff from paved roads and dumping of chemicals in ponds and streams. Many small farm and village ponds used for breeding by countless generations of newts, salamanders, frogs, and toads have been filled in for safety reasons or for convenience. They are often replaced by a galvanized trough and a hose pipe or are filled with supermarket shopping trolleys and other detritus. Even species that were common until recently have started to disappear from the countryside at an alarming rate.

On a global level conservationists have identified several other causes for declining populations. They include the depletion of ozone in the atmosphere, which may increase exposure to ultraviolet (UVB)

radiation, possibly affecting eggs and developing larvae; the accumulation of pollutants, including acid rain, in the atmosphere and water systems; changes in weather patterns; and viral and other diseases. The latter may be aggravated by stress caused by other factors and may also be spread by the movement and introduction of exotic species, so it is often difficult to separate the different causes in any particular case.

Driven to Extinction

One of the more worrying aspects is the decline of species that has taken place in some of the most pristine habitats on earth, including nature reserves and national parks. Herpetologists have monitored amphibian populations in several parts of the world since the 1980s, and in 1991 the Declining Amphibian Population Task Force (DAPTF) was established to coordinate research throughout the world. Some of the findings include 36 species that are thought to have gone extinct recently, three of which disappeared before they were even named.

⊜ *In Europe signs warn motorists of the seasonal presence of frogs and toads. Other measures are being taken to conserve local toad populations: A female toad carrying a male approaches a wide-gauge grid. They will fall through and continue their journey safely under the road.*

Amazing Statistics

The largest living amphibian is the Chinese giant salamander, *Andrias davidianus*, which can reach almost 6 feet (1.8 m) in length and weigh up to 50 pounds (22 kg). The largest frog is the Goliath frog, *Conraua goliath* from West Africa, one of which measured 34.5 inches (88 cm) and weighed just over 8 pounds (3.6 kg). The largest caecilian is *Caecilia thompsoni* (it has no common name), which grows to 5 feet (1.5 m).

Establishing the smallest species is harder. Since they all start life small, it can be difficult to know if you are measuring an adult or juvenile. The smallest caecilian is probably *Grandisonia brevis* from the Seychelles, which has a maximum size of about 4.4 inches (11 cm), and the smallest salamander is *Thorius arboreus*, one of the lungless salamanders from the highlands of Mexico.

There are several contenders for the smallest frog species, including several rain frogs in the genus *Eleutherodactylus*, a saddle-back toad, *Psyllophryne didactyla* from southern Brazil, and the stump-toed frog, *Stumpffia tridactyla* from Madagascar. They all grow to about 0.4 inches (10 mm) in length.

Many amphibians have natural life spans of one year or less, but others are more long-lived. The record is held by a Japanese giant salamander, *Andrias japonicus*, which lived 55 years in captivity, while a fire salamander, *Salamandra salamandra*, lived 50 years, and a European common toad, *Bufo bufo*, lived to the age of 36.

⊕ *In southern Cameroon a boy holds up a Goliath frog,* Conraua goliath*. These giants of the frog world can reach 34.5 inches (88 cm) in size and weigh as much as a domestic cat.*

Eleven of the extinct species are small *Atelopus* toads from the Andes of Ecuador, which (superficially at least) is one the least changed habitats in the world. In addition, another 26 species of frogs and toads have not been seen for five years or more and may well be extinct, and another 91 are Critically Endangered (IUCN).

These figures come from a small number of countries, among which Venezuela, Ecuador, Brazil, and Australia figure prominently. The situation in Central and West Africa, for instance, or in parts of Southeast Asia has not even been studied thoroughly. Secretive species such as many frogs, toads, and salamanders, and all the caecilians, are so poorly understood that they could go extinct before we even know of their existence.

Why should we care? From a purely selfish point of view we should consider that amphibians are indicators of the health of our environment. Because of their need for aquatic as well as terrestrial habitats, and because they respire across the surface of their necessarily delicate skin, amphibians react more quickly than most other animals to factors that affect their environments.

But what affects their health today may well affect ours tomorrow. Setting that fact aside, the disappearance of even one species affects anyone who values biodiversity. Frogs, newts, and salamanders are part of the web of life that makes nature so interesting and important to everyone. Some of them are attractive, many have interesting stories to tell, and all deserve their place in the world. The American environmentalist Aldo Leopold summed it up when he said, "The art of intelligent tinkering is to keep all the parts."

Amphibians as Pets

Generally speaking, amphibians are slightly more difficult to keep in captivity than reptiles because they tend to be more sensitive to environmental conditions. Because they breathe through their permeable skins, they also take up toxins that way, so they must have spotlessly clean accommodation and water that is free from chemical contaminants, including disinfectants and cleaning materials. It is a good idea to choose captive-bred specimens whenever possible because they will adapt better than wild ones, and keeping them will not contribute to the decline of wild stocks.

Aquatic species are often the easiest option because there is plenty of equipment for keeping aquarium fish that is equally suitable for species such as clawed frogs, dwarf aquarium frogs, and axolotls. The first two species are tropical, but the axolotl does not require heated water, just good filtration. Other species, such as newts, spend part of each year in the water and may refuse to feed unless they are given access to it. Several others are flexible and can be kept in water or on the land. The oriental fire-bellied toad, *Bombina orientalis*, is one of the most popular pet species and requires a setup that is roughly half land and half water. Other popular species are the horned frogs, *Ceratophrys*, which can be kept in shallow water or on a moist substrate such as moss.

Salamanders and most frogs and toads are terrestrial for almost the whole year, only needing water for a short period for breeding. Unless you are hoping to breed these species, they can be kept in a terrestrial setup all year round, with a layer of leaf litter and places to hide, such as pieces of flat stone or bark. Attractive vivaria can be built using living plants and even running water; but that is rarely necessary except in the case of certain difficult tropical species, such as poison dart frogs, which beginners should avoid.

Creating the Right Conditions

Many amphibians, even those from the tropics, prefer cooler temperatures than reptiles, and heating is often necessary only in a very cold climate. There are exceptions, however, and advice should be sought from a specialized publication or the place where the amphibians were bought. Similarly, light should be subdued because amphibians lead secretive lives, and they become stressed if they are forced to live under the glare of bright lights.

Humidity is obviously important, and even terrestrial species such as the toads, *Bufo*, should have their cage sprayed with water regularly to make sure they do not dry out. Ventilation is equally important, since amphibians do not thrive in a stagnant atmosphere.

⬆ *A rain-forest environment has been carefully created in a terrarium at a Dutch zoo. The tank is home to a number of poison dart frogs, which are highly toxic and best left to expert keepers.*

Nearly all amphibians are insectivorous: Even large species, such as the horned frogs (which will eat small mammals and other frogs), can live their entire lives on a diet of insects such as crickets and locusts. Many species (including aquatic frogs and newts) also like worms, which can be obtained (or dug up) in a variety of sizes. Most frog and toad tadpoles are herbivorous and will usually feed on algae that builds up on the surface of plants and rocks, but they will also eat flaked fish food and a variety of other special diets.

Encouraging Amphibians

It is possible to enjoy amphibians without having to keep them captive. A small garden pond with an overgrown area around the edge can provide an ideal habitat for many species of frogs, toads, newts, and salamanders,

⊕ *The oriental fire-bellied toad,* Bombina orientalis, *is probably the best terrestrial frog for the beginner to keep as a pet. It is named for its attractive underside, which is orange with black spots.*

and will help replace habitats that have been lost through urban development. Some amphibians will visit the pond to breed in the spring and then disappear into the surrounding countryside; but others will remain close by, especially if there are hiding places in the form of log piles and rockeries. Artificial substances, such as weed killers or pesticides, should be avoided. If all goes well, the garden should not need pesticides, since the amphibians will keep pests under control. Be aware that in many places it is illegal to introduce nonlocal species; however, even a small pond that provides a home to a single species of frog or newt can be very rewarding.

Common name Hellbender (mud devil, ground puppy, Allegheny alligator, big water lizard, devil dog)

Scientific name *Cryptobranchus alleganiensis*

Family Cryptobranchidae

Order Caudata (Urodela)

Size 12 in (30 cm) to 29 in (74 cm)

Key features Head and body strongly flattened; there is a wrinkled fold of skin along each flank; eyes small and gray; body yellowish brown or olive-green in color with irregular black spots, some of which may clump together to make larger blotches; eyelids absent

Habits Usually nocturnal; hides by day under rocks and submerged logs but also active in the day during rain, especially in the breeding season

Breeding Fertilization is external; females lay 150–400 eggs in an underground nest

Diet Mainly crayfish; small fish, other hellbenders, tadpoles, toads, and water snakes also recorded

Habitat Clear, fast-flowing mountain streams with no silt

Distribution North America from southern New York State to northern Alabama

Status Formerly common but becoming increasingly rare due to habitat destruction, silting, and pollution of the streams in which it lives

Similar species None in the region; the related giant salamanders of Japan and China (*Andrias japonicus* and *A. davidianus)* are similar but even larger

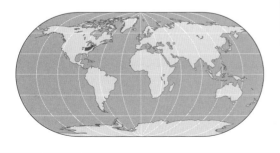

Hellbender *Cryptobranchus alleganiensis*

Hellbenders are bizarre and interesting inhabitants of the crystal-clear mountain streams flowing from the Appalachian Mountains of eastern North America. Their future is in doubt due to human activities.

LIKE THEIR CLOSE RELATIVES the giant salamanders, hellbenders require clear, shallow, well-oxygenated streams and rivers with a rocky bottom. They use the spaces between the rocks to hide in. Adults and juveniles require spaces of a different size, so a good mix of large rocks and smaller gravel is important. Flowing water keeps smaller particles from filling the gaps and also helps maintain a good level of oxygen in the water. If the river is dammed, if silt accumulates through disturbance on the banks upstream, or if the water is polluted by agricultural runoff, chemicals, or mining activity, the hellbenders disappear.

Night Feeding

Hellbenders spend much of the daytime hiding under rocks on the riverbed. They are territorial and rarely share a rock: Animals trying to crawl beneath an occupied rock are chased away. At night they venture out and crawl slowly over the bottom in search of food. Their main prey is crayfish, and they will eat up to four in one night; but they take a variety of other food as well, including small fish and fishing bait. They also eat each other, especially as eggs or larvae.

They appear to use a combination of sight and smell for finding food and will work their way upstream following its scent. They feed by means of a sideways snap or by simply opening their mouth wide, causing water (and prey) to rush into it. In captivity they will eat pieces of meat—the general feeling is that hellbenders will eat almost anything. They rarely wander far during a night's hunting and usually return to their own rock by morning. Average movement is about 30 to 60 feet (9–18 m), but males have larger home ranges than females.

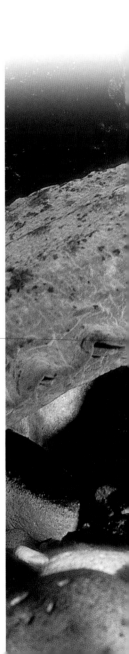

In suitable conditions hellbenders occur at high densities, with an estimated 10 animals per 120 square yards (100 sq. m) of stream in parts of the White River in Missouri. Estimates over the same area in other rivers range from one to six animals. Hellbenders occasionally leave the water voluntarily and may crawl up onto emergent rocks, but they never go far.

The color and pattern of hellbenders provide good camouflage against the jumbled rocks of the riverbed. The coloration is particularly effective against a scattering of dead oak leaves from overhanging trees in the fall, when they are more likely to be on the move during the day. Occasional animals are orange or reddish in color—the result of random mutations. They do not, as earlier writers believed, belong to a separate species that they called *Cryptobranchus fuscus*.

Hellbenders produce large amounts of slimy secretions from glands in their skin. The secretions deter some predators and parasites. They are bitter to taste and create a burning sensation if they come into contact with an open wound. Some predators seem to avoid hellbenders for this reason, but hellbenders of all ages are eaten by large fish, turtles, and water snakes.

⊕ The ideal habitat for hellbenders is among rocks of varying sizes on the beds of shallow streams and rivers. They hide under the rocks by day and make nests beneath them in the breeding season.

Breathable Skin

Hellbenders have lungs, but they hardly ever come to the surface to breathe because they can obtain nearly all their oxygen through cutaneous (skin) respiration. In experiments hellbenders were prevented from surfacing with no apparent ill effects, and one survived even after having its lungs surgically removed.

Most of their oxygen requirement is absorbed through the skin—the many folds and crenellations on the skin increase the surface area over which breathing can take place. The folds have a dense network of capillaries close to the surface and are, in effect, inside-out lungs. In quiet or warm water that is not well endowed with oxygen, hellbenders sway from side to side, causing the skin folds to undulate. The movement probably serves to send the "jacket" of oxygen-depleted water away from the surface of the folds and replace it with more highly oxygenated water.

Young larval hellbenders have feathery external gills, which they lose at about 18 months old. The generic name *Cryptobranchus*, meaning "hidden gills," is therefore inaccurate—the young have gills that are not hidden, whereas the adults have no gills. Being smaller and lacking the numerous folds in their skin, the young probably need the external gills to extract enough oxygen from the water.

Breeding

Hellbenders have a complicated and unusual breeding system. Unlike in most salamanders (but as in frogs), fertilization is external. Males and females occur in roughly equal numbers. They are similar to each other, but males may have larger skin folds along

Adaptations

Despite their ungainly appearance and ponderous lifestyle, hellbenders are superbly adapted to the shallow, fast-flowing rocky streams in which they live. Their flattened shape offers little resistance to the flowing water, allowing them to work their way upstream and also to crawl into narrow spaces under rocks. Although their eyesight is relatively poor, they have light-sensitive cells over their whole body. Those on their tail are especially finely tuned and may help them position themselves safely under rocks without their tail poking out to give the game away. They have a good sense of smell and will move upstream in search of food such as a dead fish, following the trail of scent molecules. Smell is possibly their most important sense when hunting. They also have a lateral line similar to that of fish, with which they can detect vibrations in the water.

their flanks and on the outside of the legs, and females become swollen with eggs at the start of the breeding season. They mate in the fall, from late August through mid-November, with some variation depending on where they live.

At this time they become restless. They move around on the riverbed even during the day and may congregate in unusually large numbers. They poke around among the boulders, and males choose a brooding site to develop. It is a depression in the gravel, scooped out under a large, flat rock, with its entrance facing downstream. Once it is built, the males sit in the nest with their heads poking out, waiting for females. When a ripe female comes along, the male may emerge from the chamber to drive her in; and once there, he prevents her from leaving until she has laid her eggs. While she lays them in two long strings, the male positions himself to one side and sprays them with milt (fluid containing sperm). He waves his body from side to side and raises and lowers his hind legs as he does so in order to distribute the sperm thoroughly over the eggs. Females may take two to three days to lay their full complement of 150 to 400

⊕ *Hellbenders have an unjustified reputation among fishermen for driving some fish away and inflicting poisonous bites. In reality they are harmless and eat mainly crayfish, snails, and worms.*

eggs, by which time the two strings become entangled and appear as a single, twisted mass. Females and males often eat some of the eggs as they are laid. Once the female has finished laying, the male drives her away from the nest but remains there himself, presumably to guard them. He may also attract more females, and a single nest can contain 1,000 or more eggs, the record being 1,946.

The eggs hatch after 45 to 84 days, and the hatchlings have a yolk sac that nourishes them for a few months. They also have external gills that disappear after 18 to 24 months. They live in spaces in the gravel, moving up to small stones and rocks in shallow water as they grow. They take five to eight years to reach sexual maturity, with males maturing at a slightly smaller size than females. By the time they are adult, hellbenders have relatively few predators, and they can live for 25 to 30 years in the wild. The record for a captive is 55 years.

The largest hellbender captured was just over 29 inches (74 cm) in length, and the average length of adults is 12 to 15 inches (30–38 cm). There is a good deal of variation in size from one population to another. For instance, those from Arkansas are often more than three times as large as those from some Missouri populations.

Subspecies

Hellbenders are divided into two subspecies. The typical form, *C. a. alleganiensis*, is found over most of the species' range, but the Ozark hellbender, *C. a. bishopi*, is restricted to a small part of southeastern Missouri. The latter subspecies has a blotched rather than a spotted pattern and a darker chin as well as other, less obvious differences.

The origins of the name hellbender are unclear, but it seems that the animal has always aroused strong feelings. The specific name *alleganiensis* refers to the Allegheny Mountains where it lives. Apart from hellbender, other local names include mud devil, ground puppy, Allegheny alligator, big water lizard, and devil dog—none of them particularly complimentary.

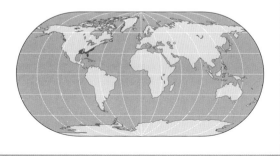

Two-toed amphiuma
(Amphiuma means)

Common name Amphiumas (Congo eels, conger eels, ditch eels)

Scientific name *Amphiuma* sp.

Family Amphiumidae

Order Caudata (Urodela)

Number of species 3

Size Up to 39 in (100 cm)

Key features Very elongated and eel-like; body cylindrical; legs tiny and vestigial with 1, 2, or 3 toes according to species; eyes small with no eyelids; external gills lacking, but pair of gill slits present just behind the head; color gray, paler underneath, with no markings

Habits Completely aquatic

Breeding Females lay long strings of 50–150 eggs and remain with them until they hatch

Diet Almost any aquatic organisms, including crayfish, frogs, fish, water snakes, and snails

Habitat Ponds, ditches, swamps, and slow-moving streams

Distribution Southeastern North America (the coastal plain from eastern Texas to southeastern Virginia)

Status Common (*A. means* and *A. tridactylum*); *A. pholeter* is rare

Similar species The 3 species resemble each other greatly, but otherwise they could only be confused with eels (however, eels have fins, because they are fish)

Amphiumas

Amphiuma sp.

Anyone who can count to three can distinguish between the three different species in the family, which is made up of the one-toed, two-toed, and three-toed amphiumas.

AMPHIUMAS' LIMBS ARE little more than tiny, spindly appendages that are slightly ridiculous and probably redundant. The legs have regressed through natural selection as the animals' lifestyle has evolved. Like the eels they resemble, amphiumas are aquatic. They live in burrows and forage through heavily vegetated or mucky water. Limbs would get in the way; and since they have become reduced, there is little need for toes either.

Despite this, they do occasionally leave the water and travel across land, and have been seen crossing roads. During droughts they burrow into the mud to estivate, and adults can survive for up to three years without feeding. Amphiumas have lungs and lack external gills but retain the gill slits (the openings through which gills emerged at the larval stage).

Amphiumas are thought to have occurred over a much wider range in North America as recently as the upper Miocene period (up to 5.3 million years ago) but retreated to the southeastern coastal plain in the Pleistocene period, 1.8 million to 10,000 years ago (the period during which humans evolved and spread). They are found nowhere else in the world, probably as a result of their specialized requirements for still or slow-moving water systems choked with vegetation or decaying matter. They often take over crayfish burrows, perhaps after having eaten the occupant, or rest among the roots of water hyacinths.

Egg Laying and Development

The two-toed amphiuma, *A. means*, is the most common and widespread species. It lives in Florida and neighboring states as far north as southeastern Virginia. The three-toed species,

⊕ **Amphiuma means,** *the two-toed amphiuma, is the largest of the amphiumas. Its tiny legs are completely out of proportion to its body size and are easy to overlook, leading people to confuse these salamanders with eels.*

A. *tridactylum*, is similar and apparently very closely related (but, of course, it has three toes). Females of these species and presumably also of the rare one-toed species, A. *pholeter*, lay 50 to 150 eggs in burrows or cavities that they first make for themselves.

The females lay their eggs in the winter and then coil around them until they hatch, which takes place several months later in summer. In the meantime, the water level may have fallen, so that by the time the eggs hatch, the nest cavities are above the water level along the edges of the pools or ditches in which they live. This may not be typical, however, because nest cavities that are not exposed are almost impossible to find.

The larval stage does not last long, and the larvae lose their external gills after about three weeks. They become sexually mature at about four to five years old and have been known to survive in captivity for up to 27 years.

Looking to the Future

Populations of the two- and three-toed amphiumas are probably quite healthy despite the loss of most of the wetlands in the southeastern United States owing to development. Habitat destruction affects some regions more than others. The one-toed amphiuma, however, has a much more limited range in southwestern Georgia and adjacent parts of northeastern Florida. Within this region populations are localized, and there is no opportunity for the salamanders to move from one to another. They are rare (or, at least, rarely seen), and there is some concern over their future.

Feeding and Defense

Amphiumas of all species are not fussy eaters. They prey most heavily on whatever animal is most common where they live. Often that is crayfish, but they also eat earthworms, fish, insects and their larvae, snails, and even clams, snakes, and turtles. Their main method of defense is to give a painful bite, but they also have a layer of slime covering their bodies that makes them difficult to grasp.

California giant salamander
**(*Dicamptodon
ensatus*)**

Common name Pacific giant salamanders

Scientific name *Dicamptodon* sp.

Family   Dicamptodontidae

Order   Caudata (Urodela)

Number of species 4 (Cope's giant salamender, *D. copei*;
coastal giant salamander, *D. tenebrosus*;
California giant salamander, *D. ensatus*; Idaho
giant salamander, *D. aterrimus*)

Size   7 in (18 cm) to 13 in (33 cm)

Key features Adults large and stout with broad, slightly
flattened heads and raised eyes; gray or
brown in color, with a dark, mottled pattern;
some never metamorphose and remain as
large larvae throughout their lives—they have
bushy external gills, 4 legs, and low tail fins
that start level with the hind limbs

Habits   Nocturnal; metamorphosed adults are
terrestrial, larvae are aquatic

Breeding   Where known, females lay clusters of eggs in
underwater cavities

Diet   Aquatic and terrestrial invertebrates; larger
prey, such as small mammals and lizards; also
cannibalistic

Habitat   Larvae live in woodland streams; adults live
alongside the streams in old-growth forest

Distribution North America in coastal central California
and the Pacific Northwest

Status   Becoming rarer as their habitat is destroyed
by clear-cutting and subsequent silting up of
forest streams

Similar species Tiger salamanders are similar but do not
occur alongside the Pacific salamanders

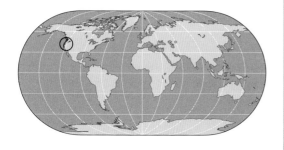

Pacific Giant Salamanders

Dicamptodon sp.

Pacific giant salamanders are only found in the Pacific Northwest of the United States and in a small part of neighboring British Columbia, Canada. They are very secretive, often burrowing down into thick moss or underground chambers. Their larvae live in streams and are more easily found than the adults.

OF THE FOUR SPECIES of Pacific giant salamander,
three are almost identical. In fact, they were
formerly regarded as a single species,
Dicamptodon ensatus. The fourth species,
Cope's giant salamander, *D. copei*, is distinct.
This salamander rarely transforms into an
adult and can reproduce while it is still a
larva, a process known as neoteny.
(Surprisingly, neoteny is quite
common in salamanders,
occurring occasionally in
the other three species

of *Dicamptodon* as well as in members of several other families.) Cope's giant salamander is, therefore, a tadpole for the whole of its life and has fins along the top and bottom of its tail and external gills, although they are very small.

The other three species, once they have metamorphosed into adults, are large and chunky. Their heads are very wide but flattened, with small eyes positioned on top. Their roughly cylindrical bodies have a row of folds down either side, known as the costal grooves, and their limbs are powerful because they use them for digging.

Adults are found under logs, bark, and rocks but never far from streams or the edges of mountain lakes. They also climb and sometimes reach heights of over 7 feet (2 m) in shrubs and trees.

⊕ *A coastal giant salamander,* **Dicamptodon tenebrosus,** *crawls on the forest floor in the Cascade Mountains of Oregon.*

Specialized Habitats

All the Pacific giant salamanders (including Cope's giant salamander) occur in very specialized habitats in the states of California, Oregon, Washington, Idaho, and British Columbia. Due to the westerly winds that bring moist air from the Pacific Ocean, these regions have a high rainfall. Over the ages the conditions have created forests of tall conifers dripping with mosses and lichens, drained by thousands of small, clear, cold streams that run down to the coast. At higher altitudes in the Rocky Mountains there are numerous small mountain lakes that also contain cold, well-oxygenated water. The forest floor is littered with rotting stumps and fallen trunks. The decaying wood is home to insects and other invertebrates, as well as small mammals.

The adult salamanders live on the forest floor during the nonbreeding season. They hide in burrows, especially during dry spells in the summer months, and emerge onto the surface only on wet, cool nights, mainly in the winter and early spring. In the spring they migrate from the surrounding forest to congregate around springs at the sources of streams, where they lay their eggs in chambers under the ground.

The larvae live in small- to medium-sized forest streams and mountain lakes. They are well

27

adapted to life there and spend most of their time on the bottom of the streams, among gravel and other sunken debris. They seem to prefer the downstream sides of pools and backwaters that occur along the watercourses. They absorb much of their oxygen and get rid of up to 80 percent of their waste carbon dioxide through their skin, which accounts for their small gills.

Where conditions are suitable, they can occur in large numbers, and in places they are the most numerous vertebrate species. The larvae take two or more years to metamorphose, and so the streams in which they live must be permanent. The forests help maintain the streams because they absorb rainwater like a sponge and release it slowly throughout the year.

Opportunistic Feeders

Adult Pacific giant salamanders are voracious feeders. Although their main prey are probably slugs, worms, and other invertebrates, they regularly take small mice and shrews. Amphibians are also eaten, including other salamanders and even smaller members of the same species. Although it is hard to study such secretive amphibians, Pacific giant salamanders almost certainly feed at night, when they emerge during rain showers to forage over the surface. However, while they are in their underground retreats, they probably feed opportunistically by capturing worms or other small animals that happen to enter the chambers in which they shelter.

The larvae are also aggressive feeders. Bearing in mind how large they can grow—to 12 inches (30 cm) in many cases—they are able to tackle just about any aquatic invertebrate. In addition, they eat fish and the eggs and tadpoles of other amphibians that share their habitat. They include the rare tailed frog, *Ascaphus truei*, whose tadpoles form

⊖ *A California giant salamander,* Dicamptodon ensatus, *eats a large banana slug. Invertebrates, small mammals, and lizards are also included in their diet as adults.*

14 percent of the diet of some populations of *D. ensatus*; the tadpoles of the northwestern salamander, *Ambystoma gracile*, make up 39 percent of their food. *Dicamptodon* larvae eat just about anything they can get their mouths around (although in experiments they spat out the larvae of rough-skinned newts, *Taricha granulosa*, which produce poisonous substances in glands in their skin). Pacific giant salamander larvae can even be caught on a hook and line—once they grab prey in their jaws, they will not let go and can be lifted out of the water.

Because they are not very discriminating and feed in response to movement, adult and larval Pacific giant salamanders often eat one another. When they are attacked on land, whether by a member of their own species or a different predator, they arch their back and hold their body high off the ground by stretching their legs out and standing on the tips of their toes. If this doesn't frighten off the predator, they lash out with their tails, which are covered with poisonous secretions. At the same time, they make loud rattling or growling sounds. They can also give a painful bite, using sharp, curved teeth. Larvae have little defense against predation, however, and the females stay with their eggs and newly hatched larvae for several months to defend them.

Reproduction

Courtship has not been observed in Pacific giant salamanders, but the adult males and females move toward the headwaters of streams and springs in the breeding season (which can be in spring or fall depending on the species). They probably find each other by following scent trails.

Mating is thought to be similar to the mole salamanders, Ambystomatidae, to which they are closely related. Fertilization is internal, and during courtship the male encourages the female to pick up a small parcel of sperm, the spermatophore, in her cloaca.

Before laying her eggs, the female digs down into the gravel at the bottom of a stream until she finds a suitable chamber or cavity

A Conservation Issue

As with many threatened animals, habitat loss is the greatest threat to the Pacific giant salamanders. The forests of redwood, Douglas fir, and hemlock where they live are known as "old-growth" forests, meaning they contain trees 250 years old or older, along with younger trees and fallen logs. The largest trees can reach 300 feet (91 m) high and over 6 feet (1.8 m) in diameter, and in places the canopy cover can be up to 80 percent, providing constant shade and cool conditions on the forest floor and in the forest streams.

Old trees, young trees, dead trees, and fallen logs all provide microhabitats for a wide range of animals whose lives are linked together. On the forest floor they provide all the microhabitats needed by the salamanders: high humidity, rotting logs and stumps to hide in, and cool, clear streams in which to breed.

Old-growth forests of this type only occur in the moist regions of the American Pacific Northwest and are the key to the continued survival of the salamanders. They were more extensive in former times, perhaps covering 15 to 17 million acres (6–7 million ha) across Oregon, Washington, and neighboring states. European settlers cleared large areas for farming and timber. More recently, commercial logging operations have reduced the area of forest even further, and now there are only about 2.4 million acres (1 million ha) left at most. Almost 90 percent of the old-growth forest has been destroyed. About half of what is left is protected in national parks or wilderness areas. The rest is earmarked for more logging. Scientists worry that when the logging is finished—in about 25 years—good habitat will be too fragmented, and the salamanders and other animals will not be able to move around freely.

Pacific giant salamanders only occur in old-growth forests or in similar habitats that are equally threatened. In particular, logging activities cause mud and silt to get into the streams. The mud clogs the gills of the salamander larvae and also makes it hard for them to find prey. After an area has been logged, the population of salamander larvae downstream falls dramatically a few years later.

The forests also provide the right habitat for a wide variety of other unique plants and animals, some of whose life cycles are linked with the salamanders in ways that we do not yet fully understand. They include the rare tailed frog, *Ascaphus truei*, several other rare salamanders, and most famously of all, the northern spotted owl, *Strix occidentalis caurina*.

It was concern over this owl in the 1970s that started an argument between the logging companies and conservationists that is ongoing. The logging companies would like to take all the large trees from the old-growth forest, and the conservationists would like to stop logging altogether. Until they can find a compromise, the future of this unique and interesting habitat and of the Pacific giant salamanders will be uncertain.

⊖ *A California redwood forest floor is an ideal hiding place for the California giant salamander,* Dicamptodon ensatus. *Unfortunately, such habitats are disappearing.*

between the rocks, using her powerful front limbs and tough, horny toes. Then she lays her eggs one at a time, attaching them individually to rocks or pieces of sunken wood. The eggs are large and white, and quite numerous.

One nest of *D. tenebrosus*, for example, contained 83 eggs, and another contained 146 eggs. Details of the eggs of the other three species are not known, but they are likely to be similar. The females stay in the water near the eggs until they hatch. This can take several weeks or even months, and the larvae also grow and develop very slowly. They may remain in the water for two or three years, growing to 12 inches (30 cm) in length before they finally change into adult salamanders and leave the water for a life on the land.

A small number of Pacific giant salamander larvae never metamorphose at all. Instead, they stay in the water throughout their entire lives. In the case of Cope's giant salamander the larvae rarely metamorphose—only four adults have ever been found, even though the larvae are quite common.

Common name Mudpuppy
(waterdog)

Scientific name *Necturus maculosus*

Family Proteidae

Order Caudata (Urodela)

Size 8 in (20 cm) to 20 in (50 cm)

Key features Adults take the form of larvae with 3 pairs
of branched, bushy external gills and with tail
fins; wide, flat head with small eyes; body
flattened from top to bottom; color brown
with lighter speckled markings; larvae have a
pair of yellow stripes down the back

Habits Totally aquatic; unable to survive long out of
water

Breeding External fertilization; female lays her clutches
of 60–120 eggs in underwater cavities in the
spring or summer; eggs hatch after 38–63
days

Diet Aquatic insects and their larvae, crustaceans,
amphibians, and fish

Habitat Rivers, lakes, ditches, and streams

Distribution Eastern North America from southeastern
Canada into the eastern United States but
not along the coastal plain

Status Common in suitable habitat

Similar species The hellbender lacks external gills as an
adult and occupies a different type of habitat;
could possibly be confused with other
mudpuppies (waterdogs), but they are
smaller, their ranges do not overlap, and they
are all comparatively rare

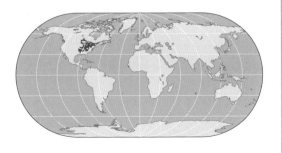

Mudpuppy

Necturus maculosus

Mudpuppies are the bulldogs of the amphibian world, tolerating a wide range of conditions and eating anything they can fit into their mouths.

THE USUAL HABITAT OF MUDPUPPIES includes canals
and ditches choked with vegetation or mud, as
well as flowing rivers with gravel bottoms and
lakes with clear, cool water. In muddy waters
they may be active during the day as well as at
night, groping their way through the muck in
search of food. In clearer waters they hide in
the day under logs and rocks or in burrows, and
only emerge at night. They have been found 60
feet (18 m) below the surface of lakes and may
be active under ice if the lakes or ditches freeze

Waterdogs

There are five species of mudpuppies, or waterdogs, all living in
North America. Although *Necturus maculosus* is very common
and wide ranging, the other four (all known as waterdogs) have
more limited ranges. The Alabama waterdog, *N. alabamensis*, lives in
Alabama and adjacent states. The Gulf Coast waterdog, *N. beyeri*,
occurs as two separate populations: one along the border between
Texas and eastern Louisiana, and the other from central Louisiana to
Mississippi. The Neuse River waterdog, *N. lewisi*, has a small
distribution in North Carolina; and finally, the dwarf water dog,
N. punctatus, occurs from southern Virginia to Georgia.

All four of these species are smaller than the common
mudpuppy, *N. maculosus,* but can be difficult to tell apart from each
other. Whereas the common species occurs inland, the others all live
on the coastal plain, along river systems draining into the Atlantic
seaboard or the Gulf Coast. Little is known about their natural
history, but they are thought to be similar to the mudpuppy in many
respects. They seem to prefer (or require) rivers and streams with log-
jams and pockets of accumulated leaf debris on the bottom in which
to hide. They tend to be less active in the summer, perhaps because
there is less food for them, or it could be to avoid predation from
fish. Populations of some species are getting fewer and smaller,
possibly due to pollution of their river systems.

over. Ohio fishermen fishing through holes in the ice often catch mudpuppies on baited hooks. In Lake Michigan and possibly elsewhere they migrate from the edges of the lake in spring and move back into deep water again during the summer.

Breeding

Mating occurs mostly in the fall but carries on throughout the winter, the timing varying according to location. After mating, the females retain the sperm in their tracts until the following spring or early summer and lay their eggs in May or June. They make nest sites in shallow water by scraping out shallow depressions under rocks, logs, or sunken trash, with the entrance holes facing downstream.

They attach the eggs singly to the underside of the roof of the cavity, turning upside down to do so. An average clutch consists of 60 to 120 eggs, and the female stays to defend them against predators until they hatch around 38 to 63 days later. The larvae prefer water that is still or moving slowly and often hide in submerged leaf litter, feeding on small invertebrates. They reach breeding size in about five years, by which time they measure around 8 inches (20 cm) in length.

Mudpuppies are successful salamanders that can occur at high densities in suitable habitats. Not so long ago they were collected in large numbers for dissection in university laboratories—a single catch in Michigan in the 1920s contained over 2,000 mudpuppies. Some authorities think that they might be important predators on fish eggs, possibly affecting commercial catches, but studies to investigate these claims have not been conducted.

⬆ *Necturus maculosus is the largest of the mudpuppies (or waterdogs). It is aptly named—Necturus comes from the Greek word for swimming, nektos, while maculosus is the Latin word for speckled or mottled.*

Common name Cascade torrent salamander

Scientific name *Rhyacotriton cascadae*

Family Rhyacotritonidae

Order Caudata (Urodela)

Size 3 in (7.5 cm) to 4.5 in (11 cm)

Key features Slender salamander with a small head, raised eyes, and a short tail; body yellowish brown above and yellow below with a distinct line where the 2 colors meet; back and sides covered with small dark spots

Habits Secretive and nocturnal, hiding by day under stones at the water's edge

Breeding Fertilization is external; females probably lay their eggs singly; eggs are relatively large

Diet Not known but probably small terrestrial and aquatic invertebrates

Habitat Streams and edges of streams in old-growth forest

Distribution Pacific Northwest (Cascade Mountains in Washington and Oregon)

Status Rare

Similar species 3 other species of *Rhyacotriton* are virtually identical, and identification is only possible through distribution

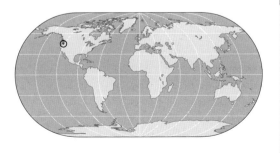

Cascade Torrent Salamander

Rhyacotriton cascadae

The Cascade torrent salamander and its three close relatives are small, secretive salamanders about whose lives little is known.

CASCADE TORRENT SALAMANDERS live in the clear, cold headwaters and springs of streams, spending most of their time under partially submerged moss-covered rocks or in fissures in wet cliff faces. They probably come out at night to forage for food but rarely wander far from water. The farthest they are found from the nearest stream is 50 yards (46 m). Their skin contains toxic substances that are apparently effective in driving off some predators, including shrews. In defensive displays the salamanders coil their tail, raising it off the ground and waving it slowly backward and forward.

Small Clutches

Torrent salamanders have internal fertilization, but courtship and the transfer of the spermatophore from male to female have never been observed. It seems that they breed throughout the summer and fall, and breeding tails off in the winter. This has been established by examining females throughout the year to see whether they contained eggs. During the breeding season females contained from two to 13 eggs, with an average of eight. Although the number of eggs is small compared with many amphibians, each one is relatively large.

The eggs of *R. cascadae* have not been found, but related species lay them singly and place them in cracks in submerged rocks or in cavities beneath them. Several females may lay their eggs in the same place, since small groups of eggs have been found together. The larvae, which are slender and of the stream type (with a flattened body and narrow fins), live in the spaces between the gravel beds of the streams, often in riffles, covered by less than 1 inch (2.5 cm) of water. In favorable conditions larvae

⬆ *The original torrent salamander,* Rhyacotriton olympicus, *is from the Olympic Peninsula in Oregon. It is very similar in appearance to its close relative, the cascade torrent salamander,* R. cascadae.

Cryptic Species

Until 1992 there was only one species of torrent salamander—the Olympic torrent salamander, *Rhyacotriton olympicus* from the Olympic Peninsula in Oregon. Close examination of this species revealed subtle differences, and three additional species were identified. They were not new in the sense that they had not been seen before, but their differences were so slight that they had been overlooked previously—one of them had been a subspecies.

When species are separated because of details that are difficult to see without looking at microscopic, biochemical, or genetic details, they are known as "cryptic," or hidden, species. The Cascade torrent salamander, *R. cascadae*, was one of the newly separated species. The other two were the Columbia torrent salamander, *R. kezeri*, and the southern torrent salamander, *R. variegatus*.

Coincidentally, around the same time—in 1989—scientists discovered that one of the other salamanders unique to the region, the Pacific giant salamander, *Dicamptodon ensatus*, was also in fact three separate cryptic species. The newly identified species were the Idaho giant salamander, *Dicamptodon aterrimus*, and the Pacific giant salamander, *Dicamptodon tenebrosus*.

live at high densities—up to 40 per square yard (1 sq. m)—and rarely move more than a few feet. If they do move, they are more likely to work their way upstream than down. They feed on small aquatic invertebrates, and their growth rate is very slow: They are three to four years old before they metamorphose.

Torrent salamanders share their old-growth forest habitat with the Pacific giant salamanders in the family Dicamptodontidae, which probably prey on them. The felling of these forests is putting populations of both groups of salamanders at risk. Like the Pacific giant salamanders, the family of torrent salamanders is found nowhere else.

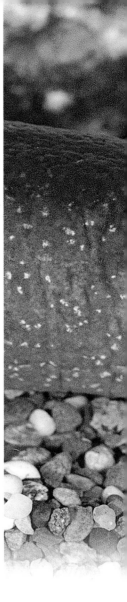

Sirens

Siren sp.

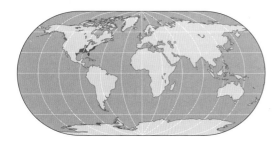

**Greater siren
(*Siren lacertina*)**

Common names Lesser siren, greater siren

Scientific names *Siren intermedia*, *Siren lacertina*

Family Sirenidae

Order Caudata (Urodela)

Size Lesser siren: 7 in (18 cm) to 27 in (69 cm); greater siren: 20 in (50 cm) to 35 in (90 cm)

Key features Both species eel-like except for a pair of small front limbs with 4 small toes and feathery external gills; gills are close to the legs and sometimes obscure them; color dark brown or olive with darker spots, sometimes entirely black; larvae and juveniles of the lesser siren often have a red patch on the snout and another along the side of the head

Habits Totally aquatic; nocturnal

Breeding Fertilization probably external; female lesser siren lays 200–550 eggs in a large clump; greater siren lays up to 1,400 eggs singly or in groups; eggs hatch after about 8 weeks

Diet Wide variety of prey taken, including invertebrates, especially insect larvae, snails, crayfish; they also eat some vegetation and amphibian eggs, including their own

Habitat Swamps, marshes, ponds, and ditches—the main requirement being plenty of mud

Distribution Lesser siren: southeastern North America from the Mexican border on the Gulf Coast to southeastern West Virginia and inland along the Mississippi Valley; greater siren: a more limited range within the same area

Status Common in suitable (but dwindling) habitats

Similar species The small front legs and absence of hind legs distinguish them from all salamanders except the dwarf sirens, which are much smaller

The mythical sea nymphs after which these salamanders were named sang to lure sailors to destruction on the rocks they inhabited. A vivid imagination is needed to see any similarities between the two!

THERE ARE TWO SPECIES of sirens in the genus *Siren*, and they are found in the southern and central United States and northeastern Mexico. Sirens are at home in the mud and are rarely seen. Unlike their mythical namesakes, they do not sing. Instead, they vocalize with a range of clicks and squeaks whenever they leave their burrows to come up for air. The sounds are thought to be a form of communication and may have a territorial function. When grasped, sirens often make a yelping sound.

Mucous Cocoons

Sirens live in almost any body of still water that is choked with vegetation or that has a good layer of decomposing leaves or mud on the bottom. The young live in shallower water than the adults. If the water dries up, neither the adults nor the young take to the land in search of somewhere else to live. Instead, they burrow down into the mud. If the mud dries out, the mucous coat covering their skin hardens to form a parchmentlike cocoon that covers the entire body except for the mouth and keeps the sirens from dehydrating. They remain inactive until the water returns.

Because they hoard large fat reserves in their tails, greater sirens, *S. lacertina*, can survive many months without feeding. The record is just over five years. Their metabolism slows down to 30 to 40 percent of its normal level while they are estivating, and they may lose three-quarters of their body weight. Lesser sirens, *S. intermedia*, also estivate but can only survive a few months in this state. Estivating

sirens are sometimes plowed up in fields that were previously flooded.

Despite the size difference, the two species have very similar lifestyles. During the day adults hide in underwater burrows built in mud banks or beneath sunken logs. At the end of each burrow is a chamber where the salamander coils when it is resting. Sirens are most active in the summer months when the water temperatures approach 86°F (30°C) and tend to forage just after dusk and immediately before dawn.

Instead of teeth, sirens have a horny beak, and they feed by suction, drawing water and prey into their mouth at the same time. Young animals live in dense clumps of vegetation through which they move at night in search of food. They eat mainly insect larvae and other invertebrates, including mollusks, but their stomachs often contain algae and pieces of plant material, perhaps ingested accidentally.

Egg Development

Courtship and mating have never been observed in either species, but evidence points to external fertilization, since in captivity eggs laid in isolation fail to develop. (If fertilization were internal, some eggs laid shortly after capture could be expected to be fertile. However, this is not the case, which indicates that fertilization occurs during, or after, laying.) Furthermore, eggs are rarely seen. Those that

The greater siren, Siren lacertina, is the largest of the sirens—the name lacertina means "little lizard." It has external gills, tiny front feet, and no back legs. Its tail has a fin above and below.

Dwarf Sirens

The family Sirenidae contains two other species of aquatic sirens, *Pseudobranchus axanthus* and *P. striatus*. They are 4 to 10 inches (10–25 cm) long and are known as dwarf sirens. They are similar in appearance to the larger sirens, but their front legs have only three toes each, and they have yellow or tan stripes running along their back and sides. They live in a wide range of water bodies from Florida to South Carolina, but they seem to be most common in small ponds and ditches that have a thick covering of water hyacinth, *Eichhornia crassipes*. In most respects this introduced weed is a menace. Dwarf sirens use their gills and skin to breathe in well-oxygenated water; but because water hyacinth reduces the oxygen-carrying capacity of the water, they also use their lungs for breathing, coming up to the surface periodically for air.

Like the other sirens, dwarf sirens sometimes live in ponds and swamps that dry up occasionally, in which case they burrow beneath the surface and estivate, reducing their metabolic rate by 50 percent or more to save energy. Estivating dwarf sirens shrink their gills, and their skin becomes dry. They can survive like this for at least two months. Living in ponds with low oxygen levels, and which may dry up occasionally, may actually benefit dwarf sirens because such conditions are unsuitable for predatory fish that would otherwise eat them. Other predators include wading birds, water snakes, and young alligators.

The breeding habits of dwarf sirens are unknown. They are assumed to have external fertilization because the males do not have the glands with which to form spermatophores, and females do not have an organ in which to store it (a spermatheca). Females lay their eggs in the winter and attach them to water hyacinth roots. In the absence of water hyacinths they use submerged aquatic plants. Nothing is known about their subsequent development.

Until recently there was only one species of dwarf siren, *Pseudobranchus striatus*, with several subspecies. However, one subspecies, *P. s. axanthus*, was promoted to a full species in 1993 based on differences in its chromosomes. These two species and the greater and lesser sirens, *Siren lacertina and S. intermedia*, make up the whole of the family Sirenidae.

The relationship of members of the family to other salamanders is a puzzle that herpetologists have yet to solve. The difficulty is that they have several primitive features, such as external fertilization, but anatomically they are similar to some of the more advanced salamanders. They also have some unique features, for example, a horny, beaklike structure instead of teeth.

⊙ *The smallest of its family, the dwarf siren,* Pseudobranchus striatus, *lives among dense, submerged vegetation. It is nocturnal and feeds on tiny invertebrate animals that it finds among the plant debris near the bottom of the water.*

↑ *The lesser siren,* Siren intermedia, *in North Carolina. Since they are nocturnal hunters, sirens spend the day hiding in debris on the bottom of bodies of still, shallow water or among the mud and vegetation.*

have been discovered have either been dredged up among aquatic plants or been found in depressions in mud on the bottom of ponds.

There have been too few observations to know if the two species have similar egg-laying habits. Both are prolific, however—the lesser siren laying up to 550 eggs, and the greater siren up to 1,400. They may be laid in large or small clumps or deposited singly. The egg-laying season appears to be late winter (in Florida), and the eggs hatch about two months later.

Lesser sirens probably mature after about two years. Their predators include water snakes, herons, egrets, large fish, and alligators, although the nocturnal habits of the sirens probably help keep predation to a minimum.

Habitat Loss

Although neither species of siren is rare, the loss of wetlands due to drainage is a problem. Also, measures to control flooding of low-lying land probably prevent sirens from dispersing across flooded areas to colonize new systems.

Common name Axolotl (Mexican mole salamander, Mexican walking fish)

Scientific name *Ambystoma mexicanum*

Family Ambystomatidae

Order Caudata (Urodela)

Size 8 in (20 cm) but exceptionally to 12 in (30 cm)

Key features 4 limbs; 3 pairs of feathery external gills; high dorsal and caudal fins; head broad and flat; mouth has a wide gape; eyes small; wild-type axolotls are dark gray in color with scattered, small black spots; laboratory strains may be white or different colors produced by selective breeding

Habits Totally aquatic; more active at night

Breeding Females lay up to 1,000 eggs attached singly or in small clumps to twigs or aquatic plants; eggs hatch after about 2 weeks

Diet Aquatic invertebrates, including insect larvae and worms; fish and tadpoles

Habitat High-altitude lakes

Distribution Lake Xochimilco and Lake Chalco on the central Mexican plateau

Status Protected (CITES); Vulnerable IUCN

Similar species 4 other Mexican *Ambystoma* species (3 from central Mexico and 1 from Puebla) are axolotls and therefore similar in appearance

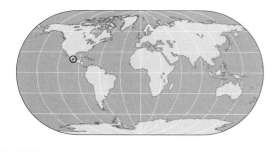

Axolotl

Ambystoma mexicanum

The axolotl is, in effect, an enormous tadpole. Adults retain many of their larval characteristics and can even reproduce as larvae.

THE AXOLOTL IS THE LARVAL FORM of the Mexican mole salamander, *Ambystoma mexicanum*. Its metamorphosis is incomplete: Although it develops small lungs and a reproductive system, it does not lose its external gills or the fins around its tail and along its back, and its skin does not take on characteristics of adult salamanders. Nor can it survive out of water.

Grown-up Axolotls

Metamorphosed axolotls are almost unheard of in the wild or in captivity. Although some sources maintain that an axolotl will metamorphose if the water level in its aquarium is lowered slowly, this is not so. Neoteny is a genetic trait in the axolotl, caused by low levels of iodine. Iodine is an essential component of hormones belonging to the thyroxin group, which are necessary for growth and development. Only by injecting axolotls with hormones of this type will they metamorphose (except in very rare cases, where they metamorphose spontaneously). Grown-up axolotls are very similar to adult tiger salamanders from Mexico, being dark gray with lighter mottling, and are closely related to them.

The axolotl's natural habitat is the montane lakes of central Mexico: Lake Xochimilco and Lake Chalco. Unfortunately, Lake Chalco exists no more, having been built over as Mexico City expanded southward. Lake Xochimilco survives as a network of canals and lagoons. It is under pressure from the growing human population nearby, but it is still rich in plants and animals.

Research Animals

The plight of wild populations of axolotls has led to the species being protected under CITES regulations and listed as Vulnerable by the

Aztec Connections

The axolotl's name has Aztec origins. It derives from two words: *atl,* meaning "water," and *xolotl,* meaning "monster." In Aztec mythology the god Xolotl was the twin brother of Quetzalcóatl, the plumed serpent god, but was disfigured and regarded as a monster. The local name for the species is *ajolote*, which has the same origins (bearing in mind that in Spanish the *x* and the *j* are pronounced as an *h). Ajolote* is also used for a completely different species, the amphisbaenian, *Bipes biporus* (a type of worm lizard), that lives in the Baja California region of Mexico. In pre-Hispanic Mexico the axolotl was a delicacy and was said to taste like an eel. Its fat was used as a medicine in the same way that cod liver oil is used nowadays.

IUCN. What is strange is that axolotls are bred in huge numbers by laboratories and amateur enthusiasts around the world. Axolotls were first bred in laboratories to provide material for teaching and research, especially in the field of embryology. They were suitable because they could be persuaded to lay fertile eggs at any time of the year and on demand. The jelly layer surrounding the eggs is also easy to remove, allowing cell division to be observed. Because of their wide availability scientists in other disciplines began to use them too.

Nearly everything we know about axolotls has been learned from captives. Wild populations, apart from being rare, are also difficult to observe. The first reference to them is in a book published in the early 17th century, but they were not named until 1789, as *Gyrinus mexicanus.* In 1830 the first reference to their local name and their eventual common name was made when they were renamed *Axolotus pisciformis.* In Paris in 1863 they were bred in captivity for the first time, and their strange life history was revealed.

⊖ *The white form of axolotl,* Ambystoma mexicanum, *is the most common. It is not a true albino because, although its skin lacks pigment, its eyes are black.*

Axolotls in Captivity

The most common axolotl is the white form, and there are probably more in captivity than in the wild. It is a genetic mutation in which pigment is lacking from cells in the skin but not from the eyes (known as leucisitic). There is an albino strain with pink eyes, but it has not been bred for as long as the white form and is seen less often. There are other, less distinctive varieties.

Axolotls need a spacious tank, but it does not have to be filled to the top—the most important factor is surface area. Axolotls eat earthworms, strips of lean meat, and other animal food. The young eat bloodworms, *Daphnia*, and pieces of each other; but the more often they are fed, the less they will mutilate each other. The tank bottom should be filled with large pebbles that the axolotls cannot ingest accidentally. They will use hiding places (broken crocks or drainpipes), but it is best to avoid building elaborate rock caves, because they are easily dislodged—sometimes with fatal results.

In the wild axolotls experience water temperatures of 41 to 68°F (5–20°C). Animals kept warmer than this will develop larger, more feathery gills but will also be prone to fungus and bacterial infections. A small filter helps keep the water clean, but axolotls dislike strong currents, so power filters should be avoided. The best way to keep them clean is to change about 20 percent of the water every week or so, using a siphon tube to take the water from the bottom of the tank. Rainwater is best; but if tapwater is used, it should be left to stand overnight before using it so that chlorine and other additives can disperse. If the replacement water is much colder than the water in the tank, the sudden temperature drop may stimulate breeding activity.

Breeding

Axolotls will breed at any time of the year, although a sudden drop in water temperature usually triggers courtship activity in males. Courtship includes nudging of the female by the male, after which she follows him until he deposits his spermatophore. Females start spawning a few hours later, laying their eggs singly or in small clusters, and attaching them to aquatic plants, twigs, or rocks. Larger females produce more eggs, and the clutch size can vary between 100 and 1,000 eggs. The eggs hatch after about two weeks, although the exact time varies with temperature. The young larvae are small at hatching and feed on very small aquatic creatures at first, such as young water fleas, *Daphnia*.

Axolotls have a characteristic method of feeding in which they remain motionless until a

suitable prey animal comes within range. Then they open their mouth so that water rushes in. At the same time, they move forward and upward slightly before sinking back to the bottom. As they grow, they become more voracious and often bite limbs and pieces of external gills from each other, especially during feeding frenzies. Under extreme circumstances a young axolotl can lose all four of its limbs. Far from being fatal, the loss does not seem to bother them, and the limbs eventually regrow.

Endangered Relatives

The axolotl is part of the tiger salamander group, but its closest relatives are the other four neotenic species that live in Mexican lakes. At least two of them are endangered—the Lake Pátzcuaro salamander, *A. dumerilii*, is listed in Appendix II of CITES, while the Lake Lerma salamander, *A. lermaense*, is listed by the IUCN as Critically Endangered. Shrinking habitats and pollution are the main reasons for the decline of these species.

⬆ *Axolotls are easy to keep in captivity, but their status in the wild is under threat. Today there are many more living in fish tanks than there are in Mexican lakes.*

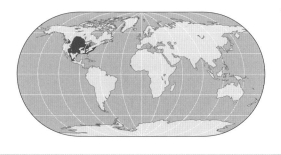

Common name Tiger salamander

Scientific name *Ambystoma tigrinum*

Family Ambystomatidae

Order Caudata (Urodela)

Size 7 in (18 cm) to 14 in (35 cm)

Key features Head broad and flattened; mouth wide, eyes raised; limbs and feet short and stocky; tail relatively short and rounded in cross-section, although it becomes flattened from side to side in breeding males; males have slightly longer tails than females; coloration usually black, gray, or dark brown with lighter markings in yellow or cream or pale brown depending on the subspecies; neotenic individuals are common in some populations

Habits Terrestrial as an adult; nocturnal

Breeding Internal fertilization; females lay clumps of 5–100 eggs (the average is about 50) attached to aquatic plants or twigs; eggs hatch after 20–50 days

Diet Invertebrates and small vertebrates, including other salamanders; cannibalistic individuals occur

Habitat Forests, fields, meadows, and even desert and semidesert areas when breeding pools are available

Distribution North America, almost coast to coast, and from Canada to Central Mexico

Status Generally common, but some forms are extremely rare

Similar species Pacific giant salamanders, *Dicamptodon* species, the spotted salamander, *A. maculatum*, and other well-marked large species could be confused with tiger salamanders

Tiger Salamander

Ambystoma tigrinum

The tiger salamander, which occurs in a wide variety of colors and patterns, is probably the most familiar salamander over much of the United States and Canada.

THE TIGER SALAMANDER IS divided into subspecies that vary somewhat in color and markings. Patterns include those in which black-and-yellow or black-and-cream areas are roughly equal in extent, with the lighter color arranged in irregular crossbars, for example, the barred tiger salamander, *A. t. mavortium*. In some subspecies the lighter areas are more extensive than the dark ones, as in the blotched tiger salamander, *A. t. melanostictum*, and in others the light markings consist of small round or oval spots distributed over the animal's body, for example, the eastern tiger salamander, *A. t. tigrinum*. Finally, there is a form in which the lighter markings are olive-green or gray, and the small black spots are hardly visible, as in the Arizona tiger salamander, *A. t. nebulosum*. Some of these local forms are widely distributed and are so common that they are used as fishing bait, whereas others are extremely rare and enjoy total state and federal protection.

Lifestyle Variations

As well as the color and geographical variations, there are variations in lifestyle within and between populations. Six forms, or "morphs," are recognized; some populations have only two, but others can include all six. For example, most tiger salamanders eat invertebrates and occasionally small vertebrates, but cannibalism is sometimes present in certain morphs. Cannibalistic salamanders can be immature larvae, mature aquatic larvae that fail to metamorphose (neotenous larvae), or terrestrial adults. The cannibalistic morph is usually larger than the normal morph and has a broader

⊕ *The barred tiger salamander,* Ambystoma tigrinum mavortium, *was named the Kansas State amphibian in 1994. As well as having bright yellow or olive spots, blotches, or bars on its back and sides, it has a distinctive "grin" on its face.*

head, larger skull, and an extra row of teeth. The teeth are longer than those of normal tiger salamanders and may be curved backward.

The different morphs are not evenly distributed across subspecies—cannibals are rare in the eastern tiger salamander, *A. t. tigrinum*, for instance. The barred subspecies, *A. t. mavortium*, varies in that some larvae metamorphose at a smaller size than others. The small larvae live in temporary pools and develop more quickly than the larger ones that live in permanent bodies of water. Like spadefoot toads, their development is probably accelerated so that they have a better chance of leaving their pools before they dry up.

In general, however, tiger salamander larvae grow slowly and can reach large sizes before metamorphosing, especially if they are not overcrowded and there is plenty of food to go around. Eastern populations are more likely to stay in the water for extended periods. They often reach sexual maturity shortly after they leave the water. They may travel

A Tiger Salamander Rarity

The rarest tiger salamander is *A. t. stebbinsi*. It lives on hillsides and meadows in the Huachuca and Patagonia mountain ranges in southeastern Arizona. The population was only recognized as a separate subspecies in 1988 when it was found to have been cut off from other tiger salamanders by large areas of unsuitable habitat. It breeds only in a limited number of cattle tanks and modified water holes. Historically it would have bred in naturally occurring water holes and springs, but about 90 percent of suitable habitat in the area has been lost, degraded, or altered. Several water holes where it was known to breed in the 1960s have dried up in times of drought, killing any larvae in them (although metamorphosed individuals living nearby may have recolonized them when they filled up again).

Disease killed all the salamanders at three sites in 1985, and diseased individuals were also found at another seven sites. An associated problem is the introduction of nonlocal species of amphibians, especially the American bullfrog, *Rana catesbeiana*, and fish, which may prey on the tiger salamanders or their larvae and can also spread disease. Larvae of tiger salamanders are widely used as fishing bait in Arizona, and subspecies from other parts of the state have been introduced to the area for bait propagation, so there is also a danger that the native form will be diluted by interbreeding.

several hundred yards after they leave the ponds, or they may remain nearby, perhaps returning to shallow water to feed on frog tadpoles and other aquatic prey. Adults sometimes migrate to temporary ponds even if they have already bred in permanent ponds, presumably because prey such as insect larvae and frog tadpoles become concentrated as the water evaporates. Such migrations, whether to breed or to move from one pond to another, nearly always take place during rainstorms in summer and fall.

In the west of their range tiger salamanders tend to live in the burrows of small mammals, but in the east they usually dig their own burrows with their powerful front limbs. The burrows are often only a few inches deep;

⊕ Adult Arizona tiger salamanders, Ambystoma tigrinum nebulosum, are brownish gray with small, dark spots. The subspecies is found in parts of Colorado, Utah, New Mexico, and central Arizona.

but an eastern tiger salamander was found 7 feet (2 m) deep, and a blotched tiger salamander in Alberta, Canada, was found using a rattlesnake den for shelter in the winter.

Life Cycle

The breeding pattern is typical of the family. Males may try to interfere with courting pairs by nudging the male or the female out of the way or by covering spermatophores with their own. Spermatophores are larger than in other mole salamanders. Males can lay up to 37 during a single night, but the average number is 21. Females lay their eggs singly or in clumps depending on subspecies, but an average egg mass numbers around 50 eggs, which are attached to twigs

A Close Relative

The California tiger salamander, *Ambystoma californiense*, used to be part of the tiger salamander complex, but most scientists now recognize it as a separate species. Its status is based on genetic studies, its geographic isolation from other forms of the tiger salamander, and its distinctive markings, which consist of round, lemon-yellow spots on a jet-black background. The species lives only in the Central Valley and a few localities farther west. Once widespread, now it is found only in small scattered colonies where suitable habitat still remains. Most populations have been eliminated due to urban and agricultural development. Another factor in its decline may be the programs to control ground squirrels and pocket gophers in the region: California tiger salamanders rely on the burrows of both species to retreat from the hot, dry California summers.

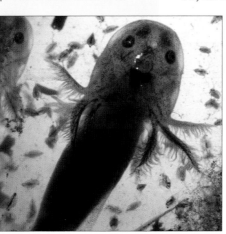

⋔ *California tiger salamander,* Ambystoma californiense *larvae, from the pools that occur during spring in a national wildlife refuge in California.*

and plant stems. In the north of the range total clutch sizes average 421 eggs, but farther south they are bigger—with 2,385 for small morphs and 5,670 for large morphs in Texas. The biggest recorded clutch was 7,651 eggs, the largest of any salamander.

The larvae are voracious feeders and can alter the ecology of their ponds by preying heavily on certain species of invertebrates. Even large larvae will eat small invertebrates, but they are capable of taking larger prey, such as frog tadpoles, when they are available. Cannibalistic larvae eat larger prey than typical larvae.

The growth rate of the larvae varies tremendously. In lowland ponds where the water is warm they usually transform in two to three months, after growing relatively quickly. Under extreme conditions the larvae in playa lakes in Texas can reach sexual maturity and transform when they are only five or six weeks old. In montane regions, on the other hand, they often overwinter and leave the water the following summer. Some fail to metamorphose at all, perhaps because the terrestrial habitat is more hostile than the aquatic one. Where they occur, cannibalistic larvae grow more quickly than normal ones and metamorphose sooner.

In summary, the life cycle of the tiger salamander is extremely variable. It changes with location (and therefore climate); but even at the same location some larvae are programed to feed more heavily, grow more quickly, and metamorphose sooner than others. However, larvae that take longer to grow usually metamorphose at a larger size. If the population contains cannibals, they are more likely to do well if the normal larvae vary in size (because they will be assured of suitable prey). In many populations some of the larvae do not metamorphose at all. They are neotenic—they become sexually mature while retaining some of their larval characteristics.

Common name Black-bellied salamander

Scientific name *Desmognathus quadramaculatus*

Subfamily Desmognathinae

Family Plethodontidae

Order Caudata (Urodela)

Size 4 in (10 cm) to 8 in (20 cm)

Key features Stocky; appears rubbery rather than slimy; limbs well developed; 14 conspicuous costal grooves along its flanks; tail is flattened from side to side and has a ridge along the top; mainly brown in color, peppered with small spots of greenish yellow or rust brown, becoming overall darker with age; body black below

Habits Nocturnal; terrestrial or semiaquatic

Breeding Fertilization is internal; female lays small clutches of eggs on the undersides of rocks in shallow water; eggs hatch after 8–12 weeks into free-living, aquatic larvae

Diet Larvae eat small invertebrates, such as mayflies, stoneflies, beetles, ants, and bugs; adults eat a range of terrestrial prey, including other salamanders

Habitat Alongside, at the edge of, or in fast-flowing woodland streams

Distribution North America in the Allegheny Mountains from southern West Virginia to northern Georgia

Status Numerous in suitable habitats

Similar species Plethodontid salamanders can be difficult to tell apart, but the black-bellied salamander is one of the larger, more robust species of *Desmognathus*

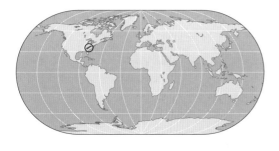

Black-Bellied Salamander

Desmognathus quadramaculatus

The black-bellied salamander and its close relatives live among waterfalls on the clear, boulder-strewn streams that drain the Appalachian mountain chain.

THE BLACK-BELLIED SALAMANDER is a robust, lively species and is one of the few plethodontids that may be active during the day. It is quick and agile; if disturbed, it darts away into a new crevice or into the water, where it may swim upstream. It lives along rushing watercourses, preferring small streams with plenty of large boulders, often in the vicinity of small cascades and waterfalls. Juveniles prefer slower-moving streams and seepages with plenty of stones of various sizes, which they use for cover.

Adults sometimes stray several yards from their streams, especially on damp nights, to hunt for food, but most individuals stay near the water in rock crevices or burrows in the bank. As they grow larger, they are less inclined to move and prefer to remain in or near their burrows, from where they ambush prey. They defend their burrows from other members of the species, and many have bite scars on their heads from fights. Over 40 percent of adults have lost their tails at some time.

Progressive Diet

The black-bellied salamander changes its diet markedly as it develops, thereby avoiding too much competition between the ages. Larvae eat small aquatic invertebrates, including the larvae of flies such as mayflies, stoneflies, and crane flies. Larger larvae also eat small crayfish and other salamander larvae. Juveniles usually stay in the water and eat flying insects when they touch the water's surface to breed, or when newly emerged. Adults eat a variety of terrestrial prey, including other salamanders, such as *Plethodon* and *Eurycea* species and the spring salamanders, *Gyrinophilus*. On the other

⊕ *Although nocturnal, the black-bellied salamander sometimes basks by day on wet rocks. It rarely ventures far from the side of a stream.*

hand, black-bellied salamanders are preyed on by a wide variety of predators such as shrews and garter snakes, although they defend themselves by biting vigorously. Faced with a shrew, a black-bellied salamander opens its jaws to display the white lining of its mouth and lunges forward while snapping its jaws.

Eggs on Stalks

Courtship and mating have not been seen in this species but probably occur in late summer and fall. Females lay their eggs the next spring and attach them in layers or clumps to the undersides of rocks. Each egg is suspended by a short stalk, and two or more eggs may share a stalk. If the eggs are in contact with flowing water, they are constantly agitated and aerated by the current. The female stays with them until they hatch two or three months later.

The small larvae find shelter beneath and between stones on the streambed and grow slowly. They metamorphose after two to four years, by which time they will have reached about 1.6 inches (4 cm) from snout to vent, although at higher elevations they may develop more slowly and metamorphose at 2.1 inches (5.4 cm). They become sexually mature after a further five to seven years; so, including its larval stage, a breeding salamander may be 10 years old or more.

Interacting Species

The black-bellied salamander often lives alongside other species of *Desmognathus*, including the seal salamander, *D. monticola*, and the Ocoee salamander, *D. ocoee*. They probably prey on each other's young and also affect the population structure by competing for burrows and other cover. The seal salamander (and probably other species) uses chemical signals to detect other salamanders; if they are present, it may avoid them. Experiments in which one or more species of *Desmognathus* have been removed from a small area have yielded interesting results: Some species increase while others decrease, showing that they interact strongly, often in ways that are not yet fully understood.

Common name Three-lined salamander

Scientific name *Eurycea guttolineata*

Subfamily Plethodontinae

Family Plethodontidae

Order Caudata (Urodela)

Size 4 in (10 cm) to 7 in (18 cm) including tail

Key features Slender with long tail accounting for 60–65 percent of the total length; limbs well developed; body has a pattern of three black stripes, 1 on each flank and 1 down the center of the back, on a tan or light-brown background; central stripe stops at the base of the tail, which is plain brown above

Habits Nocturnal; terrestrial

Breeding Fertilization is internal; female lays up to 100 eggs in winter; eggs hatch after 4–12 weeks

Diet Wide variety of invertebrates, including snails and snail eggs

Habitat Forests; never far from streams, ditches, or ponds

Distribution Southeastern North America along the Appalachian chain onto the Coastal Plain and up the eastern Mississippi Valley as far as southwestern Kentucky

Status Common in suitable habitat

Similar species The species used to be a subspecies of the long-tailed salamander, *E. longicauda*, which is similar and whose range it abuts; the two-lined salamander, *E. bislineata*, is also similar but lacks the dark dorsal stripe

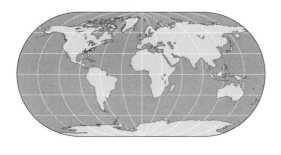

Three-Lined Salamander

Eurycea guttolineata

The three-lined salamander is a typical terrestrial plethodontid. It lives in forest litter or under logs in hardwood forests, emerging on damp and rainy nights to search for food.

THE THREE-LINED SALAMANDER is most active during the first few hours of darkness. Its diet is made up of a long list of small invertebrates such as beetles, flies, ants, spiders, crickets, and caterpillars. Adults are not territorial and may be found in groups.

The Reproductive Cycle

Their movements and breeding habits are similar to those of the long-tailed salamander, *E. longicauda*, with which they used to be classified, but they may differ in small details. Males are smaller than females, have elongated teeth in their upper jaws, and tentacles (or "cirri") below their nostrils. Adults feed throughout the spring and summer, and in fall they become less active on the surface.

Females move to breeding sites at that time, seeking out springs, streams (or ponds into which springs flow), caves, and abandoned mine shafts. They lay their eggs in fall or in the early spring, attaching them to the undersides of rocks, either in flowing water or just above it. Females have been found with small groups of eggs, but it is not clear if they stay with them until they hatch. They lay a total of 100 eggs. Based on clutches that have been found, they must lay them in several batches, which would make egg guarding impossible. The eggs hatch in four to 12 weeks depending on the water temperature, so newly hatched larvae may make an appearance in late fall or early spring.

The larvae live in cool springs, sometimes in caves, and eat small invertebrates, especially ostracods and copepods (minute aquatic crustaceans such as *Daphnia* and *Cyclops* species), fly larvae, and mayfly nymphs. Like many small salamander larvae, they live among dense aquatic vegetation, waterlogged leaf litter, and stones but emerge after dark to forage out in the open. Most of them metamorphose by the end of their first summer, but some overwinter as larvae and transform the following summer. Juveniles take about two years to reach breeding size.

Tail Waving

Like several other species in the genus *Eurycea*, the three-lined salamander uses its tail in defense, raising it above its head and waving it from side to side. At the same time, it coils its body so that its head is hidden under the tail. The purpose of the display is to encourage a predator to attack its tail (which the salamander can shed) rather than its head.

⬅ *The three-lined salamander can be identified by its markings and its long tail, which is about two-thirds of its total length. Its name comes from three dark stripes—one on its back and one on each side.*

Related Species

There are 14 species in the genus *Eurycea*. Seven are typical terrestrial salamanders like the three-lined salamander, and seven are aquatic and pedomorphic (retaining juvenile characteristics), for example, the Barton Springs salamander, *E. sosorum*. All the terrestrial species are similar to each other and can present problems in identification. Scientists are still working on the relationships, and some species, such as the two-lined salamander, *E. bislineata*, are likely to be split into two or more different species.

Of the pedomorphic species, three live in surface waters and have functional eyes and pigment, three live permanently in caves and are effectively blind, and one (the Texas salamander, *E. neotenes*) occurs in both situations. Six of the pedomorphic species live in Texas, but the Oklahoma salamander, *E. tynerensis*, lives around the area where three states—Oklahoma, Missouri, and Arkansas—meet.

Common name Barton Springs salamander

Scientific name *Eurycea sosorum*

Subfamily Plethodontinae

Family Plethodontidae

Order Caudata (Urodela)

Size 2.5 in (6 cm)

Key features Gills external; legs spindly; snout distinctive and squared off; eyes small and pigmented; color variable, may be pale purple-brown, yellow, or cream with small flecks of color creating a mottled "salt and pepper" effect; groups of reflective scales appear as light patches

Habits Totally aquatic, living in deep water that stays at a constant 68°F (20°C)

Breeding Egg laying probably occurs in winter, otherwise habits not known

Diet Small aquatic invertebrates, especially amphipods

Habitat Springs in limestone rock formations, under rocks, in gravel, and among plants and algae

Distribution Four springs within Zilker Park, Austin, Texas

Status Extremely rare

Similar species Other pedomorphic salamanders occur in the area, including *E. nana, E. rathbuni, E. neotenes,* and *E. robusta*, but this is the only one that lives in Barton Springs

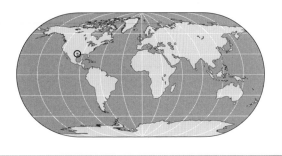

Barton Springs Salamander
Eurycea sosorum

The Barton Springs salamander was described to science only in 1993, but its existence was known as early as 1946. Today it is extremely rare and lives only in four springs within a small area of Austin, Texas.

THE BARTON SPRINGS SALAMANDER has a highly specialized lifestyle and a narrow ecological niche. In Barton Springs pool, for instance, it occurs only within a layer of gravel and small rocks overlying a coarse, sandy (or bare limestone) substrate near where the spring enters the pool. The water there is crystal clear, extremely pure, and contains no mud or silt.

Although nothing definite is known of the salamander's breeding habits, it is likely that they are similar to those of related species: Small numbers of eggs are probably attached to the stones and gravel on the bed of the stream or pool where it lives. Because of the low water temperature it takes a relatively long time for the eggs to hatch into tiny replicas of the adult.

The Barton Springs salamander is pedomorphic (meaning that the adults retain juvenile characteristics, such as external gills). There are other related pedomorphic species in the genus *Eurycea* from Texas and neighboring states, and some of them are restricted to underground streams.

Threatened Species
The Barton Springs salamander is extremely rare. Its known natural range is one of the smallest of any vertebrate species; and because it lies entirely within the city of Austin, Texas, there are grave concerns over its continued existence. A recent survey by the University of Texas using scuba equipment found only one individual. Furthermore, the salamander's continued survival depends entirely on the pristine water quality of the springs and the pools into which they empty.

⊕ *Well adapted to its aquatic lifestyle, the adult Barton Springs salamander retains many juvenile characteristics, for example, its long, slender body, three pairs of external gills, and a relatively short, finned tail.*

Pedomorphic Relatives

The Barton Springs salamander is not the only rare pedomorphic species of *Eurycea* in Texas. The San Marcos salamander, *E. nana*, lives along the north bank of Spring Lake, which forms the headwaters of the San Marcos River in Texas. The Texas blind salamander, *E. rathbuni*, is a cave-dwelling species without functional eyes or pigment, also living near San Marcos. Both these species are endangered and protected by federal law, like the Barton Springs salamander. The Blanco blind salamander, *E. robusta*, is in the greatest danger, and it may already be too late to save it. Four specimens were found by a group of workmen opening up a spring in a dry riverbed in the Blanco River in 1951. The site was later filled in with gravel by the river, and the species has not been seen again.

The Texas salamander, *E. neotenes*, by contrast, is relatively common and well studied. It lives on the Edwards Plateau of central Texas (like the other pedomorphic forms) but has an extensive range throughout the system of caves and underground streams and the springs that emerge from the limestone.

The springs are fed by an underground lake, or aquifer, that extends to the south and west of Austin, and the rapid growth of the city is threatening to contaminate the watershed. The amounts of silt, heavy metals, petroleum by-products, pesticides, and other toxins entering the system have increased dramatically in recent years. The small invertebrates on which the salamander feeds (and therefore the salamander itself) are extremely sensitive to such changes. More specifically, a large multinational corporation wanted to develop a 4,000-acre (1,600-ha) site within the Barton Springs watershed despite overwhelming opposition from the citizens of Austin.

Amid accusations of corruption and intimidation, the Save Our Springs (SOS) movement was formed in order to fight any future development. The Barton Springs salamander become a symbol of the organization's efforts because it acts as an indicator for the water quality. The health of the salamander population is totally dependent on the health of the Springs, and so its scientific name, *sosorum*, was created in recognition of the organization's efforts.

Conservation

To protect both the salamander and the springs, in 1992 the federal government was formally requested to list the salamander as an endangered and threatened species. But the government failed to act, and the battle between the citizens of Austin, the United States Fish and Wildlife Service, and the developers continued until April 1994, when the relevant city authorities agreed on guidelines for the management of the springs. Finally, on April 30, 1997, the Barton Springs salamander was given total legal protection.

Slimy Salamander

Plethodon glutinosus

Common name Slimy salamander

Scientific name *Plethodon glutinosus*

Subfamily Plethodontinae

Family Plethodontidae

Order Caudata (Urodela)

Size 4.5 in (11 cm) to 8 in (20 cm)

Key features Body slender; legs well developed; tail is round and about the same length as the head and body combined; color black or dark gray with small sliver-white spots over all its surfaces; secretions from its tail give the skin a more slimy appearance than that of other salamanders

Habits Nocturnal; terrestrial

Breeding Fertilization is internal; females suspend clusters of 5–34 eggs from overhanging rocks and coil around them until they hatch after 2–3 months

Diet Invertebrates, especially ants and small beetles, but also a wide variety of other species

Habitat Floors of hardwood forests, swamp forests, and pine woods

Distribution Southeastern North America from Texas and Florida to New York; distribution patchy toward the south of its range

Status Common

Similar species Several other species of *Plethodon*, notably the white-spotted salamander, *P. punctatus*, and the Cumberland Plateau salamander, *P. kentucki*

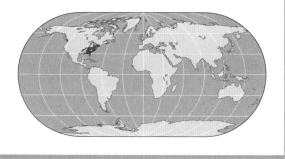

The slimy salamander lives up to both its common and scientific names. It secretes a slimy, sticky substance from glands in its tail as a defense against predators.

MANY SALAMANDERS HAVE poison glands in their skin to deter predators, but the slimy salamander is especially well endowed. Faced with a potential enemy, it raises its tail and lashes out with it. The secretions are distasteful, toxic, and may help incapacitate predators by smearing their eyes and mouth with goo. Even so, slimy salamanders fall prey to garter snakes copperheads, and probably other amphibian-eating snakes, as well as to birds, small mammals, and other salamanders.

The timing of courtship and breeding varies from one population to another. In the south it starts in February and goes on until summer, when females lay their eggs. In the north it starts in late summer or fall, and females lay the next spring or summer. Females from southern populations breed every year, but those in the north may breed only every other year.

Elaborate Courtship

The courting male goes through a sequence of maneuvers that identify him as a member of the correct species and stimulate the female to pick up his spermatophore. First, he presses his mental gland and nasolabial grooves against her head, body, or tail. Then he begins a courtship "dance," lifting and lowering his hind legs together or alternately. If he lifts them together, he uses his tail to prop up the rear of his body.

After a while he begins to raise and lower his front limbs as well, and gradually moves toward the female's head before rubbing his nasolabial grooves over her. He bites her body or tail gently, holds on for a short time, and then releases her. Next, he rubs his mental gland over the female's head and nasolabial grooves. He then pushes his head under her

chin and walks under her, keeping in contact all the time. As his tail passes under her chin, he waves it from side to side and stops moving forward. The female steps over his tail until she is straddling it, and they move forward together, the male still waving his tail and the back part of his body. They can cover up to 15 feet (4.6 m) in this position.

When they stop, the male begins to wriggle the base of his tail from side to side, and the female follows the movement with her head. The male lowers his vent and deposits his spermatophore on the ground. They both move forward again with the female's chin in contact with the base of the male's tail until she moves over the spermatophore, which she picks up with her cloaca. This ends the sequence, and the pair go their separate ways.

When seeking females to court, males approach any other salamanders. If they happen to be other males, a fight may break out, during which they bite one another. At other times, however, the male that

After rain showers the slimy salamander moves around the forest floor looking for invertebrate prey. If touched by human fingers, the gluelike secretions on its skin are almost impossible to remove.

has been approached may act like a female, encouraging the courting male to deposit (and therefore waste) his spermatophore.

Smell is an important factor in identifying other salamanders of the same species, and experiments have shown that females prefer the odor of male slimy salamanders to those of related species. Scent and elaborate courtship help prevent females from mating with the wrong species and therefore laying infertile eggs. Having said that, the whole *Plethodon glutinosus* species complex seems to consist of up to 13 recognized populations, some of which interbreed, and some of which do not.

Scientists think that the species became fragmented thousands of years ago; and while some populations differentiated to the point where they no longer recognize each other as belonging to the same species, others only went part of the way down that evolutionary path. Two salamanders, the Cumberland Plateau salamander, *P. kentucki,* and the rare Tellico salamander, *P. aureolus*, have been elevated from subspecies to full species, but scientists are waiting for more information before deciding on the validity of several other proposed species.

Common name Red salamander

Scientific name *Pseudotriton ruber*

Subamily Plethodontinae

Family Plethodontidae

Order Caudata (Urodela)

Size 3.8 in (9.6 cm) to 7 in (18 cm)

Key features Body stout; tail relatively short compared to many others in the family; skin appears rubbery; color varies from orange to crimson or purplish red; covered with small black spots that are more numerous on the back than the sides; juveniles more brilliantly marked than adults, which become dull with age

Habits Nocturnal; terrestrial or semiaquatic, often living in mud or under logs

Breeding Fertilization is internal; females lay clutches of 70–90 eggs that they attach to the undersides of rocks; they probably brood them until they hatch after about 12 weeks

Diet Small invertebrates and smaller salamanders

Habitat Seepages, streams, and bogs in deciduous forests and meadows

Distribution North America from southern New York to Indiana and the Gulf Coast; absent from much of the Atlantic coastal plain

Status Common in suitable habitat

Similar species The mud salamander, *Pseudotriton montanus*, is very similar but is usually orange-brown in color

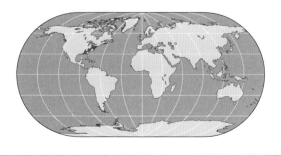

Red Salamander

Pseudotriton ruber

The red salamander is one of the most colorful salamanders in North America, although its bright coloration sometimes darkens as it ages.

THE RED COLORATION DOES not necessarily indicate that red salamanders are unpalatable: Many birds, mammals, and reptiles apparently eat them without ill effect. However, the species' range falls entirely within that of the eastern newt, *Notophthalmus viridescens*. Juveniles of that species, which are bright orange and are known as "red efts," produce powerful toxins in their skin. Therefore the red salamander might be a Batesian (harmless) mimic of the juvenile stage of the eastern newt.

Experiments show that birds learn to avoid red salamanders after they have had an unpleasant experience with red efts. Also, red salamanders defend themselves by raising their tail and coiling their body around in a manner similar to that adopted by red efts. As red efts grow to maturity, they lose their bright coloration and become brown, which might explain why adult red salamanders are not as brightly colored as juveniles.

Other research has concluded that red salamanders are Müllerian mimics because they produce some skin toxins, although they are not as strong as those of the eastern newt. (Müllerian mimics belong to a group of species that are all toxic and benefit by being similar to each other.) Other mildly toxic salamanders, such as the mud salamander, *Pseudotriton montanus*, posssibly the dusky salamander, *Desmognathus fuscus*, and other red-backed species that resemble each other (and the red salamander) superficially, may also benefit.

Simple Courtship

Compared with other plethodontids, red salamanders have a simple courtship. Males approach females and rub their snout over the

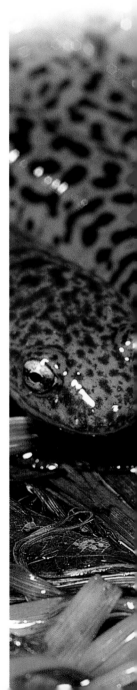

Red salamanders can be found by turning over stones or logs in or near small springs or brooks that run through woods or meadows.

female's head. Then the male forces his head under the female's chin and begins to wave his tail. She holds her chin against the base of his tail and straddles it before they walk forward for a short distance. The male then deposits his spermatophore, and the female picks it up.

Females are capable of storing sperm for very long periods after courtship, often for several months. They lay their eggs in fall or winter, selecting a shallow aquatic site such as a spring or bog through which water is continually seeping. Each egg is attached to the underside of a rock or stone by a narrow stalk and is often submerged in the water. A typical clutch consists of about 70 to 90 eggs, and the female probably stays with them, although an attended nest has not been found yet.

The eggs hatch after about three months, and the larvae make their way to slow-moving backwaters and pools where leaves and other debris collect. This provides them with somewhere to hide and is home to the large numbers of small invertebrates on which they feed. The larvae are slow growing and can take one and a half to three and a half years to metamorphose. Newly metamorphosed juveniles are relatively large and reach maturity about one year later.

Red salamanders do not seem to be territorial in the way that some related species are. They are sometimes found in large aggregations, especially in fall, when they make their way to springs and small streams to overwinter. They leave their wintering sites in the early spring and become more or less terrestrial until early summer, when they begin to gravitate back toward aquatic sites.

During their terrestrial phase they live in burrows in soft mud at the side of streams or beneath logs. Red salamanders feed on a wide variety of invertebrates; but being relatively large, they can also tackle small vertebrates, especially other salamanders. Known prey items include red-backed salamanders, *Plethodon cinereus*, and frogs.

Red eft stage

Common name Eastern newt (red-spotted newt)

Scientific name *Notophthalmus viridescens*

Family   Salamandridae

Order   Caudata (Urodela)

Size   2.5 in (6.3 cm) to 4.5 in (11 cm)

Key features Small newt with velvety skin; tail accounts
for about half the total length and has a
narrow keel above and below; adults are olive
above and yellow below with both surfaces
speckled with tiny black flecks; row of small,
round, bright-red spots bordered with black
on each side, sometimes joined together to
form broken stripes; juveniles bright to dull
orange

Habits   Aquatic, semiaquatic, and terrestrial
depending on stage of life and other factors

Breeding   Fertilization is internal; females lay eggs singly
over a long period; total eggs laid can
number 25–350; eggs hatch after 20–35 days

Diet   Small invertebrates on the land and in water

Habitat   Permanent and semipermanent ponds, lakes,
reservoirs, ditches, and swamps in forests or
open farmland

Distribution Eastern North America

Status   Very common

Similar species 2 other species of *Notophthalmus* are
similar but lack the small red markings

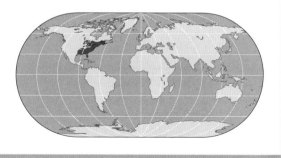

Eastern Newt

Notophthalmus viridescens

The eastern newt is found in quiet pools or backwaters of rivers in forests or in meadows. Juvenile red efts can be seen during the day near woodlands after rain.

THE EASTERN NEWT TYPICALLY goes through three stages: It begins life as an aquatic larva, metamorphoses to become a terrestrial juvenile (known as an eft), and then develops into an aquatic adult. To further complicate a confusing sequence of events, there is great variation.

Some individuals skip the intermediate terrestrial juvenile stage and remain in the water after they have metamorphosed into aquatic juveniles. Others reach adulthood without having metamorphosed completely, so they become neotenous adults with external gills. Adults may return to the water after they have matured and stay there for the rest of their lives. Alternatively, they may remain there as long as possible but leave temporarily if the ponds begin to dry up or become overheated; or they may simply return to the water and breed, leaving once the breeding season is over. Some, but not all, of this variation is related to locality, although some populations include individuals that have different life cycles.

Red Efts

The most familiar form is probably the red eft. It is a small, bright- to dull-orange newt that lives among leaf litter. Red efts are more likely to be active in the day than other amphibians because they gain some protection through the bright coloration that warns of poisonous secretions from glands in their skin. Red efts are ten times as toxic as adult eastern newts and are avoided by many predators, including American toads, garter snakes, red-tailed hawks, and raccoons. Their defense is not as effective against nocturnal hunters (because the bright colors are not easily visible), and bullfrogs and some turtles will eat them. There is a record of a hognose snake eating one, and another of a Boy Scout in New York State in the 1940s

eating several red
efts wrapped in bread.
Neither the hognose snake
nor the scout apparently
suffered any ill effects!

Breeding

Courtship in eastern newts is variable. At its
simplest the male displays in front of the
female, she nudges his tail, he drops his
spermatophore, and she picks it up in her
cloaca. This occurs in less than 30 percent of
encounters. In the others the male has to work
harder to stimulate the female, and courtship
involves a form of amplexus—the male grasps
the female just behind her front limbs with his
hind limbs. At the same time, he rubs her snout
with his front limbs and the sides of his head.
He curls his tail around and wafts secretions

from his cloaca past her nostrils. After an hour
or more he releases her and deposits his
spermatophore. If all goes well, the female
gradually moves forward until she is over the
spermatophore and picks it up. Unfortunately,
in just over half the encounters the female
swims away without picking it up. In other
cases another male darts between the male and
female at the last minute and deposits his own
spermatophore, sometimes eating that of the
first male. Surprisingly, females are as likely to
pick up the cheater's spermatophore as that of
their courtship partner.

Females lay their eggs singly, attaching
each one to the leaf of an aquatic plant and
carefully folding the leaf over it with their hind
legs. Since they lay only a few eggs each day,
and they can total 25 to 350, egg laying can
take several weeks to complete.

↑ *Adult eastern newts*
usually live among
vegetation in shallow
water. They are voracious
feeders, preying on
worms, insects, small
crustaceans and mollusks,
as well as amphibian
eggs and larvae.

Common name Rough-skinned newt

Scientific name *Taricha granulosa*

Family Salamandridae

Order Caudata (Urodela)

Size 6.1 in (15.5 cm) to 8.6 in (22 cm)

Key features Heavily built newt; skin rough due to its covering of small warts; color dark brown or black with an orange or yellow underside, sometimes with a few dark markings

Habits Adults and juveniles terrestrial; larvae aquatic; adults secretive, emerging at night to feed

Breeding Fertilization is internal and follows courtship in which amplexus takes place; female lays eggs that she attaches singly to aquatic plants or debris

Diet Small invertebrates, such as insects and worms; frogs' eggs and tadpoles

Habitat Damp forests, sometimes fields and meadows, in hilly or mountainous countryside; larvae live in temporary or permanent ponds, lakes, and ditches

Distribution Western North America from southeastern Alaska to San Francisco Bay but not extending far inland

Status Common

Similar species 2 related species, the red-bellied newt, *Taricha rivularis*, and the California newt, *T. torosa*, live in the same region; they are all very similar, but *T. rivularis* has a rich red underside (the others have orange bellies), and *T. torosa* has larger eyes; distinguishing the latter species from *T. granulosa* in places where they both occur is difficult

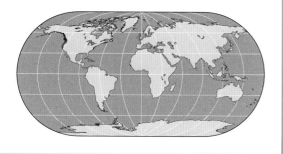

Rough-Skinned Newt

Taricha granulosa

The skin of the rough-skinned newt contains powerful poisons—easily enough to kill or repel a potential predator. The toxins are even capable of killing a human foolhardy enough to eat one.

THE ROUGH-SKINNED NEWT is far more toxic than the two other species of *Taricha* (*T. rivularis*, the red-bellied newt, and *T. torosa*, the California newt), but the eggs of all three species are equally toxic. In experiments an amount of preparation from its skin too small to visualize killed a laboratory mouse in under 10 minutes. Surprisingly, however, one of its main predators, the red-spotted garter snake, *Thamnophis sirtalis concinnus*, seems to be immune to its effects, while other species of garter snakes become paralyzed. On Vancouver Island the newts are less toxic than elsewhere, and the garter snakes there are less resistant to the newt toxin.

As a second means of defense, rough-skinned newts arch their backs, close their eyes, and raise their tail and head to reveal their bright undersides in a warning display.

Locating Breeding Ponds

In the spring adult rough-skinned newts make their way to breeding ponds, which may be temporary pools, beaver ponds, or larger bodies of water. However, the timing can vary from place to place—at high altitudes breeding may not take place until October, while nearer the coast they breed from January to April. The newts move mostly at night and especially during wet weather.

Several experiments have been conducted to test the species' homing instinct. Results have shown that animals that are moved over 500 yards (450 m) from their home ranges always return, sometimes in less than 12 hours. They seem to orient themselves using scent and celestial cues, and they may also use memory.

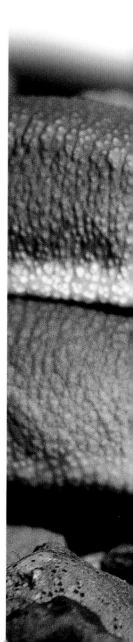

Many move along small streams until they arrive at the breeding pools.

Most females breed every year, but some breed every second year. There is also regional variation in their behavior after breeding: In some places they leave the water once egg laying is finished, but in others they stay for the remainder of the year, leaving only in the fall to find somewhere to hibernate. In California adults usually remain in the water throughout the year unless heavy rain washes them out. Even during the breeding season individual newts may leave the pond temporarily, perhaps to search for food.

Courtship consists of a dorsal amplexus in which the male grasps the female just behind her front

Mysterious Gatherings

For reasons that are not fully understood, rough-skinned newts sometimes come together to form large aggregations. One contained about 5,000 males and females that had recently bred. They were in the channel of a reservoir, and covered an area of about 22 square yards (18 sq. m). They gradually dispersed over the next few weeks, probably to their overwintering sites.

Another record involved a group of 259 newts, including large larvae, juveniles, and adults grouped together under objects along the shore of Crater Lake, Oregon. Newts from Crater Lake are unusual in having dark blotches on their bellies, and they are considered to be a distinct subspecies, *T. granulosa mazamae*.

⊕ Amplexus in rough-skinned newts can last for up to two days. Should they need to come to the surface to breathe during this time, they do so still locked together.

limbs and just in front of her hind limbs. While in this position, he uses his chin and his hind limbs to stroke various parts of the female's body. They can remain coupled like this for up to two days until the female raises her head, presumably to signal that she is ready to pick up a spermatophore. The male releases his grip and moves around to the front of the female. She places her snout in contact with his cloaca. After depositing the spermatophore, he swings his body around, while the female keeps her snout in contact with his cloaca. Eventually, she will be positioned directly over the spermatophore, which she picks up with her cloaca. At this point the male may go back into amplexus again, and the process may be repeated several times.

The female begins egg laying shortly after mating and attaches the eggs singly to aquatic plants or underwater debris. The larvae usually grow to metamorphosis by the end of the summer, but at high elevations they overwinter and transform the following year.

Common name
Tailed frog

Scientific name
Ascaphus truei

Family Ascaphidae (sometimes placed in the Leiopelmatidae)

Order Anura

Size From 1 in (2.5 cm) to 2 in (5 cm)

Key features Fairly ordinary looking; skin slightly rough; body brown, olive, gray, or reddish-brown with some irregular mottling; dark stripe through the eye; males have a short "tail" consisting of an extension of the cloaca used for transferring sperm into the cloaca of females; eardrum lacking

Habits Nocturnal; semiaquatic or terrestrial

Breeding Very unusual; fertilization is internal; females lays 40–80 eggs that hatch after about 30 days; larvae take several years to metamorphose

Diet Invertebrates

Habitat Cold, clear, rocky streams flowing through ancient forests

Distribution North America (Pacific Northwest from southern British Columbia, Canada, to northern California), with many separated populations

Status Rare and endangered in Canada (and protected nationally) but no protection in the U.S.

Similar species A second species, *Ascaphus montanus*, the Rocky Mountain tailed frog, is sometimes recognized, but it differs only slightly from *A. truei*

Tailed Frog
Ascaphus truei

The unique little tailed frog is the most primitive frog species in the world. As with the New Zealand frogs, the adults retain the same tail-wagging muscles that allow tadpoles to swim.

SOME AUTHORITIES GROUP the New Zealand frogs and the tailed frog (or frogs) together in one family because they share several primitive characteristics, but they also differ in several important ways. Apart from some anatomical differences, the tailed frog has aquatic larvae, while those of the New Zealand frogs develop directly inside the egg capsule. The tailed frog also has internal fertilization, aided by the male's "tail." In reality, it is a fleshy, tubular extension of the cloaca that becomes swollen during amplexus and is inserted into the cloaca of the female to transfer sperm.

The breeding season lasts from May until October, but activity is greatest in the fall. Females may only breed every alternate year. Tailed frogs do not have eardrums, and they probably do not call. Males have roughened pads of skin on the front limbs and the palms of their "hands," which darken in the breeding season, and they use them to grip the female.

Necklace of Eggs
Amplexus is inguinal, meaning that the male grasps the female just in front of her hind limbs and maneuvers his "tail" into her cloaca by arching his back. They remain together for 24 to 30 hours. The female stores the sperm in her oviduct until the following year, laying between 40 and 80 eggs in July. They are joined together in a long string with constrictions in the jelly between each egg, resembling a necklace. The female attaches them to the underside of rocks on the bed of the stream.

The eggs consume less oxygen than almost any other amphibian eggs due to the cold temperatures of the stream in which they develop. They hatch in 30 days, in August or

⊕ *The tiny tailed frogs do not have true tails. Males have a tail-like organ for sperm transfer, and all adults have tiny tail-wagging muscles, a reminder of the fact that they evolved from tailed ancestors.*

September. The larvae are highly adapted to life in fast-flowing streams. They have broad bodies with a large, round, suckerlike disk on the underside with which they attach themselves to stones. Without it they would be in danger of being swept away, and they stick so tightly to the rocks that they are hard to remove.

Other torrent-dwelling frogs, such as the African ghost frogs, *Heleophryne* species, and the *Amolops* species from Asia, have similar tadpoles. They feed on the bacterial and algal slime that develops on rocks, and to a lesser extent, on organic material suspended in the water. They shun the light, hiding away during the day and becoming more active at night. Despite this, in places where they occur in the same streams, larvae of the Pacific giant salamander, *Dicamptodon ensatus*, prey heavily on them—tailed frog tadpoles may make up 14 percent of their diet. They grow slowly and take from

One Species or Two?

Until recently only one tailed frog, *Ascaphus truei,* was known, with a degree of variation between isolated populations. In 2001, however, scientists reported variation in the DNA between populations and proposed a new species, the Rocky Mountain tailed frog, *Ascaphus montanus*. It is possible that other new species will be described. However, these species cannot be distinguished from each other using visual characteristics alone.

two to four years to metamorphose. It can be another five or six years until they are large enough to breed.

Adult tailed frogs remain in the vicinity of the streams in which they breed but sometimes stray up to 25 yards (23 m) from the water's edge at night to feed. During dry weather they stay near the streamside. They feed on a wide variety of small invertebrates.

Common name Mexican
burrowing frog

Scientific name *Rhinophrynus dorsalis*

Family   Rhinophrynidae

Order   Anura

Size   From 2.5 in (6.5 cm) to 3 in (7.5 cm)

Key features Adult body almost as broad as it is long;
head tiny and blunt; snout cone shaped;
limbs short, better suited to burrowing than
locomotion; dark gray in color with a few
scattered white or pinkish-white spots around
its face and on its flanks; conspicuous orange
or pink stripe down the center of its back

Habits   Strictly burrowing; emerges only during heavy
rain

Breeding   In temporary pools and flooded fields after
heavy rain; female lays thousands of small
eggs that hatch after a few days

Diet   Ants, termites, and their larvae

Habitat   Lowland forests and coastal plains

Distribution Central America, barely entering the United
States along the Gulf Coast of Texas,
extending along the east coast of Mexico into
the Yucatán Peninsula, Costa Rica, and just
into northeastern Honduras

Status   Common but rarely seen

Similar species None; some of the narrow-mouthed
toads, Microhylidae, have the same body
shape, but they are significantly smaller and
lack the brightly colored dorsal stripe

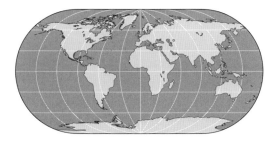

Mexican Burrowing Frog

Rhinophrynus dorsalis

Mexican burrowing frogs are unusual to look at and have a unique way of feeding. After heavy rainstorms, males of this species emerge from the ground. They call in large choruses while floating on the surface of the flooded land.

THE MEXICAN BURROWING FROGS are opportunistic breeders. They emerge from their underground chambers to mate and lay eggs whenever torrential rain floods the flat countryside where they live. Their front legs are short and have no webbing, but the hind legs are heavily webbed to aid in swimming and have two elongated tubercles, or "spades," for digging.

When they are not calling, their body is flaccid, and their skin seems several sizes too large for them. Males have a pair of internal vocal sacs, and they inflate themselves like balloons and float on the surface while calling. They make a loud, resonant "whoooooo....." call and form large choruses that can be heard over half a mile (1 km) away.

Females are larger than males and lay several thousand small eggs following a period of inguinal amplexus. The eggs float to the surface and hatch a few days later.

Toads' Tongues

Broadly speaking, frogs and toads have one of three types of tongue. Most commonly, as in the treefrogs in the Hylidae, the tongue is attached at the front of the jaw so that it can be flipped out to catch small prey at some distance from the toad's snout. Other species, especially from the more primitive families, such as the fire-bellied toads (Bombinatoridae), have tongues that are attached at the back of the mouth (like ours) so they capture prey by lunging at it. The burrowing toad may be the only species with a tongue that can change shape and be projected right ahead.

They have no teeth, and they lack the hard, bony beak that most tadpoles use to scrape food from rocks and other hard surfaces. In many respects the tadpoles of this species are like those of the clawed toads, *Xenopus*, and their relatives.

Synchronized Swimming

Rhinophrynus tadpoles tend to live in large shoals numbering from 50 to several hundred individuals, all pointing the same way and moving in synchrony with each other. Shoals can contain tadpoles of widely differing sizes —they may include tadpoles from different parents, hatched at different times. This may help reduce predation or increase feeding efficiency, or both. As the tadpoles feed, their tails set up small water currents that bring food particles toward their mouths. Although each individual can produce its own current, a large number working together can increase the flow and therefore the amount of food. In experiments scientists found that tadpoles kept together in shoals grew more quickly than those raised individually.

Feeding

The adult frog has an unusual method of feeding, possibly unique among frogs. Its tongue is flat and triangular in shape when contracted, but it can be made stiff and rod shaped by increasing the hydrostatic pressure in a chamber, or sinus, within it. The tongue can then be protruded through a small groove at the front of the lower jaw. Because it feeds underground, the technique has never been observed, but scientists think that the frog pushes its hard, calloused snout through the wall of a termite nest or tunnel and flicks out its tongue to capture the prey inside.

Unusual Tadpoles

The tadpoles of the Mexican burrowing toad live in midwater, maintaining a horizontal position by constantly vibrating their tail. They feed by filtering large quantities of water and extracting suspended organic material. They have a flattened head, and their eyes are positioned on either side of the mouth. The mouth itself is wide, slitlike, and is surrounded by 11 sensitive barbels that presumably help direct food particles into the mouth.

↑ *Mexican burrowing frogs are well adapted for their underground lifestyle, having spadelike hind feet and toes and a flattened body. Their tongue is also modified for a specialized diet of termites.*

Couch's Spadefoot

Scaphiopus couchi

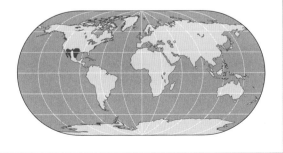

Common name Couch's spadefoot

Scientific name *Scaphiopus couchi*

Family Pelobatidae

Order Anura

Size From 2.3 in (5.5 cm) to 3.5 in (9 cm)

Key features Body plump with soft, fairly smooth skin; eyes large with yellow irises and vertically elliptical pupils; limbs short and powerful; hind limbs have hard black ridges on their "heels," used for burrowing backward into the ground; color yellowish or greenish brown; females have brown mottled markings on the back but males are plain; underside of males and females mostly white; females larger than males

Habits Nocturnal; terrestrial, spending most of their life underground

Breeding In temporary pools following rain; females lay up to 3,000 eggs that hatch within a few days

Diet Invertebrates

Habitat Plains, vegetated deserts, and other semiarid places

Distribution Southern United States and northern Mexico, including Baja California

Status Common but rarely seen

Similar species There are a number of other spadefoot toads in North America, but Couch's is the only yellow one

Many parts of the dry American Southwest reverberate with the calls of Couch's spadefoot toads following heavy summer rains. The loud choruses of these toads are an important way of bringing breeding animals together.

COUCH'S SPADEFOOT TOADS, which can be present in high densities, spend most of their life underground in cocoons formed from several layers of shed skin. This helps prevent dehydration, and they may spend many months in a form of "suspended animation" during dry weather. As soon as the summer rains fall, however, they quickly dig their way to the surface to take advantage of temporary pools that form in the desert. At such times the ground may be covered with spadefoot toads.

Choruses can number several thousand calling males, and the sound they produce can be heard over 1 mile (1.6 km) away. Scientists think they call so loudly because their breeding sites can change from year to year as localized rainstorms move across the desert. The loud calls help direct females (and other males) to the right place. Other species from the region, such as western spadefoots, *S. hammondi*, plains spadefoots, *S. bombifrons,* green toads, *Bufo debilis*, and Sonoran desert toads, *Bufo alvarius*, have similar lifestyles, and choruses can contain several species, all with different calls.

⊕ *A Couch's spadefoot toad hides in a sandy burrow in Arizona. Because of the unfavorable conditions where most of them live, and the need to avoid dehydration, these toads live underground and only emerge at night.*

Explosive Breeders

Spadefoot toads are good examples of "explosive breeders," species in which all individuals breed within a short space of time. Females of explosive breeders do not "choose" their mates as they do in other species in which males might be spaced out along a pond or stream edge, for example. Instead, each male

Distant Thunder?

Scientists are worried that off-road vehicles are disrupting the Couch's spadefoot toads' breeding behavior. Apparently the toads mistake the noise of the vehicles thundering across the desert surface for real thunder and, assuming a rainstorm is imminent, burrow up to the surface at an inappropriate time.

tries to elbow his way to a female and gain one or more matings before the brief breeding season is over. This is known as "scramble competition." Females of the species are larger than the males. In the case of Couch's spadefoot toads a breeding season may last just two or three days, during which time every female toad in a given locality digs her way to the surface, finds a mate, and produces eggs.

Although the toads may be active for a time after breeding, while they feed and build up food reserves for another 10 or 11 months' estivation, they burrow down to form another cocoon as soon as the ground begins to dry out again. Meanwhile, their eggs hatch within a few days, and the tadpoles develop rapidly. Under extreme circumstances they can metamorphose 14 to 15 days after hatching. They grow at different rates, however. Some tadpoles grow more slowly and metamorphose at a larger size. In years when rain falls several

times, keeping the temporary ponds full of water, these individuals have an advantage. In dry years they perish before they metamorphose, so producing two types of tadpoles acts as insurance against the total loss of the batch.

Because of the very nature of the ponds in which they develop, spadefoot tadpoles are exposed to extremely hot conditions and can tolerate temperatures above 98°F (41°C). Most other frog and toad tadpoles cannot survive temperatures much higher than 86°F (30°C), and species from cool environments, such as the tailed frog, *Ascaphus truei*, prefer to live at 68°F (20°C) or less. In addition, while most frog and toad tadpoles need to acclimatize to exceptionally high temperatures over a period of several days, Couch's spadefoots' eggs are tolerant of high temperatures even before development begins.

Common name Cane
toad (marine toad, giant toad)

Scientific name *Bufo marinus*

Family Bufonidae

Order Anura

Size 4 in (10 cm) to 9.5 in (24 cm); the largest
wild specimen weighed 3 lb (1.36 kg)

Key features Very large, possibly the world's largest toad;
head large; neck bears elongated parotid
glands; hind thighs have large poison glands;
the whole of the back liberally sprinkled with
warts; color brown, often plain, but
sometimes with a pattern of slightly darker
blotches

Habits Nocturnal; terrestrial

Breeding In water; females lay up to 35,000 eggs in a
long string; eggs hatch within 48 hours;
tadpoles metamorphose in 12–60 days

Diet Most edible things, including insects, small
vertebrates, and even dog food

Habitat Absent from very few habitats within its
range, including villages and towns

Distribution Natural distribution is Central and South
America, just reaching the United States in
extreme southern Texas; it has been
deliberately introduced to numerous other
countries, notably Australia

Status Common, to plague proportions in places

Similar species Several other large brown toads that live
in the same region, including the rococo
toad, *Bufo paracnemis*

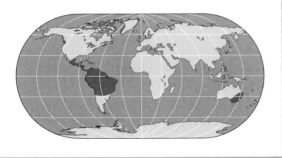

Cane Toad

Bufo marinus

*Few amphibians can claim as much notoriety as the
cane toad. Its introduction to Australia and
subsequent depredations of the native fauna are well
documented and are often used to illustrate the
dangers of ill-conceived biological control.*

THE CANE TOAD, WHICH IS also called the marine
toad (even though it is not marine), was
introduced to Australia in the 1930s in an
attempt to control pests of sugarcane, notably
the beetle *Phyllophaga vandinei*. This pest was
causing great concern in several parts of the
world where sugar was produced. It had
brought the agricultural community to its knees
in several countries because there were no
pesticides available in those days. The cane
toads, which can eat on average 12.5 beetles a
night, were the answer to the growers' prayers.
A thousand toads could potentially eliminate
over 4 million beetles in one year.

Australia's decision to introduce the toads
was also based on earlier introductions starting
in the middle of the 19th century. At that time
the toads were released on several West Indian
Islands that were suffering at the hands of the
same beetle (which also eats the leaves and
roots of other tropical crops such as banana,
coconut, and breadfruit).

Seasoned Traveler
The cane toad was also introduced to Hawaii in
1932, to the Philippines in 1934, and to
Formosa (now Taiwan) in 1935 for the same
purpose. Some of these introductions were
from populations that had in turn been
introduced from elsewhere, so the offspring of
toads from Trinidad were introduced to Puerto
Rico, Puerto Rico then provided stock for
Hawaii, and Hawaii passed some on to Australia
and Taiwan. Australia generously sent toads to
New Guinea some time around 1937.
Altogether, cane toads have been introduced
into at least 15 different countries at one time

→ *Cane toads are
various shades of brown
depending on their
habitat. Their skin is
covered with warts, and
their head has distinctive
horned ridges.*

The Heavyweights

or another. The globetrotting toad has rapidly expanded its horizons.

The original Australian introduction took place in 1935 at the Sugar Experimental Station in Meringa, Queensland, and involved 101 toads. They bred immediately, and 3,400 young toads were released into neighboring sugar-growing areas the same year. There was some concern from conservationists even then that the toads would also eat beneficial insects along with the pest species, and further importations were banned later that year. The ban was not well received by the farmers, and it was lifted in 1936.

The largest cane toad ever recorded was a captive male called "Prinsen," owned by an enthusiast in Sweden. It measured 15 in (38 cm) in length and weighed 5.6 pounds (2.54 kg). The largest female was called "Totally Awesome" and was owned by a zoo in Des Moines, Iowa. It weighed in at 5.1 pounds (2.31 kg) and measured 9.5 inches (24.1 cm) long.

Other large toads include Blomberg's toad, *Bufo blombergi*, from Colombia. It is around 8 inches (20 cm) long and weighs 2.2 pounds (1 kg), which is larger than the average cane toad. The rococo toad, *Bufo paracnemis*, also from South America, is similar to the cane toad and almost as large. In Southeast Asia the largest species are the giant river toad, *Bufo juxtasper*, that reaches 8.5 inches (21.5 cm) and the river toad, *Bufo asper*, that grows to 5.5 inches (14 cm). The largest North American species is the Colorado River toad, *Bufo alvarius*, at 7 inches (18 cm) long. In Europe the southern version of the common toad, *Bufo bufo spinosus*, can exceptionally reach 8 inches (20 cm) in parts of Spain and Italy. By comparison, most members of the genus *Bufo* are about 1.5 to 2.5 inches (4–6 cm) long.

→ *Cane toads are sometimes called giant toads, with good reason. As this Guyanese specimen shows, they can grow to an enormous size and weight.*

Needless to say, the toads thrived in their new home, due in part to their adaptability and in part because they had no predators and very few competitors. By 1974 they had spread into 225,000 square miles (584,000 sq. km) of Queensland—about one-third of the state. They are still spreading today and increase their range by about 8.1 percent each year.

Breakout

As well as the spread of existing toad populations, small numbers have escaped while being transported to other parts of Australia. In Perth, for example, a box containing about 50 toads broke open at the airport, and the toads

69

made off into the surrounding countryside. Honey producers were alarmed because the toads eat large numbers of bees. The airport was searched, and a substantial reward was offered for any toad recovered. Although several toads remained unaccounted for, they appear not to have bred, and the region is still toad-free. The beekeepers (and probably the bees, too) breathed a huge sigh of relief.

What makes the cane toad such a good colonizer? In a word: adaptability. Cane toads are like rats—they are able to modify their lifestyles, diets, and breeding habits according to whatever is available. Although they originate in tropical rain forests, they are equally at home in fields, plantations, parks, golf courses, and gardens. They even occur in the heart of cities, where they hide under buildings by day and emerge at night to sit around the bases of street lamps to snap up insects attracted by the light.

Avid Foragers

The feeding habits of cane toads are legendary. They will eat anything that fits in their mouths, and that includes all the usual insects and other invertebrates, but also smaller frogs and toads, lizards, small snakes, mammals, and birds.

The most significant factor in their feeding habits, however, is their ability to recognize food that is not moving. While most other frogs and toads will only stalk moving prey, cane toads seem to use their sense of smell when out foraging. They recognize the smell of dog food, for instance, and will even learn when it is due to be placed out in a bowl. They congregate in numbers (along with the dog) and wait for the bowl to arrive, just as they wait at the entrances of beehives, ready to pick

⊙ *In Australia native species of mammals and marsupials, such as this pygmy possum, are at risk of predation by the formidable cane toad.*

A Bad Press

Apart from beekeepers, conservationists and the public at large have become concerned about the presence of the cane toads. Some of the fears are unjustified. In 1959 one commentator in Florida wrote: "monstrous toads which threaten housewives in their backyards, seize dogs by the head, and hang on with a death-resulting grip, or attack and kill with their virulent poison the innocent neighborhood cats." There is no doubt that cane toads produce virulent poisons that can easily kill a dog or a cat. However, they do not go out of their way to do so, nor (as far as we know) do they seize dogs by the head!

The biggest problem they pose is that they eat and compete with indigenous species of amphibians, many of which are unique to Australia. Having said that, the lifestyles of Australian toads vary so much that competition may be limited to a few breeding pools. The appetite and sheer size of the cane toads must take a toll on local

populations, but again surveys seem to show that they do not appear to have had a serious effect. Predators that attempt to eat them, including several species of snakes, often die. Much of the reaction against them may be prejudice: Humans do not much like large toads that eat the food they put out for their pets.

Cane toads have suffered a bad press among beekeepers, since they can devour large numbers of bees. This toad is attacking a hive in Queensland, Australia.

off returning bees. They also visit garbage dumps and eat vegetable scraps such as corn on the cob, broccoli, and rice. This implies a certain intelligent approach to food gathering.

In places where the cane toad lives side by side with other members of the genus *Bufo*, it competes so strongly that it may almost eliminate them. For example, in the United States in southern Texas and in Florida (where it was introduced) few other species can compete with the cane toad. In experiments scientists found that the American toads, *Bufo americanus*, nearly always died whenever they were kept in cages with cane toads. That was not because they were attacked, but because they gave up trying to get to the food before the cane toads.

ⓘ *A cane toad attempts to make itself look even bigger when threatened by a toad-eating snake,* Xenodon rhabdocephalus, *in Costa Rica, its natural home.*

Poison Glands

Cane toads are immune to attack from almost any predator. Their skin contains numerous poison glands, two of which are greatly enlarged and positioned just behind the head. They secrete potent toxins in the form of a sticky, milky fluid. When the toads are provoked, they can squirt the liquid up to 3 feet (1 m), but it usually just oozes out.

If the toxin enters the mouth, eyes, or open wound of a victim, it causes immediate excruciating pain and forces the predator to drop the toad. Unless they have a method of skinning the toads and avoiding their most poisonous parts, predators would almost certainly die if they ate one.

Examples of species that have died as a result of eating cane toads include several mammals, notably cats and dogs, crows and other birds, large monitor lizards, and snakes—even venomous species in Australia such as death adders. Predators from countries where the toads have been introduced may be more at risk because they are not genetically programmed to avoid them.

25,000 small black eggs. The eggs usually hatch within 48 hours, and the tadpoles metamorphose between 12 and 60 days later. The newly metamorphosed toadlets are surprisingly small and swarm over the banks of the pond like black flies. Although the tadpoles are distasteful to fish and most other animals, they lose some of their toxicity when they change, and that is the time when they are most vulnerable. It is just as well, considering the large numbers produced.

Another defense mechanism involves posture. When a toad is threatened, it flattens its body and tilts it toward the aggressor by straightening the two legs on the far side. This makes it look even larger than it is.

Breeding
Cane toads breed at any time of the year provided the conditions are right for them. In places where it rains throughout the year, marine toads have an extended breeding season, with different individuals breeding at different times. This helps their tadpoles avoid competition with each other and also insures against random catastrophes, such as ponds drying up. Cane toads will breed in most types of water, including ponds, ditches, and streams. The male's call is loud and tuneless, like a small outboard motor.

The females lay their eggs in long strands that can measure up to 20 yards (18 m) long and contain up to

⊕ *The poison glands of cane toads are particularly large and ooze a sticky, milky fluid that is highly toxic.*

"Marine" Misnomer
The scientific name, *Bufo marinus*, and one of the common names for the species suggest that it is in someway associated with the marine environment. This is not so, and the name may have been coined when tadpoles were found close to the seashore. They must have been living in fresh water draining down to the sea, however, since experiments have shown that they die in water containing more than 15 percent saltwater. That is far less than the amount tolerated by several other species, for example, the clawed toad, *Xenopus laevis*, which can live in water with a concentration of nearly three times that amount.

Adding to Our Knowledge

The cane toad has some beneficial qualities, especially in parts of Australia where it is plentiful and where native species are protected. For example, it was routinely used for pregnancy testing before the development of chemical tests. (The traditional animal used, the African clawed toad, *Xenopus laevis*, does not occur in Australia, and it is illegal to import it in case it spreads and becomes a nuisance.) The urine of pregnant women contains a hormone called chorionic gonadotrophin (HCG); its presence causes toads injected with an extract from the urine to lay eggs.

The cane toad was later used for testing a variety of other drugs. It is also widely used for dissection in biology classes, and a business has grown around the collection and sale of the toads for that purpose. Attempts to use the flesh of the toad as chicken feed and to use the skin for tanning have, however, proved unsuccessful.

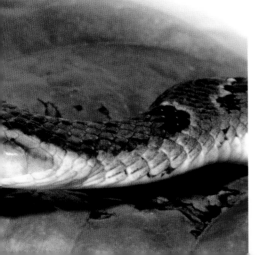

Eleutherodactylus
abbotti

Common names Rain frogs, leaf-litter frogs, robber
frogs, stream frogs

Scientific name *Eleutherodactylus* sp.

Family   Leptodactylidae

Order   Anura

Size   From 0.4 in (10 mm) to 4 in (10 cm)

Key features Mostly fairly nondescript, small, and
brownish in color; some have brighter green,
tan, or orange coloration; fingers and toes
lack webbing; some have large heads and
eyes; a large round disk on the underside
helps them cling to smooth surfaces; digits
have expanded tips for climbing

Habits   Mostly nocturnal; usually seen in leaf litter
immediately before, during, and after rain;
some climb into low shrubs and bushes;
others live among rocks and boulders

Breeding   Terrestrial breeders; females lay from 3 to
over 20 eggs that hatch directly into
miniature versions of the adults

Diet   Small invertebrates

Habitat   Deciduous and rain forests, plantations,
gardens, and parks

Distribution From extreme south of Texas and Arizona
through Central America and the West Indies
to Argentina and Brazil; introduced to Florida
and Louisiana

Status   Some very abundant, others known from only
a few specimens; several are thought to be
recently extinct

Similar species Distinguishing between different species
can be very difficult; they may also look like
juveniles of many other types of frogs

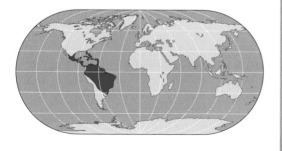

Rain Frogs

Eleutherodactylus sp.

*Eleutherodactylus is not only the largest genus of frogs
but the largest of all vertebrate genera. There are 48
species in Cuba alone. While there is variation between
species, they are all small and mainly terrestrial.*

ESTIMATES OF THE NUMBER of species OF rain frogs
vary from 600 to 700, but an accurate count is
difficult. Most *Eleutherodactylus* are small and
insignificant, and therefore easily overlooked.
Even if they are collected, distinguishing one
species from another is not easy. Many single
species have turned out to consist of two or
more species after close examination. Some
species occur in a number of different color
forms, or "morphs," and may look like separate
species at first but later turn out to be just one.
New species are being added every year, either
as completely new frogs are discovered, or as
old museum specimens are examined more
closely. At the same time, many species have
not been seen in recent years and are feared

The Greenhouse Frog

The greenhouse frog, *Eleutherodactylus planirostris*, is from Cuba
and several small islands in the West Indies. It was introduced to
Florida in 1875, where it is now the commonest frog in many places,
and it arrived in Louisiana in 1975.

Wherever they go, greenhouse frogs are a success. They live
among leaves and other debris, often in greenhouses, gardens, and
parks. At night or during rainstorms they make a short, chirping
noise. They breed throughout the warmer months, usually May to
September in Florida. The female lays three to 26 eggs in a cluster on
damp soil and stays nearby until 13 days later, when the eggs hatch.
The newly hatched froglets are just 0.16 to 0.24 inches (4–6 mm)
long and feed on tiny invertebrates. Adults are 1.5 in (3.8 cm)
long and eat ants, beetles, spiders, and other arthropods. They are
reddish-brown (with a mottled or striped pattern) with a dark patch
between their eyes and bands on their legs. They have long, slender
toes with no webbing but with squared-off expanded tips.

extinct. Species may be disappearing as fast or faster than they are being discovered.

Rain frogs are nearly all terrestrial, living among leaf litter and other forest debris or under stones and trash. Because of their small size they are vulnerable to desiccation in dry habitats, so some live alongside streams where humidity is constantly high. Others remain among the roots of grasses and leaves, where the microhabitat is moist even when the habitat overall is dry. Several climb into the branches and leaves of low trees, bushes, and shrubs at night but return to the ground by daybreak. For example, the coqui frog from Puerto Rico, *E. coqui*, climbs trees at night to call and to forage for food; but as dawn approaches and the humidity drops, it returns to the ground.

Small and Compact

Rain frogs are all relatively small and of compact build with long hind limbs. The smallest species, including *E. limbatus* from Cuba, are as small as 0.4 inches (10 mm) long. The largest, probably *E. gulosus* from Central America, is ten times as long. Most have smooth skin, but a few are toadlike in build with warty skin, such as *E. bufoniformis* from Central America. *Eleutherodactylus megacephalus,* also from Central America, is heavily built with a huge bony head. Many others, such as the greenhouse frog, *E. planirostris* from Cuba, and the whistling frog, *E. johnstonei* (which is native to the Lesser Antilles but has been introduced to other islands and mainland countries), are dainty, agile species with long limbs and toes.

Many species have a circular disk on their underside that helps them cling to smooth

⚠ Eleutherodactylus acuminatus on a fern in lowland rain forest in Ecuador. As in all rain frogs, the end of each toe is expanded to help the frog climb over low branches and foliage.

surfaces. Typically, they have expanded tips to their toes for climbing, but they are better developed in some species than in others.

Cryptic Coloration

The most common type of coloring among rain frogs is brown, often with mottled markings of lighter and darker shades. This is known as cryptic coloration—it helps the animal hide among dead leaves or other natural features. A recurring theme is a dark stripe through the eye that lines up with a stripe on the head. This breaks up the outline of the eye and makes it harder for predators to "lock onto." Many species are dimorphic (meaning they have two different color forms), with striped and mottled individuals occurring in a single population.

A few species are very colorful; *E. altae* from central Costa Rica and northern Panama is black with a bright red spot in its groin that can only be seen when it moves. This is known as "flash" coloration—when the frog jumps, the brightly colored area "flashes" up; but as soon as it lands and folds its limbs again, the color disappears, leaving the predator looking for a spot of color that is no longer there.

One species, *E. gaigae*, is brown with an orange stripe down either side of its back. Scientists believe that it imitates a highly toxic poison dart frog, *Phyllobates lugubris*, that lives in the same region. This is an example of Batesian mimicry—predators that have learned to avoid the poisonous dart frog also leave the rain frog alone, even though it is harmless.

Predatory Frogs and Snakes

It is not surprising that rain frogs use camouflage and various other mechanisms to avoid being eaten. Being small and defenseless, they are ideal food for many predatory forest inhabitants. Among their main enemies are other frogs, and large rain frogs eat small ones too. There are many small snakes in the region that live in leaf litter, including rear-fanged species such as *Coniophanes fissidens*—over 50 percent of its diet consists of rain frogs. The blunt-headed vine snake, *Imantodes cenchoa*

from Central America, prowls for frogs and sleeping lizards in low bushes at night, and eats a high proportion of rain frogs, as do several other small colubrids. Juvenile pit vipers, *Bothriechis lateralis*, lure rain frogs closer by twitching the brightly colored tip of their tail.

Small rain frogs are also eaten by invertebrates such as crab spiders, and they are occasionally caught up in the webs of large *Nephila* and other orb-weaving spider species. To defend themselves, rain frogs often make one long leap and remain motionless where they land. That confuses predators, which are often unable to locate them again.

Why So Many Species?

Whereas some species of rain frogs are generalists and have a wide distribution that encompasses a variety of habitats, others are highly specialized in their requirements. Even where several species occur in a small area, each one will have specific preferences for temperature, humidity, shelter, and other factors, some of which are so subtle that we cannot easily distinguish them. This means that just a few miles apart, where conditions may be slightly different, "species one" gives way to "species two," and so on. The end result is a patchwork of distribution patterns, with many small pockets of specialized species superimposed on a smaller number of more widespread, "general-purpose" species.

The coqui frog, *E. coqui*, is common and widespread in Puerto Rico, for example, while another rain frog, *E. antillensis*, has a more restricted range. Perhaps because it is smaller and therefore more prone to drying out, it can only live in areas that are permanently damp. Studies on four other species show that they all have differences in microhabitats and activity patterns based on their temperature and humidity preferences. This allows a number of similar species to coexist without undue

⊖ *Camouflage and cryptic coloring play an important part in defense for the rain frogs. Here* Eleutherodactylus noblei *mimics a dead leaf in a Costa Rican rain forest.*

competition. On the Central American mainland the rain frogs, by being active at night, are thought to avoid competition with diurnal poison dart frogs, which are of similar size and have similar ecological requirements .

Scientists have hardly scratched the surface when it comes to understanding the ways in which these small frogs—some of which occur in huge numbers—affect each other. Nor do they fully understand the effects they have on the other animals (predators and prey) with which they coexist and on the ecosystem as a whole. The coqui frog is the most studied species. Scientists found that its population density reached 0.459 frogs to every 1.2 square yards (1 sq. m) in places but was only 0.0017 to every 1.2 square yards (1 sq. m) elsewhere.

Numbers seem to vary according to the available resources, the most important of which is probably shelter for hiding and laying eggs. In an experiment in which more hiding places (lengths of hollow bamboo) were added, the number of frogs increased. The number of predators present is also probably significant.

Reproduction

All *Eleutherodactylus* species lay their eggs on the land, and the embryos develop inside the capsule before hatching as miniature versions of their parents. Males are significantly smaller than females in most species and have larger eardrums, sometimes twice the size of the females'. Males' calls vary according to species, but many consist of an incessant repeated note, often sounding like the call of an insect. They usually call from the same place every night, often a leaf low down on a bush or shrub, or from the ground. The males are territorial, and the calls help define their territories and attract females. Approaching males are often confronted by the incumbent male, and fights can ensue. Male coqui frogs bite intruders during territorial bouts.

Females that are ready to lay approach a calling male, and they go into amplexus with the male gripping the female behind her forelimbs. They move to a suitable site for egg

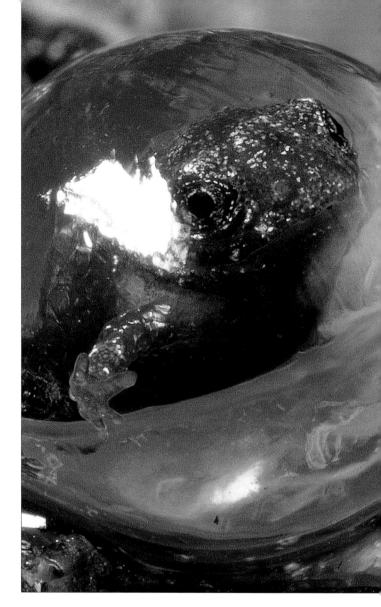

Escaping from the Egg

In most frog species the tadpoles need to break through the egg capsule. They do this by secreting chemicals from their snout and neck. The chemicals dissolve gelatin, which is the main component of the egg membrane. Of course, the eggs of most frogs do not have a tough outer membrane, because they are laid in water.

Rain-frog embryos probably secrete enzymes early on in their development, too, and use them to dissolve the inner membrane so that they can move into the large outer capsule in order to continue their development to froglet.

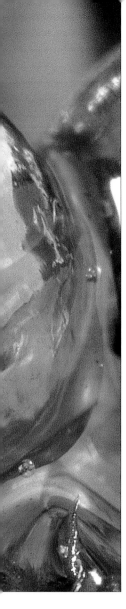

laying, usually a patch of soil or leaf litter that is protected by an overhanging leaf or log. The eggs, which number from three to more than 20, are large and unpigmented, and are laid in a cluster. The eggs are unlike most other frogs' eggs because they have a thickened outer capsule and an inner capsule that turns to water shortly after the eggs are laid. This provides the embryo with a suitable environment in which to develop.

Parental Care

The female usually stays with the eggs, sitting nearby or on top of the clutch, but in a few species it is the male that attends. Because he is territorial, he may continue to call and attract additional females and have more than one clutch to look after.

There are two advantages to staying with the eggs. First, the attending frog can keep them from drying out by emptying the contents of its bladder over them, and second, it can protect them against predators or parasites. Flies of several types will try to lay their eggs on the egg mass, and the maggots will burrow into the eggs and feed on them if an adult is not close by. The frog larvae do not feed—their yolk contains enough nourishment for them to develop to metamorphosis.

Development time for the larvae varies from 15 to 49 days depending on species. The froglet breaks through the tough outer membrane of the egg with an egg tooth, a small spine that grows in the middle of the frog's upper lip and that is not present in other frogs. The frog makes side-to-side slashing

A developing froglet (Eleutherodactylus species) inside its egg capsule on a rain-forest leaf in Costa Rica.

Expanding his vocal sac, a male rain frog, Eleutherodactylus martiniquensis from St. Lucia, calls to establish his territory and attract a mate.

Live-Bearing Frogs

Although *Eleutherodactylus jasperi* from Puerto Rico has internal fertilization, the embryos do not obtain any nourishment from the mother. Strictly speaking, therefore, the species is ovoviviparous (meaning the female keeps the eggs in her body until just before they are ready to hatch). Only two frog species are truly viviparous (live bearing), with the young obtaining nourishment from the parent as they develop. They are the African species *Nectophrynoides liberiensis* and *N. occidentalis*. The developing embryos feed on a substance produced from the walls lining the oviduct (sometimes called "uterine milk").

Two other *Nectophrynoides* species are ovoviviparous. The Australian gastric-brooding frogs, *Rheobatrachus*, also "give birth," but the females actually swallow their newly laid eggs, and the eggs continue developing in the mother's stomach. These frogs are not "live bearing" in the true sense of the word, because fertilization is external. Several other frogs carry eggs or tadpoles (or both) in pouches or chambers until they are fully formed.

movements with its head when it is ready to emerge; and once it has made an opening, it climbs out.

All *Eleutherodactylus* species have direct development; of the species studied, all deposit their eggs on the land except one—*E. jasperi* from Puerto Rico. This species has internal fertilization, and the female retains the developing eggs in her oviducts for the 33 days they take to develop. She usually produces four offspring, which are simply "born" via her cloaca. One other species, the coqui frog, has internal fertilization, but the female goes on to lay eggs in the normal way.

Having said that, the reproductive pattern in rain frogs is only known for a very small proportion of species. Given their ability to develop without feeding, it is possible that other species also give birth to live young. Much remains to be discovered in this area.

Common name Great Plains
narrow-mouthed toad (western narrow-
mouthed toad)

Scientific name *Gastrophryne olivacea*

Subfamily Microhylinae

Family Microhylidae

Order Anura

Size From 1 in (2.5 cm) to 1.5 in (3.2 cm)

Key features Small; from above it appears teardrop
shaped with a rounded body tapering to a
pointed head; there is a distinctive fold of
skin behind the head; limbs short; color gray
or olive-green either without markings or
with a few small, scattered dark spots

Habits Secretive; nocturnal; terrestrial

Breeding In flooded fields, ruts, and small pools;
female lays very small eggs; tadpoles
metamorphose after 30–50 days

Diet Small invertebrates, especially ants

Habitat Grasslands, open woods, and deserts

Distribution North America from Nebraska south to the
Gulf Coast and across to Arizona, then into
the lowlands of northern Mexico

Status Common

Similar species The eastern narrow-mouthed toad,
G. carolinensis, has a more easterly
distribution, although the 2 species overlap in
parts of Texas and adjacent states; it is brown
rather than gray in color and has a strongly
patterned back

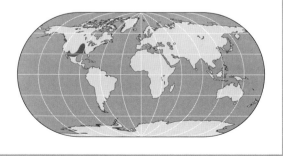

Great Plains Narrow-Mouthed Toad

Gastrophryne olivacea

Anyone who is not in the habit of searching under flat rocks or boards could easily overlook the small Great Plains narrow-mouthed toad. During the day or during short spells of dry weather it can often be found crouching in such places.

A SECRETIVE ANIMAL, the Great Plains narrow-
mouthed toad can go deep underground,
retreating into cracks in drying mud or entering
the burrows of rodents or reptiles. It favors nest
holes belonging to the tarantula, *Dugesiella
hentzi*, and an unusual relationship has evolved
between the two species.

Living in Harmony

The spider, which is several times the size of the
toad and could easily kill and eat it, tolerates
the presence of the toad in its burrows and may
even encourage it. If a predator such as snake
enters the spider's burrow, the toad wriggles
under the tarantula's body in the knowledge
that the tarantula will defend itself and the
toad. For its part, the toad does not eat the
young tarantulas when they hatch, even though
they are of similar size to its main prey—ants. In
return for the spider's protection the toad eats
the ants, which are the tarantula's most
destructive enemy. They enter the burrow in
search of eggs or spiderlings to eat. It is
thought to be the only example of a symbiotic
relationship (one in which both species benefit)
between a frog and an invertebrate. In fact,
spiders in other parts of the world frequently
prey on small frogs, which sometimes become
entangled in their webs.

Because of its diet of ants the narrow-
mouthed toad accumulates toxins in its body
and secretes distasteful substances if molested.
In humans the substances can cause a burning

⊕ *Although closely
related to the Great
Plains narrow-mouthed
toad, the eastern narrow-
mouthed toad,
Gastrophryne
carolinensis, is reddish
brown in color and lives
around ponds and
ditches in eastern
North America.*

⊕ *Great Plains narrow-mouthed toads,* Gastrophryne olivacea, *are more terrestrial than aquatic, as in this toad from Kansas. They use a running or hopping (rather than leaping) form of movement to escape danger.*

sensation if they come into contact with the mucous membranes, such as the lips, tongue, or eyes: Never suck your fingers or rub your eyes after handling a narrow-mouthed toad! In any case, catching narrow-mouthed toads is not easy. Despite their short limbs, they run fast or make short, rapid hops if disturbed, often wriggling quickly through grass or other vegetation (like a small mouse or vole).

High-Pitched Calls

Male narrow-mouthed toads make a short buzzing call sometimes likened to a sheep's bleating but much higher in pitch. They call from flooded fields, swamps, and temporary pools and puddles after rain, and cattle tanks are also used. At times they may use deeper, more permanent bodies of water if they are choked

with plants. The eggs are very small, black and white, and form a film on the surface. The tadpoles are small and have no horny beak or rasping teeth. They metamorphose after 30 to 50 days, and the small toads measure about 0. 5 inches (13 mm).

The Relatives

The family Microhylidae is poorly represented in North America. The only other widespread species is the eastern narrow-mouthed toad, *Gastrophryne carolinensis*. The sheep frog, *Hypopachus variolosus*, just reaches Texas, but most of its range is farther south—it reaches Costa Rica in Central America.

Even in Central and South America microhylids tend to be small, dull in color, and secretive, living in leaf litter and under rocks and logs. They have been unable to break out of that niche because the region has such a diverse frog fauna. In contrast, microhylids in other parts of the world where competition is less intense have conquered many different environments. In Southeast Asia *Metaphrynella pollicaris* breed in tree holes several yards off the ground and have expanded toe pads. Others, such as the African *Breviceps* species, are confirmed burrowers and have small "spades" on their hind feet. At least one species, *Sphenophryne palmipes* from New Guinea, is aquatic. These habits and the adaptations involved have resulted in a variety of shapes, sizes, and colors.

American Green Treefrog

Hyla cinerea

The American green treefrog is a characteristic inhabitant of the subtropical American Southeast. Familiar to residents by sound if not by sight, it can occur in vast numbers.

Common name
American green treefrog (rain frog)

Scientific name *Hyla cinerea*

Subfamily Hylinae

Family Hylidae

Order Anura

Size From 1.25 in (3 cm) to 2.5 in (6 cm)

Key features Body slender; eyes golden; skin slightly granular; color bright green with a thick, creamy-white stripe running around the upper lips and extending down each side of the face and onto the flanks; some individuals may lack the side stripe, especially in the north of its range; a few scattered cream or golden spots often present on its back; hind legs longer than those of most treefrogs

Habits Arboreal; nocturnal

Breeding In ponds and the edges of lakes and backwaters; eggs laid in small clumps attached to aquatic vegetation

Diet Insects, especially flying species

Habitat In wetlands, in reed beds, palms, Spanish moss, and on large leaves

Distribution Southeastern United States

Status Very common in places

Similar species None in the area; the squirrel treefrog, *Hyla squirella*, is sometimes green but has a plumper shape and lacks the side stripe

THE AMERICAN GREEN TREEFROG is an agile climber. It often hangs by one or two of its toes when climbing among reeds and bushes in search of food. Because its hind legs are longer than those of most other treefrogs, it can also make long leaps. It becomes active at dusk and is a busy forager, finding its prey by sight and catching it after a short chase. During the day it rests on stems above the water, moving down at night to hunt around the water's surface. It sometimes rests on lily pads, especially the leaves of the water hyacinth, *Eichhornia crassipes*, which was introduced into Florida and neighboring states from Southeast Asia.

Familiar Choruses

Its call is loud and unmistakable. Although at a distance it is said to resemble a cow bell, at close quarters it sounds more like a duck. It is most noisy around dusk when the frogs start calling one at a time until the chorus builds to a crescendo. Then it stops suddenly, only to start up again after a short break. Choruses are mainly associated with breeding activities, but they also occur just before rain or if the weather is especially still and humid. Certain sounds can also start them off—the clattering of typewriter keys (now a thing of the past in most places) being one of them.

Breeding starts in April and continues throughout the summer to the middle of August. The eggs are laid in small clumps that are attached to aquatic vegetation floating near the surface. The tadpoles are greenish in color, and the pale stripe on the side appears before they metamorphose.

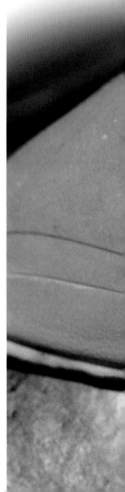

The American green treefrog is characterized by a prominent white stripe extending from the mouth along the sides of the body. It also has enlarged toe pads.

Color-Change Artists

Like many other treefrogs, the American green treefrog can change color. It tends to turn darker, approaching olive-green or brown, if it is cold and when light levels are low. In warm, bright conditions it is light yellowish green. Males also turn lighter when they are calling. They can also change according to the color of the background on which they are resting, but all the reasons for their color changes are not completely understood. Sometimes groups of treefrogs of various colors can occur in the same place at the same time. A cage full of captives may range from light grass-green to dark olive and brown at any given time.

The physical aspects of color change are well understood, however. Cells containing the dark pigment melanin (called melanophores) spread out when the frog "wants" to turn darker, and they surround the other color-producing cells (xanthophores and iridophores). At the same time, the color-producing cells change shape and realign themselves so that their influence over the frog's color is reduced.

Treefrog Neighbors

Florida and adjacent states have more species of treefrogs than any other part of North America. Other species that might be found alongside the green treefrog include the barking treefrog, *Hyla gratiosa*—a large, toadlike species with a characteristic call—the squirrel treefrog, *H. squirella*, and the pine woods treefrog, *H. femoralis*.

In northern Florida and along the eastern seaboard these species are joined by several others: the spring peeper, *H. crucifer,* and the gray treefrogs, *H. versicolor* and *H. chrysoscelis*. The Cuban treefrog, *Osteopilus septentrionalus*, is an introduction from Cuba that continues to extend its range, possibly at the expense of smaller species, which it eats.

Cuban Treefrog

Osteopilus septentrionalis

The Cuban treefrog is an adaptable species that thrives in a range of conditions. Its versatility has helped it become a "weed" species in places where it has been introduced, such as Florida.

Common name Cuban treefrog (giant treefrog)

Scientific name *Osteopilus septentrionalis*

Subfamily Hylinae

Family Hylidae

Order Anura

Size From 2 in (5 cm) to 4.9 in (12.5 cm)

Key features Body large; skin slightly warty; usually light brown or buff in color, but some have extensive areas of green; irregular, darker patches often present on the back as well as bars on the hind legs; head flat and bony; toe pads conspicuous; females are considerably larger than males

Habits Nocturnal; arboreal

Breeding In pools and cisterns; female lays clutches of 130 large eggs in floating rafts; eggs hatch after 2 days

Diet Large insects; other frogs

Habitat Often common around houses, in plant pots, drainpipes, and outhouses; also in leaf axils of palms and other plants

Distribution Cuba (including the Isla de Juventud), Cayman Islands, and Bahamas; introduced to Puerto Rico, Virgin Islands, Anguilla, and southern Florida

Status Extremely common

Similar species Large body size, toe pads, and warty skin make adults unmistakable; juveniles may look like a number of other smaller, mostly brown treefrogs

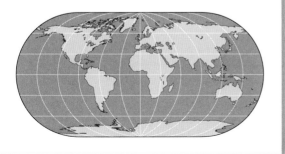

THE CUBAN TREEFROG'S LARGE BODY SIZE means that it can tackle a wide variety of prey, including large insects such as adult cockroaches as well as smaller species of treefrogs. It is strongly associated with human activities, although its natural habitat includes forests, the edges of ponds and lakes, and rocky outcrops.

The frogs withstand dry conditions by retreating into cracks and crevices; but given the chance, they will set up home in gardens, well-watered plant pots and window boxes, and around the edges of artificial ponds. They are especially numerous in ornamental gardens surrounding hotels. They learn to hunt near lights to which moths and other flying insects are attracted, and sometimes they wait on window panes for food to come within range. They also occur in cisterns, wells, and drainpipes, which make good substitutes for their natural hiding places in leaf axils and bromeliad "vases."

They live throughout the island of Cuba but are most common in places where human activities have altered the landscape, especially in and around banana plantations. They do not live in heavily forested areas (of which there are few remaining).

Fast Breeders

Cuban treefrogs are efficient and prolific breeders, often using temporary pools of water collected in old cisterns and the flooded basements of ruined buildings. They tolerate water with a high salinity. Females are much larger than males and lay clutches of about 130 large eggs in floating rafts or clumps. They hatch within two days, and the tadpoles

⊕ A Cuban treefrog emerges from its hiding place inside a bromeliad "vase." The adaptable little frogs are equally at home in man-made habitats.

metamorphose in as little
as three weeks. The young frogs grow quickly,
and males mature within a few months, when
they measure just over 1.5 inches (4 cm).

Threats

Very few frogs have negative effects on their
local ecology, but the Cuban treefrog and the
African clawed toad, *Xenopus laevis*, are
notable exceptions. The latter was introduced
to California, where it eats the tadpoles of
other frogs and probably other native aquatic
life. The Cuban treefrog has been introduced to
Florida, where it eats smaller frogs and their
tadpoles. Squirrel treefrogs, *Hyla squirella*, and
the American green treefrogs, *H. cinerea*, are
probably the most badly affected species. In
addition, the introduced frogs compete with
native species for food and breeding sites.

Arrival in Florida

Cuban treefrogs were first reported in Florida in 1931, when three
were collected at Key West. From there they spread throughout
the Florida Keys, and by 1952 they had reached mainland Florida
near Miami. By the 1970s they had spread up the Gulf Coast to Fort
Myers, Naples, and Sanibel Island. They managed to extend their
range naturally or possibly by hitching a lift with trucks transporting
fruit and vegetables or among garden plants.

There is no way to rid Florida of the Cuban treefrogs. Like many
other animals (and plants) that have been introduced into the state,
they thrive in the near-perfect conditions. Occasional frosts reduce
numbers, but the frogs breed so readily that they quickly replace the
ones that die, and they are continuing to extend their range.

One reason for the rapid spread of Cuban
treefrogs in Florida is the lack of natural
predators. The frogs produce toxic skin
secretions that cause irritation in humans and
presumably give them some protection against
predators. Crows and some other birds appear
to avoid them, although snakes do not.

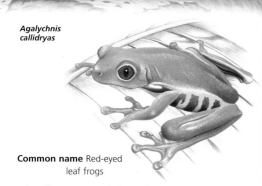

*Agalychnis
callidryas*

Common name Red-eyed
leaf frogs

Scientific names *Agalychnis callidryas* and *A. saltator*

Subfamily Phyllomedusinae

Family Hylidae

Order Anura

Size *A. callidryas* 2.8 in (7 cm); *A. saltator* 2.4 in
(6 cm)

Key features Body slender; waist narrow; legs long and
spindly; feet webbed; toes have expanded
sticky pads; eyes very large with brilliant-red
irises; pupils vertical, separating them from all
other treefrogs except other members of the
Phyllomedusinae; *A. callidryas* has blue-and-
cream markings on its flanks, varying
according to location

Habits Highly arboreal; mostly nocturnal

Breeding Eggs laid on leaves overhanging small pools;
on average female lays 29–51 eggs, possibly
in several clutches; eggs hatch after 5 days
(*A. callidryas*); 21–72 eggs that hatch after
about 6 days (*A. saltator*)

Diet Invertebrates

Habitat Lowland rain forests

Distribution Central America from southern Veracruz
and the Yucatán Peninsula, Mexico, to the
Canal Zone, Panama (*A. callidryas*); *A. saltator*
has a more restricted range from
northeastern Nicaragua to northeastern
Costa Rica

Status Common in suitable habitat but declining

Similar species Several other *Agalychnis* species occur in
the region but none with bright red eyes

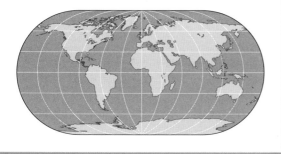

Red-Eyed Leaf Frogs

Agalychnis callidryas and *A. saltator*

*No other frogs characterize the exotic fauna of the rain
forests, or "jungles," of South America as well as the
red-eyed frogs. Their distinctive image is often
used to represent the countries where they live.*

INSTANTLY RECOGNIZABLE, the more common species
of red-eyed leaf frog, *A. callidryas*, appears on
posters, postage stamps, and in numerous
books and magazines throughout the world.
The smaller species, *A. saltator*, sometimes
called the lesser red-eyed leaf frog, is only
found where *A. callidryas* also lives but has a
more restricted range. Both species are limited
to primary rain forests, living in the canopies of
tall forest trees such as palms or in bromeliads
and other epiphytic plants (plants that live on
other plants). They rest by day and become
active at dusk, often descending to lower levels,
especially in the breeding season.

Calling Positions

Agalychnis callidryas breeds during the rainy
season in small forest pools, including
temporary ones. As soon as the sun sets, males
call from high up in the branches where they
have spent the day. These preliminary calls are
sometimes called "rain calls." As they descend,
they stop calling until they take up positions
near the breeding sites. Once they have arrived
there, their calls are different from the rain calls
and consist of single- or double-note "chock"
or "chock-chock," with a pause of anything
from eight seconds to one minute between
calls. Calling males usually position themselves
on the stems of shrubs, sitting across the stem
at right angles. Sites are typically 3 to 9 feet
(0.9–2.7 m) above small ponds. Unless the
population is very dense, the frogs are usually
well spaced out.

Females in breeding condition approach,
attracted by the males' calls. When a female is

⊕ Agalychnis saltator *in Costa Rica. Like many red-eyed animals, the red-eyed leaf frogs hunt at night.*

a few inches from a male, he stops calling, moves toward her, and climbs on her back. If the female approaches from behind where the male cannot see her, she places a hand on his back. Once they are in amplexus, the female descends to the water, where she fills her bladder. She uses the water to produce the jelly that will surround her eggs. Then she climbs back into the bush or tree and walks around until she finds a suitable egg-laying site.

While this is going on, the male (which is substantially smaller than the female) simply

Red Eyes

Red eyes are associated with nocturnal species. Apart from the species described here, there are several treefrogs, *Hyla* species, with red eyes as well as a large Australian red-eyed frog, *Litoria chloris*. On Madagascar a number of frogs belonging to the genus *Boophis* also have red or pink eyes.

⊕ *Perched on a Heliconia bract, a red-eyed leaf frog,* Agalychnis callidryas, *perfectly matches the colors of the plant.*

87

hangs on and may close his eyes. Eventually, the female walks along a stem until she arrives at a leaf that is hanging over the water. She crawls to the tip of the leaf and turns so that she is facing upward. As she lays her eggs, she moves slowly up the leaf so that the egg mass is elongated. The male fertilizes the eggs while this is happening.

Clutch size seems to vary according to locality: In Veracruz, Mexico, females lay an average of 51 eggs, while in Guatemala the average is 29. It is likely that they lay several clutches, because dissected females contain significantly more eggs than these figures suggest, although it is not known if they are laid during a single breeding session.

⬅ *Moving along a leaf in a Costa Rican rain forest, a female* Agalychnis calcarifer *lays her eggs in an elongated shape. The male, still attached, fertilizes them as they are laid.*

⬇ *In Costa Rica a pair of flap-heeled leaf frogs,* Agalychnis calcarifer, *mate while an overenthusiastic male of a different species tries to get in on the act.*

If the leaf is shaken, however, as it may be if a snake is approaching the nest, the tadpoles are likely to hatch whether it is raining or not. A human can also trigger hatching by shaking the leaf. This is not thought to be a defense mechanism, simply reaction to a movement similar to that caused by heavy rain.

Assuming they do not get eaten, the tadpoles hang with their tail pointing downward in the water near the surface, often in a patch of sunshine. They metamorphose after about 60 to 80 days. The newly changed young are green but have yellow eyes at first; the red pigment appears after about two weeks, starting at the outer edges of the irises and spreading inward until the eyes are completely red.

Taking to the Water

The eggs take about five days to hatch. At the time of hatching the jelly mass begins to liquefy so the tadpoles can move around in their nest. Hatching is usually triggered by rain, and the tadpoles wriggle until they slide down the leaf and drip off the end into the pond below. When they hit the surface, they swim to the bottom and remain there for a minute or two before reappearing at the surface.

Sometimes things go slightly wrong, and the tadpoles miss the water. If the distance is only an inch or two, they can usually flip themselves into it. If they hatch during dry weather, they stay in the nest to avoid the possibility of dripping onto mud or into a shrinking pool.

The purpose of laying eggs on leaves rather than in the water is to avoid predation by fish, other tadpoles, and aquatic invertebrates and their larvae. The strategy is only partially successful, however. At least two species of snakes, the plain blunt-headed snake, *Imantodes inornatus*, and one of the cat-eyed snakes, *Leptodeira septentrionalis*, have learned to search for the eggs among the leaves of pond-side shrubs. The snakes, which also eat adult frogs as well as lizards, swallow mouthfuls of the jelly as they pull the eggs off the leaf.

⤒ *A juvenile red-eyed leaf frog,* A. callidryas, *emerges from the water in Belize. Its eyes will turn red after about two weeks.*

Breeding Differences

All the *Agalychnis* have a similar breeding system, but the details vary slightly. The smaller red-eyed leaf frog, *A. saltator,* for instance, is an explosive breeder (meaning that the breeding season is very short, and large numbers of the frogs all mate simultaneously). On suitable nights, usually immediately after torrential rain, several hundreds may congregate on vines hanging over ponds. The females plaster their egg masses to clumps of moss surrounding epiphytic plants or to their roots. Although each clump is separate at the time of laying, the vigorous activity of the frogs (both single males and breeding pairs) tends to mix the clutches together into a single mass. This species lays its

Origins of the Names

*A*galychnis is derived from two Latin words, *aga,* meaning "very," and *Lychnis*, the name of a genus of plants containing several species with bright red flowers. The reference is presumably to the red eyes of the two species. *Saltator* is a straightforward translation from Latin, meaning "the jumper," and *callidryas* comes from two words: the Greek *kallos*, meaning "beautiful," and dryad (from Greek origins), meaning a tree or wood nymph.

eggs in the early morning, and some pairs are still around the laying sites at noon the following day. They lay between 21 and 72 eggs that hatch after about six days. Apart from the snakes mentioned above, their eggs are eaten by ants, warblers, and capuchin monkeys.

The flap-heeled leaf frog, *Agalychnis calcarifer*, is a large, spectacular, and rarely seen species. It breeds throughout the year, not just in the rainy season. It does not use forest ponds but lays its eggs on leaves above water-filled cavities in fallen tree trunks. Males call from standing trees nearby; once a female has appeared, the pair make their way to a suitable site while in amplexus. Egg laying usually takes place the next morning.

⊖ *Not a flying frog but, more accurately, a gliding frog.* Agalychnis spurrelli *uses the enormous areas of webbing between its fingers and toes as a parachute.*

Flying Frogs

No reptiles or amphibians have mastered flight, but a few have evolved the shape and ability to glide. They include two groups of lizards, the flying geckos, *Ptychozoon*, and the flying lizards, *Draco*, and the so-called flying snake, *Chrysopelea*, all from Southeast Asia. As far as we know, no American reptiles can glide.

Some leaf frogs, for example, *Agalychnis saltator* and *A. spurrelli*, also glide. They have extensive webbing on their front and hind feet, which they spread widely to parachute from high branches. It is not controlled flight, and their trajectory is less than 45 degrees: A frog that launches itself from a height of about 15 feet (4.6 m) would at best land about 12 horizontal feet (3.6 m) away. *Agalychnis callidryas* is also able to parachute and can perform as well as *A. spurrelli* but does not do so very often. In any case, parachuting seems to be a strategy of last resort in response to danger rather than a quick means of moving from treetop to ground level.

It is likely that most members of the genus can glide; since they do not swim, their webbed feet must serve some purpose. In Southeast Asia, the home of gliding lizards and snakes, there is also a group of gliding frogs in the genus *Rhacophorus*. This genus and *Agalychnis* parallel each other closely.

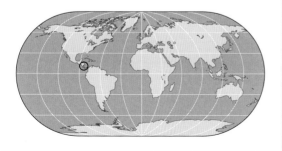

Strawberry Poison Dart Frog

Dendrobates pumilio

Common name Strawberry poison dart frog (strawberry frog)

Scientific name Dendrobates pumilio

Family Dendrobatidae

Order Anura

Size From 0.7 in (1.8 cm) to 1 in (2.5 cm)

Key features Body small but quite plump; snout short and blunt; eyes large and black; limbs thin; in its most common color form the head and body are bright strawberry-red or orange-red; back legs and lower parts of the front legs are black or dark blue; sometimes small dark-blue or black spots occur on the back; males have a buff-colored patch on the throat

Habits Diurnal; terrestrial

Breeding Mating and egg laying take place on the ground; female lays several clutches of up to 5 eggs; eggs hatch after 7 days; parental care exhibited

Diet Small invertebrates, especially ants and forest mites

Habitat Lowland rain forests, including some secondary forests and clearings

Distribution Central America on the Atlantic watersheds of eastern Nicaragua, Costa Rica, and northern Panama

Status Very numerous in suitable habitats

Similar species 2 similar species, both predominantly red: *Dendrobates granuliferus* (but it has a granular back, while *D. pumilio* has a smooth back) and *D. speciosus*, which is red all over; other red species occur in South America

Nobody who sees the little strawberry poison dart frog in its natural habitat can fail to be enchanted by its bright colors, busy lifestyle, and cheerful, buzzing call.

THE LITTLE STRAWBERRY POISON DART frog, measuring just 1 inch (2.5 cm) long, has helped put Costa Rica firmly on the ecotourist's map. The frogs have a limited range in the country but are especially common around one or two of the main tourist lodges, where they are the main attraction. They can be seen constantly hopping around in a characteristic jerky manner in the leaf litter at the edge of the forest and among the undergrowth right up to the edge of paths and buildings. Their popularity has led to numerous appearances on postage stamps, souvenirs, and T-shirts.

In parts of lowland Costa Rica they occur in very high densities during the wettest months— over 800 per 2.5 acres (1 ha)—and in slightly lower densities during the short dry season. Males call constantly at all times of the year, pausing in their travels to raise their body up and make surprisingly loud, chirping trills that can last for up to 30 seconds.

Territorial Tussles

Males are territorial; and if a calling male ventures into another male's territory, the calling rate intensifies between them. Under extreme provocation the territory holder will jump on top of the intruder, and they will wrestle off and on for up to 20 minutes, standing up on their hind legs and trying to force each other to the ground with their front legs.

While they are engaged in tussling and tumbling backward and forward, they appear oblivious to their surroundings and are easy to observe. Eventually one male, usually the intruder, is pinned to the ground and is allowed

⤒ *After they have hatched, strawberry poison dart tadpoles are transported to a suitable plant, such as a bromeliad, where they continue their development in safety.*

to leave after a few seconds. Females, juveniles, and noncalling males are ignored by the calling male. Females can also be territorial when breeding and may occasionally fight.

Breeding and Care of the Eggs

The strawberry poison dart frogs breed at any time of the year. Females that are ready to lay eggs are attracted to calling males and approach them. The male leads the female to a site that he has prepared, usually a large leaf that he has cleaned of debris. There is no amplexus: The two adults sit facing in opposite directions with their cloacae touching. The female lays up to five eggs (more in captivity) and can lay a clutch every week. After egg

laying and fertilization the male and female return to the clutch every day. The male moistens the eggs by sitting over them and emptying his bladder.

When the eggs hatch about seven days later, the mother returns. The tadpoles climb onto her back, sometimes singly and sometimes

Two male strawberry poison dart frogs are locked in combat as they wrestle for dominance over a territory in a Costa Rican rain forest.

Feeding the Tadpoles

Frogs and toads that lay their eggs in small bodies of water such as tree holes and the leaf axils of plants avoid, or at least minimize, the possibility of predation. The trouble is that they also deprive the tadpoles of a regular food supply, such as aquatic plants and algae. Some species have solved this problem by providing their eggs with enough yolk to see the tadpoles through their development. Others need to provide a separate food supply for the tadpoles, and the only way they can do that is by laying eggs for them.

Eggs for Breakfast

Apart from the strawberry poison dart frog there are several other species in South America that lay eggs for their developing tadpoles. They are the granular poison dart frog, *D. granuliferus*, the red poison dart frog, *D. speciosus*, the harlequin poison dart frog, *D. histrionicus*, and Lehmann's poison dart frog, *D. lehmanni*. The latter two species are very closely related to each other and are possibly two forms of the same species. Staying in Latin America, the crowned treefrog, *Anotheca spinosa*, lays its eggs in water-filled tree holes, and the female returns to lay fertile eggs for the growing tadpoles.

Two other hylid treefrogs, *Hyla picadoi* and *H. zeteki* from Costa Rica and western Panama, have a similar system but use bromeliads in which to deposit their tadpoles. The tadpoles eat frogs' eggs—probably their own but possibly also those of other species. The same applies to tadpoles of at least one of the bony-headed treefrogs, the well-named *Osteocephalus oophagus* (the Latinized form of "oophageous," which means "egg-eater"). Bromeliad plants only grow in the Americas, and there is no equivalent in the Old World (perhaps one of the reasons why the New World is comparatively rich in treefrogs).

Species in Asia and Africa have to find alternative accommodation for their eggs and tadpoles if they are to place them above ground level, so they use holes in tree trunks and bamboo stems. All these Asian and African species, which include members of several families, simply lay large, yolky eggs, and their tadpoles do not need to feed.

However, a Japanese species—Effinger's treefrog, *Chirixalus effingeri* from Taiwan and Japan—lays its eggs in tree holes, often in a small mass just above the water. As in the strawberry poison dart frog and other dendrobatids, the male remains nearby and may moisten them if necessary. When the tadpoles hatch, they slide down into the water. Females return to the tree hole regularly and produce more spawn; and when the female enters the water, the tadpoles already there pick at her cloaca to encourage her to lay infertile eggs, which they eat. Finally, there is circumstantial evidence that two other Asian tree-hole breeders, *Theloderma horridum* and an unidentified *Philautus* species, also feed their tadpoles on infertile young.

In summary, out of a total of nearly 5,000 species of frogs throughout the world, only 12 feed their tadpoles on their own eggs. Four of them are poison dart frogs. Having said that, the life histories of many frogs, especially those in remote corners of the world, are unknown, and others may yet come to light.

several together. She carries them up into bromeliad plants, usually a few feet from the ground on tree branches and fallen trunks. She places a single tadpole in each bromeliad "vase" (but only if it is empty when she arrives).

Begging for Food

Following the careful placement of her tadpoles, she returns to each bromeliad every day or so, usually in the morning, and lays up to five infertile eggs on which the tadpole feeds. She backs down into the water in the base of the plant until her vent (the opening of her cloaca) is submerged. The tadpole approaches, stiffens its body, and vibrates. This "begging" behavior is only successful with the tadpole's mother—females refuse to feed tadpoles that are not their own. Young tadpoles bite a hole in the jelly surrounding the eggs and suck them out, but larger tadpoles eat the jelly as well. The tadpoles take 43 to 52 days to develop, during which time they eat up to 40 infertile eggs. They measure 0.4 inches (10 mm) at metamorphosis and are a uniform, dark blood-red color.

Occasionally the system breaks down, and a male carries a tadpole to a bromeliad (as they do in many other dendrobatid species). If that happens, the female cannot find the tadpole; and because it cannot eat any food other than eggs, the tadpole starves to death.

Since it is one of the smaller species of poison dart frog, the strawberry poison dart frog feeds only on small invertebrates. Ants form half the diet of the adults, and forest mites found among leaf litter make up another 40 percent. The remainder of their diet consists of small flies, spiders, and other small invertebrates. Juveniles, which are less than 0.5 inches (13 mm) long when they metamorphose, eat mainly mites, springtails, and rotifers (microscopic aquatic invertebrates of the phylum Aschelminthes).

Because their prey is so small, each frog needs to feed almost continuously when it is active. On average the frogs' stomachs contain just under 35 items each. They do not have a specialized method of hunting and simply hop around in the leaf litter picking off small invertebrates as they encounter them.

Color Variants

In keeping with its name, the strawberry poison dart frog is usually bright red in color with dark-blue legs. (This is sometimes called the "blue jean" form.) Off the coast of Panama, however, color variants of the same species—orange or red with black spots or white with black spots—all occur on a single island. Other forms from offshore islands include uniform blue, green, brown, or black frogs, or green frogs

with large brown or black blotches. Not surprisingly, many of them have been described as separate species at different times. Another Central American species, the green-and-black poison dart frog, *D. auratus*, can sometimes, in fact, be blue and black.

⟵ The blue poison dart frog, Dendrobates azureus, is a close relative of the strawberry poison dart frog. It gets its colors from the other end of the spectrum but is equally dazzling.

⟱ Not all strawberry poison dart frogs live up to their colorful name. Various forms exist, such as this black-and-white one, and are often mistakenly described as different species.

Common name American bullfrog

Scientific name *Rana catesbeiana*

Subfamily Raninae

Family Ranidae

Order Anura

Size From 3.5 in (9 cm) to 8 in (20 cm); when stretched out, they can measure 36 in (91 cm)

Key features A large frog (the largest in North America) with long, powerful hind legs and heavily webbed feet; eardrum prominent and larger in males than in females; color mottled olive, brown, or green above and lighter green on the head; legs are banded or spotted with dark brown or black; chin and throat also have dark markings; its bellowing call is loud and distinctive

Habits Semiaquatic, rarely seen far from water

Breeding Female lays masses of spawn in water in spring and summer; eggs hatch after 4 days

Diet Large invertebrates and small vertebrates, including other frogs

Habitat Large ponds and lakes; usually stays near the water's edge or rests among floating vegetation

Distribution Eastern and central North America; introduced to western United States and other regions

Status Common

Similar species Adults are distinctive on account of their size; juveniles could be confused with several other medium-sized ranids from the region

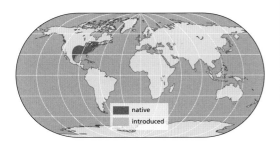

native
introduced

American Bullfrog

Rana catesbeiana

Large, powerful hind legs launch the bullfrog on a long, arching trajectory when it makes its enormous leaps. They also propel it through the water at great speed when it swims.

THE BULLFROG IS THOROUGHLY AQUATIC, with heavily webbed hind feet. It is often seen basking at the water's edge, facing the water or floating just below the surface with only the top of its head and its eyes visible. It is wary, however; if disturbed on land, it jumps into the water, making a considerable splash, and swims away rapidly. With one or two kicks it covers several feet and can dive to the bottom. Equally, it can jump into nearby vegetation on land.

Bellowing Calls

Bullfrogs come ashore at night to hunt for food, and males also come ashore in spring and summer to call. The breeding season varies with locality: In the north it is during May, June, and July, but in the south it is extended and can last from February to October. Males produce their famous bellowing calls and defend territories from other males, fighting if necessary to drive them away.

Males have much larger tympana than females, but nobody knows why. Both sexes apparently hear equally well. Territory holders puff up their bodies and raise themselves out of the water. The males with the best territories have higher success rates in terms of breeding. Females are attracted to males with "good" territories even though they often swim off to another part of the pond to lay their eggs after they have paired up.

Females lay huge masses of spawn averaging over 11,000 eggs that float near the surface in a foamy film. The record is 47,840 eggs, more than any other frog or toad. Females usually produce just one clutch of eggs in their first breeding year, but they produce two or more in subsequent years. The frequency depends on the local climatic conditions, and in places where the summer is short, they may only lay one clutch regardless of their age. An average female probably produces over 80,000 eggs in her lifetime.

The eggs take about four days to hatch. The tadpoles' development depends on climate. In the north they can take three or more years to grow, but they metamorphose at a larger size than in the south. Northern frogs grow more slowly after metamorphosis, however. It is not uncommon for bullfrogs to become mature within a year of metamorphosing, but females can take an extra year. They can spend more time as tadpoles than as growing juveniles.

Huge Tadpoles

The tadpoles are spotted and grow very large, with bodies as big as golf balls. In northern regions they may overwinter for two successive

⊕ *Bullfrogs often spend two years in the tadpole stage and are very large. This tadpole already has well-developed legs.*

⊕ *Adult bullfrogs are very large and robust with big golden eyes. Both sexes have a pronounced tympanum ("eardrum") just behind and below the eye.*

97

years, living beneath the ice in frozen ponds. Compared with other frogs, tadpole survival rates are good—about 15 percent. Considering the number of eggs laid, subsequent mortality must be high, or bullfrogs would have overrun the world by now.

Metamorphosed juveniles from the center of their range (for example, Illinois) grow quickly for the first two years until they weigh about 7 ounces (200 g). Then they slow down and take two more years to reach just under 9 ounces (250 g).

Bullfrogs are the largest frogs in North America. Taking the measurement from the tip of the snout to the tip of their toes with the feet held straight out behind them, they are the longest in the world, measuring 36 inches (91 cm). A frog this size was recorded as weighing 7.25 pounds (3.3 kg). Although it has shorter limbs, the Goliath frog, *Conraua goliath* from West Africa, is much bulkier: The largest one weighed 8.1 pounds (3.7 kg).

Unwelcome Visitors

Bullfrog tadpoles have been imported into Britain in large numbers since the 1980s and sold in garden centers and pet stores. They were often released into garden ponds either as tadpoles or young frogs. They prefer larger bodies of water, however, and mostly migrated to lakes and flooded gravel pits where, because they are shy, they often went unnoticed for a while.

Since they grew slowly, the effects were not immediately apparent, but some began to terrorize local amphibians. Calling males have been heard in various localities, and breeding was first reported in 1999 on the border of Surrey and Kent in the southeast of England, where thousands of young dispersed. The bullfrogs have also bred in the Netherlands and northern Italy.

Temperature Control

The bullfrog experiences a wide range of temperatures throughout its large north-south distribution. Although other species of frogs and toads have evolved different temperature preferences according to where they live, the bullfrog appears not to have adapted in that way. It prefers the same temperatures whether it lives in Florida or Nova Scotia.

⊕ *Always ready to take on a challenge, a voracious bullfrog attempts to eat a ribbon snake.*

It regulates its temperature by basking. In cold places it basks as long and as often as possible, exposing the greatest part of its body to the sun. But in warmer spots it may seek shade or reduce the amount of heat it absorbs by changing the shape and orientation of its body. In particular, it can tolerate very high temperatures by sitting in water. As water evaporates, it cools the frog's body. The frog replaces the water by absorbing more through its skin, so there is a continual movement of water into the frog through its underside and out again through its upper surfaces.

Competing for Food

Bullfrogs are voracious predators, taking small mammals, lizards, snakes, and other frogs, including smaller members of their own species. In places where they have been introduced (California and several other western states, Mexico, Cuba, Puerto Rico, Hispaniola, and Jamaica in the Americas; the Netherlands, France, Spain, and Italy in Europe; and Java, Japan, Thailand, and Taiwan in Asia) they are often implicated in the disappearance or reduction in numbers of native species living in similar habitats. In California, for instance, they are one of the causes of the decline of the red-legged frog, *Rana aurora*.

Their method of feeding is to sit and wait for prey to come within range, but there is some evidence that they are attracted to the distress calls of other frogs, including those of other bullfrogs (presumably in the hope of getting an easy meal). Food is taken with a lunge, and the frog may use its short front legs to help stuff the food into its mouth.

Similar Species

There are two other large green frogs from eastern North America. The pig frog, *Rana grylio*, named for its call (as is the bullfrog, of course) has a more limited range mainly in Florida and neighboring states. It is even more aquatic than the bullfrog and lives in weedy places such as lakes, swamps, and ditches. It is hunted for its legs, which are edible. It grows to over 6 inches (15 cm) and, confusingly, is also known as the bullfrog in places.

The green frog, *Rana clamitans*, is smaller, growing to about 4 inches (10 cm). Its range coincides almost exactly with that of the bullfrog, but it prefers shallower water. Whereas the bullfrog and the pig frog both have smooth backs, the green frog has a pair of fleshy ridges running down either side of its back.

The frog-jumping contest held annually in Jubilee, California, dates back to 1928. Today thousands of contestants from all over the world give the unique event international acclaim.

"The Celebrated Jumping Frog of Calaveras County"

In the 1860s the author Mark Twain visited Calaveras County, California, as a struggling journalist and heard a tale about a frog-jumping contest. In 1865 he turned it into a short story that became his first success and put him on the road to fame. The story is celebrated every year in the small town of Jubilee with a bullfrog-jumping competition in which participants catch bullfrogs and persuade them to compete with each other in the long jump. More than 2,000 frogs take part every year, and after the event they are returned to the ponds from which they were taken.

Each frog makes three consecutive jumps, and the winner is the frog that covers the greatest combined distance. The event attracts 40,000 tourists during May, and past champions, such as "Splashdown," "Ripple," and "Wet Bet," are commemorated on bronze plaques displayed along some of the town's sidewalks. Pride of place goes to the current world record holder, "Rosie the Ribiter," who leaped 21.48 feet (6.5 m) in May 1986.

Ironically, the bullfrog probably did not occur in Calaveras County in Twain's day, although it does today. Much controversy surrounds the origin of the story: Does it refer to the local red-legged frog, *Rana aurora*, or is it simply a fiction? Either way, the frogs used nowadays in the competition are descendants of the bullfrogs that were introduced into the Sierra Nevada in the late 19th century and are now gradually replacing the native species.

WHAT IS A REPTILE?

The reptiles form the class Reptilia. There are just over 8,000 species in total, and they are divided into four groups, or orders: the Testudines (turtles and tortoises), the Squamata (lizards, amphisbaenians, and snakes), the Crocodylia (crocodiles and alligators), and the Rhynchocephalia (tuataras). The numbers are unevenly divided among the orders, with the Squamata being the largest group in terms of numbers of species. It is also the most widespread group with almost global distribution. It is divided further into three suborders: the Amphisbaenia (amphisbaenians, or worm lizards), the Sauria (lizards), and the Serpentes (snakes).

Although reptiles are less conspicuous than many other animal groups, they form a unit within the system of biological classification that puts them on a par with other major groups such as insects, birds, and mammals.

Like fish, amphibians, birds, and mammals, reptiles are vertebrates (animals with a backbone). However, they obtain their body heat from outside sources (they are ectotherms) rather than producing it metabolically from their food. This ability separates them from birds and mammals, which are endothermic. They are separated from the fish and the amphibians by their reproductive biology: Reptile embryos are surrounded by three special membranes: the amnion, chorion, and allantois. The evolution of the "amniotic egg," as it is called, was a significant step and one that led subsequently to the evolution of birds and mammals.

Reptiles lay shelled eggs or produce live young depending on species. That means they are not closely tied to water, unlike most amphibians (although perversely some reptiles, such as crocodilians and sea turtles, have become aquatic as adults and have to come back to the land to lay their eggs, the very opposite of amphibians). In contrast to amphibians, reptiles are covered in dry, horny scales that are relatively impermeable to water. These two factors (their scales and their amniotic eggs) allowed them to move away from watery habitats and colonize the interiors of continents, even though some still favor wet or aquatic habitats.

⊙ *Representatives of reptile groups: tuatara (***Sphenodon punctatus,*** order Rhyncocephala) (1); female false gharial (***Tomistoma schlegelii,*** order Crocodylia) (2); worm lizard (order Squamata, suborder Amphisbaenia) (3); Alabama red-bellied turtle (***Pseudemys alabamensis,*** order Testudines) (4); green tree python (***Morelia viridis,*** order Squamata, suborder Serpentes) (5); Madagascan day gecko (***Phelsuma laticauda,*** order Squamata, suborder Sauria) (6).*

Temperature Regulation

Understanding how reptiles operate at different temperatures is the key to understanding their behavior, biology, and ecology. Each species has a "preferred body temperature" at which they are best able to move around to hunt for and digest their food, to produce eggs or sperm, and so on. The temperature varies according to species but is often about 85 to 100°F (30–37°C). They may still be active at lower temperatures but they slow down, and at some point conditions will become too cold for them to move at all. This is known as the "critical lower temperature." If they have not found shelter at this point, they become stranded and are vulnerable to

5

6

predation. If the temperature continues to fall, they are at risk of freezing (they reach their "lethal minimum temperature"). The same thing happens with rising temperatures. Critical maximum temperatures are often quite close to preferred body temperatures, so even a small rise can spell trouble. The reptile must find a place away from the heat (in the shade, under a rock, or in a burrow) to keep its body from becoming overheated. Reptiles trapped in the sun (if they fall into a trench, for instance) succumb and die in minutes on hot days.

Reptiles living in different climates clearly need to use different strategies to maintain a suitable temperature. In the tropics they may need to do little by way of thermoregulation because the ambient temperature may be close to their optimum for much of the time. In cooler climates, such as North America, South Africa, and Europe, they can raise their body temperature during the warmest part of the day in spring and summer, perhaps by basking, but nighttime temperatures may be too cool for them on all but the warmest nights.

Species living in these climates tend to be diurnal, but depending on their locality, they may become nocturnal during midsummer. Of course, different species have different preferred body temperatures,

so even in the same locality some may be diurnal and some nocturnal. In winter none of them can reach their preferred temperature at any time of the day, and they need to retreat to a safe place and remain there in hibernation until the following spring.

At the other extreme, reptiles living in very hot places are often active at night and seek shelter during the day. Another advantage is that they can reduce the risk of predation by daytime hunters such as birds of prey (but not by nocturnal predators, of course). Where conditions are too harsh, they may retreat underground for days or even weeks at a time to "sit out" the worst excesses of the climate before returning to the surface (this is known as estivation). In practice, most reptiles that estivate usually do so in order to avoid extreme dryness rather

⊕ *Many reptiles need to bask in the sun to reach their body's preferred temperature. In central Oman a spiny-tailed lizard,* Uromastyx aegyptia microlepis, *stretches out on a rock to warm up.*

⊖ *Right: A chart demonstrating the main lines of reptilian evolution. The four subclasses of reptiles (Euryapsida, Anapsida, Diapsida, and Synapsida) are distinguished by the arched recesses, or apses, in the skull behind the eye sockets.*

Below right: Anapsida (1) have no apses, and today they are represented by the turtles and tortoises. Synapsida (2) have one apse, and this line led to the evolution of mammals. Diapsids (3), with two apses, included the now extinct dinosaurs and are represented today by all other reptile groups apart from turtles and tortoises. The Euryapsids (4) had one apse high on the skull and are represented by the now extinct marine reptiles of the Mesozoic.

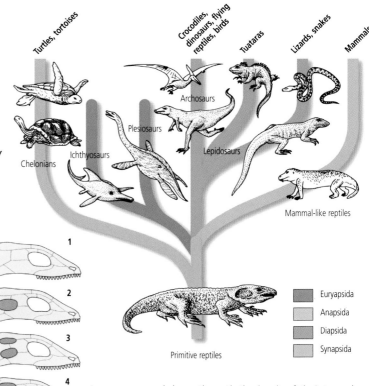

Euryapsida
Anapsida
Diapsida
Synapsida

than heat, and they tend to be species that normally rely on water, for example, crocodilians and freshwater turtles.

Maintaining the correct body temperature by thermoregulation takes several forms in reptiles. Species that live in open environments shuttle backward and forward between areas of sun and areas of shade. Some of them are dark in color so that they absorb heat more quickly. They may also flatten or orient their body in a particular way to help absorb heat more quickly: American fence lizards, *Sceloporus* species, side-blotched lizards in the genus *Uta*, and European vipers, *Vipera* species, are good examples.

Forest dwellers have less opportunity to bask, but they can move into small open areas where the sun gets through or move up into the canopy. Aquatic species, such as crocodilians and turtles, have limited opportunities to control their body temperatures and must often "make do" with whatever temperature the water happens to be; most of them come from warmer climates where typical temperatures are suitable. Crocodiles, alligators, and freshwater turtles may "haul out" for long periods to bask on the riverbank or on logs or rocks that stick out. Sea turtles do not usually bask, except perhaps at the water's surface, and so they are restricted to the tropics. Burrowing species, such as the worm lizards, may be able

to move up and down through the levels of their tunnels; but by and large they do not actively thermoregulate, and they are sometimes known as "thermal conformers."

Origins of Reptiles

Reptiles evolved from four-legged amphibians about 350 million years ago. However, species that would pinpoint their exact origins have not been positively identified from fossil records. They are known to have laid amniotic eggs, which was a significant development. By 310 million years ago the early land-dwelling animals that laid amniotic eggs split into two branches, one that would lead to the mammals and the other to reptiles and birds. The implications of this division are, perhaps surprisingly, that birds are more closely related to reptiles than to mammals—some scientists even maintain that they are reptiles.

⊖ *A scene from an early Jurassic landscape shows the diversity of reptilian life. A pterosaur, Rhamphorhyncus (1); a stegosaur, Kentrosaurus (2); theropod dinosaurs, Elaphrosaurus (3) and Ceratosaurus (4); sauropod dinosaurs, Dicraeosaurus (5), and Brachiosaurus (6).*

By the end of the Triassic Period (about 208 million years ago) the oldest lineages of reptiles that we know today had appeared. They were the early chelonians, or shelled reptiles (turtles and tortoises), the crocodilians, and the rhynchocephalians (the ancestors of the tuataras). The lizards, worm lizards, and snakes came later, first appearing during the Jurassic Period about 208 to 144 million years ago. The worm lizards are thought to be the most recently evolved of the major groups. Many other branches of the reptile lineage led to evolutionary dead ends but only after they had been highly successful for very long periods of time before eventually dying out.

Form and Function

Compared with birds or mammals, living reptiles form a diverse group. There are species with and without shells. Some have four limbs, some have two, and some have none. All are covered in scales, but the scales can be massive, knobby, and stonelike or tiny, granular, and silky to the touch. Compare a snapping turtle or an alligator with an anole lizard or a gecko to get an idea of the wide range of forms and sizes in the order. The sizes, shapes, and colors

of reptiles are not there to help us tell one species from another: They have been finetuned through the evolutionary process to help each species adapt to its particular place in the scheme of things. Even small groups of closely related species contain very diverse species occupying different ecological niches.

We know that stout snakes with short tails are likely to be slow-moving, burrowing reptiles, and that long, thin ones with long tails are likely to be fast-moving, terrestrial types (unless they have prehensile tails, in which case they will be climbers). Flattened turtles with streamlined shells are aquatic, while species with domed shells and elephantlike feet are terrestrial, and so on.

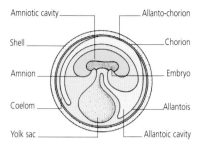

Amniotic cavity — Allanto-chorion
Shell — Chorion
Amnion — Embryo
Coelom — Allantois
Yolk sac — Allantoic cavity

⬅ *Developing egg, showing layers of membrane between shell and embryo. The partly fused chorion and allantois on the inner surface of the shell are supplied with blood vessels, enabling the embryo to breathe through pores in the shell. The allantois also acts as a repository for the embryo's waste products. The amnion is a fluid-filled sac around the embryo that keeps it from drying out. The yolk sac contains the embryonic food supply, rich in protein and fats. Eggs of this type, such as those of birds, are called cleidoic ("closed-box") eggs, since apart from respiration and some absorption of water from the environment, they are self-sufficient. Water absorption by the eggs of many reptiles, especially the softer-shelled types, is higher than by birds' eggs.*

➡ *Reptilian hearts. In most reptiles the chambers of the ventricles are incompletely separated (1). In crocodilians complete separation exists, although there is a small connection, the foramen of Panizza, between the outlet vessels (2). Even in the unseparated ventricle a system of valves and blood pressure differences ensures that there is little mixing of arterial and venous blood under normal conditions. In all reptiles, however, the potential exists to shunt the blood from one side of the heart to the other. This helps them adapt, especially aquatic animals, since blood can be recycled when breathing is interrupted.*

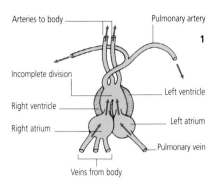

Arteries to body — Pulmonary artery
1
Incomplete division — Left ventricle
Right ventricle — Left atrium
Right atrium — Pulmonary vein
Veins from body

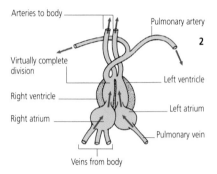

Arteries to body — Pulmonary artery
2
Virtually complete division — Left ventricle
Right ventricle — Left atrium
Right atrium — Pulmonary vein
Veins from body

Within several families of lizards there has been a tendency to lose limbs, which is also related to lifestyle. The skinks are a particularly good example of "adaptive radiation"—the process by which related species evolve in different ways to suit different conditions. Skinks range from tiny, legless, burrowing forms through elongated, grass-dwelling species with tiny reduced limbs to chunky, heavy-bodied, terrestrial forms.

Coloration is usually related to defense. Cryptic, or disguised, species are colored to match their surroundings, and other species have disruptive geometric markings that help break up their outline. Some species are so well camouflaged that they are nearly impossible to make out even when you know where they are. Other reptiles, however, are brightly colored to warn that they are venomous. On the other hand, there are species that are harmless but also brightly colored to fool predators into thinking that they are venomous (known as Batesian mimicry). Some camouflaged species have brightly colored patches or extensions to their body that they can flash when they want to display to other members of their own species or to deter potential predators.

Who Lives Where and Why?

Because they are dependent on temperature, reptiles are most at home in tropical and subtropical regions, with the greatest numbers of species and individuals occurring in the tropical rain forests of Central and South America, West and Central Africa, and Southeast Asia. Farther away from the tropics toward the poles the numbers fall dramatically. Species that do not have the ability to thermoregulate, such as burrowing and aquatic reptiles, are even more restricted to warm places.

Superimposed on this pattern are the historical events that have affected the way in which reptiles have been able to spread across the globe. At about the time they were diversifying most rapidly, the landmasses and "supercontinents" were changing shape through continental drift. Areas that had been connected were breaking apart, while in other places landmasses collided. Evolving reptiles were "passengers" on these landmasses; and lacking the ability to cover large tracts of water (with the obvious exception of the sea turtles), they became isolated in some places but were presented with opportunities to expand in others.

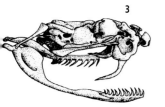

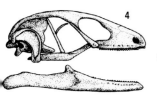

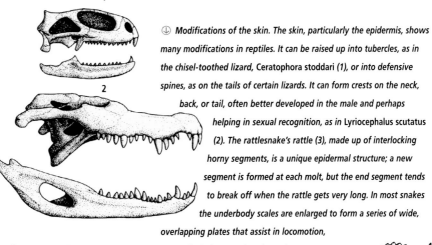

⊕ Modifications of the skin. The skin, particularly the epidermis, shows many modifications in reptiles. It can be raised up into tubercles, as in the chisel-toothed lizard, Ceratophora stoddari (1), or into defensive spines, as on the tails of certain lizards. It can form crests on the neck, back, or tail, often better developed in the male and perhaps helping in sexual recognition, as in Lyriocephalus scutatus (2). The rattlesnake's rattle (3), made up of interlocking horny segments, is a unique epidermal structure; a new segment is formed at each molt, but the end segment tends to break off when the rattle gets very long. In most snakes the underbody scales are enlarged to form a series of wide, overlapping plates that assist in locomotion, especially in forms such as boas that can crawl stretched out almost straight. The modified scales, or lamellae, on the toe pads of geckos (4) have fine bristles (setae) that allow them to climb smooth surfaces.

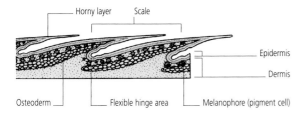

↑ The skulls of living reptiles: tuatara (1), crocodile (2), snake (3), lizard (4), and turtle (5).

Horny layer   Scale

Epidermis

Dermis

Osteoderm   Flexible hinge area   Melanophore (pigment cell)

↑ Cross-sectional diagram of the skin of a slowworm. All anguimorphs such as this are heavily armored, having mostly nonoverlapping scales with underlying osteoderms.

"Older" lineages (those that appeared early on) were able to spread onto most landmasses and travel with them. Some of them subsequently thrived and became widespread (the geckos, for example), while the success of others diminished as more adaptable groups ousted them. For the "newer" families, however, some options were closed because they were already isolated by the time they appeared. That is why there are no vipers in Australasia and no monitor lizards in the Americas.

Isolated island groups are often very poor in reptile species, but their patterns of colonization and speciation (species formation) are especially interesting to biologists because they can add to our understanding of the processes of evolution and natural selection. The most obvious example is the Galápagos archipelago. Reptiles first spread to places like this accidentally (and perhaps only on one or two occasions), possibly by "rafting" on mats of floating vegetation.

Reproduction

Unlike the amphibians, reptiles have internal fertilization. The male introduces the sperm directly into the female's reproductive tract through the cloaca, which is the opening for the digestive and reproductive systems. In all reptiles except the tuataras males have copulatory organs. In lizards, snakes, and worm lizards they are paired and are called the hemipenes. There is usually competition among males for access to females, which can take various forms. In species that use visual clues for communication, such as some lizards, males often display crests, frills, or brightly colored parts of their anatomy to

105

⊕ *A clutch of eggs laid by a female milksnake hatches out. Most snakes lay eggs, but other reptiles, including some snakes, are live-bearers. Reproductive patterns are often determined by lifestyle and habitat.*

attract mates and to advertise their ownership of territory. Color change can also be involved, most famously in chameleons. The courtship process in many species, especially secretive ones such as skinks and worm lizards, is poorly known, but chemical communication almost certainly plays an important part.

Reproductive cycles vary greatly according to species and where they live. Some tropical species breed all year around, while some from colder climates breed only once every two or three years. Tuataras breed only every five or more years. Most temperate species breed in the spring and summer, but again there is some variation.

Reptiles may lay eggs or give birth to live young. This is an evolutionary "decision" with important tradeoffs. Laying eggs frees the female to continue feeding and may enable her to produce a second clutch quickly; on the other hand, the eggs are vulnerable to predation and are at the mercy of the elements. Giving birth to live young enables the female to care for her developing embryos more effectively because she is carrying them around with her, but it is an added burden for several months. The "choice" she makes (in evolutionary terms) will depend on factors such as climate and lifestyle.

Superimposed on this, however, is an ancestral element: Reptiles in some families seem "locked into" a particular reproductive mode (for example, all pythons lay eggs, but nearly all boas give birth to live young). The crocodilians, turtles, and tuataras do not seem to have evolved the facility to give birth—they lay eggs, which is the "ancestral mode" for all reptiles. Among lizards and snakes most lay eggs, but a significant proportion are live-bearers. Many aquatic snakes, including the sea snakes, give birth because finding a suitable place to lay their eggs presents a problem (although some species, notably the sea kraits, come ashore to lay eggs). Worm lizards are all egg layers as far as is known, but the natural history of many of these obscure reptiles remains a mystery.

Food and Feeding

Among them reptiles eat just about anything organic. There are divisions along taxonomic lines, however. All snakes are carnivorous, for instance, although their prey can vary from ants to antelopes. Crocodilians are also carnivorous—their prey ranges from insects to large mammals such as zebras and wildebeests. Worm lizards are probably all carnivorous too and feed largely on burrowing insects such as ants and termites, but the larger species also take small vertebrates, including lizards. Lizards feed on a wide variety of items— many eat insects, but many others are herbivores. Large monitors are ferocious predators of vertebrates such as other lizards, birds, and mammals. Marine and freshwater turtles eat animal and plant material depending on species, and some eat both. Land turtles tend to be herbivores but are not averse to eating animals when they can catch them, which is not very often. A number of reptiles, perhaps more than we realize, eat carrion as a sideline.

Methods of finding and overcoming food are equally diverse. Finding and catching plant material is not very hard, although plants are well known for producing toxins to deter grazers and browsers. Many reptiles are amazingly oblivious to spines and bitter substances, and can eat plant species that other herbivores reject.

Catching animal prey takes a number of different forms. Many are "sit-and-wait" predators, setting themselves up in a likely place and waiting for prey to blunder past. American horned lizards, *Phrynosoma* species, and Australian thorny devils, *Moloch horridus*, position themselves next to ant trails and simply mop up the ants as they walk past. Overpowering larger prey—especially if it can fight back—calls for more cunning and specialized equipment. The ultimate weapon is the evolution of venom in some snakes, which enables them to dispense death in the blink of an eye even to animals many times their own size.

Classification of Species

Compared with other groups of zoology, the naming and reclassification of reptiles seems to be always in a state of change. In 2003, for example, there were 59 new species described, 3 subspecies were elevated to full species, and 18 species were suppressed (because it turned out that they had been named twice). In 2002 there were 60 new species, in 2001 80 new species were named, and 72 new species were described in 2000. In just four years, then, 271 completely new species were added to the reptiles. In the same period there were few, if any, new birds or mammals. What is more, scientists are constantly reclassifying and renaming existing species to try to represent more accurately the relationships between them. This can make life difficult for those studying or writing about reptiles.

Many new reptile species are discovered in places that have hardly been explored from a herpetological point of view, such as Madagascar. Other species belong to groups that are hard to find or difficult to work with (or both), such as the blind and thread snakes, Leptotyphlopidae and Typhlopidae. Others are still turning up in parts of the world where herpetologists have been working for years and belong to conspicuous groups of reptiles. The reptile lists of South Africa and Australia, for example, have grown significantly in the last 10 years or so—by 20 percent in South Africa, an average of one new species every 44 days!

⊕ *The Galápagos Islands are home to some of the most unusual reptiles, including the marine iguanas, Amblyrhynchus cristatus. They are the only lizards that enter the sea and feed on seaweed.*

Declining Species

Until 200 years ago the Galápagos Islands were home to hundreds of thousands of giant tortoises. During the 19th century visiting whaling ships began to collect the tortoises to stock their holds with fresh meat. They left behind a number of destructive, introduced mammals—rats, cats, pigs, and goats—that preyed on the tortoises' eggs and young or competed with them for food. By the mid-20th century three of the original 14 subspecies of giant tortoise were extinct. Only four subspecies are considered to be safe from extinction. Six out of a total of seven marine turtle species are classed as Endangered or Critically Endangered (IUCN) as are seven of just 22 surviving species of crocodilians.

According to the IUCN 21 species of reptiles have become extinct in recent times. Sixteen of them lived on islands. Island species are especially vulnerable because their environment is easily affected by human impacts, especially the introduction of predatory animals. On Round Island in the Indian Ocean every native reptile species is extinct or on the brink of extinction, while Mauritius has lost eight species.

Not all the news is bad, however. The surviving Galápagos tortoises are being bred successfully in captivity, goats and rats have been eliminated on some islands, and the vegetation is beginning to recover. The Jamaican iguana, *Cyclura collei*, was believed extinct since the 1940s but turned up in small numbers in 1990 on a

Reptiles as Pets

Reptiles have become popular pets. Species available range from small geckos to huge pythons and the common boa (*Boa constrictor*). Many are now being selectively bred to give the enthusiast a wide selection of color and pattern forms. Their care varies greatly according to the species, so always seek the advice of the vendor, and consult a specialist book for the relevant information.

Captive-bred animals should be obtained wherever possible. There are a number of reasons for this. First, they will be better adapted to captivity than wild ones and will therefore calm down sooner and be more inclined to accept an unnatural diet. Second, they are likely to be free from parasites and infections that often plague specimens captured from the wild. Third, the fact that they were produced in captivity means that they are an adaptable species. Finally, many wild reptile populations are under threat, and to encourage trade in them is irresponsible. Many species are protected internationally, nationally, or locally, and you may be breaking the law by keeping them. Similarly, collecting species from national or state parks is not allowed.

Accommodation

Accommodation can range from plastic containers for the smallest species (or for rearing juveniles of some of the larger species) to huge, room-sized cages that will

↩ *Green iguanas lie trussed up ready for sale at a market in Guyana. These animals are destined for the cooking pot; their flesh is often used in stews and curries in that part of the world.*

be necessary to house the large constricting snakes or large, active lizards such as iguanas and monitors. As a rule, however, beginners are advised to avoid any large, active species. Venomous snakes and lizards do not make good pets either, for obvious reasons.

Environment

Background reading about the natural history of your chosen species will provide clues to its requirements. Heating of some sort will probably be necessary depending on the species you keep and where you live. Diurnal lizards and snakes prefer an overhead light source such as a heat lamp or spotlight because they are used to basking in the sun. Others fare better if a gentle heat is applied under their cage by means of a heat mat or heat strip. The best plan is to arrange the heating at one end of the cage only: That will create a thermal gradient, and the reptile will be able to move from one part of the cage to another to take advantage of different temperatures.

In addition, many lizards and turtles require a source of ultraviolet light because it enables them to synthesize vitamin D, which they need in order to absorb calcium into their skeleton. In the wild they would obtain vitamin D from sunlight, but in captivity special lights, together with dietary supplements, are often necessary to provide the correct nutritional balance. Lighting is not normally required for most of the more popular snakes such as corn snakes because in nature they shun the light and are most active in the evening and at night. Garter snakes, however, do like to bask.

Some species are very sensitive to humidity, and it is important to make sure that they are neither too damp nor too dry. Some species are particularly susceptible to shedding problems if they are kept too dry. If their skin becomes dry or comes away in many pieces, that is a sure sign they are being kept in conditions that are too dry. Clearly, freshwater turtles require an area of water, and some species can be kept in totally aquatic accommodation such as an aquarium; but most will need an area where they can crawl out to bask under a light source.

Feeding

There are almost as many types of reptile food as there are reptiles. However, it is best to choose a species whose diet is easily catered to in captivity. Insectivorous lizards, snakes, and turtles will usually eat crickets, which can be bought from pet stores, or you may be able to collect enough insects, at least during the summer.

Earthworms are another good source of food for species that will eat them. Many snakes require vertebrate food, of which the most convenient is rodents, which can be bought frozen and then thawed out as required. Again, captive-bred individuals are more likely to accept food that has been stored in this way; wild snakes often insist on having, at best, freshly killed prey, which is not always convenient (or legal).

remote hillside. Eggs have been collected, a captive-breeding program is underway, and young iguanas will be released into the wild once they are no longer vulnerable.

Cause for Concern

Despite these measures hundreds of reptile species may disappear over the next century. Habitat destruction through agricultural development, urbanization, mineral extraction, erosion, and pollution, is the most important cause. On top of this thousands of reptiles are killed by traffic on the roads every day, and several populations have been lost through the flooding of valleys for hydro-electrical projects. Reptiles are also hunted for food, their eggs, or the pet trade. Sea turtles enjoy total protection throughout the world but poachers still take adults and eggs in many of the poorer parts of the world, and wild crocodilians are still hunted illegally for their skins.

Not only rare species are affected. Some species that were widespread a few decades ago are becoming scarce. Many people will grow up without ever seeing a wild lizard, snake, or turtle. The challenge for the future will be to find ways to reconcile the human race's need to expand and feed itself with the preservation of the wild places needed by reptiles and other animals.

Common name Loggerhead turtle

Scientific name *Caretta caretta*

Family	Cheloniidae
Suborder	Cryptodira
Order	Testudines
Size	Carapace 41 in (104 cm) long
Weight	Up to 1,200 lb (544 kg)
Key features	Very big head and powerful jaws; carapace heart shaped, lacking ridges in adults (but juvenile's carapace is ridged); carapace brown, often with light brown, reddish-brown, or black markings; plastron yellowish-brown in color; limbs paddlelike and have 2 claws on each
Habits	Tends to breed farther from the equator than many turtles; relatively aggressive
Breeding	Nesting interval typically 2–3 years but can range from 1–6 years; females come ashore to lay clutches of 100 eggs 4–7 times during the breeding season; eggs hatch after 54–68 days
Diet	Mainly shellfish, including mussels, clams, and crabs; may eat some seaweed
Habitat	Coastal areas, often in relatively shallow water; occurs in muddy waters as well as clear tropical seas
Distribution	Wide range through the Pacific, Indian, and Atlantic Oceans, especially in southeastern United States; occurs as far north as Newfoundland and as far south as Argentina
Status	Endangered (IUCN); listed on CITES Appendix I

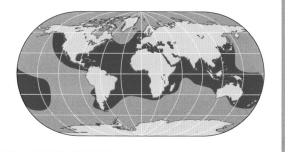

Loggerhead Turtle
Caretta caretta

The loggerhead turtle is one of the largest of the hard-shelled turtles. Despite a ban on international trade, the turtle is still considered to be vulnerable worldwide.

THE LOGGERHEAD IS THE LARGEST MEMBER of its family. Its skull length alone can be almost 12 inches (30 cm) and gives the turtle its common name. Its powerful jaws are used to crush the shells of invertebrates such as horseshoe crabs that feature prominently in its diet. The southeastern United States is one of its strongholds, with the beaches here being used by over one-third of the world's population. It is the commonest species seen by divers off the coast of Florida, where it frequents relatively shallow waters.

Nesting typically occurs between late August and the end of September in Florida, which is the most significant nesting area in the region. Small numbers of female loggerheads also lay their eggs on beaches in the Carolinas and Georgia. In both places they dig holes in which to lay their eggs, and the eggs take on average 54 days to hatch in Florida, extending to between 63 and 68 days in Georgia.

Cutting the Egg

When it is ready to hatch, the young turtle uses the sharp projection on the end of its nose, the egg tooth, to cut its way out. The plastron is curved when it hatches and straightens out later. Having nourished the young turtle during its development in the egg and for a while immediately after hatching, the yolk sac is soon absorbed into the body.

It usually takes about five days from the time that young loggerheads start breaking out of their shells until they appear at the surface of the sand. They often rest during this period, especially during the day when the sand above them is hotter. This instinctive reaction ensures that they only emerge under cover of darkness, when it is safer. The young loggerhead hatchlings measure just 2 inches (5 cm) and vary in color from light to dark brown on the carapace with yellowish underparts. The flippers are brown with very distinctive white edges.

Drawn to the Light

As in other sea turtles, young loggerheads orient themselves by light at first. They are instinctively drawn to the sea, where the light above is usually brighter than on land. Unfortunately, in areas where there has been marked beachfront development, the light from the

The Threat of Nets

Because they live mainly in relatively shallow coastal waters where they look for rich shellfish beds, loggerhead turtles are vulnerable to becoming entangled in shrimp nets and drowning as a result. Although they generally do not catch fish, they sometimes scavenge on dead fish used as bait; this habit can also lead to the turtles becoming caught in traps.

⊕ *The head of the loggerhead turtle is relatively large compared with that of other turtles. In open sea loggerheads spend much of the time floating on the surface and feed on sponges, jellyfish, mussels, clams, oysters, shrimp, as well as a variety of fish.*

land confuses young turtles and pulls them away from the sea. Weakened and disoriented, they are vulnerable to predators on the beach when dawn breaks.

Hatchling loggerheads that reach the water swim during the day and rest at night as they head to areas of sargassum in the ocean. It is thought that they drift in the fields of sargassum, traveling as far the Azores, which lie some 2,500 miles (4,023 km) from the beaches of Florida where they hatched. They remain there until they attain a shell length of about 20 in (50 cm) and probably return to the area around Florida for the first time 10 years later. Loggerheads are as likely to be found in muddy waters with poor visibility as they are to occur in clear tropical seas.

The turtles range along a vast area of the Atlantic coast and have been seen as far north as Newfoundland and as far south as Argentina. Juveniles in particular are found in large numbers well away from their traditional haunts. As many as 10,000 loggerheads are estimated to spend the summer months off the Chesapeake Bay region of the eastern United States, appearing from May onward. They overwinter in warmer waters farther south.

Young turtles that hatch in the Indian and Pacific Oceans are thought to head for the coast of Baja California. Huge numbers of juvenile loggerheads have been found there, and their movements have been confirmed by satellite tracking.

Green Turtle

Chelonia mydas

The green turtle was once common in the warm oceans of the world. Unfortunately, it has become increasingly rare in some areas, where it suffers from commercial exploitation and is at risk of extinction.

Common name Green turtle

Scientific name *Chelonia mydas*

Family   Cheloniidae

Suborder   Cryptodira

Order   Testudines

Size   Carapace usually over 36 in (91 cm) long

Weight   Up to 352 lb (160 kg) when adult

Key features Head relatively small with a prominent pair of scales in front of the eyes; jaw is serrated along its edges; distinctive differences in appearance between Atlantic and Pacific populations, the latter having a significantly darker plastron; carapace dome shaped and appears green; limbs paddlelike, usually with a single claw on each one

Habits   A marine turtle occurring in coastal areas rather than roaming across the open ocean; some populations bask during the day

Breeding Female lays about 115 eggs per clutch on average 3–5 times during a season; interval between laying is usually 2–3 years; eggs hatch after about 65 days

Diet   Small individuals feed on small crustaceans and similar creatures; larger individuals are entirely herbivorous, eating sea grass and marine algae

Habitat   Coastal areas, bays, and shallow water in tropical and temperate seas

Distribution Pacific and Atlantic Oceans

Status   Endangered (IUCN); listed on CITES Appendix I

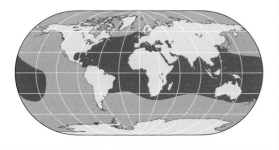

THE NAME GREEN TURTLE COMES FROM the color of the fat beneath the shell in these marine turtles. It varies among individuals: In some there may be light stripes radiating across the carapace with yellow and brown areas apparent as well. The Pacific population is often described as black sea turtles because they typically have a much darker, grayish, or even black carapace. Their shells also appear more domed than those of their Atlantic relatives.

Green turtles are probably the slowest growing of all vertebrates thanks largely to their diet. Although initially they hunt small crustaceans, they soon become vegetarian, feeding mainly on sea grass and marine algae once their carapace measures approximately 8 inches (20 cm) long. In areas where sea grass is prevalent, regular grazing by the turtles encourages the plant's growth. This is important to the turtles' own well-being, since fresh shoots are more nutritious. As in herbivorous mammals, the green turtles rely on a beneficial population of microbes in their intestinal tract to aid the digestion of plant matter.

Dietary Adaptations

Green turtles are quite adaptable in their feeding habits, and their diet varies significantly throughout their range. In northern Australia, for example, they have learned to snap the leaves off mangrove trees, adding to their feeding options. The serrations on the sides of their jaws help them tear off mouthfuls that can be swallowed easily, and they will sometimes even pluck leaves growing above the water's surface.

In areas where sea grass is not present, notably around Hawaii and on Australia's Great

↑ *A green turtle feeds on marine algae growing on coral in waters off the coast of Malaysia. Its other favorite food is sea grass.*

← *The beautiful markings of the carapace can be seen clearly on this green turtle from Malaysia. The green effect comes from the layer of fat beneath the shell.*

Barrier Reef, the lack of sea grass may explain why green turtles there are so slow to reach sexual maturity. Studies involving Hawaiian green turtles revealed that some were mature by 11 years old, but others were not capable of breeding for the first time until they were 59. In the case of some green turtles living off the coast of Queensland, Australia, sexual maturity may not occur until the turtles are 70 years old. Growth and therefore breeding capability relate largely to the availability of food. Ultimately,

Temperature-Dependent Sex Determination

It was in green turtles that researchers first discovered the phenomenon of temperature-dependent sex determination (TDSD). It is now known to apply quite widely to many chelonians that lack sex chromosomes to regulate gender. In such cases the temperature at which the eggs are incubated is significant in determining the sex of the hatchlings. Clutches exposed to higher temperatures contain female offspring, while those that hatch under cooler conditions are likely to produce mainly males. However, the exact details vary according to species, and TDSD does not apply to all species.

however, the green turtle can grow larger than any other member of its family. Those in the Atlantic are bigger on average than their Pacific counterparts.

Sand Pits

When they come ashore to nest, females dig a pit for their eggs, using their hind flippers. This laborious task usually takes about two hours. A nesting female must do this roughly every two weeks during the breeding season, since she lays from two to seven clutches. As in other marine turtles, the eggs have relatively rubbery shells and are laid with mucus around them. This stops them from being damaged as they fall on top of each other in the pit. The female uses her flippers to cover the eggs with sand.

Because the eggs are laid above the high-tide line, they are free from the risk of flooding and should hatch about 65 days later. Hatchling green turtles

Basking

A very unusual behavior pattern has been observed in green turtles found in the northwestern area of the Hawaiian archipelago. Individuals haul themselves out of the water onto the beaches of isolated islands to bask during the day. Why they do this is unclear, but it may be a way of avoiding attacks from tiger sharks, *Galeocerdo cuvier*, which are prevalent in the area. Basking is almost completely unknown in other marine turtles.

Once established in an area, the turtles are unlikely to leave except to nest. They also seem to be particular about their feeding preferences. In Hawaiian waters green turtles regularly look for just nine out of over 400 species of marine algae growing in the region.

⊕ *Using her hind flippers and becoming covered in sand in the process, a nesting female green turtle digs a pit for her eggs on a beach on Ascension Island.*

are about 2 inches (5 cm) long and weigh roughly 0.9 ounces (25g). Their carapace is dark above and lighter below. Young green turtles that hatch on Hawaiian beaches face relatively few predators. Seabirds do not seriously affect their numbers, nor do large fish waiting offshore in the ocean.

Populations around the World

Green turtles are widely distributed throughout temperate and tropical seas, and have been seen off the North American coast as far north as Massachusetts.

In the past green turtles were heavily hunted as a source of food, but in many parts of their range they are now strictly protected. Nicaragua shut its turtle-processing plants in 1976, a move that has probably also helped the important Tortuguero population in neighboring Costa Rica—today turtles of all ages can be seen feeding together there.

Although it is nearly 30 years since green turtles were given legal protection in Hawaii, their numbers have not increased dramatically. This is partly because of changes in their habitat that have reduced the amount of food available. In addition, a significant number are affected by skin tumors known as fibropapillomas, which may be linked with harmful environmental conditions. In the vicinity of the island of Honokowai over 90 percent of the green turtles are suffering with these viral growths on their bodies.

The green turtle population in the Atlantic has fallen dramatically in some areas, and the species has become extinct on the Cayman Islands and Bermuda. Breeding populations occur on the mainland right around the Caribbean from the coast of Florida to Costa Rica and down to Surinam in South America as well as on islands throughout the region.

Success Story

One of the most significant breeding colonies can be found on Ascension Island. The turtles nesting there have been tracked back to the coast of Brazil, which means that they must migrate over 1,600 miles (1,000 km) to their nesting grounds. Individuals within the Ascension Island breeding population represent some of the largest living examples of the species, possibly because they have not been subjected to heavy predation.

Even so, they would have been dwarfed by some of the monsters recorded from

centuries ago. Particularly large specimens weighing as much as 1,000 pounds (454 kg) have been recorded from the Cedar Key region of Florida.

Ranching

One of the practical ways of safeguarding wild populations of green turtles is by ranching. This entails collecting a percentage of the eggs laid by the turtles and hatching them artificially. The young hatchlings are reared in captivity and ultimately used to meet the demand for soup and other by-products.

By legitimizing trade in this way, it is hoped that wild turtles will be left alone. However, a number of welfare issues have arisen surrounding programs of this type, especially with regard to the turtles' growth rates. Young green turtles raised in this way grow at a much faster rate than in the wild. This affects their physical appearance, causing the carapace to appear more domed.

Fears have also been expressed that these programs simply encourage trade and could provide cover for the illegal collection of wild turtles, which are killed and sold as if they were reared in captivity. International trade in marine turtles (and various associated products ranging from soup to shells that may be sold to unsuspecting tourists) remains illegal under the Conservation in International Trade in Endangered Species (CITES) treaty.

⊕ It is hoped that turtle farms such as this one on Grand Cayman Island will prevent the hunting of green turtles in the wild.

Common name
Hawksbill turtle

Scientific name *Eretmochelys imbricata*

Family Cheloniidae

Suborder Cryptodira

Order Testudines

Size Carapace up to 36 in (91 cm) long

Weight Up to 150 lb (68 kg)

Key features Head narrow and distinctive with a
hawklike bill; 2 pairs of scales in front of the
eyes; carapace elliptical with an attractive
blend of yellow or orange mixed with brown,
but coloration is highly individual; scutes
overlap behind each other on the carapace;
2 claws present on each flipper; serrations
present on side of carapace

Habits Often encountered looking for prey on coral
reefs

Breeding Female usually lays up to 160 eggs in a
season but breeds on average only every 2–4
years; eggs hatch after 58–75 days

Diet Invertebrates, mainly sponges, but also squid
and shrimp

Habitat Mainly tropical waters

Distribution Occurs in the Atlantic and in parts of the
Indian and Pacific oceans

Status Endangered (IUCN); listed on CITES
Appendix I

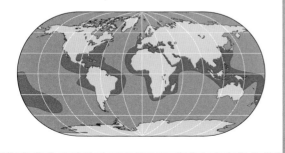

Hawksbill Turtle

Eretmochelys imbricata

The name imbricata *describes the overlapping plates
on the hawksbill's upper shell. Unfortunately, it is the
beautiful carapace, known as "tortoiseshell," that has
led to widespread hunting of this small sea turtle.*

RECENT SURVEYS SUGGEST THAT numbers of the
hawksbill turtle have declined more seriously
and rapidly in recent years than was previously
thought. This is true especially throughout the
Caribbean and the western Atlantic Ocean in
spite of the widespread protection given to the
species. In the past huge numbers of these
turtles were caught. Their shells were used to
create "tortoiseshell" objects ranging from tea
caddies to hair combs, which were highly
fashionable in the late 19th and early 20th
centuries. The scutes that extend over the
carapace are the most highly prized because of
the amber mottling that is apparent once the
upper shell of the turtle is polished. In Japan,
where the use of tortoiseshell has been elevated
to an art form, this material is known as *bekko*.

Deadly Sponges

The hawksbill turtles get their name from the
shape of their narrow mouthparts. Their "v"-
shaped lower jaw is used to reach and pluck
sponges from inaccessible areas of a reef. Some
species of sponge protect themselves by toxins
in their bodies, but they do not seem to harm
the hawksbill turtle. Bizarrely, the sponge toxins
remain potent, a fact confirmed by cases in
which humans died from eating the flesh of
hawksbill turtles that had eaten the sponges.

The turtles depend on sponges as their
major food source. Any deterioration in the
conditions on a reef will cause a decline in the
number of sponges and leave the turtles
vulnerable to starvation.

Hawksbill turtles are relatively small and
agile, and can therefore reach nesting beaches

Hitching a Ride

Sea turtles in general carry a number of other creatures on their shell, particularly barnacles and various types of coral. Hawksbills from the Atlantic region often have Columbus crabs, *Planes minutus*, attached to the rear of their body. They are probably acquired when the hatchling turtles are feeding in the sargassum, where young crabs are frequently found.

In contrast, it is normally adult crabs that are seen on mature turtles. They help keep the reptile's body clean, feeding on algae and other creatures that may also attach themselves. If the crabs did not keep these organisms in check, they could make swimming much harder for the reptile by reducing its streamlined profile.

over reefs that would exclude larger, heavier species. They lay their eggs quite high up on the beach, often in sites partially concealed by vegetation. Once on land, the nesting process can be completed in an hour, although it often takes longer. Females lay a total of up to 160 eggs, returning to the same beach to lay at intervals of roughly 14 days about four or five times during the season. The number of eggs laid is determined by the size of the female, with larger turtles laying more eggs.

Dangerous Detritus

The hatchlings have a carapace length of just over 1.5 in (3.8 cm), and they generally weigh less than 0.7 ounces (20 g). They head into areas of sargassum at first and are vulnerable to floating detritus, including pieces of styrofoam, which can sometimes lodge in their digestive tracts with fatal consequences. Assuming they survive, the young turtles head back to reef areas once they have grown to 8 inches (20 cm) long—they often retreat under rocky overhangs and similar safe places.

The carapace alters in shape as young hawksbills mature, taking on a more elongated outline. The serrations running down the sides toward the rear of the carapace may have a protective function, but they shrink as the turtle grows older. Their ultimate disappearance in adults is regarded as a sign of old age.

Many hawksbill turtles do not seem to travel long distances to their nesting grounds, but there are exceptions, discovered as a result of tagging. One female caught and marked in the Torres Strait region of northern Australia was caught again 11 months later approximately 2,240 miles (3,600 km) away in the Solomon Islands, where she came on land to nest.

⊖ *A hawksbill turtle swims near the Virgin Islands in the Caribbean. The closeup shows the beaklike mouthparts that give the turtle its common name.*

117

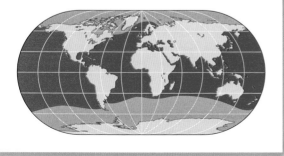

Leatherback Turtle

Dermochelys coriacea

The leatherback turtles are true giants. They are the largest of all marine turtles and the heaviest reptiles in the world. Their very distinctive shells have a leathery appearance.

Common name Leatherback turtle

Scientific name *Dermochelys coriacea*

Family Dermochelyidae

Suborder Cryptodira

Order Testudines

Size Carapace can be up to 8 ft (2.4 m) in length

Weight Up to 1,650 lb (750 kg)

Key features Carapace very distinctive with 7 ridges running down its length; surface of the carapace is effectively a rubbery skin rather than made up of scales; skin strengthened with very small bony plates; color dark with whitish markings; plastron bears about 5 ridges and varies in color from a whitish shade to black; flippers lack claws; front flippers extremely long; carapace of hatchlings has rows of white scales

Habits Often favors open sea, swimming widely through the world's oceans

Breeding Clutches consist of about 80 viable eggs; female typically produces 6–9 clutches per season; egg-laying interval typically 2–3 years; youngsters emerge after about 65 days

Diet Almost exclusively jellyfish

Habitat Temperate and tropical waters

Distribution Has the largest range of any marine turtle; found in all the world's oceans from Alaska to New Zealand

Status Critically Endangered (IUCN); listed on CITES Appendix I

AT ABOUT 8 FEET (2.4 M) LONG and weighing up to 1,650 pounds (750 kg), the leatherback's bulk probably enables it to maintain a sufficiently high core body temperature that allows it to venture farther into temperate waters than any other species of marine turtle. Leatherbacks are apparently unaffected by sea temperatures even below 41°F (5°C), and they range as far north as the seas around Alaska. Their body is actually slightly warmer than that of their surroundings in these cold waters, which suggests that they have a basic mechanism to regulate their body temperature.

These turtles are also found in the oceans below the southern tip of Africa and off the Chilean coast as well as close to New Zealand. In fact, the largest leatherback recorded was not found in the tropics but was discovered stranded on a beach on the coast of Wales in the British Isles in 1988. It is possible that global warming and its effects on sea temperature are affecting the range of these turtles.

Remote Nesting Sites

Leatherbacks return to the tropics to breed. They often choose remote areas for this purpose, although there are about 50 nests recorded along the Florida coastline each year. They traditionally use beaches onto which they can haul themselves up without difficulty, and where they can come directly out of deep sea rather than swimming across reefs. This is possibly to protect their vulnerable underparts from injury and may explain why they tend to nest more commonly on mainland areas rather than islands. Unfortunately, these beaches can be badly eroded in storms, leaving the leatherback's developing eggs at greater risk of being lost than those of other marine turtles.

Egg stealing has been a threat in some areas in the past, but improved protective measures mean that it is less of a problem today. The oil in the leatherback's body was also used for the manufacture of many products, including cosmetics and medicines, but the introduction of synthetic substitutes has ended this trade. Leatherbacks are not hunted for their meat, which is regarded as unpalatable.

Although leatherbacks often lay eggs on their own, they sometimes nest in small groups. Their breeding range extends almost all the way around the world—from the Caribbean region across to the western coast of South Africa to India, Sri Lanka, Thailand, and Australia right across the Pacific to the shores of

Long Journeys

Tagging studies have revealed the remarkable distances that leatherbacks can cover in the world's oceans—one individual tagged on its nesting ground in Surinam, northern South America, was rediscovered on the eastern side of the Atlantic over 4,226 miles (6,800 km) from the original tagging site. Unfortunately, leatherbacks have tended to lose their tags more readily than other turtles, so fewer data are available, but it certainly appears that those encountered along the northern coast of South America regularly undertake journeys of over 3,125 miles (5,028 km). Switching the tag site on the leatherback's body from the front flipper to the inner side of the back flipper has helped, however, since the tags are exposed to less physical force in this area of the body. This should ensure that more information about their movements can be obtained.

Mexico. Clutch sizes laid by leatherbacks in the eastern Pacific region tend to be smaller than those produced in other parts of their range.

What is suspected to be the largest breeding colony of leatherbacks in the world was only discovered as

Female leatherbacks, such as this one in Trinidad, come ashore to nest every two to three years on the warm sands of remote tropical beaches.

recently as 1976 thanks to the confiscation of a large number of leatherback eggs that were on their way to Mexico City. The trail led to an area known as Tierra Colorado on the Pacific coast.

Studies have since revealed that up to 500 leatherback females may come ashore to lay eggs there every night during the nesting period, mainly in December and January each year. It appears that, at least in this area, female leatherbacks return on their own with no males congregating offshore in search of mates.

An unusual phenomenon is the presence of small, apparently immature eggs found in the nests of leatherback turtles. Their presence may be linked in some way to the interval of time between the laying of the clutches, which is much shorter than in other marine species. It is often no more than seven to 10 days, and some eggs do not develop fully in this time. It takes about 65 days for the young leatherbacks to hatch and emerge at the surface, by which stage they are about 2.5 inches (6.3 cm) long. The hatchlings are unmistakable: The longitudinal ridges are well defined, and there are rows of white scales that appear as stripes along the length of the flippers.

It is quite straightforward to determine the sex of leatherback turtles, since males have much longer tails than females and, as in many other chelonians, a slightly concave plastron.

Imprinting Behavior

One strange phenomenon that has been repeatedly documented is the way in which, after she has completed the task of egg laying, a female leatherback circles the nest site, just as the young do once they hatch. It may be that this behavior somehow imprints onto the memories of the youngsters, aiding their return to the same place in due course. Current estimates suggest that there could be between 100,000 and 115,000 breeding female leatherbacks in the world's oceans today.

Predators

Leatherbacks tend to dive deeper than other turtles, which may give them some protection against being attacked. They are also well equipped to swim fast out of harm's way thanks to the propulsive power of their front flippers. They are longer than those of any other marine turtle and can extend to nearly 9 feet (2.7 m) in length.

Even once they are fully grown, however, these turtles still face a number of predators. Various sharks, including the notorious great

Death at the Hands of Humans

The leatherback's wide range means that it is very difficult to build up an accurate population estimate, but there are signs that the species is in trouble. This is not essentially because of hunting pressure but largely as a result of its feeding habits. Its rather slender jaws with their scissorlike action are used to capture jellyfish, which form the basis of its diet. Unfortunately, these turtles find it hard to distinguish between jellyfish and plastic detritus such as plastic bags and other similar waste floating on the surface of the sea. When seized and swallowed, these items are likely to get stuck in the turtle's gut, resulting in a slow and painful death. Controlling losses of leatherback turtles is exceptionally difficult, and there is no easy way of solving this problem.

There has been progress, however, in addressing some of the other threats facing leatherback populations. It was estimated that about 640 of these turtles were being accidentally captured in nets in U.S. waters annually. Many of them died through drowning or injuries sustained during their capture. Devices to keep turtles out of the nets were developed, and the law was changed to make their use mandatory in U.S. waters. Elsewhere, however (often in international waters), problems remain, with the turtles being caught in fishing nets or becoming entangled in ropes or lines. Even if the leatherback can free itself, the resulting injury can prove fatal. The leatherback's urge to swim, together with its specialized feeding habits, mean that nursing it back to health in captivity is often a difficult task too.

⊕ *A leatherback turtle hatching on the Virgin Islands in the Caribbean. Hatchlings use a sharp tooth called an "egg tooth" to break through the eggshell.*

⊕ *In French Guiana a group of young hatchlings have just emerged from their eggs. They must make their way to the ocean quickly to avoid predatory seabirds.*

white shark, *Carcharodon carcharias* from Australian waters, represent a hazard; killer whales, *Orcinus orca*, are also known to prey on leatherback turtles, the reptile's size being of little use against such fearsome predators.

Virtually nothing is known about the potential life span of these turtles, but for individuals that escape being hunted, it is thought to be measured in decades, as in the case of other sea turtles. While it is generally assumed that the leatherback turtle is solitary by nature, there have been accounts of sightings at sea of groups numbering as many as 100 individuals. Whether or not the groups are drawn together for mating purposes is unclear; it could simply be that they tend to congregate in areas where food is plentiful.

Common name Alligator snapping turtle

Scientific name *Macroclemys temminckii*

Family   Chelydridae

Suborder Cryptodira

Order   Testudines

Size   Carapace about 26 in (66 cm) in length

Weight   219 lb (99.5 kg)

Key features Head large; jaws prominent and hooked; tail long; carapace varies in color from brown to gray depending on the individual and has 3 distinctive keels arranged in ridges, resembling those on the back of an alligator; feet on all four limbs end in sharp claws; lure present in mouth to attract prey

Habits   Sedentary predator usually found in deep stretches of water; lures prey within reach especially during the daytime; may become more active as a hunter at night; strictly aquatic, but females leave the water to lay their eggs; relatively weak swimmer

Breeding Occurs in spring and early summer; clutches contain up to 50 eggs that hatch after about 100 days

Diet   Eats anything it can catch, including birds, small mammals, other turtles, fish, and mussels where available; also eats fruit and nuts

Habitat   Relatively sluggish stretches of water

Distribution North America from Kansas, Illinois, and Indiana to the Gulf of Mexico, including Florida and eastern Texas

Status   Declining; now rare in many parts of its range; protected locally in parts of United States; Vulnerable (IUCN)

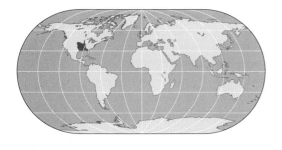

Alligator Snapping Turtle

Macroclemys temminckii

The alligator snapping turtle ranks among the largest of all freshwater turtles, as well as being the biggest found in the United States. However, giant specimens are very rarely encountered these days.

ALLIGATOR SNAPPING TURTLES get their common name from the keeled ridges on their carapace, which resembles the back of an alligator. They used to be heavily hunted to make turtle soup, which was a popular dish in the southern states. During a three-year period in the mid-1980s more than 37,736 pounds (17,117 kg) of their meat was bought by a single dealer in Louisiana. Even today hunting is a potential problem in some areas, and habitat change has generally had a harmful effect on the populations of alligator snapping turtles.

An exception has occurred in Florida, however, as a result of drainage of the Apalachicola River. The silt that was dredged out of the river was deposited on the floodplain. Clutches laid there by alligator snapping turtles were subsequently exposed to raised temperatures during the incubation period, giving rise to a higher percentage of female offspring among the hatchlings.

This occurred as a result of temperature-dependent sex determination (TDSD), in which ambient temperature during incubation plays an important part in determining the sex of the developing young. The extra females should help increase the reproductive potential of the species in this area, since a greater number of females in the population will mean that more eggs are laid.

Luring Prey

The alligator snapping turtle's bulky body means that it is not well suited to being an active predator. As a result, the species has developed a very distinctive method of obtaining prey.

⊕ The alligator snapping turtle is unusual in being able to pump blood to its tongue, creating a lure to entice fish into its mouth. It feeds mainly on fish but will also capture and eat small turtles.

These turtles are well camouflaged in their surroundings thanks in part to their dark coloration, and they often feed during the day. An individual will rest in a characteristic hunting pose on the muddy bottom with its mouth open. A projection on its tongue turns pink as it fills with blood and acts as a lure to entice prey into its jaws. The turtle can even move this structure to make it look like a wriggling worm. As soon as the prey enters its mouth, the turtle snaps shut its jaws. At other times, however, the lure is relatively inconspicuous and whitish in color, drained of blood and lying on the floor of the mouth.

This method of feeding is especially common in juvenile alligator snapping turtles. As they grow older, their feeding preferences and tastes change. It has been suggested that the main type of food in the diet of these turtles was once freshwater mussels; but thanks to the effects of water pollution and overexploitation of stocks the mussels have become rare, and the turtles have been forced to switch to other food. In areas where the mussels are available, however, they feature significantly in the turtles' diet.

Their powerful jaws also enable them to feed on smaller turtles occurring in their habitat, such as the common musk turtle, *Sternotherus odoratus*, and even their smaller relative, the common snapping turtle, *Chelydra serpentina*. There is virtually nothing that large alligator snapping turtles will not prey on—they eat all types of creatures, including birds such as wood ducks, *Aix sponsa*, and even mammals such as raccoons, which they seize in their massive jaws. The turtle drags them under water and drowns them before eating them. The alligator snapping turtle is not exclusively predatory by nature, however. It has a keen sense of smell, which makes it an effective scavenger. One turtle was even trained to find human corpses in the waterways of Indiana. It was released on a wire leash into the water close to where a person had disappeared, and it was followed by observers in a boat as it picked up the corpse's scent. It also feeds opportunistically on vegetable matter such as persimmons and acorns, gathering these seasonal foods as they fall

⤊ The three dorsal ridges can be seen clearly on the carapace of this alligator snapping turtle. The irregular outline together with the brownish body color give it a degree of camouflage on the riverbed.

from trees and bushes overhanging the water— acorns in particular form a significant part of the turtle's diet in some places.

Breeding Behavior

The mating period of alligator snapping turtles begins in February and usually lasts until April. Where several males congregate hoping to mate with a single female, they often behave aggressively toward their potential rivals in an attempt to drive them away. A male that wants to mate with a female first sniffs her body

carefully starting in the vicinity of her head. He then moves down the side of her body to the cloaca before mounting her under water. He grips her with his claws, anchoring on slightly to one side of her body. This enables him to direct his tail beneath the female's so that he can introduce his sperm into her body.

As in many other chelonians, the gap between the base of the tail and the opening in the anogenital region is longer in males, which aids mating. Copulation itself can last anywhere from five to 25 minutes, with the male

she can deposit her eggs. It seems that the number laid depends to a significant extent on the size of the female, with larger individuals laying comparatively bigger clutches of up to 50 eggs. The eggs themselves are hard shelled and relatively spherical in shape.

The nests of alligator snapping turtles can sometimes be raided by predators like raccoons. It typically takes about 100 days or so for the eggs to hatch. The carapace of the hatchlings measures about 1.8 inches (4.6 cm) in length at this stage.

Mossbacks

Although alligator snapping turtles naturally inhabit rivers in the Mississippi drainage area of southern parts of the United States, they are relatively weak swimmers. They prefer to move by walking on the riverbed. They do not come onto land to bask, yet the heavy growth of green algae present on the carapace of many larger individuals suggests that they regularly spend time in shallow areas of water. Relatively intense sunlight falling on their backs is responsible for triggering the development of the plant growth, and it may even spread farther along the upper surfaces of the head and tail in some cases. As a result, the turtles are often referred to as "mossbacks" by people in the Deep South.

A dense covering of algae (not, in fact, moss as suggested by its nickname) often coats the shells of alligator snapping turtles that frequent shallow waters.

releasing a steady stream of air bubbles out of his nose during this period.

When she is ready to lay, the female alligator snapping turtle hauls herself onto land and digs a nesting chamber with her hind feet. This activity often takes place during the day. The nest is enlarged at the base to accommodate the eggs. It may extend over 12 inches (30 cm) down into the ground.

The female starts by digging a pit into which she can lower much of her body. She then creates a smaller hole beneath, into which

Giants of the Past

Although there are only two surviving species in the family Chelydridae (the other being the snapping turtle, *Chelydra serpentina* from Canada to Ecuador), snapping turtles used to be much more widely distributed, including in Europe. Another species of alligator snapping turtle, *Macroclemys schmidti*, lived in North America about 26 million years ago near present-day South Dakota. Records suggest that the largest alligator snapping turtles were found in northern parts of the species' range, possibly migrating there from farther south. It is also likely that much larger specimens than those officially known to zoologists existed.

One of the most celebrated "giants" was the so-called "Beast of Busco," or Oscar, as it became known. It was originally reported by a farmer in the summer of 1948. He spotted the monstrous turtle in Fulk's Lake, a stretch of water covering some 7 acres (2.8 ha) near the town of Churubusco in Indiana. It was seen again in March 1949, and some townsfolk made an attempt to corral the turtle in a small area of the lake. They constructed a stockade using stakes and managed to keep the giant reptile confined in 20 feet (6 m) of water. Unfortunately, it managed to break out of the enclosure. Those who observed the turtle said that it was about the same size as a dinner table, with a heavy covering of algal growth on its back. Its weight was estimated as being about 500 pounds (227 kg). A film of the event was taken at the time but has subsequently been lost.

More than 200 witnesses saw the turtle try to seize a duck that was being used as a lure to catch it. It was then decided to drain the lake to expose the "Beast of Busco," but the attempt nearly ended in tragedy when two people became trapped in the treacherous mud that coats the bottom of the deep lake and almost drowned. After that the turtle was left alone, and nothing more appears to have been written about it. However, the story has been immortalized in a unique annual turtle festival held in the town that takes place during June. It lasts for four days and includes a carnival parade as well as turtle racing, and now even the town's official logo features a turtle!

Other myths surround these turtles, not least that their jaws are reputed to be strong enough to break a broom handle with a single bite. Tests have shown that even a large alligator snapping turtle weighing 40 pounds (18 kg) would have difficulty snapping a pencil in this way, although the shearing effects of the jaws are such that they can bite chunks out of boats when lifted aboard. Big specimens are very dangerous to handle not just because of their strong jaws but because of their powerful flippers, which have sharp claws.

Once they are in the water, the young turtles may occasionally fall victim to larger individuals of their own species, but they are more likely to be caught and eaten by alligators. While these turtles will prey on small gars, *Lepisosteus* species, larger examples of these fish, which can reach 10 feet (3 m) in length, regularly hunt small alligator snapping turtles in return.

Forced to Move

There is some evidence that alligator snapping turtles are territorial. Established individuals may actively resent the incursion of smaller turtles into their territory. This may be related to the fact that the turtles can be forced to shift regularly from one locality to another in order to guarantee a food supply. In some areas at least it appears that the lure in their mouth often becomes less effective at attracting prey over the course of several years, and fish tend to avoid it. This may be particularly significant in view of the fact that these turtles are potentially very long-lived. There are reliable records of individual alligator snapping turtles in zoological collections living for over 60 years, and it is thought that their life expectancy could be much longer, possibly more than 100 years.

↑ Twenty-one years after it was stolen from a reptile park, this 110-pound (50-kg) alligator snapping turtle was found in sewers in Sydney, Australia. It has since been returned to the park.

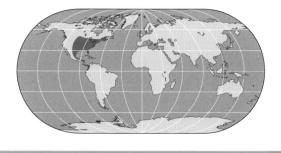

Common Snapping Turtle

Chelydra serpentina

Common name Common snapping turtle

Scientific name *Chelydra serpentina*

Family Chelydridae

Suborder Cryptodira

Order Testudines

Size Carapace length up to 24 in (61 cm)

Weight Up to 82 lb (37.2 kg)

Key features Head powerful; jaw hooked; barbels present on lower jaw with small tubercles on the neck and underparts; eyes prominently located near the snout; carapace brown and relatively smooth in older individuals but with a more pronounced keel in younger turtles; plastron relatively small in area with no patterning and varies from whitish to coppery brown; tail quite long with a crest running down the upper surface

Habits Relatively shy; spends long periods concealed in mud or vegetation; usually more active at night; often rests during the day, floating just under the surface with the eyes protruding

Breeding Female lays single clutch of 25–80 eggs (but may lay more than once a year); eggs hatch after minimum of 2 months

Diet Predominantly carnivorous; eats fish, amphibians, other turtles, birds, snakes, and small mammals; also eats plant matter

Habitat Occurs in virtually any type of standing or flowing fresh water, especially where there is a muddy base and vegetation

Distribution Southern parts of Canada through the United States and Central America south to Ecuador

Status Reasonably common

Although it does not grow as large as its relative, the alligator snapping turtle, Macroclemys temminckii, *the snapping turtle is a voracious predator. It has powerful jaws that can inflict a painful, damaging bite.*

THERE IS SOME DISPUTE over the taxonomy of the snapping turtle. Its range extends from southern parts of Canada through the United States and Central America as far south as Ecuador. Although it is traditionally divided into four subspecies within this range, DNA studies have led to the suggestion that the population should be split into two or three distinct species, with those in southern areas being recognized as separate from the northern populations. In the east the Florida snapping turtle, *C. s. osceola*, is also considered to be a separate species by some taxonomists. It is restricted entirely to the Florida peninsula but appears to differ little from examples occurring elsewhere in North America.

Musky Females

The mating period of snapping turtles varies from April to November in different parts of their range. It is thought that females emit a pheromone from a gland in the cloaca that attracts males when they are ready to mate. The secretion has a distinctive, musklike odor. Courtship is aggressive: The male pursues the female, snapping initially at her head and legs to slow her down. If she accepts his advances, she raises her hindquarters, and both turtles then face each other for a period, while moving their head from side to side. The male then moves around the female's body and climbs on top of her, anchoring himself with his feet. Mating lasts for about 10 minutes.

Female common snapping turtles do not need to mate every year in order to lay fertile eggs. In common with many other chelonians females are able to store viable sperm in their reproductive tract from previous matings, which will fertilize future egg clutches. As a result, the eggs laid by a female of this species can produce hatchlings of different parentages.

Nesting begins in May, peaks in June, and can continue until as late as September. A rise in air temperature above 50°F (10°C), especially in combination with some rain, triggers nesting behavior. Egg laying begins either at dusk or dawn. Larger females tend to nest earlier in the season and lay proportionately more eggs in a clutch than younger individuals laying for the first time.

Dug in a wide variety of soil conditions usually in the open and often some distance from water, the nests themselves are vulnerable to predators, including skunks and raccoons. Some snakes, notably the eastern king snake, *Lampropeltis getulus getulus*, will also eat turtle eggs readily. Often what happens is that eggs at the top of the nest are destroyed

⟵ **Female snapping turtles make a bowl-shaped cavity in loose sand, loam, or plant debris. In the nest the eggs are vulnerable to predators, and this female in Ohio takes no chances and stays close by.**

⟳ **An average of 40 eggs are laid, and incubation lasts at least two months. The young emerge from the nest and head for water, where they hide under cover from predators.**

as a result of predation, but those at the bottom survive and hatch.

The incubation period tends to vary markedly through the snapping turtle's range. Eggs hatch after just two months in warm surroundings but take much longer in northern parts, where the young may even overwinter in the nest before emerging the following spring. If the nest is shallow, however, they may be killed by frost over this period. The young hatchlings emerge under cover of darkness and are directed toward the water by the light reflecting off its surface. (Marine turtle hatchlings, notably loggerhead turtles, *Caretta caretta*, use a similar method of finding their way to the sea.)

Predators and Prey

Common snapping turtles measure about 1 inch (2.5 cm) when they hatch, and their long, flexible tail is similar in length to their shell. They may use the tail as an anchor at first, clasping onto vegetation to keep themselves from being swept away by the current once they enter the water.

They spend much of their early life concealed in these surroundings, often lying partly hidden in the streambed to avoid drawing attention to themselves. This is a particularly dangerous time for the young turtles—they face many predators, from wading birds such as herons to amphibians such as large bullfrogs, *Rana catesbeiana*.

Young snapping turtles have voracious appetites of their own, however, enabling them to grow rapidly. Males eventually reach a larger size than females. Both sexes are sexually mature once their carapace has grown to about 8 inches (20 cm) long, by which time they are between five and six years old. Their growth then slows significantly. Other changes in appearance are evident as they grow: The shell becomes relatively long compared with its width, and the tail is proportionately shorter compared with their overall size.

Their hunting habits also tend to change as they grow older, with mammals and birds more

likely to fall prey to them at this stage. Muskrats, for example, may be seized and dragged under water. They are held under until they drown and are then eaten. Adult ducks may suffer a similar fate. Larger individuals have even been seen preying on smaller members of their own kind, and carrion also features in their diet. But even adult snapping turtles are not entirely safe from predators, particularly in southeastern parts of the United States, where their distribution overlaps with that of the American alligator, *Alligator mississippiensis*. These large reptiles will eat the whole turtle, including the shell, which is crushed in their powerful jaws.

Snapping turtles are also hunted on a wide scale for their meat. The equivalent of over 6,000 adults were caught commercially in Minnesota in the late 1980s, for example, and 8,000 in southern Ontario. Regulations are in force to regulate this trade, certainly in the northern part of the species' range, but trade in the subspecies *C. s. rossignonii* from Central America and *C. s. acutirostris* from South America is less well documented and could be endangering these populations.

Nasty Bite

Estimating numbers of snapping turtles in a given area is not easy because they are less inclined to enter baited traps than other turtles whose range overlaps with theirs. Handling common snapping turtles is not straightforward either, since they can be a genuine danger to the unwary. While most turtles can be safely held by the sides of their shells, common snapping turtles are able to reach around with their head and inflict a serious bite. They are highly aggressive when restrained, and the safest way to move an individual is by grasping the upper and lower ends of the carapace and holding it away from your body.

Few turtles occur in such a wide range of aquatic habitats as the common snapping turtles. They can be found anywhere from muddy pools to fast-flowing rivers and readily move across land if food becomes short, or if

water levels fall significantly. They often travel under cover of darkness, when they are naturally more active. During the day they often rest by floating just under the water's surface with their eyes protruding, keeping a watch on their surroundings. As a result, their shell develops a covering of green algae, which helps conceal their presence even more.

They rarely bask on land, however, unless plagued by leeches. In that case they are forced to dry off in order to make the parasites dehydrate and let go. Their disinclination to bask is probably related to the relatively large amount of water they lose from their body when on land as well as to their dislike of high temperatures.

During the winter, however, individuals in northern areas will hibernate in the mud on the bottom of a river or pond. They dig themselves in usually by the end of October and then emerge the following March. In areas closer to the equator the turtles may bury themselves in mud and wait for the rains to return if the pools in which they are living dry up. While common snapping turtles are essentially found only in fresh water throughout their range, on rare occasions they can be encountered in brackish areas.

⊕ *Not afraid to tackle even venomous prey, a snapping turtle eats a rattlesnake, Crotalus viridis.*

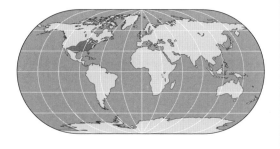

Spiny Softshell

Apalone spinifera

The highly aquatic spiny softshells seldom venture out of water except to bask. The Latin name spinifera *means "bearing thorns," a reference to the spinelike tubercles on the carapace edge just behind the head.*

Common name Spiny softshell

Scientific name *Apalone spinifera*

Family Trionychidae

Suborder Cryptodira

Order Testudines

Size Carapace length 6.5 in (16.5 cm) to 18 in (46 cm) in females; from 5 in (13 cm) to 9.3 in (23.5 cm) in males

Weight Approximately 2.2 lb (1 kg) to 3.3 lb (1.5 kg)

Key features Flattened, leathery shell lacks scutes and is circular; underlying color varies from olive to tan; patterning highly variable; spots (ocelli) on carapace have black edges; distinctive spiny tubercles on the front edge of shell are unique to this species; neck long with dark-edged lighter stripes; nostrils elongated and snorkel-like; limbs powerful and paddlelike

Habits Fast swimmer; predominantly aquatic but will emerge to bask on occasions; burrows into mud or sand beneath the water to hide with just the head exposed

Breeding Female lays 4–32 white, spherical eggs; eggs probably hatch after about 8–10 weeks

Diet Carnivorous; eats mainly invertebrates such as crayfish; larger individuals may take fish and amphibians

Habitat Still or slow-flowing waters that are often shallow with sandy or muddy bottom; may also occur in faster-flowing waters

Distribution North America from southern Canada south across the southern United States, including the Florida Peninsula, and around the Gulf Coast in Mexico

Status Generally quite common

MEMBERS OF THE FAMILY TRIONYCHIDAE, to which the spiny softshell belongs, are widespread. They occur in parts of Africa and Asia as well as North America. The spiny softshell is one of the most widely distributed species. Its range extends from southern parts of Canada across much of the southern United States and south as far as Mexico.

Six distinctive subspecies have been identified. The eastern softshell, *Apalone spinifera spiniferus*, is relatively large with black borders around the spots (ocelli) on the carapace. In contrast, the western race, *A. s. hartwegi*, has much smaller ocelli as well as dots on its carapace. Unlike these two forms, the Gulf Coast spiny softshell, *A. s. asper*, has at least two lines at the rear of the carapace. The Texas race, *A. s emoryi*, has a pale rim to its carapace, which is much wider along the rear edge, and there are also white tubercles present on the rear third of the carapace. In the pallid subspecies, *A. s. pallidus* from west of the Mississippi and east of the Brazos River, the tubercles are more prominent, extending over the back half of the carapace. In the case of the Guadalupe spiny softshell, *A. s. guadalupensis*, the white tubercles cover most of the carapace and are encircled by black rings. In places where two different races overlap, however, they can be difficult to distinguish because they show characteristics of both populations.

Pancake Turtles

Turtles in this family are sometimes known as pancake turtles due to their flat, circular shape. Spiny softshell turtles are adept at burrowing in mud or sand beneath the water, hiding away and leaving just their head exposed above the surface. They do not need to surface in order to breathe as frequently as other turtles, since they can absorb oxygen directly in the pharyngeal region of their throat as well as through their leathery shell. In extreme cases they are able to remain under the water for up to five hours. During the winter period in northern parts of their range they will hibernate in the water by burying themselves under several inches of mud. During this time they slow down their respiratory rate.

Mating occurs in the spring, and egg laying peaks during June and July. Females haul themselves onto land and dig a nest site quite rapidly using their hind feet. They sometimes complete this task in under 15 minutes.

It is not uncommon for the nesting turtles to empty their bladder

⊕ *A female spiny softshell basks at the side of a river with its head raised, revealing the unusual long, piglike nose that is characteristic of the species.*

into the hole as they dig to make the soil particles stick together and help the excavation process. They invariably choose a sunny site close to water.

Young spiny softshells start to emerge from the end of August through to October, but in the far north of their range the young may overwinter in the nest, emerging for the first time the following spring. They measure about 1.4 inches (3.6 cm). They appear to be relatively slow growing and only reach sexual maturity when they are about 10 years of age.

The species is known for its longevity—the largest females can be over 50 years old. They face relatively few threats except for pollution of the water, which can be a major hazard in some areas. Adults are sometimes caught for food, but generally these softshells are not subjected to heavy hunting pressure.

Their powerful feet mean that the spiny softshells are able to live in fast-flowing rivers but are equally at home in ditches. When seeking food, they often prefer to comb the bottom rather than swim actively in search of prey. Invertebrates such as crayfish are their main prey items, but larger individuals also prey on fish and amphibians, notably frogs.

Common name Yellow mud turtle

Scientific name *Kinosternon flavescens*

Family   Kinosternidae

Suborder   Cryptodira

Order   Testudines

Size   Length of carapace 6.3 in (16 cm) maximum

Weight   Approximately 1.3 lb (0.6 kg)

Key features Carapace predominantly olive-brown and smooth with an oval shape; yellow coloration confined largely to the jaw and throat area, including the 2 barbels on the chin; plastron relatively large and light brown in color (darker in some individuals than others) with distinct hinges at either end; males have a concave plastron and patches of scales on the inner side of the hind legs; tail long, ending in a spiny tip

Habits   Spends daytime in water, often emerging to feed on land at night; most active during June and July

Breeding Female typically lays 1 clutch containing 4 eggs, but numbers vary from 1–6 in total; eggs hatch after about 75 days

Diet   Omnivorous; eats mainly aquatic invertebrates; on land eats snails and other terrestrial invertebrates

Habitat   Slow-flowing streams and similar stretches of fresh water, especially where there is plenty of aquatic vegetation

Distribution Central and southern United States to Mexico

Status   Reasonably common, although the subspecies *K. f. spooneri* is regarded as State Endangered in Illinois, Iowa, and Missouri

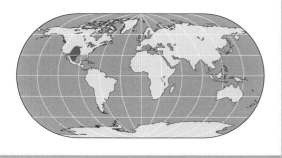

Yellow Mud Turtle

Kinosternon flavescens

The common name of the yellow mud turtle comes from the yellow areas on its throat, head, and neck. The plastron has two hinges, allowing the turtle to retreat into its shell and seal each end separately.

MUD TURTLES ARE WIDELY DISTRIBUTED throughout northern and central parts of America, extending down to Colombia in South America. The yellow mud turtle occurs in central parts of the United States from northern Nebraska south to Texas. It can be distinguished in all cases by the presence of an elevated ninth marginal scute. Its range also covers parts of New Mexico and southeastern Arizona extending across the Mexican border.

Several distinctive subspecies are recognized throughout its range. The most northerly form, *Kinosternon flavescens flavescens*, also displays the most pronounced yellow coloration, which extends onto its carapace. The Mexican form, *K. f. stejnegeri*, has an olive carapace with a particularly long gular scute compared with the front lobe of the plastron. The dark-shelled Illinois yellow mud turtle, *K. f. spooneri*, is the rarest subspecies, and its existence is threatened largely by the effects of water pollution. It occurs in the northwest of Illinois and adjacent parts of Iowa and Missouri. Habitat conservation will be vital in the future to ensure its continued survival.

Yellow mud turtles can be found in a wide range of aquatic environments, including both natural and artificial areas of calm water, ranging from swamps to sinkholes and even cattle troughs. They are often seen basking during the day, especially when the weather is warm and sunny. Their level of activity varies through the year, however. It peaks during June and July, when they are active during the day, particularly in the late afternoon, and at night. They feed largely on the bottom and rely on

The scorpion mud turtle, Kinosternon scorpoides *from Costa Rica, is related to the yellow mud turtle. However, its carapace is slightly more domed.*

their keen sense of smell to locate edible items, sometimes even scavenging on carrion. Occasionally they also feed on land.

Breeding takes place during July and August. They have sometimes been seen mating out of the water. The hard-shelled eggs are buried—females occasionally lay them in heaps of vegetation rather than straight into the ground. The raised temperature resulting from the decomposition of the plant matter may help speed up the development of the embryos. Unlike many chelonians, female yellow mud turtles prefer to start digging their nest hole using their front feet at first, completing the task with their hind legs.

The eggs usually take about 75 days to hatch, and the young measure approximately 1.2 inches (3 cm) when they emerge. Young Illinois yellow mud turtles are quite different compared with the adults and display a series of pale spots on their chin and a dark shell.

⊕ Yellow mud turtles frequent small bodies of water that can dry up in summer. They spend the cooler months under leaf litter, in tree stumps or muskrat dens, or buried in mud under water.

All yellow mud turtles grow quite slowly. As a result, males are unlikely to breed for the first time until they are at least four years old, and the females are usually slightly older.

Digging in for the Winter

As the fall advances in the northern parts of their range, the mud turtles often emerge onto land to find suitable areas for hibernation. They may dig themselves in under logs or burrow straight into the soil. They may invade muskrat dens. Since they often occur in areas of water surrounded by open woodland, these turtles may even hibernate in old tree stumps on occasions as well.

Yellow mud turtles are most likely to be encountered on land when it is raining or soon afterward. During dry periods they prefer to immerse themselves in standing areas of water.

Adults face relatively few predators, possibly because they have scent glands that give off a repellent smell if they are directly threatened. In addition, the yellow mud turtles can seal themselves into their shell thanks to two hinges on the plastron. They prefer to defend themselves in this way rather than by attempting to bite. The young are more at risk of predation, however, because of their small size. This makes them vulnerable to various predatory fish, for example, as well as other reptiles, including snakes.

135

Common name Painted turtle

Scientific name *Chrysemys picta*

Family Emydidae

Suborder Cryptodira

Order Testudines

Size Carapace up to 10 in (25 cm) long

Weight Approximately 2.2 lb (1 kg)

Key features Shell smooth with no keel or serrations along the rear of the carapace; in eastern painted turtle the central vertebral shields and adjacent side shields are aligned rather than overlapping; different subspecies identified easily by distinctive coloring and patterning; pattern of yellow stripes on head, becoming reddish on the sides of head and front legs; females grow larger than males; males have longer front claws than females

Habits Semiaquatic; often leaves the water to bask

Breeding Female may produce clutches of anything from 2 to 20 eggs; eggs hatch after 10–11 weeks on average

Diet Young tend to be carnivorous; mature painted turtles eat a higher percentage of aquatic vegetation

Habitat Relatively tranquil stretches of water, ranging from smaller streams to lakes and rivers; eastern form occasionally found in brackish water

Distribution Central and eastern parts of North America from Canada in the north to Mexico in the south

Status Relatively common

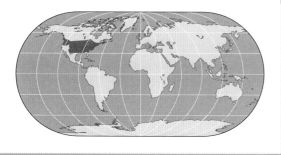

Painted Turtle
Chrysemys picta

The painted turtle is the most widely distributed North American turtle and the only one whose range extends across the entire continent. Because of their size and attractive colors, painted turtles are often kept as pets.

PAINTED TURTLES GET THEIR NAME from their bright coloration. Four distinct subspecies are recognized through their range. The eastern painted turtle, *Chrysemys picta picta*, occurs farthest east and is found from southeastern Canada down the Eastern Seaboard of the United States to northern Georgia and Alabama. A particular feature of this subspecies, which makes it virtually unique, is the way in which the central vertebral shields running down the back and the adjacent shields on either side are aligned rather than overlapping. This creates a distinctive pattern of lines running across the shell.

The eastern painted turtle can also be identified easily by its unmarked yellow plastron. This helps distinguish it from the midland painted turtle, *C. p. marginata*, which also has a blackish carapace but has a dark patch at the center of the plastron. This feature is apparent even in young hatchlings, although the exact pattern of markings on the underside of the shell differs according to the individual. As its name suggests, the range of this subspecies lies to the west of its near relative, extending across Canada from southern Quebec to Ontario and occurring as far south as Oklahoma and Alabama.

The southern painted turtle, *C. p. dorsalis*, is perhaps the most distinctive subspecies of all thanks to the yellow or sometimes reddish stripe that runs down the center of the carapace. The plastron is yellowish in color with no markings. As its name suggests, its range does not extend as far north as Canada; it is confined to the United States from southern Illinois southward to the Gulf of Mexico, ranging from Oklahoma to Alabama.

⊕ *The eastern painted turtle,* Chrysemys picta picta, *has a greenish carapace with thick lines between the aligned scutes and red markings around the edge. The plastron is yellow.*

The western painted turtle, *C. p. belli*, occurs farther west. It is found over a wider area than the other subspecies. It ranges farther north into British Columbia as well and is found in a number of localities in the southwestern United States—it even occurs in an area in Chihuahua, Mexico. It has distinctive lines over the carapace as well as elaborate patterning that extends to the edge of the plastron. It has potentially the largest size of all the subspecies. Where the different races of painted turtle overlap, however, they interbreed, giving rise to offspring with intermediate characteristics. This is known as intergradation.

Courtship and Breeding

Courtship begins in April. At this stage the reason for the male's longer front claws becomes apparent. He swims up in front of a female, approaching her headfirst. He gently uses his claws to fan water close to her face and then starts to touch her face. Assuming she is receptive, she responds by touching his face. The pair then swim to the bottom. The male grips onto the female, placing his legs at each corner of her shell, and mating takes place. A pair may remained joined in this way for up to 15 minutes.

The nesting period itself usually extends from May to July. Females typically emerge from the water to lay either soon after dawn or in the late afternoon. To make digging easier, they

⊕ Chrysemys picta belli, *the western painted turtle, is the most widespread of the four subspecies and grows to a larger size than the others—up to 10 inches (25 cm).*

choose a site that has soft soil, often moving up onto a bank or even near a road, where the area is unlikely to become flooded. The nest itself is usually quite shallow, often less than 4 inches (10 cm) deep.

In northern parts female painted turtles tend to lay only once or twice during this period. Farther south they can lay throughout the season and produce up to four clutches. There are differences among the subspecies as well, with the relatively large western painted turtle producing more eggs per clutch than the southern race, which is the smallest. In any population large females invariably lay more eggs compared with smaller individuals. Breeding is unlikely to occur until the female is six years old; in some areas females may not lay every year if the temperature is too cold.

How Did the Subspecies Evolve?

There is a tendency to think that species are created as individual populations become isolated. However, this process can occur in reverse, which may be true in the case of the painted turtle. It is believed that at the time of the last Ice Age (about 18,000 years ago), today's painted turtles existed as three separate species. Their distribution was somewhat similar to their current ranges, except that they did not extend as far north because of the presence of the ice sheet.

The western painted turtle was present in the Southwest, and the southern painted turtle was confined in the vicinity of the lower Mississippi region. As the climate warmed, it is thought that these two distinct populations followed the retreating glaciers northward. They met around what is now known as the Missouri River, and thus began a process of hybridization that ultimately resulted in the development of the midland painted turtle.

In turn the midland painted turtles traveled northward as far as the eastern area of the Great Lakes. Sandwiched between their two ancestral forms, they occupied the area where they are found today. The movement of the eastern painted turtle up the Atlantic coast also resulted in contact with the southern painted turtle on the western side of its distribution. Instead of remaining isolated, therefore, the three original species came together, with the result that the painted turtle now enjoys the widest distribution of any aquatic chelonian on the North American continent.

The time taken for the eggs to hatch varies depending on local conditions, but incubation usually takes between 65 and 80 days. The gender of the offspring is determined by the temperature at which the eggs hatch—at higher temperatures of about 87°F (30.5°C) females are produced, but at temperatures below 77°F (25°C) males develop. It is unclear whether the female is influenced in this respect when choosing her nesting site. Young painted turtles have a rounded carapace. They are little more than 1 inch (2.5 cm) in length, but they grow fast at first, doubling their size within a year. This makes them less vulnerable to the many predators that they face when young.

Basking in Groups

It is quite common to see painted turtles basking out of water, often with their hind legs stretched out behind them. This helps keep

⊕ *Although they spend most of the time in water, painted turtles often sun themselves on a log, a rock, or the shore. They are often seen in large groups.*

⊙ *The different subspecies of painted turtles are distinctive. This is a southern painted turtle, C. picta dorsalis, distinguished by a reddish-orange stripe running down the center of the carapace.*

their shells healthy and raises their body temperature. In some areas it is not uncommon for up to 50 turtles to share a partially submerged rock or log when basking, often lying on top of each other. This may make them less vulnerable to predators—if one individual detects possible danger and dives back into the water, all the others will follow very rapidly.

Painted turtles display a regular daily routine, emerging to bask early in the morning. This means that they can raise their body temperature and therefore their level of activity at this stage, plunging back into the water to feed before basking again in the early afternoon. They then look for more food and finally burrow into the bottom of their stream or pond overnight.

Basking is particularly significant in temperate areas because, even if the water temperature is relatively low, the turtles can take advantage of any additional warmth provided by the sun. Painted turtles may enter a dormant period in northern parts of their range during the winter months; but although they become sluggish, they may not be completely inactive—they have been seen swimming even in ice-covered water. Their body temperature under these circumstances has been shown to be higher than that of their surroundings, suggesting that they have a primitive mechanism for heat regulation.

Common name Pond slider

Scientific name *Chrysemys scripta*

Family Emydidae

Suborder Cryptodira

Order Testudines

Size Varies from 8.3 in (21 cm) to 24 in (60 cm) depending on subspecies; females in all cases grow larger than males

Weight Approximately 2.2 lb (1 kg) to 4.4 lb (2 kg)

Key features Vary with subspecies; the well-known red-eared slider (*T. s. elegans*) has distinctive red flashes on either side of the head behind the eyes, which are pale green with a dark horizontal stripe; body has a striped pattern consisting of yellow and green markings; carapace greenish with darker markings, especially in older individuals; plastron yellowish with individual dark markings

Habits Semiaquatic; emerges regularly to bask

Breeding Female lays 12–15 eggs in a clutch, often nesting several times in a season; eggs hatch after 6–10 weeks on average

Diet Invertebrates, including tadpoles and aquatic snails; small fish; adults also eat plant matter

Habitat Slow-flowing stretches of water with plenty of vegetation

Distribution North, Central, and South America

Status Relatively common

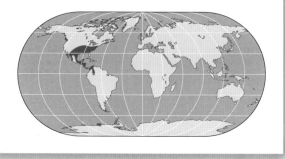

Pond Slider

Chrysemys scripta

Pond sliders love to bask on logs or rocks near water. Sometimes two or three can be seen piled on top of each other. "Slider" describes the way they retreat quietly into the water at the slightest threat.

NO OTHER SPECIES OF TURTLE is so variable in appearance throughout its range as the pond slider, whose distribution extends from southeastern Virginia in the United States south through Mexico as far as Brazil. There are 14 distinctive subspecies recognized over this area, of which the red-eared slider, *Chrysemys scripta elegans*, is by far the best known thanks to its popularity in the pet trade. Its natural range extends through the Mississippi Valley from the Gulf of Mexico up to Illinois.

Large numbers of hatchlings were once exported to Europe. However, fears that unwanted pets dumped in waterways could prove harmful to native wildlife led to an importation ban by the European Community in 1997. Nevertheless, red-eared sliders are still being bred commercially in the United States and also now on a large scale in parts of the Far East, where most are sold for food rather than as pets. This may help protect native Asiatic turtles, which have been subjected to heavy hunting pressures over recent years.

Riverine Life

The name "slider" refers to the way in which the turtles slip into the water if disturbed while basking. In southern parts of their range they are more commonly seen in river habitats.

Breeding behavior varies according to location. In temperate areas females lay in the early summer, typically between April and July. Courtship varies markedly among the different subspecies depending on whether or not the males have elongated claws on their front feet. Where they are present, as in the red-eared slider, the male approaches his intended mate from the front, fanning her face with water and

⊕ *The red-eared slider,* Chrysemys scripta elegans, *can be distinguished from all other North American turtles by the presence of a broad red stripe behind the eye.*

using his claws to stroke her face. In the case of the Mexican race, *T. s. taylori*, however, males adopt a more aggressive style of courtship. They simply bite at the rear of the female's shell and snap at her legs. It is possible that the female releases a particular scent when she is receptive, which may trigger this behavior.

In South America, where pond sliders occur more often in rivers, nesting habits are less influenced by temperature than by rainfall. Egg laying in this region tends to occur during the dry season, when the sandbars are exposed. The young turtles take from about six to nine weeks to hatch and have a circular shape when they first emerge from the egg. They also tend to be more brightly marked on the carapace than adults, in which the patterning becomes obscured with age.

Color Changes

Older male pond sliders can end up being almost black. This phenomenon is known as acquired melanism because of the increased presence of the black pigment melanin in the shell of older individuals. (This process is a little like hair turning gray with age.) Other types of color change can be found in these turtles.

Occasionally what are known as leucistic slider hatchlings are recorded. They are the result of a genetic mutation that causes them to have no melanin, a characteristic that can be passed from one generation to the next. Their entire body and shell tend to be a muddy yellow color overall, and the distinctive color flash on the head of most sliders appears paler than normal in these mutated individuals.

Young sliders are highly carnivorous at first, and the relatively large percentage of animal protein in their diet fuels their fast growth. They prey on a variety of small aquatic creatures ranging from tadpoles to aquatic snails and small fish. Once they are older, however, pond sliders tend to eat more plant matter and become omnivorous in their feeding habits.

Eastern Box Turtle

Terrapene carolina

Common name	Eastern box turtle
Scientific name	*Terrapene carolina*
Family	Emydidae
Suborder	Cryptodira
Order	Testudines
Size	Carapace up to 8 in (20 cm) in length
Weight	Approximately 2.2 lb (1 kg)
Key features	Carapace relatively domed, usually brownish in color often with variable markings; body predominantly brown with yellow and orange markings particularly on the chin and front legs (depending to some extent on the subspecies and the individual); plastron relatively plain with distinctive hinged flaps front and back, allowing the turtle to seal itself into its shell completely; males generally have reddish irises, but those of females are brownish
Habits	Spends much of its time on land but usually remains close to water; may immerse itself for long periods, especially during dry spells
Breeding	Female lays 3–8 eggs in a clutch, sometimes more than once in a season; eggs hatch after 9–18 weeks
Diet	A wide variety of invertebrates as well as smaller vertebrates and carrion; also feeds on vegetable matter and fruit
Habitat	Most likely to be encountered in open areas of woodland; sometimes also occurs in marshy areas
Distribution	Eastern United States to northern Mexico
Status	Has declined in various parts of its range

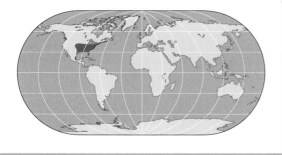

Eastern box turtles are among the most well-known turtles and have even appeared on a U.S. postage stamp. Their appearance is variable, and some individuals are thought to live for over 130 years.

THE DOMED CARAPACE of the eastern box turtle is a clue that these turtles spend much of their time on land—more aquatic species have a more streamlined shape. The turtles range widely across eastern parts of the United States from Maine to Florida and south to northern Mexico.

The species is divided into six subspecies that differ in size, markings, and shell shape. The largest race is the Gulf Coast box turtle, *Terrapene carolina major*, which also displays flaring of the hind marginal shields. Its shell is dull in color compared with that of the northern nominate race, *T. c. carolina*. Both these subspecies have four toes on each hind foot. The other two subspecies in the United States are *T. c. triunguis* from Missouri south to Alabama and Texas, and *T. c. bauri* from Florida. Both have three rather than four toes on each of the hind feet. However, *T. c. bauri* can be distinguished by the light pattern of lines radiating across the carapace and two stripes on each side of the head. The carapace of the Mexican races, *T. c. yucatana* and *T. c. mexicana*, is particularly domed—in the latter it is yellow with dark spots.

Hibernation Sites

In northern parts of their range eastern box turtles hibernate in a variety of different places and often use the same site each year. They may prefer to hibernate under water in mud or bury down into soil or under vegetation. Some sites are shared by several box turtles, and they will continue burrowing if the winter proves severe, sometimes digging down distances as great as 24 inches (60 cm). On occasion they

→ *Box turtles have two hinges on the plastron, allowing them to close up like a box when threatened. This is the Florida box turtle, Terrapene carolina bauri.*

"Old 1844"

In the past it was something of a tradition for people to carve their initials or dates into the shells of eastern box turtles, particularly in northeastern parts of the United States. Since studies have shown that these turtles are sedentary, researchers have tried to correlate the initials carved on shells of individual turtles with local parish records to come up with a novel way of estimating their age. This led to the discovery of the Hope Valley turtle, also known as "Old 1844," which is believed to be the oldest living vertebrate recorded in the United States.

This particular box turtle had two sets of initials, one of which was E. B. K., and two dates etched on its plastron. It was discovered that in 1844 there was a 19-year-old farmhand called Edward Barber Kenyon working on the land where the turtle was found. The fact that there was no distortion of the carving suggested that the reptile was fully grown then and would therefore have been at least 20 years old at the time. Although it proved impossible to match the second set of initials, G. V. B., alongside the date of July 11, 1860, it was discovered that two families (the Bitgoods and the Bigwoods) had owned the land during that period. It could have been one of their family members who found the turtle again. These two pieces of evidence suggested that Old 1844 was therefore about 138 years old at the date when these enquiries were made.

may also move from one site to another during mild spells, but this can prove fatal if the weather takes an unexpected turn for the worse—the turtles are left stranded and defenseless against the frost.

Those that survive over the winter usually emerge during April, and mating begins soon after. Their domed shells mean that males have to balance themselves at a semivertical angle when mating. It can be very dangerous for them if they fall over and are unable to right themselves. In most cases, however, they can use their powerful neck to flip their body over if they should fall while mating.

Females lay their eggs typically between May and July, digging the nest site under cover of darkness. The incubation period depends greatly on the temperature and can range from nine weeks to 18 weeks.

⊖ *A closeup of the eastern box turtle shows bright yellow markings on the chin and head. Males have red irises, while those of females are usually brown.*

Common name Spotted turtle

Scientific name *Clemmys guttata*

Family   Emydidae

Suborder   Cryptodira

Order   Testudines

Size   Carapace to a maximum of 5 in (13 cm)

Weight   Approximately 1.1 lb (0.5 kg)

Key features Carapace relatively low and blackish with
                an overlying pattern of yellowish spots (which
                may be more orange in some cases); plastron
                varies from yellowish to orange in color with
                variable black blotching; males have brownish
                chin and eyes; females are more colorful with
                orange irises and a yellow chin as well as a
                flatter plastron

Habits   Semiaquatic, often wandering on land as well
                as being found in water

Breeding   Female lays a single clutch of 3–8 eggs that
                hatch after about 10 weeks

Diet   Omnivorous; eats especially invertebrates of
                various types, some of which may be
                captured on land

Habitat   Typically found in marshy areas, sometimes in
                association with woodland

Distribution North America from the Great Lakes in
                southern Canada south to northern Florida

Status   May be under threat in some areas from
                habitat disturbance and loss

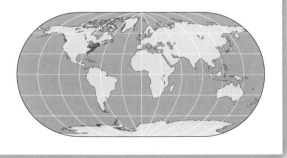

Spotted Turtle

Clemmys guttata

The best time to see one of the cool-weather spotted turtles is spring—in summer they hide on land waiting for the fall rains before moving back to water, and in winter they hibernate in abandoned muskrat nests.

THE SPOTTED TURTLE is a widely distributed species found in the region of the Great Lakes in southern Canada. Its range extends southward along the Eastern Seaboard of the United States reaching as far as northern Florida, although its distribution becomes more sporadic farther south. Spotted turtles sometimes congregate together in suitable areas. It is not uncommon to see a group basking on a log out of the water; but if disturbed, the turtles will plunge straight back into the water and bury themselves immediately in the mud at the bottom. On land they simply withdraw into their shell if threatened, remaining there until the danger has passed.

Spotted turtles thrive at relatively low temperatures. They may even estivate during the hottest part of the summer, concealing themselves in mud under the water.

These turtles mate quite early in the year, often during March, when the temperature of their surroundings can be just over 43°F (8°C). The female is pursued by one or more males as part of the courtship ritual. The chase can last for up to half an hour, during which time the males may fight among themselves. Mating tends to take place more frequently in the water than on land.

Carefully Constructed Nests

Females usually lay their eggs in June. The female digs a nest in a sunny place, sometimes in quite dry soil. It is not unknown for several different sites to be partially dug and then abandoned before she finds a suitable spot. She uses her hind feet alternately when scooping out the soil. She gives the nest a relatively narrow neck and then widens it

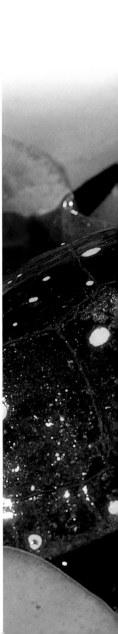

below to create a chamber. Once the nest is completed, the female uses her feet to channel the eggs safely into position. Finally, after a brief pause she fills in the nest using the soil that she dug out previously. She then flattens the surface, using her plastron for this purpose. The whole process lasts for about two hours.

It takes at least 10 weeks before the young hatchlings begin to emerge. In the case of eggs laid in dry ground the young turtles emerge later. In some northern parts of their range the hatchlings may even remain in the ground until the following spring. Young spotted turtles usually have a single yellow spot on each of the

⊕ *Spotted turtles are usually found in marshy meadows, bogs, swamps, ponds, or ditches and prefer areas with relatively still water.*

scutes on the carapace apart from the cervical (neck) scute, which is plain. However, a few youngsters may display no markings at all on the carapace, although they have spots on their head and neck.

Hatchlings in general are less heavily spotted than the adults. The extent of spotting also appears to relate to location—one study suggests that individuals from Virginia have smaller, less conspicuous spotting than those occurring farther north. The carapace in hatchlings is about 1.2 inches (3 cm) long, and their slender tail is proportionately longer than that of adults. The plastron is smaller in length relative to the carapace at this stage, but it grows quickly during the first year.

Spotted turtles usually reach sexual maturity at between seven and eight years of age, once they have grown to about 3 inches (8 cm) long. They can live for over half a century. The spots tend to fade in older individuals to the extent that their carapace can appear smooth and black.

Spotted turtles tend to be quite sedentary. They display affinity to their home territory: Studies have shown that they can find their way home from a distance of 0.5 miles (0.8 km).

Spotted turtles spend the winter hibernating either in the mud under water or in a suitable site on land, such as a pile of vegetation. Occasionally a small group can be found together in an abandoned muskrat nest.

145

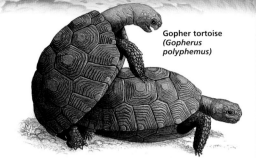

Gopher tortoise
(*Gopherus
polyphemus*)

Common/Scientific names Desert gopher, *Gopherus agassizii;* gopher tortoise, *G. polyphemus;* Berlandier's gopher, *G. berlandieri;* Bolson tortoise, *G. flavomarginatus*

Family Testudinidae

Suborder Cryptodira

Order Testudines

Size Carapace length from 9 in (23 cm) in *G. berlandieri* to 20 in (50 cm) in *G. agassizii*

Weight Approximately 8 lb (3.6 kg) to 15 lb (6.8 kg)

Key features Carapace domed; front limbs flattened for burrowing and bear thick hard scales; hind feet stumpy and elephantine; all feet lack webbing; plastron in males is concave; carapace generally some shade of brown or tan but variable according to species; plastron usually yellowish

Habits Strictly terrestrial; retreat into burrows to avoid excessive temperatures; desert gophers and Bolson tortoises may hibernate

Breeding Most mate in spring, and females may nest 2 or 3 times a season; all are egg layers, with clutch sizes ranging from 2–15 eggs that hatch in late summer or fall

Diet Herbivores; diet includes plants, fruits, and grasses

Habitat Prefer sandy soil; varies from arid desert to scrub woodlands, grasslands, and forests

Distribution Southern United States south to Mexico

Status Numbers in decline due to habitat change and land development; *G. polypheumus, G. flavomarginatus,* and *G. agassizii* are Vulnerable (IUCN); all species listed on CITES Appendix I or II

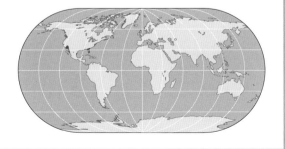

Gopher Tortoises *Gopherus* sp.

The gopher tortoises are the only remaining land tortoises found in North America today. Sadly, all four species are declining in number and need to be protected.

GOPHER TORTOISES ARE MORE DEPENDENT on their underground burrows than other tortoises and most of them dig much longer tunnels. They are not social by nature, however, and do not share their burrows with their own kind.

There are four species in the genus *Gopherus*. First, the desert gopher, *G. agassizii*, ranges from northern California down to parts of Mexico including Baja California and Sonora. It is well equipped for tunneling thanks to its powerful front legs. It is the largest species, reaching a maximum carapace length of about 20 inches (50 cm). Many invertebrates invade its tunnels, and they in turn attract predatory species such as the gopher frog, *Rana capito*, various rodents, and rattlesnakes, *Crotalus* species. However, they all seem to coexist quite peacefully with the tortoise. These gophers emerge to feed on vegetation such as cacti in the arid areas where they occur.

The second species, the gopher tortoise, *G. polyphemus*, occurs from South Carolina through Florida south to Louisiana. It is quite small with a carapace of up to 12 inches (30 cm) long. Females lay their eggs from April to June. Unfortunately, studies have shown that nest predation by mammals, including armadillos, *Dasypus novemcinctus*, and striped skunks, *Mephitis mephitis*, can be high. Estimates suggest that fewer than 6 percent of eggs laid give rise to young tortoises that survive their first year. They are about 20 years old before they can breed for the first time.

Third, Berlandier's gopher, *G. berlandieri,* is found in more western areas from southern

⊕ *The gopher tortoise, Gopher polyphemus, digs its burrows in well-drained, sandy soil in places such as sandhill oak forests, pine flatwoods, oak hammocks, and beach scrub forests.*

Texas across the Mexican border. (It is also known as the Texas desert tortoise.) It is the smallest member of the genus with a maximum carapace length of about 9 inches (23 cm). Unlike its bigger relatives, it does not dig tunnels itself—it prefers to invade those dug by other animals. If necessary, however, it will excavate a simple retreat in the ground using the gular prong at the front of the plastron. The hollow is usually well concealed in vegetation.

The fourth member of the genus is the Bolson tortoise, *G. flavomarginatus*. It occurs in Mexico in a limited area approximately 75 miles (121 km) long between Chihuahua, Coahuila, and Durango. It is well equipped to dig, and its tunnels can be over 33 feet (10 m) long. In the past this species used to extend as far north as Oklahoma; but its range has contracted dramatically, and it is now considered to be highly endangered.

Burrowing Experts

In normal circumstances young gophers start to create their burrows soon after hatching and may remain there throughout their potentially

long lives, digging at intervals. The tunnel is not just a refuge to escape the worst of the desert sun; it also helps provide the tortoises with a more humid environment below ground. When they emerge, they follow paths that can be clearly made out by the pattern of flat, shortened vegetation where they have been grazing. Gophers benefit from water present in the plants and fruits that they eat, so they do not need to drink regularly, although they may drink condensation in their burrows.

A Health Concern

Unfortunately, there are serious risks involved in moving populations of gopher tortoises for conservation purposes, including the endangered Bolson tortoise, *G. flavomarginatus*. The dry environment in which the gophers occur may be one reason why they appear extremely vulnerable to mycoplasmosis, which often results in a fatal infection of the upper respiratory tract. Some tortoises can be carriers of the mycoplasma microbes that cause this illness, so that they represent an unseen hazard to other individuals with which they come into contact.

Common name Plumed basilisk
(Jesus Christ lizard)

Scientific name *Basiliscus plumifrons*

Subfamily Corytophaninae

Family Iguanidae

Suborder Sauria

Order Squamata

Size Males to 36 inches (91 cm); females to 20
inches (51 cm), of which the tail can account
for three-quarters

Key features Adults green with black bars on the tail
and lighter green or white spots on the
flanks; both sexes have a crest on their head
(the male's has two lobes); male also has
separate crests on the back and tail; body
and tail flattened from side to side; front legs
and tail very long; juveniles are spidery in
appearance with long, thin legs

Habits Arboreal or semiarboreal; diurnal

Breeding Egg layer that breeds throughout the year;
female lays 4–17 eggs that hatch after about
65 days

Diet Small vertebrates, invertebrates, and plant
material

Habitat Forests (usually in the vicinity of water)

Distribution Central America (eastern Honduras to
southwestern Costa Rica)

Status Common in suitable habitat

Similar species There are other basilisks in the region,
but *B. plumifrons* is the only bright green
one; other green iguanids of similar size
lack crests

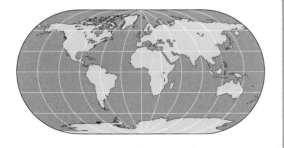

Plumed Basilisk

Basiliscus plumifrons

*The colorful plumed basilisk lives in the forests of
Central America. It is never far from water, which
often provides it with an escape route when
faced with danger.*

BASILISKS HAVE AN AMAZING ability to run across the
surface of still water, a habit that has given
them the alternative common name of Jesus
Christ lizard. Their long toes have a fringe of
rectangular, projecting scales that can rest on
the surface film without breaking through, as
long as the basilisk keeps moving. Once they
get going, they lift the front of their body up,
hold their front legs against their chest, and run
on their long hinds legs, curving their tail up in
an arc to act as a counterbalance. Small
individuals do not even need to move very fast
to remain on the surface and often seem to
move in slow motion at first before accelerating
across a patch of open water, leaving a twin
trail of ripples. Sometimes a small group will
break cover and run off together in formation.
They are also good swimmers and can swim
underwater for long distances.

Daytime Foragers

Basilisks usually occur in dense vegetation along
streams and rivers, and often sleep on branches
overhanging water. If they are disturbed by a
predator, they are quick to drop into the water
and may swim to the bottom. During the day
they forage among the vegetation, eating more
or less anything they find. Juveniles are almost
entirely insectivorous; but as they grow, their
diet becomes more varied, and they will also
take leaves, fruit, and berries. Large adults
sometimes tackle crustaceans such as shrimp
and crabs, and have even been known to eat
snakes and sleeping bats.

Like many tropical lizards, they breed
throughout the year, although most activity
takes place during the rainy season (May to
September in Costa Rica, for instance). The

⊕ *The plumed basilisk,* Basiliscus plumifrons, *is one of the fastest lizards, able to run at speeds in excess of 6.5 feet (2 m) per second. It is also the most colorful species in the genus, the others being dull brown in color.*

female lays four to 17 eggs in a short nest chamber that the lizards excavate themselves. The eggs take about 65 days to hatch. The babies are dull in color and show no signs of the crests, which develop later as low ridges of skin that gradually increase in size. The crests on the head are fleshy and often become torn and somewhat ragged, while those on the back and tail of males are supported by elongated, bony spines projecting up from the vertebrae.

The Relatives

There are four species of basilisk altogether, ranging from Mexico to Ecuador and western Venezuela. All have crests, but only the plumed basilisk is bright green in color. They favor waterside habitats, except for the striped basilisk, *B. vittatus*, which can be found far from water in open places, including disturbed habitats such as pastures and coconut plantations. Like *B. plumifrons*, it is capable of walking on two legs (bipedal locomotion) across water if the need arises.

Mythological Creature

The basilisk is an ancient mythological beast with the legs and head of a rooster, the body, tail, and tongue of a snake, and the wings of a bat. The similarities to the basilisk lizard, therefore, are the crest (which is like the comb of a rooster), the long, snakelike tail, and the bright, staring eyes. The basilisk from mythology could kill everything it encountered with its stare, and the only defense against it was to hold up a mirror, whereupon its own reflection would frighten it to death.

The English playwright William Shakespeare often used herpetological metaphors, including one about a basilisk. In *Richard III* (Act I, Scene 2) Lady Anne responds to Richard's compliment about her eyes, "Would they were basilisk's, to strike thee dead!" It seems there is just no pleasing some folk!

Common name Collared lizard

Scientific name *Crotaphytus collaris*

Subfamily Crotaphytinae

Family Iguanidae

Suborder Sauria

Order Squamata

Size To 10 in (25cm); males are larger than females

Key features Head massive; 2 black rings around the neck; tail long and cylindrical; hind limbs long; body covered in small scales, giving the skin a silky texture; body color varies among populations and with the season but is typically green in males, dull green, brown, or yellowish in females, all with light spots loosely arranged into transverse lines; juveniles have distinct banding across the back that gradually fades as the animal grows

Habits Diurnal and heat loving; lives on the ground and rarely climbs, except among boulders

Breeding Egg layer with more than one clutch each year; female lays 1–13 eggs that hatch after about 45 days

Diet Large invertebrates and smaller lizards; also some vegetable material, including leaves and flowers

Habitat Hot, rocky hillsides with sparse vegetation

Distribution Western United States in desert regions

Status Common

Similar species There are other collared lizards, but their ranges do not overlap; the leopard lizards, *Gambelia*, are their only other close relatives

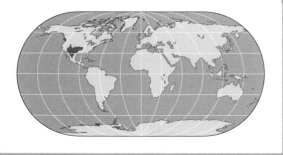

Collared Lizard

Crotaphytus collaris

Collared lizards are noted for running upright on their hind legs, making them look like miniature Tyrannosaurus rex. *They are powerful hunters and have an unusual way of waving their tail, like a cat, before grabbing at prey.*

THERE ARE EIGHT SPECIES OF COLLARED LIZARDS and three species of leopard lizards. Together they make up the subfamily Crotaphytinae, which is sometimes regarded as a full family, the Crotaphytidae. All collared lizards are broadly similar in size and shape, and all have two black collars separated by a white or light-colored one, although their general coloration varies. For instance, *C. vestigium* from Baja California and California, is rich chocolate-brown with pure white spots and bands fading to dull orange or green on its flanks. The spectacular Dickerson's collared lizard, *C. dickersonae*, is sometimes regarded as a subspecies of *C. collaris*. The males are deep blue in color.

The other half of the family, the leopard lizards, consists of three species with slightly more slender heads and bodies than the collared lizards. They prefer open habitat, such as sand and gravel flats with sparse vegetation, for example, creosote bush scrub. They shelter in burrows at night. They are pale buff or sandy brown in color and often wait for prey at the base of a small bush, where the dappled shadow helps disguise their outline. When approached by predators, leopard lizards often flatten themselves to the surface and rely on their pale camouflage colors to escape notice.

Fearless Terrorists

Collared lizards are powerful hunters—they are likely to terrorize smaller lizards from the region. They chase them down and crush them in their powerful jaws before swallowing them whole. Collared lizards also eat large invertebrates such as grasshoppers and beetles. They dominate south-facing rocky ridges and

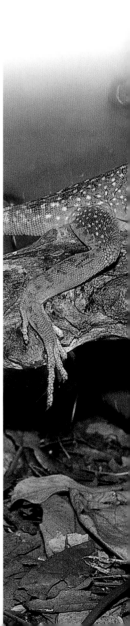

Collared lizards exhibit sexual dimorphism, as seen in this pair of Crotaphytus collaris *from Texas. The male (left) is predominantly green, while the female (right) is yellowish brown in color. Males are also larger than females.*

hillsides by taking up positions on prominent boulders. From there they can survey the large area over which they hunt. Males are especially territorial. They stand up on stiff limbs and bob their body up and down if another collared lizard approaches. They will even display to humans, standing their ground until the last minute. Then they dash off, sometimes lifting the front part of their body off the ground and taking huge strides with their hind legs. At the same time, they raise their tail as a counterweight. Their aggressive behavior has persuaded local people, especially in Mexico, that collared lizards are venomous.

Breeding Coloration

Collared lizards come into breeding condition in the spring, often in late March or early April after several months in hibernation. At that time of year the male's colors really glow once he has warmed up by basking on the hottest exposed rocks. Dominant males mate with all the females living within their territory. Once females have mated and their eggs begin to develop, they too undergo a color change. Large patches of bright orange appear on their flanks and the sides of their neck, showing that they are full of eggs (this is known as "gravid coloration"). The color probably indicates to the male that she is not receptive to more mating attempts. This prevents further attempts at courtship and saves both of them time and energy.

Gravid coloration is not unique to collared lizards: It is present in many other iguanids and in some agamid lizards and chameleons. The exact color varies from species to species, but it is invariably bright, distinctive, and easily visible from a distance. Females lay one to 13 eggs, which they bury, and which hatch after about 45 days. Each female lays two or more clutches throughout the summer provided she can find enough food to replenish her reserves. The hatchlings, the last of which emerges in late summer or early fall, lack the bright colors of adults and are mostly brown with a black collar.

Common name Green Iguana (common iguana)

Scientific name *Iguana iguana*

Subfamily Iguaninae

Family Iguanidae

Suborder Sauria

Order Squamata

Size Males to 6.6 ft (2 m), females to 4.8 ft (1.4 m)

Key features Very large green or greenish lizards; adults have crest of tooth-shaped scales along the back and the first third of the tail; tail has broad, dark bands around it; limbs long; each toe is also long and has claws for grasping; large males develop a flap of skin (dewlap) under the chin (in females it is smaller); a single, very large smooth scale present on each side of the head below the eardrum in both males and females

Habits Arboreal; diurnal

Breeding Egg layers with large clutches of 9–71 eggs; eggs hatch after 65–115 days

Diet Mostly vegetation, especially leaves

Habitat Forests, especially rain forests but also dry deciduous forests in some places

Distribution Central and South America (northwestern Mexico in the north to Ecuador, northern Bolivia, Paraguay, and southern Brazil to the south); also on some West Indian islands and introduced to Florida

Status Common in places but under pressure from humans in others

Similar species The closely related *Iguana delicatissima* from the Lesser Antilles (West Indies)

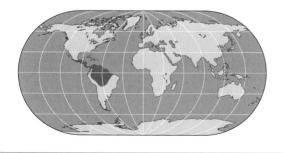

Green Iguana

Iguana iguana

The green iguana is an instantly recognizable lizard from Central and South America. It is a dinosaurlike lizard of impressive proportions that lives in the highest tree canopies.

ALTHOUGH THE GREEN IGUANA is not tied to the water to the same extent as some other iguanids, such as the plumed basilisk, *Basiliscus plumifrons*, it is most often seen along the edges of rivers. Since it is easier to see into the tops of tall trees that are isolated at the edge of rivers than those that are surrounded by other trees, it is possible that green iguanas are everywhere in the forest but that we only see them near rivers. Iguanas often use water as an escape route and are good swimmers.

Life Cycle

Iguanas go through several life phases. Starting with the eggs, female iguanas lay them in burrows that they dig themselves. The burrows are usually between 3 and 6 feet (0.9–1.8 m) in length and 12 to 24 inches (30–60 cm) below the surface. They end in a chamber that is large enough to allow the female to turn around. Where populations are dense or where nest sites are scarce, a number of females (sometimes as many as eight) may dig interconnecting tunnels with several entrance holes and egg-laying chambers.

The female green iguana lays a clutch of nine to 71 eggs. In western Costa Rica an average clutch numbers about 35 eggs (it may vary in other localities). Where egg-laying sites are scarce, females may remain near their nests and defend them from other females, which may otherwise dig up the eggs in the course of their own excavations.

The eggs hatch after 65 to 115 days, and clutches often hatch simultaneously. The mass hatching may limit predation, because predators can only eat so many young iguanas at one time. If the eggs hatched over an extended period, the predators would be able to pick off the young lizards as they emerged. Also, large numbers of young iguanas together are more likely to spot potential danger or may even intimidate predators.

Even before they leave their nest chamber, the juveniles eat some soil, which is thought to provide their gut with bacteria that aid digestion. After emerging, they move off into low shrubbery, still maintaining contact with each other. Contact involves tongue licking, rubbing their chins over each other, and nipping each other with their jaws, and is similar to the grooming behavior seen in many social birds and mammals.

The group of young iguanas may forage on the ground at first, but they always sleep on branches, often in small groups. After a few days they move into low shrubs and gradually move farther up into the canopy. By feeding below the adults and larger juveniles, they eat their feces (either deliberately or inadvertently),

⊖ *Green iguanas have small, granular scales and long claws on their fingers and toes to help them climb. The prominent dewlap shows that this individual is a male.*

Tasty Cousin

The genus *Iguana* has one other member, *I. delicatissima*, which means "delicious iguana." Before it became rare, it was valued as food on the Lesser Antilles islands. It is almost identical to the green iguana, but it is slightly smaller and lacks the enlarged scales on its jowls. It was once abundant on every island from Anguilla to Martinique, but habitat destruction, harvesting for food, and introduced predators such as dogs, cats, and mongooses have finished it off on St. Kitts, Nevis, and Antigua. Numbers on the other islands have been reduced to critical levels. To raise awareness of the situation, the Anguilla Post Office issued a set of stamps featuring the species in 1997.

153

which inoculate their gut with the bacteria needed to help them break down plant material containing cellulose.

Young iguanas have many enemies, including a variety of snakes, birds of prey, and birds such as anis and toucans. A number of small opportunistic mammals, such as coatis and kinkajous, also prey on them. As the iguanas grow, some smaller predators are no longer a problem; but they can attract the attention of larger ones such as crocodiles, caimans, and wild cats. Assuming they survive, they reach breeding size in two or three years. Females and young adult males maintain their green coloration, but they are rarely as bright as the hatchlings. Older males are often gray or tan in color and may turn orange at the height of the breeding season.

Social Behavior and Courtship

A typical colony consists of a large dominant male, a few smaller but also mature males, several subadult males, and four to six females. The large male maintains his dominance by perching at the top of large, prominent rain-forest trees and rarely comes down to the ground. He displays to neighboring males at regular intervals by lowering his large throat flap (dewlap) and nodding his head vigorously.

If close encounters between two large males occur, they raise themselves to their full height, compress their bodies, and lower their dewlaps to make themselves look as large as possible. They circle each other, hissing all the time. If neither is intimidated, they may begin to fight using their long, whiplike tails to thrash each other and bite their opponent's neck until

⊕ Young green iguanas like this juvenile from Costa Rica are more brightly colored than the adults. Young iguanas mature after about two years; and as they grow, the bright green color fades.

Spiny-Tailed Iguanas

In Central America the spiny-tailed iguanas, *Ctenosaura* species, are the terrestrial counterparts of the green iguana and are also herbivorous. There are 14 species in the genus altogether, some with small ranges, including the small islands in the Gulf of California, although the most widespread species, *C. similis*, is found from Mexico to Panama. This species is as large as the green iguana but is less colorful, being pale gray with darker markings. Its tail is strongly banded and has rings of thorny scales around it. Spiny-tailed iguanas dwell among rocks and are often common in forest clearings and around human settlements, where they dig extensive tunnels. Juveniles are bright green and can easily be mistaken for young green iguanas.

⊘ *The clubtail iguana, Ctenosaura quinquecarinata from Central America, is a lesser-known relative of the green iguana. Like the other members of its genus, it can be distinguished by the thorny scales around its tail.*

one turns dark and retreats. The dominant male mates with all the females in his territory.

Courtship can last for two weeks or more before the pair finally mate. A male approaches a receptive female from behind and vibrates his head. The female moves her tail to one side, inviting the male to mount her. He continues to bob his head while he climbs on top of her, grips her neck in his jaws, and twists his tail beneath hers so that mating can take place. Small males living nearby look like females, and the large male may not drive them away; in fact, they sometimes try to mate with receptive females while the large male is otherwise occupied.

Once mating is over, females with mature eggs come down from the trees and move to places where they can dig nests. The sites are often open, sandy patches along the riverbank or clearings in the forest. Females may need to travel up to 1.5 miles (2.4 km) to find a suitable egg-laying site.

A significant predator of iguana eggs is the American sunbeam snake, *Loxocemus bicolor*. Although the snake eats a variety of food, including small mammals, frogs, and lizards, it specializes in digging up reptile nests and eating the eggs. In western Costa Rica where it is fairly common it enters iguana nest tunnels in search of the lizards or digs them out with its pointed snout. First, it slits the iguana eggs to make them collapse, then pushes them against a loop of its body and swallows them whole. One snake that was examined contained 23 green iguana eggs in its stomach, and another had eaten 32 eggs of a spiny-tailed iguana, *Ctenosaura* species.

Large adults are fairly safe from predators (except humans) because of their sheer size. Iguanas basking near water often drop from their branches and swim to safety or disappear under the surface. Females from Barro Colorado Island in Panama even swim to a small, sandy island to lay their eggs.

If they are captured, green iguanas struggle frantically, using their long claws to scratch and tear at their captor and their whiplike tail to thrash it. Handling an angry iguana is no easy matter. Having said that, they are no match for a determined human, and iguanas are routinely sold as food on the streets of Mexico, Guyana, and other parts of Latin America. To reduce the effect on wild populations, iguana "farms" have been set up to provide a supply of animals for both the food and the pet markets.

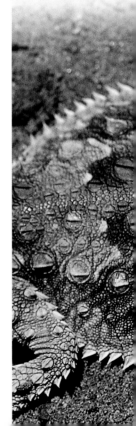

Coast Horned Lizard

Phrynosoma coronatum

Horned lizards are among the strangest creatures to inhabit the American Southwest and have always been objects of curiosity among the people of the region.

THE ANASAZI INDIANS AND THEIR DESCENDANTS had many stories and superstitions centered on the horned lizard, including beliefs that it could bring about or cure various ailments depending on how it was treated. Stylized horned lizards often feature on pottery, rock paintings, and the small carvings known as fetishes. Modern inhabitants of the Southwest find them no less interesting. They are studied by scientists and kept as pets by well-meaning enthusiasts (usually with poor results). Until recently they were displayed along with rattlesnakes in roadside animal shows, often labeled as "horned toads" (or sometimes "horny toads") because of their squat shape. (The name *Phrynosoma* means "toad bodied.")

Horned lizards are superbly adapted to their environment. In the case of the coast horned lizard the habitat includes the dry woodlands and chaparral as well as desert and semidesert areas in valleys and foothills at elevations up to 6,000 feet (1,830 m).

Early in the morning they often bask with only their head showing above the sand or soil. A mass of capillaries running just under the surface allows their blood to warm up quickly, and from there it moves around the rest of the body. In this way they can reach a temperature at which they can be active without completely exposing themselves and at the same time avoid the possibility of encountering a predator while they are still in a torpid state.

Following this they use their disk-shaped bodies as solar panels, flattening and tilting them toward the sun to absorb as much warmth as possible until they reach their preferred temperature. Only then will they go in

⊕ *The coast horned lizard,* Phrynosoma coronatum, *is relatively large and less rounded than other horned lizards. Its "coronet" is made of long, backward-pointing spines.*

Common name Coast horned lizard

Scientific name *Phrynosoma coronatum*

Subfamily Phrynosomatinae

Family Iguanidae

Suborder Sauria

Order Squamata

Size From 2.5 in (6 cm) to 4 in (10 cm)

Key features Body flattened and oval or disk shaped; head has a crest, or "coronet," of long, backward-pointing spines, the central 2 (the "horns") being longer than the others; a fringe of smaller thorny spines runs along the edge on each side of its body; large spiny scales also scattered over its back; color yellow, beige, or pale pink with irregular darker crossbands and a paler stripe down the center, providing camouflage colors to match the sand or gravel on which it is resting

Habits Diurnal; terrestrial

Breeding Egg layer with an average of 25 eggs laid in the summer; eggs hatch after about 60 days

Diet Small invertebrates, especially ants

Habitat Dry scrub and sandy washes with scattered bushes; also in dry forest clearings

Distribution Western California south to the tip of Baja California, Mexico

Status Common but easily overlooked

Similar species There are other horned lizards in the American Southwest, but none of their ranges overlap that of this species; the 2 long spines on the back of its head are also distinctive

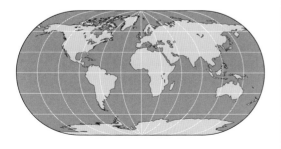

→ *Like the coast horned lizard, the related P. douglassi, the short-horned lizard, inflates its body to appear bigger and more intimidating when threatened.*

search of food. As the day wears on, they may reorient themselves, contracting their body to a more cylindrical shape and raising themselves off the ground to reduce heat absorption and prevent overheating. At that point other lizards simply seek shade, but horned lizards have an unusual feeding strategy that involves staying out in the open longer than other species.

Ants on the Menu

Horned lizards are ant specialists. Although the proportion of ants in their diet depends on the species, the coast horned lizard is probably typical, with ants making up more than 50 percent of its food. The bones of its skull are modified to make it more effective at snapping up many small food items in rapid succession. Because ants are small and contain a high proportion of indigestible chitin, horned lizards need to eat a lot of them.

They move between anthills until they find a predictable ant trail. Then they sit and wait for the ants to go by, flicking out their tongue and snapping them up one at a time. Only when the supply of ants dries up do they move to another anthill. Their modified skull and large gape may help them flick their tongue in and out rapidly, and they often eat over 200 ants in a single day. To accommodate all the ants, they need a large stomach: Horned lizards' stomachs are proportionately much larger than the stomachs of other lizards of similar overall size. It is the large stomach that gives the horned lizard its short, bulky body plan, and it has other implications too.

Camouflage

Their body shape prevents horned lizards from being swift movers. Although they sometimes scamper into the shelter of a nearby bush, their usual plan is to escape the notice of a predator.

They manage to disguise themselves in several ways. First, their coloration always matches the surface on which they live, so coast horned lizards in different parts of the range are different colors depending on the soil type. Because they rely so heavily on camouflage, they tend to remain motionless if they are approached. They crouch low against the ground, where their disklike shape and the fringes of large scales help eliminate shadows and break up their outline—a horned lizard can be nearly impossible to see even when you know where it is!

If the camouflage fails to work, the lizards move on to the next level of defense. They can inflate their body, which has the effect of making them look larger and more intimidating, and also displays their spines more prominently. They tilt their body toward the predator to emphasize their spikiness. Snakes and birds that

⊕ **Phrynosoma cornutum,** *the Texas horned lizard, is one of several species in the genus that can deter predators by squirting foul-tasting blood from its eyes.*

clearly did not heed these warnings have been found with horned lizards in their throats and spines sticking out through their skin.

Finally, the last line of defense is to squirt blood. The coast horned lizard is one of several species that can cause small blood vessels around the rim of their eyes to burst, resulting in a thin jet of blood that travels for several inches. Experiments have shown that horned lizards are more likely to squirt blood if they are attacked by members of the dog family (foxes, coyotes, and domestic dogs) than other types of predators. Naturalists have seen the animals drop horned lizards and shake their head vigorously in an effort to get the blood out of their mouth.

Some researchers believe that horned lizards obtain toxins from the ants they eat and store them in their blood to make it taste bitter. If this proves to be the case, the horned lizards would provide an interesting parallel with the poison dart frogs and the mantella frogs (families Mantellidae and Dendrobatidae), which also gather toxins from the bodies of ants they eat and use them for defense.

Large Clutch Sizes

The horned lizard's ant diet is responsible for its rotund body shape and therefore its inability to run quickly. These factors have in turn led to the evolution of cryptic (disguise) coloration and other methods of defense. The carryover effects do not stop there, however. The large body size allows female horned lizards to produce larger clutches of eggs. Not only do they have a greater volume to fill, but the extra bulk of large clutches does not burden the female to the same extent as it would more slender, agile species that rely on speed to escape from predators or to hunt food.

The reproductive effort of reptiles is sometimes measured in terms of relative clutch mass (RCM), which is calculated by dividing the weight of the female by the weight of the eggs or young she produces. Typical RCMs for snakes are about 20 percent; generally speaking, RCMs in lizards are significantly lower. The coast

⊕ *A newborn short-horned lizard,* **Phrynosoma hernandesi,** *in the Chiricahua Mountains of Arizona. Species such as this that live in cool, montane habitats give birth, whereas lowland, desert species are egg layers.*

horned lizard has an RCM approaching 35 percent, which is considerably larger than that of other species from the same region.

The other evolutionary "decision" the coast horned lizard has had to make is whether to direct the reproductive effort into producing a few large eggs or young, or a lot of small ones. In fact, it does the latter. Coast horned lizards have relatively large clutch sizes with an average of 25 and a maximum of 40 eggs. An example of the other extreme is the related side-blotched lizard, *Uta stansburiana*, which lays just one to five eggs.

Eggs or Live Young?

As a rule, species in a single genus either lay eggs or give birth to live young, but there are a few exceptions, including the horned lizards. Of the 13 species six lay eggs and seven are live-bearers. All the live-bearing species live in montane environments that are cooler than the regions inhabited by the egg layers. This is because species that retain their eggs inside their bodies are in a better position to speed up the development of the eggs by basking than those that simply bury them and let the environment provide the heat. On the other hand, species from the warmer lowlands, such as the coast horned lizard, may have time to develop a second clutch before the summer ends (provided they can deposit their first clutch in an early stage of development). In this way they double the potential number of young per year. A very similar situation exists among the alligator lizards in the family Anguidae and the small wall lizards in the family Lacertidae.

Common name Green anole (American chameleon)

Scientific name *Anolis carolinensis*

Subfamily Polychrotinae

Family Iguanidae

Suborder Sauria

Order Squamata

Size From 4.5 in (11 cm) to 8 in (20 cm)

Key features A graceful lizard; head long and narrow; snout pointed; body long and slender; tail is nearly twice as long as head and body combined; legs long and thin; toes have small pads just behind the claws for climbing; color usually bright green but can change to brown or buff; males have a pink dewlap (throat flap)

Habits Diurnal; arboreal, climbing mainly in shrubs and on tree trunks

Breeding Egg layer; female lays several clutches containing a single egg throughout the summer

Diet Small invertebrates

Habitat Open woodland, hedges, parks, and gardens

Distribution Southeastern North America

Status Formerly common, now becoming increasingly rare

Similar species None in the area; small introduced anoles in Florida lack the bright green coloration; the knight anole, *Anolis equestris*, is much larger and lives only in the extreme south of Florida

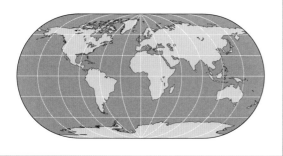

Green Anole

Anolis carolinensis

The green anole is the only member of its genus in the United States, although its relatives have been among the most successful colonizers of Central and South America.

WITH ABOUT 350 SPECIES the genus *Anolis* is one of the most numerous of all lizard genera. Anoles live in South and Central America, especially the West Indies, but the green anole is the only one to occur in the United States, where it is endemic. This colorful lizard was once a familiar sight climbing into low bushes and making graceful leaps in search of prey or flicking its pink dewlap to attract the attention of other members of its species. In recent years its numbers have declined dramatically, perhaps because of competition with introduced species such as the Cuban anole, *Anolis sagrei*, which has done particularly well in its new home.

The green anole is slightly larger than the introduced Cuban species, but it is not as adaptable. Cuban anoles are common wherever they live, setting up territories on and around houses in towns as well as in the countryside. Green anoles also occur in gardens but not to the same extent. The interactions between the two species have not been properly studied, but the fact that one is declining while the other is increasing is a good indicator that competition of one form or another is taking place.

Multiple Clutches

Anoles, unlike the horned lizards, *Phrynosoma* species, are not prolific breeders. Because they rely on speed and agility to catch prey and to evade predators, a bulky clutch of developing eggs would be a real hindrance. To overcome the problem, females mate once and lay several clutches containing a single elongated egg at

⊕ The green anole can be anything from bright green to brown or gray. Brown phases such as this male from Florida may also be induced when the temperature drops below 70°F (21°C) or if the lizard is threatened or stressed. The usual pink dewlap also turns brown.

Unsurprisingly, larger and older males are more successful than younger ones at finding mates, but another factor that determines success is activity levels. Males that remain in the same territory defend it easily but only mate with females in that territory. By moving around and continuously setting up new territories, males gain access to more females; but as a result, they come into conflict with other males that may already be present.

regular intervals over a long period. Under ideal conditions females can lay an egg every seven days throughout the spring and summer. Not only does this keep the female's body in good shape, it also allows her to hedge her bets by choosing different egg-laying sites—in a large once-a-year clutch females are gambling with the survival of all their offspring in one go; but by spreading the eggs in different places, there is a better chance of some of them surviving. Eggs are usually laid in damp soil or leaf litter at the base of trees.

Male green anoles are territorial, and their behavior has been studied in greater detail than any of the tropical species. Males display ownership of a territory by rapidly flicking their brightly colored dewlaps up and down. Although the movement can attract predators, when the dewlaps are folded down again, the predator tends to lose sight of the lizard and is left looking for a pink "prey image" rather than a green one.

Species' Recognition

Green anoles in the American Southeast had no need to share their resources with other species until recently when the Cuban anole, *Anolis sagrei*, appeared. Nor could they mistake each other for related anoles and mate with the "wrong" partner. In the Caribbean and elsewhere, however, many species can occur together, and confusion could be a problem. (There are 55 species on Cuba, for example, and 40 on Hispaniola.)

They avoid confusion and direct competition in two ways. First, the various species in a given area occupy different ecological niches. For example, there will be different species living on the ground, in grasses, on bushes, tree trunks, twigs, and in the crowns of forest trees. Second, species' recognition is made easy by having differently colored dewlaps (throat flaps). Within a small area there may be species with orange, yellow, white, or even blue dewlaps, and each responds only to the "correct" color when interacting with others.

Side-Blotched Lizard

Uta stansburiana

Common name Side-blotched lizard (common side-blotched lizard)

Scientific name *Uta stansburiana*

Subfamily Phrynosomatinae

Family Iguanidae

Suborder Sauria

Order Squamata

Size From 3 in (7.5 cm) to 5 in (13 cm)

Key features Body small, brownish or gray; small rounded scales give it a smooth appearance; no dorsal crest; a dark black or bluish blotch usually present on either side of the body just behind the front limbs; males may have blue flecks and orange or yellow on their throat and sides

Habits Diurnal; terrestrial, may climb into low shrubs

Breeding Egg layer; female lays several clutches during the summer; eggs hatch after about 60 days

Diet Insects and other invertebrates

Habitat Anywhere dry; sand dunes and washes, scrub, places with scattered rocks and thin woodlands

Distribution Southwestern United States from Washington to western Texas south to Baja California, Sonora, and north-central Mexico

Status Very common

Similar species Tree lizard, *Urosaurus microscutatus*, has a double row of large scales along its midline interrupted by a single row of small ones down the center; long-tailed brush lizard, *U. graciosus*, has a wide band of large scales down its back; both lack the characteristic dark blotch of *Uta stansburiana*

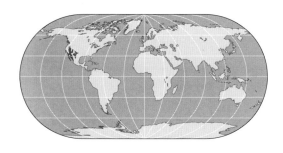

Despite its nondescript appearance, the side-blotched lizard is one of the most important species in the ecology of reptiles in the southwestern United States.

THE SIDE-BLOTCHED LIZARD is one of the most numerous and adaptable species, and it can live in practically any dry environment. It is also one of the most studied lizards anywhere in the world. Because it is so common and can easily be observed during the day, scientists have been able to carry out some interesting research. Much of what they have found out probably applies to several other similar species.

It has a preferred body temperature of 95°F (35°C), substantially lower than that of many other lizards from the region. As a result, it can be active throughout the year in some places, especially in the south of its range. It is an important prey species for many predatory birds and snakes, and in places it may be the main prey of the collared lizards, *Crotaphytus* species.

Sexual Strategies

Careful observations of side-blotched lizard colonies have revealed some interesting sexual behavior. Males fall into one of three categories distinguished by behavior and coloration.

Most mature males have orange throats. They form the first category. They defend large territories that contain a number of females, and they attempt to mate with all of them. Other males have bluish throats. These males do not try to hold down large territories. Instead, they remain with a single female for several days while she is most receptive. In effect, they "guard" the female from other males.

Finally, there are the yellow-throated males. They wander in and out of other males' territories, but they avoid conflict because they look like females. Their strategy is to attempt to mate with females when the territory holder is not looking. They are therefore known as "sneaky" males.

The system is very complicated, but it works well: Sneaky males "steal" matings from territorial males but not from mate-guarding males; territorial males gain almost exclusive access to a number of females but are susceptible to sneaky males; and mate-guarding males protect their females from sneaky males but can be driven off by the more powerful territorial males.

Side-blotched lizards can be very prolific. Females can lay several clutches of up to eight eggs throughout the summer, although there are geographical variations. Winter rainfall seems to be the key to how many eggs they lay: In wetter years the lizards' insect food is more abundant, and they eat enough to divert a large amount of energy into egg production. Gravid females develop orange markings on their flanks to signal to males that they are not receptive to mating.

⊖ **The side-blotched lizard is very common. Its most distinguishing feature is the blue or black blotch on its side just behind the front legs.**

Hatchlings emerge from mid- to late summer. They grow quickly and are sexually mature within a year, so turnover is high. Rapid generation times help species adapt to changing conditions, because the opportunities for variation and mutation are increased.

The Relatives

At some point in the past the side-blotched lizard found its way to several small islands in the Gulf of California, where it evolved into six new species, each with a very small range. Some make a living around seabird colonies, feeding on spilled fish and flies, while others forage for sea slaters along the rocky coastline. They are:

U. palmeri, Palmer's side-blotched lizard from the small island of San Pedro Martír

U. nolascensi from San Pedro Nolascoa, a tiny island between the shores of Baja California and Sonora; unique in the genus because of its bright greenish-blue coloration

U. tumidarostra, the swollen-nosed side-blotched lizard from the island of Coloradito

U. encantadae from the Islas Encantadas

U. squamata from the island of Santa Catalina

U. lowei from the sinister-named Isla El Muerto (Dead-Man Island)

Common name Western banded gecko

Scientific name *Coleonyx variegatus*

Subfamily Eublepharinae

Family Eublepharidae

Suborder Sauria

Order Squamata

Size From 3.3 in (8 cm) to 4.3 in (12 cm)

Key features A delicate-looking gecko with thin, translucent skin and tiny scales; eyes are large and have functional eyelids; limbs long and thin; toes end in small claws; color variable but usually cream, buff, or yellow with dark-brown crossbands; tail has black-and-white bands

Habits Terrestrial; strictly nocturnal

Breeding Female lays 2 soft-shelled eggs; eggs hatch after about 45 days

Diet Insects, spiders, and small scorpions

Habitat Rocky deserts

Distribution Southwestern United Sates and northwestern Mexico, including Baja California

Status Common

Similar species There are 6 other members of the genus, but a combination of range, size, and markings makes it unlikely that they would be confused with the western banded gecko (or each other)

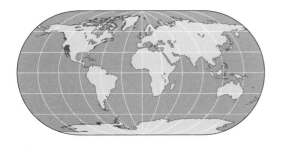

Western Banded Gecko

Coleonyx variegatus

The delicate appearance of the western banded gecko makes it seem an unlikely inhabitant of the hot, dry, environment in which it lives.

THE WESTERN BANDED GECKO'S HABITAT is one of the harshest environments in North America: the rock piles, cacti, and agaves of the American Southwest and adjacent parts of Mexico. Scientists think that the banded geckos, *Coleonyx* species, spread over the region long ago, when conditions were wetter and more humid, and the vegetation was lush.

As the region dried out gradually, the western banded gecko and some of the others adapted to a more arid environment by developing skin that did not lose water as quickly and by limiting themselves to being

Banded Geckos and Superstitions

There are six other members of the genus *Coleonyx*. Two of them, the Texas banded gecko, *C. brevis,* and the Big Bend banded gecko, *C. reticulatus*, live in the southern United States and northern Mexico, but their ranges do not overlap that of the western species. The barefoot gecko, *C. switaki*, lives in southern California and Baja California but is larger than the western banded gecko and not easily confused with it. Two species, *C. elegans* and *C. mitratus*, are restricted to Central America. The remaining species, the black banded gecko, *C. fasciatus* from northwestern Mexico, is very similar in appearance to the western banded gecko, and some scientists consider it to be a subspecies. There is a possible eighth species, *C. gypsicolus* from Isla San Marcos in the Gulf of California. It is very similar in appearance to the barefoot gecko.

People living in Baja California are very afraid of banded geckos of all species, and several superstitions are associated with them. For example, they think that if a gecko walks across your skin, the skin will slough away. Seri Indians believe that the gecko will cause a fatal lung disease if touched and that touching a gecko will cause the flesh to fall off your hands and body.

active on cool nights. In spring before the ground heats up too much, they often shelter closer to the surface during the day under rocks and among the litter of dead agave leaves and cactus pads. But during summer days, when temperatures can rise to lethal levels, they retreat deep underground in burrows and crevices. Two related species, the Yucatán banded gecko, *Coleonyx elegans*, and the Central American banded gecko, *C. mitratus*, live farther south in habitats that are thought to be similar to those in which the ancestral banded geckos lived.

Western banded geckos are often seen wandering around on desert roads at night, usually in the two or three hours before midnight. From a car they look like little white moving twigs or cigarette ends and are easily overlooked if you are traveling at speed. Closer inspection reveals that they walk with their tail curled over their back, and in dim light they can

look like scorpions. They may do this to mimic scorpions in order to deter predators, or it may be a way of deflecting attack away from their head. It may be both, of course.

Juveniles' tails are more boldly banded than those of the adults, and all banded geckos are liable to discard their tails if they are grasped.

Social Interaction

Western banded geckos live in small colonies. Males are highly territorial, and dominant males drive off strange males but tolerate juveniles and females. Breeding starts in early spring, and the females usually begin to lay eggs in May, but this varies slightly according to locality. They lay clutches of two (occasionally one or three) soft-shelled eggs. They bury them in damp sand or soil, usually under a rock or among the roots of a plant. Each female can produce up to three clutches in a single breeding season.

⊕ *The fragile-looking western banded gecko has several ways of defending itself. It curls its tail over the back to resemble a scorpion, and its tail can break off easily. The gecko can also make a high-pitched squeak and squirt sticky liquid over an enemy.*

Common name Ashy gecko

Scientific name *Sphaerodactylus elegans*

Subfamily Sphaerodactylinae

Family Gekkonidae

Suborder Sauria

Order Squamata

Size 2.8 in (7.1 cm) long

Key features Head pointed and flattened; body and tail cylindrical with a speckled pattern of yellowish-brown markings on a darker background; markings sometimes run together to form stripes or parts of stripes, especially on the head; toe pads present on digits, but they are small and easily overlooked; juveniles are gray with dark crossbands and a reddish tail

Habits Diurnal and terrestrial or arboreal

Breeding Female lays a single hard-shelled egg; further detail unkown

Diet Small insects and spiders

Habitat Rarely seen away from buildings but thought to live naturally in forests and plantations

Distribution Cuba, Hispaniola; introduced to Florida

Status Common

Similar species All *Sphaerodactylus* species look similar; in Florida it is the only small gecko with many small pale spots covering the entire head, body, and tail; separation from other West Indian species can be very difficult

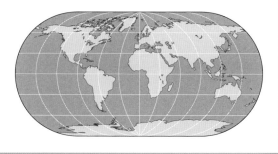

Ashy Gecko *Sphaerodactylus elegans*

The ashy gecko is a tiny lizard that often goes unnoticed. Nonetheless, it is a successful and adaptable colonizer and often lives in houses and gardens.

THE ASHY GECKO IS NATIVE TO CUBA and Hispaniola but was introduced to Key West many years ago, probably on a shipment of wood or fruit. Since then it has spread up the Florida Keys and has also been seen on the Gulf Coast. In time it may spread from the south to many more parts of the state. Interestingly, there may be as many as 14 gecko species in Florida, but only one is native. It is another *Sphaerodactylus* species, the Florida reef gecko, *S. notatus*, found also in the south of the state and on the Dry Tortugas islands. It is thought to be native to the region, although related forms occur on Cuba and the Bahamas.

The ashy gecko tends to live around houses, especially on vertical walls. It is diurnal by nature but occasionally comes out at night to feed on insects that are attracted to an outside light. The reef gecko is more likely to occur on the ground among debris such as boards, coconut husks, and garbage. It is even smaller than the ashy gecko, and at 2.5 inches (6.3 cm) when fully grown, it is the smallest North American lizard.

Fast and Agile

The ashy gecko has minute granular scales. Those on the top of the tail are slightly rough, although the reason for this is not clear. *Sphaerodactylus* means "ball feet," and this gecko has very small pads with rounded surfaces. Since it is small and light, it does not need the adhesive power of some of the larger geckos. It is quick and agile, however, and difficult to catch.

In its native Cuba the ashy gecko often lives in houses, hiding behind furniture and pictures. It does not appear to have a voice,

⊕ *In Florida an ashy gecko sheds its skin. Unlike snakes, lizards usually shed their skin in pieces.*

⊕ *The genus* Gonatodes *contains 17 species of dwarf geckos distributed throughout the Central and northern South American region. This is a* Gonatodes ceciliae *male from Trinidad.*

their eggs in the same place, and the remains of many eggs are sometimes found together in especially favored places. Hatchlings are correspondingly small, barely 1 inch (2.5 cm) in length. They are light gray in color with several narrow, dark crossbands on their head, neck, and body. The bands extend onto the tail but become shorter and more like spots. The rest of the tail is rosy red in color. The difference between juveniles and adults is so great that they were once thought to belong to separate species.

and individuals recognize each other by tongue-licking.

Details of courtship are completely lacking, but females lay a single, pea-sized egg that has a hard shell. The egg can go through the female's cloaca because it is flexible when laid and only becomes hardened when exposed to air. Eggs are laid in cracks in wood or in small spaces among debris. Several females may lay

Dwarf Geckos

The ashy gecko is one of about 95 species in the genus *Sphaerodactylus*. Its stronghold is the Caribbean region, with most species occurring on the large and small islands and just a few reaching the mainland. Together with four other genera—*Coleodactylus* (five species), *Lepidoblepharis* (17 species), *Gonatodes* (17 species), and *Pseudogonatodes* (seven species)—they make up a group of dwarf geckos that are sometimes placed in a separate subfamily, the Sphaerodactylinae. All the members of this group occur in South or Central America, all are small, and all lay a single egg.

They are mostly diurnal, and some are brightly colored, especially the males. In the striped day gecko, *Gonatodes vittatus*, for example, males are tan in color with a wide, black-edged white stripe down the back and over the head between the eyes. Females have only faint traces of the stripe and are mottled brown. The yellow-headed gecko, *G. albogularis,* comes from Central America and many West Indian islands but, like the ashy gecko, has also made a home for itself in Florida. The males have a dark blue body and a tan or yellowish head, while the females have mottled brown bodies with a light collar. Colonies of these geckos live on the trunks of large forest trees.

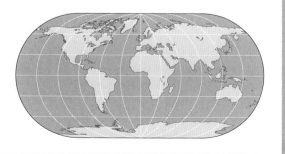

Common name Granite
                 night lizard

Scientific name *Xantusia henshawi*

Family   Xantusiidae

Suborder   Sauria

Order   Squamata

Size   From 4 in (10 cm) to 5 in (13 cm) long

Key features A small, flattened lizard with smooth, shiny
                 skin made up of a large number of small
                 scales; eyes moderately large with vertical
                 pupils but no movable eyelids; head wide and
                 flattened and covered with large, symmetrical
                 scales; markings consist of large dark-brown
                 blotches separated by narrow white or yellow
                 netting; limbs thin with long claws for
                 climbing

Habits   Very secretive; active in the evening

Breeding   Female gives birth to 1–2 young in the fall;
                gestation period about 3 months

Diet   Small invertebrates and some plant material

Habitat   Rocky outcrops and hillsides in canyons,
                where it hides in crevices

Distribution Southern California and northern Baja
                 California, Mexico

Status   Common in suitable habitat

Similar species *Xantusia bezyi*, recently described from
                Arizona, is very similar, as is *X. bolsonae* from
                Durango, Mexico

Granite Night Lizard

Xantusia henshawi

The granite night lizard is easily overlooked, since it lives in crevices in massive rocks and boulders. It rarely ventures out in the open until after dark.

RECENTLY HERPETOLOGISTS HAVE QUESTIONED the term "night" lizard, especially in relation to the granite night lizards, because they are probably active during the day. However, the activity takes place deep in crevices in large boulders, where they cannot be seen.

Granite night lizards are colonial lizards living in quite small areas of suitable habitat. They often live on granite rocks in canyons and gullies, where they are protected from direct sunlight for part of the day, and where a little humidity remains well into the summer.

Because the granite night lizard has such a specialized habitat, its occurrence is patchy even within the small area over which it occurs, and there are large gaps in its distribution. Some populations differ superficially from others, and several subspecies have been described. One form discovered in Arizona was originally considered to be a variation of the desert night lizard, *X. vigilis*. But its markings are similar to those of the granite night lizard, and in 2001 it was described as a separate species, *X. bezyi*.

Spring Breeding

Male granite night lizards have a small gland on the inside of their thighs as well as a row of femoral pores. These pores probably produce substances that allow the males to mark their territories, although little is known about communications or social interactions.

Breeding takes place in spring, and the female gives birth to one or two young in the fall after a gestation of about three months. The young take two or more years to reach maturity. This is unusual for a small lizard, most of which grow rapidly and breed quickly. For example, the side-blotched lizard,

Predators are limited to larger lizards, snakes, and predatory birds. In recent times their biggest threat has come from people collecting them for the pet trade and for research.

The only way of catching them is to pry off the large flakes of rock under which they shelter. This causes permanent damage to the habitat, since there are only a limited number of rock flakes for them to live under, and tens of thousands of years will have to pass before the weathering process will produce more flakes. Many areas have been badly damaged in the past by collectors, and the species is now protected not because it is particularly rare, but because the collecting method is so destructive.

⊖ As its name suggests, the granite night lizard can usually be found under pieces of flaking granite in rocky areas of southern California and Mexico.

Uta stansburiana, which comes from the same part of the world but belongs to the Iguanidae, is practically "annual," with almost a complete turnover of individuals between one breeding season and the next.

Threats

The survival rate of the young is thought to be very high because they rarely stray from the crevices in which they live, even at night.

Close Relatives

The desert night lizard, *Xantusia vigilis* from North America, is smaller than the granite night lizard and more widespread. It is not quite as specialized in its habitat requirements and lives in small colonies among rocks or between the overlapping leaves in the bases of live and dead yucca plants. Interestingly, colonies living in yucca debris have cylindrical bodies, whereas those living among rocks have flattened bodies like that of the granite night lizard.

The island night lizard, *X. riversiana,* is just like a desert night lizard but several times bigger. This species is restricted to three small islands off the coast of southern California, where it has federal protection. Because insect food is hard to come by, this species has adopted an omnivorous diet and eats the flowers and seeds of succulent plants and annuals that grow on the islands. Two Mexican species, *X. bolsonae* from Durango and *X. sanchezi* (described in 1999 from Zacatecas, Mexico), are poorly known.

Common name Desert grassland whiptail

Scientific name *Cnemidophorus uniparens*

Family Teiidae

Suborder Sauria

Order Squamata

Size 9 in (23 cm) long

Key features A small, graceful lizard with a long cylindrical body; long tail accounts for about two-thirds of total length if complete; head narrow and pointed; limbs long, especially the back ones, which also have long toes; color rich brown with 6 unbroken cream stripes from the back of the head to the base of the tail; juveniles have blue tails

Habits Terrestrial and diurnal

Breeding Parthenogenetic; females lay 1–4 eggs without the help of males; eggs hatch into more females in 50–55 days

Diet Insects and spiders

Habitat Dry scrub and grassland; open forests in mountain foothills

Distribution North America (southeastern Arizona, southwestern New Mexico, and adjacent parts of Mexico to the south)

Status Common

Similar species Other whiptails, of which there are a number in the region

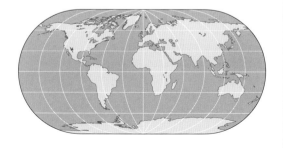

Desert Grassland Whiptail

Cnemidophorus uniparens

The desert grassland whiptail is a fast-moving, sun-loving lizard with a terrific capacity for speed and an interesting life history.

THE DESERT GRASSLAND WHIPTAIL lives in arid parts of the American Southwest, rarely emerging until temperatures reach 86°F (30°C) or more and basking on the most exposed patches of sand or rock. Where it extends up into the desert foothills, it also lives between evergreen oak trees, sometimes basking on their bases or on the boulders surrounding them.

Like other whiptails, this lizard is a fast mover; similar species have been clocked at 15 mph (25 km/h), which is the speed achieved during a four-minute mile! What's more, it can keep up this speed for a considerable time. If it is trying to run down a meal or escape from a predator, it can race across open ground without a pause and change direction in the blink of an eye. It rarely resorts to cover and prefers to stay in the open and outrun its enemies. This is a challenging species to catch!

On the other hand, it is sometimes hunted successfully by whip snakes, such as the Sonoran whip snake, *Masticophis bilineatus*, and the coachwhip, *M. flagellum*. Nocturnal lizard-eating snakes, such as lyre snakes, *Trimorphodon biscutatus*, long-nosed snakes, *Rhinocheilus lecontei*, and spotted night snakes, *Hypsiglena torquata*, are plentiful in the region where it lives, and they are probably its most effective predators. Their strategy is to nose around in crevices and burrows at night, hoping to catch diurnal lizards while they are sleeping.

Single Parents

The aspect of its natural history that separates the desert grassland whiptail from most other lizards is its reproductive biology. The clue is in its scientific name—*uniparens* means "one

Parthenogenesis—How Widespread Is It?

Although many invertebrates are parthenogenetic (aphids and water fleas, for example), there are only a few fish, a few amphibians, one snake, and about 30 species of lizards that reproduce in this way (that we know of). Since not all the species are closely related to each other, parthenogenesis has evidently evolved independently among lizards several times.

Parthenogenetic species are found among the Agamidae (the butterfly agamas, *Leiolepis* species); the Chamaeleonidae (a dwarf chameleon, *Brookesia affinis*); several geckos (including *Hemidactylus garnotii* and *Lepidodactylus lugubris*); the Gymnophthalmidae (Underwood's spectacled lizard, *Gymnophthalmus underwoodi*); the Teiidae (several whiptail lizards and also *Kentropyx suquiensis* from Argentina); and the Xantusiidae (the yellow-spotted night lizard, *Lepidophyma flavimaculatus*). It is also possible that a member of the Iguanidae, one of the chuckwallalike *Phymaturus* species from southern Chile and Argentina, reproduces by parthenogenesis.

parent." This is an all-female species that can reproduce without having mated. There are no males, and all individuals are female clones. Occasionally females will behave like males and go through a false courtship and copulation sequence. In whiptail lizards this behavior increases the clutch size of the female, but in some other parthenogenetic species it has the opposite effect (in other words, it lowers the reproductive output). The reasons for this anomaly are not understood.

Parthenogenesis in lizards was first discovered in 1958 by the Russian herpetologist Ilya Darevsky. The first species known to be parthenogenetic was a lacertid, *Lacerta saxicola*, since renamed (fittingly) *Darevskia saxicola*. Following this, other parthenogenetic species were discovered, including several more lacertids from the Caucasian region, often after workers realized that all museum specimens were females. It later turned out that

⊖ *Although it has many predators, few can outrun the desert grassland whiptail. Because it is so fast and agile, it is able to spend much of its time in the open.*

parthenogenesis is especially common among whiptail lizards, and the species most thoroughly investigated is the desert whiptail lizard. Confirmation came with an experiment in which skin grafts were made on desert grassland whiptail lizards from widely separated parts of their range. They all accepted small patches of skin from each other, as you would expect if they were all clones. Grafts made between individuals of a sexually reproducing species, the western whiptail lizard, *C. tigris*, were invariably rejected.

How Parthenogenesis Works

There are several ways in which all-female species reproduce. The European pool frogs, *Rana* species, reproduce by a method called hybridogenesis, and some North American mole salamanders, *Ambystoma* species, use a method called gynogenesis. Both systems require a male to initiate cell division, even though his genetic material is not incorporated into the resultant eggs. The desert whiptail lizard follows a third system, parthenogenesis, in which males are not required at all.

The desert grassland whiptail is the result of hybridization and back-crossing between the little striped whiptail, *C. inornatus*, and the Texas spotted whiptail, *C. gularis*. In normal sex cells each chromosome divides once, and each resulting strand becomes part of a gamete (that is, sperm or ovum) that then combines with the equivalent chromosome from the opposite sex in a process known as meiosis. In the desert grassland whiptail, however, division of the sex cells is abnormal—the cells undergo a

⊕ *The rainbow lizard, Cnemidophorus deppei from Costa Rica, has beautiful bright markings. Like the desert grassland whiptail, it is very fast and agile.*

⊖ *The coastal whiptail, Cnemidophorus tigris multiscutatus from Baja California, Mexico, has a checkered appearance. It is closely related to the desert grassland whiptail.*

preliminary doubling of the chromosomes before meiosis, resulting in cells with four strands of each chromosome (4N). They divide to give 2N (diploid) instead of the normal 1N (haploid) pattern, and the ova develop into offspring that are genetically identical to the mother. They do not need the complementary chromosomes that would normally be provided by the male. All the young produced are also females and can lay eggs without mating.

Parthenogenesis—Pros and Cons

A parthenogenetic breeding system has advantages and disadvantages. On the plus side, species can reproduce without males and are therefore more likely to colonize fresh territory—it only takes a single female (even a juvenile or an egg) to move in. This is especially helpful to species such as some geckos that often raft to new islands.

Another advantage, and one that applies to the desert grassland whiptail, is the very fast rate at which populations can increase. In a population with the usual 50:50 sex ratio only half produce eggs or young, whereas in parthenogenetic species they all produce offspring. Since population growth is exponential, there is a dramatic incrase after just a few generations. Assuming that every female lays 10 eggs a year, the population is 10 at the end of the first year. Each of those females will produce 10 eggs the following year, making 100. By the end of the third year there will be 1,000, and so on.

In contrast, in a sexually breeding species there will be five females at the end of the first year. They will produce a total of 50 by the end of the second year, but about half will be males. The 25 females will produce a total of 250 young the third year, but again, only half will be females. Leaving predation and other dangers aside, the reproductive population of the parthenogenetic species after just three years will already be eight times that of the normal species (1,000 versus 125).

But if parthenogenetic species are so successful, why aren't there more of them? Parthenogenetic individuals are all clones. They are genetically identical to each other; unlike in sexually reproducing species, there is no variability. Because the adaptation of a species is based on natural selection, where those most suited to the environment survive and the others do not, variability becomes important if the environment changes—at least some will be able to survive. Because parthenogenetic species consist of identical clones, if the conditions change drastically even over a long period, they will probably all die off.

There are two conclusions to be drawn. First, many parthenogenetic species are probably quite "young." They arose only a few hundred years ago, have thrived until now, but may not survive very much longer. Others will take their place if conditions change. The other scenario is that they will act like "weeds," moving from place to place to track patches of suitable habitat. They are quick to exploit new opportunities, increase quickly, and then move on.

Five-Lined Skink

Eumeces fasciatus

Five-lined skinks can be seen in woods where there are plenty of logs, stumps, rock piles, and leaf litter. The brightly colored juveniles are more distinctive than the adults, whose colors fade with age.

THE FIVE-LINED SKINK IS PROBABLY the most common member of the genus found in the United States. Although its habitat varies, it prefers moist areas. It lives in wooded and partly wooded places as well as disturbed environments such as forest edges and cleared areas. It favors sites with wood and brush piles, stumps, logs, buildings, and outcrops, all of which provide shelter and basking places.

Five-lined skinks are diurnal and mainly terrestrial creatures, although they will climb onto stumps and small rotting trees to bask and search for insects. During the hottest part of the day in midsummer they often take refuge under rocks or logs. They are also accomplished burrowers and excavate dugouts under rocks. At night or when hibernating, they seek shelter in rotting logs, rock crevices, and sawdust piles.

They have a wedge-shaped head and a long, slender, cylindrical body. Males are slightly larger than females and grow up to 8 inches (20 cm) long, of which about 60 percent is the tail. The limbs are small but powerful with five clawed digits on each. The species can be distinguished from similar species by a middle row of enlarged scales under the tail and 26 to 30 longitudinal rows of scales around the center of the body. The skin is supported by small bones called osteoderms that lie beneath each scale, giving it greater strength.

Diet and Predators

Small invertebrates such as spiders, crickets, grasshoppers, beetles, millipedes, and caterpillars make up most of the skinks' diet. Snails and small vertebrates, including smaller lizards and newborn small mammals, are also

⊙ *The cream stripes and bright-blue tail indicate that this five-lined skink in Florida is a juvenile. The long, tapering tail can be broken off in the presence of a predator.*

Common name	Five-lined skink
Scientific name	*Eumeces fasciatus*
Family	Scincidae
Suborder	Sauria
Order	Squamata
Size	Up to 8 in (20 cm)
Key features	Body slender and elongated; body color tan, bronze, or grayish olive-green with pale stripes; juveniles have 5 longitudinal bright-cream to yellow stripes on a black background; tail is blue in juveniles and some females but fades to gray in adult males; head wedge shaped; ear opening distinct; limbs short, each bearing five digits with claws; scales smooth
Habits	Diurnal; terrestrial; may climb onto tree stumps to bask and look for insects; also burrows under rocks
Breeding	Egg layer; clutch containing 4–15 eggs laid in a nest dug in moist soil; eggs hatch after 33–35 days
Diet	Insects, spiders, earthworms, crustaceans, and small lizards
Habitat	Humid woods with leaf litter and tree stumps; may also be seen around human habitations
Distribution	Southern New England to northern Florida west to Texas, Kansas, Wisconsin, and southern Ontario; isolated groups may occur farther west
Status	Common but listed as being of special concern in some parts of its range, e.g., Iowa
Similar species	*Eumeces inexpectatus* and *E. laticeps* have similar colors and longitudinal stripes

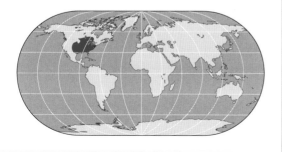

eaten. The skinks are often seen climbing on houses and are regarded as beneficial, since they eat a number of insect pests. They crush food in their strong jaws prior to swallowing it.

The skinks rely on speed to escape from predators, including snakes, crows, hawks, racoons, and foxes. However, if it is grabbed, the skink can break off its tail voluntarily, a process known as autotomy. While the skink runs for shelter, the predator is distracted by the disconnected tail, which continues to twitch. The skink regenerates a new tail, but it is usually not as long as the original.

Reproduction

In spring the snout and jaws of mature males develop a reddish-orange coloration. Mating occurs between mid-May and the end of June, and females lay a clutch of up to 15 eggs some four to five weeks later. They prefer secluded nest sites under cover such as logs, boards, rocks, or partially decayed stumps.

They also prefer areas where the soil has a higher moisture content. The eggs absorb moisture from the soil, which enables them to

Bright Youngsters

Juvenile five-lined skinks are attractive animals with five narrow, longitudinal cream to yellow stripes running along the back from the snout to the tail. The background body color is black, and the tail is blue. A light-colored "v" shape on the head merges with the mid-dorsal stripe. The tail color dulls with age and turns gray, although some females may retain some of the blue coloration. Body coloration also changes to a tan, bronze, or grayish olive-green with pale stripes. In old males only faint traces of stripes may remain.

Male five-lined skinks will attack other males and smaller lizards. However, they do not attack lizards with blue tails. This enables both the adults and the juveniles to feed on different sizes of food in the same area and reduces the risk of juveniles being killed by aggressive, mature adults.

swell. Incubation time varies from 33 to 55 days depending on temperature. During this time the female coils around the eggs, feeding on any passing insects and exhibiting defensive biting behavior toward small predators.

She also regulates the temperature of the eggs by moving them up or down in the nest site; if there is a danger of it flooding or the eggs becoming too moist, she moves them to safety. After the eggs hatch, the female plays no further part in looking after the young.

Common name Eastern glass
lizard (Florida glass lizard)

Scientific name *Ophisaurus ventralis*

Subfamily Anguinae

Family Anguidae

Suborder Sauria

Order Squamata

Size 39 in (99 cm)

Key features A stiff, legless lizard with eyelids and
external ear openings; a groove along its side
marks the change from grayish-brown flanks
with white bars to the plain, off-white
underside; the back is plain brown in color;
side of the head is marked with dark-edged,
whitish bars, but they may disappear
with age

Habits Diurnal; terrestrial

Breeding Female lays 8–17 eggs that hatch after 8–9
weeks

Diet Invertebrates, especially slugs, snails, and
earthworms

Habitat Grassland, open woods, fields, and parks

Distribution Southeastern United Sates (North Carolina,
the whole of Florida, eastern Louisiana)

Status Common

Similar species The ranges of 3 other glass lizards—
the slender, the island, and the mimic
(*Ophisaurus attenuatus*, *O. compressus*, and
O. mimicus)—overlap the range of the
eastern glass lizard; the first 2 usually have
some black striping along their back or
flanks, while the mimic glass lizard is much
smaller, about 15 in (38 cm)

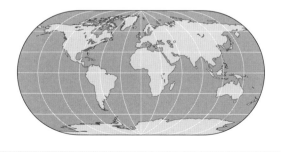

Eastern Glass Lizard
Ophisaurus ventralis

Glass lizards are well named: If their tail is held or attacked, it can shatter into several pieces, each of which continues to move independently.

GLASS LIZARDS SHOULD BE EASY TO DISTINGUISH from snakes because they have movable eyelids and external ear openings, whereas snakes do not. The head and body are only half as long as the tail (showing that it is a terrestrial rather than a burrowing species), while a snake's tail is generally about one-fifth of its total length. Glass lizards also have a distinct groove along each side of the body that allows it to expand when the lizard is distended with food or eggs.

A characteristic shared by all four North American glass lizards is the ability to lose and regrow the tail. A new, shorter tail will grow in its place, and adults with complete and original tails are rare. (The tail of the island glass lizard, *O. compressus*, does not have fracture planes like the other three species, and its tail is therefore not shed as easily.) The only other means of defense for glass lizards is to wriggle furiously and empty the contents of their cloacal glands, smearing and spraying them over their enemy.

Eastern glass lizards are usually found sheltering under objects lying on the ground, often pieces of board, tin, old carpet, or sacking. They are active during the day, especially early in the morning when the humidity is high, and their prey—slugs, snails, and earthworms—are most easily found.

Guarding the Eggs
Eastern glass lizards usually mate in the spring and lay eight to 17 eggs in May, June, or July. The eggs are laid in hollows in the ground, often under a log or flat rock. The female

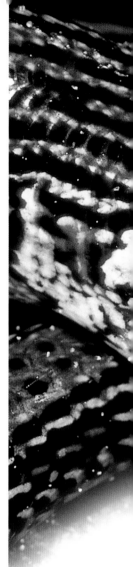

⊕ *A mating pair of* Ophisaurus ventralis *glass lizards in Florida. Eastern glass lizards breed in spring; unusually among lizards, the females care for their eggs by coiling around them until they hatch.*

Lateral Folds

All the glass lizards and many other members of the family (except the legless lizards, *Anniella*, and the slow worm, *Anguis fragilis*) have folds of skin along the sides of the body from the front legs to the back legs. The folded area is covered with small, soft scales, making it very flexible. The lizards need the fold because they have osteoderms (small bones) under their other scales. The bones make them so stiff that without the fold the lizards would not be able to expand their body to breathe, to take in large meals, or in the case of females, to hold developing eggs or young.

remains coiled around the eggs to guard them until they hatch during August and September.

Egg brooding in lizards is very rare. The only other species in which females are known to brood their eggs are the oviparous (egg-laying) members of the skink genus *Eumeces*, such as the prairie skink, *E. septentrionalis*, and the five-lined skink, *E. fasciatus*. Coincidentally, several of these species live in the same region as the glass lizards. The other members of the genus are viviparous (live-bearers). Some authorities think that egg brooding is the first evolutionary step toward viviparity.

Rare Relative

The mimic glass lizard, *O. mimicus*, was described to science only in 1987. It is the smallest glass lizard in North America, rarely exceeding 15 inches (38 cm) in total length, and is light tan to golden brown in color with several stripes. It is found in pine grasslands of northern Florida, coastal North Carolina, Georgia, and Mississippi.

177

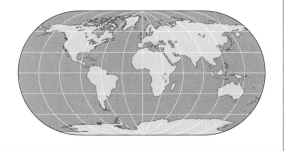

Anniella geronomensis

Common names

Baja California legless lizard (*A. geronomensis*); California legless lizard (*A. pulchra*)

Scientific names *Anniella geronomensis* and *A. pulchra*

Subfamily Anniellinae

Family Anguidae

Suborder Sauria

Order Squamata

Size From 6 in (15 cm) to 7 in (18 cm)

Key features Small legless lizards with few distinguishing marks; head small and pointed (when seen from the side) and not distinct from the neck; lower jaw deeply countersunk; eyes also sunk within the head and reduced to narrow horizontal slits; *A. geronomensis* is coppery or silvery brown in color with 7 or 8 thin black stripes running the length of the body; *A. pulchra* is similar but has 1 black line along the center of its back, another along each flank, and its underside is yellow

Habits Burrowers; sometimes bask on dunes but avoid extreme temperatures by moving around

Breeding Poorly known; may give birth to one or two live young in late summer or early fall

Diet Small invertebrates

Habitat Sand dunes (*A. geronomensis*) and sandy soils (*A. pulchra*)

Distribution Baja California, Mexico (*A. geronomensis*), southern California (*A. pulchra*)

Status Probably common in suitable habitat but localized and hard to find

Similar species None in the region

North American Legless Lizards

Anniella geronomensis and *A. pulchra*

Although common in some areas of their range, the North American legless lizards are considered species of special concern locally, and collecting them is restricted by law.

THE LITTLE NORTH AMERICAN legless lizards look superficially like young glass lizards, *Ophisaurus* species, or European slow worms, *Anguis fragilis*, but they are far more specialized. They spend most of their lives below the ground. Because they are burrowing species, they have long bodies and short tails (unlike all the other legless anguids, which have short bodies and long tails).

Sand Specialists

The Baja California species lives in the loose, windblown sand that forms a dune system stretching for about 54 miles (87 km) along the coast in the northern half of the peninsula. They are found nowhere else. They live among the roots of shrubs that grow on the dunes and travel between them by "swimming" through the sand just below the surface, leaving characteristic winding tracks. Early in the morning when the weather is cool, the lizards stay buried deep in the sand but come closer to the surface as soon as the sun begins to warm up the dunes.

Because the dunes are aligned north-south, the seaward, west-facing sides become very cool in the afternoon when the sun moves lower in the sky and the onshore breezes bring cold air. The inland side, however, does not benefit from the breezes, and the sun heats this side of the dunes up to temperatures that are dangerously high for the lizards. It seems that the lizards avoid the extremes of heat and cold by moving around to find the optimum

⤴ *California legless lizards, Anniella pulchra, are often seen among leaf litter and commonly burrow in soil near the surface. They differ from A. geronomensis in having three black lines along the body (rather than seven or eight) and a yellow underside.*

temperature. By late afternoon they often emerge to bask on the tops of the dunes where there is a fine balance between the heat of the sun and the cool breezes. They may stay on the surface to forage for food in the early part of the night before they become too cold. They also feed in the sand on burrowing insects and their larvae and small scorpions.

Farther north the California legless lizard is not so specialized. It lives on sandy and loamy soils, and can be found under stones and dead wood. It occurs on beaches, under debris, and among shrubs but in more compacted sand than the dunes farther south. In parts of California it is common in loose soil under juniper trees, where dead leaves provide an ideal habitat for the termites on which it feeds.

This species sometimes comes up toward the surface in the morning to bask under a flat rock or in the upper layer of soil and then emerges to hunt small insects and spiders. Where both species occur together, the Baja California species is the most common, but the California legless lizard can live farther inland

because it is not as strongly associated with loose sand as its coastal counterpart.

The Baja California species is inactive in midwinter, but the more northerly California legless lizard is active throughout the year. That is because the habitats along the Baja coast are more susceptible to the cooling effects of the Humboldt current, which brings cold fogs in from the sea. They burn off by the time they are a few miles inland, and the climate behind the fog zone is also far warmer in winter.

Little is known about the breeding habits of either species. Observations are based on a few captured specimens, making it hard to draw any firm conclusions. Female Baja California legless lizards have been found containing single embryos late in the year. Juveniles have been found in the spring and summer. This suggests that they mate in the spring and give birth late in the year. Similarly, the California legless lizard appears to give birth in late summer or early fall, and females of this species have been found with two embryos inside them.

Common name
  Southern alligator lizard

Scientific name *Elgaria multicarinata*

Subfamily Gerrhonotinae

Family Anguidae

Suborder Sauria

Order Squamata

Size From 10 in (25 cm) to 16 in (41 cm)

Key features A large lizard with a wide, triangular head
  covered with large scales; forelimbs small;
  hind limbs slightly larger; a fold runs along
  each flank between the fore- and hind limbs;
  scales on its back and flanks are roughly
  square and keeled, giving it a ridged
  appearance; color reddish brown or tan on
  the back fading to grayish on the flanks,
  usually with irregular black bands

Habits Diurnal; semiarboreal

Breeding Female lays 2–3 clutches of eggs each year

Diet Insects and spiders; occasional small lizards,
  nestling birds and mice; also eats carrion

Habitat Moist grasslands and woodlands, especially in
  foothills

Distribution Western North America (southern
  Washington State south to Baja California
  along a fairly narrow coastal belt)

Status Common

Similar species Several other alligator lizards live in the
  same region; the northern alligator lizard,
  Elgaria coerulea, is slightly smaller and has a
  more speckled pattern

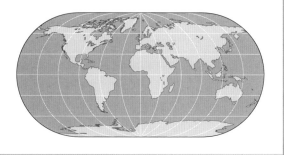

Southern Alligator Lizard

Elgaria multicarinata

Alligator lizards are so-called because they look like tiny alligators. They can also swim well and have a strong bite. Sometimes they even bite and then twist their entire body, like their larger namesakes.

THE SOUTHERN ALLIGATOR LIZARD is very much a generalist, occupying a range of different habitats and eating a wide variety of food. It has a stiff body and a prehensile tail that it uses when clambering about in bushes and shrubs, although it is equally at home on the ground.

It has a wide range throughout the conifer forests of California and Baja California, and is most common at the edges of fields, especially where there are rocks. It also lives in semidesert habitats and on mountain slopes, but it prefers moist places with some vegetation and ground cover, such as the bottom of canyons and gulleys. It is active during the day even when it is cool and overcast.

Slow and Steady

This species is not the most agile of lizards, owing to the layer of bony plates, or osteoderms, beneath its scales. Unless it is disturbed, it moves at a leisurely pace, inspecting every new thing with its thick, notched tongue. Its gait is deliberate and almost snakelike—pushing itself along with its limbs but also using its body to provide some thrust. It seems to slide gracefully through the vegetation. It is more easily captured than many small lizards, but it is capable of giving a painful bite. It will also part company with its tail at the slightest excuse, sometimes releasing it before it is actually grasped by an enemy.

The southern alligator lizard is an active hunter, foraging for prey among shrubs, leaf litter, and long grass. Its head is wide, and its jaws are powerful, enabling it to crush hard-shelled insects such as beetles. It will also take small vertebrates such as mammals, birds, and

other lizards. Skinks and abandoned skink tails have been found in the stomachs of several specimens.

Reproduction

The lizards breed in the spring. Females may lay two or three clutches of eggs in the course of the summer. However, the northern alligator lizard, *E. coerulea*, which comes from a cooler region but is otherwise similar, gives birth to live young. Both methods have advantages and disadvantages according to circumstances.

There are usually good reasons why some members of a family lay eggs and others give birth to live young. Egg-laying females,

for example, only have to carry their brood for a limited time before laying them. In the case of the southern alligator lizard this means that females can go on to produce one or even two more clutches in the course of a year. Live-bearers have to carry the developing embryos around with them for longer, which may put a strain on them; but they can raise their body temperature by basking, which allows the embryos to develop more quickly. They can also protect them from predators.

Close Relatives

There are eight species in the genus *Elgaria*. Apart from the northern and southern alligator lizards, *E. coerulea* and *E. multicarinata*, another four occur in Baja California (*E. velazquezi*, *E. paucicarinata*, *E. cedrosensis*, and *E. nana*). The latter two are restricted to the small islands of Cedros and Coronado. None have common names, although they are collectively known as *ajolote* in Mexico. The remaining species, the Madrean alligator lizard, *E. kingii*, and the Panamint alligator lizard, *E. panamintina*, live around the Arizona-New Mexico-Mexico borders and in eastern California respectively. Two other alligator lizards are included in the genus *Gerrhonotus*. They are the Texas alligator lizard, *G. liocephalus*, and Lugo's alligator lizard, *G. lugoi* from Mexico.

⊖ *The California form of the southern alligator lizard is found in grassy or rocky areas in northern California. Like all southern alligator lizards, it is aggressive and can lose its tail if it is grabbed.*

Diploglossus monotropis

Common name Giant galliwasps

Scientific names *Celestus* sp. and *Diploglossus* sp.

Subfamily Diploglossinae

Family Anguidae

Suborder Sauria

Order Squamata

Size Body length over 12 in (30 cm); up to 18 in (46 cm) including tail

Key features Bulky, skinklike lizards with thick bodies, short limbs, and pointed snouts; heads covered with large, platelike scales; body scales shiny and overlapping with a rounded edge (cycloid); they have parallel ridges running down them (striations) that are better defined on some species than others; coloration varies, but most are shades of brown with orange or yellow markings; male *D. monotropis* are brightly marked in orange and yellow

Habits Diurnal or nocturnal depending on species; ground dwellers or semiburrowers

Breeding *Celestus* sp. are live-bearers; *Diploglossus* sp. may be live-bearers or egg layers; related species of egg-laying *Diploglossus* apparently coil around their incubating eggs

Diet Poorly known; large species are thought to be partly herbivorous; *C. occiduus* is reported to eat fish

Habitat Rain forests (among leaf litter) and swamps

Distribution Central America (*D. monotropis*) and the West Indies (Jamaica and Hispaniola)

Status Extremely rare, some possibly extinct

Similar species None in the region

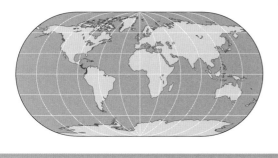

Giant Galliwasps

Celestus and *Diploglossus* sp.

Giant galliwasps form a very special group of six rare species. Some of them are threatened with imminent extinction.

THE GENERA *CELESTUS* AND *DIPLOGLOSSUS* contain 28 and 11 species respectively. Most are small to moderate in size. However, four species of *Celestus* (the Jamaican galliwasp, *C. occiduus*, the Haitian galliwasp, *C. warreni*, and two species from the Dominican Republic, *C. anelpistus* and *C. carraui*) and two species of *Diploglossus* (*D. monotropis* from Central America and *D. millepunctatus* from a tiny island off Colombia) are much larger with combined head and body lengths of over 8 inches (20 cm). They are known collectively as giant galliwasps, and the largest species is the one from Jamaica with a combined head and body length of over 12 inches (30 cm).

Endangered or Extinct

The only giant galliwasp that is not endangered is the Central American species, *D. monotropis*, which is rarely seen but widespread. The Jamaican galliwasp, *C. occiduus*, has not been seen since 1840, and many scientists think it is already extinct. However, it lives a secretive life in remote parts of the island, and a small population may have escaped notice. The Dominican species, *C. anelpistus*, lives (or lived) only in a small forest that was being destroyed even as the only four known specimens were collected in 1977. *Diploglossus millepunctatus* lives exclusively on the barren Malpelo Island west of Colombia. The other two species are rare but not critically endangered at present.

The main reasons for the decline of the giant galliwasps are habitat destruction resulting from land clearance for agricultural planting and the introduction of predators such as cats. A further pressure is that of wanton

⊖ *In Costa Rica a female galliwasp lizard,* **Diploglossus bilobatus,** *guards her clutch of eggs. Captive breeding programs involving similar, less rare members of the genus may ensure the future survival of the critically endangered species.*

Disappearing Giants

Reptiles that evolve on islands often exhibit gigantism (they are significantly larger than their relatives on the mainland). They have another, less welcome characteristic: They are more likely to go extinct because it takes less to upset the ecological balance on islands. Among the other giant island lizards that have disappeared in historical times are the Martinique giant ameiva, *Ameiva major* (Teiidae); the Cape Verde giant skink, *Macroscincus coctei* (Scincidae); and the Rodrigues giant day gecko, *Phelsuma gigas* (Gekkonidae).

Both species of giant tortoise, *Geochelone nigra* from the Galápagos Islands and *Dipsochelys dussumieri* from Aldabra, have been close to extinction, while others from Indian Ocean islands have disappeared in more recent times. In 1997 the last 12 Seychelles giant tortoises, *Dipsochelys hololissa*, were discovered in captivity on the islands and have been the subject of captive breeding programs in zoos throughout the world.

killing by indigenous people who often fear galliwasps and assume that they are venomous.

Galliwasps are the subject of several myths: People in Jamaica used to think that if you were bitten by a galliwasp and the galliwasp reached water first, you would die; but if you reached water first, the galliwasp would die. In parts of Panama and Costa Rica *D. monotropis* is called *el escorpion coral,* or the "coral snake lizard," because it is colored like a coral snake. Other variations include *la madre de coral,* "the

mother of coral snakes." In Haiti galliwasps are associated with voodoo superstitions and are often found hacked into pieces.

Experiment in Captive Breeding

The last hope for many of the giant galliwasps is to establish a captive breeding program to boost their numbers before releasing them into a secure habitat. Because they are so rare, the first step has been to set up breeding colonies of *C. warreni* (a more common species from Hispaniola) at Nashville Zoo in order to develop the necessary technique. It has proved very successful—over 300 offspring have been produced from nine pairs of lizards collected from the wild. The next step will be to use the knowledge gained to breed another large species, *D. monotropis,* before working with the critically endangered species.

It is also hoped that educational programs in places where the giant galliwasps occur naturally will lead to a better understanding of them and may help find previously unknown populations of the Jamaican galliwasp.

Common name Gila monster (Aztec lizard)

Scientific name *Heloderma suspectum*

Family   Helodermatidae

Suborder   Sauria

Order   Squamata

Size   From 13 in (33 cm) to 22 in (56 cm)

Key features Head rounded and bears a patch of light-colored scales; nose blunt; neck short; body heavy with short, powerful limbs and long claws; tail short and fat; scales beadlike; eyelids movable; camouflage colors of black, orange, yellow, and pink on the body; has 2 elongated cloacal scales

Habits   Active by day, at dusk, or at night depending on season and temperatures; spends much of the time in burrows or in shaded areas

Breeding Female lays 1 clutch of up to 12 eggs in late summer; eggs hatch 10 months later

Diet   Small mammals, eggs of birds and reptiles, insects

Habitat   Dry grassland, deserts, and foothills of mountains

Distribution Southwestern United States and northwestern Mexico

Status   Vulnerable (IUCN); listed in CITES Appendix II

Similar species *Heloderma horridum*

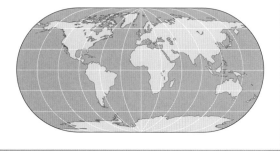

Gila Monster

Heloderma suspectum

Surrounded by myths and superstitions, the Gila monster is one of just two venomous lizards. Although potent, its venom has hardly ever been known to kill a human.

THE GILA MONSTER is named after the Gila basin in Arizona where numbers of the lizard are plentiful. It is sometimes referred to as the Aztec lizard, since it has featured in paintings by the Aztecs. Although it has a wide distribution in southern Nevada, southeastern California, southwestern New Mexico, and Arizona, numbers are concentrated in small pockets. There are two subspecies: *Heloderma suspectum suspectum*, the Gila monster, and *H. s. cinctum*, the banded Gila monster, which is slightly smaller and whose coloration contains lighter-colored bands. Its range includes southwest Utah and southern Nevada.

The habitat of Gila monsters varies from desert grassland, Mohave and Sonoran desert scrub, to Sonoran thorn scrub. They can be found on lower mountain slopes in arid and semiarid areas and also on adjacent plains and occasionally irrigated areas. They inhabit canyon bottoms—deep ravines with streams that may dry up for part of the year. In parts of Arizona the Gila monster's range extends into oak woodland and in Sonora onto beaches.

Seeking Shade
Within its habitat it seeks shelter under rocks, in dense thickets, and in wood-rat nests. It also digs burrows as well as making use of those belonging to other animals. Although Gila monsters are adapted to an extremely dry habitat, their optimum temperature is only about 86°F (30°C), which is considerably lower than other desert lizards. To avoid the high daytime temperatures during the summer, Gila monsters tend to be active at dawn and dusk. They spend the rest of the day in burrows, often dug using their powerful limbs and long

claws, or under rocks and shrubs. In Arizona Gila monsters spend 98 percent of their active season underground, and in Utah they live for 95 percent of the time in burrows.

During winter when temperatures fall below 50°F (10°C), they hibernate in burrows that have a south-facing entrance. On sunny days they wake and emerge to bask at the entrance. During the rainy season they become active at dusk and nocturnal; but after emerging from hibernation when temperatures are still relatively low, they are diurnal.

The Gila monster has a more rounded head, a shorter tail, and is a smaller species overall than its close relative the Mexican beaded lizard, *H. horridum*. Its long claws are useful when climbing trees, which it frequently does in the rainy season to escape the threat of torrential rain flooding its burrows. In spring it eats insects, but in June and July it changes to small mammals and birds. It can live for several months without food, although loss of weight shows mainly in the tail, which can lose 20 percent of its girth in one month without food.

⊖ *Distinctively patterned in colors of light yellow, orange, pink, and black, the Gila monster is hard to spot against a dark background or in dappled shade.*

Camouflage and Warning Coloration

Coloration of Gila monsters consists of irregular bands and blotches of black, orange, yellow, and pink. Younger specimens have more extensive lighter areas. Unusually for lizards these colors act both as camouflage and as a warning to enemies. Since the Gila monster is active primarily at dawn and dusk, the bands of color are difficult to see in the dappled shade when it moves or shelters beneath creosote bushes and other shrubs. Against a dark background the black markings blend in, and the light markings resemble gravel. Its nose is black, providing excellent camouflage when peering from burrows.

When it moves away from vegetation, its bright body markings become warning coloration, advertising its toxicity. In response to a threat the Gila monster will hiss and gape, revealing the pink venom glands that contrast with the dark lining of the mouth—yet another warning signal.

185

Beaded Lizard Venom

Venom in reptiles is usually associated with snakes. However, the two species of beaded lizard (the Gila monster and the Mexican beaded lizard) are the only venomous lizards. At first scientists debated whether or not they were venomous and gave the Gila monster the name *Heloderma suspectum*, since at the time it was only suspected to be venomous.

Beaded lizards have 10 teeth in each jaw. When compared with snakes, their venom-delivery mechanism is rather primitive. There is a gland on each side of the jaw with ducts next to the points where the teeth emerge from the jaw. When the animal bites, venom is expelled from the glands some distance from the teeth. The venom flows along a mucous fold between the lip and the lower jaw before reaching the front surface of the teeth. This is an inefficient method compared with the stabbing or biting stroke of vipers and cobras. Instead, Gila monsters must grip the prey or enemy tightly with both jaws and hang on to allow time for the venom to flow into the wound. Its jaws are very strong and difficult to disengage.

The poison produced is a neurotoxin that causes swelling, dizziness, drowsiness, vomiting, palpitations, swollen tongue, paralysis, labored breathing, and a fall in blood pressure. Some people unfortunate enough to have been bitten may experience just one or two symptoms. The swelling and pain that accompany a bite are due to the way in which the venom is injected. The lizard uses its vicelike grip to hold on, and chews with a sideways action of the teeth. It is possible for the elongated, inwardly curved, sharp teeth to break off and remain embedded in the victim. Teeth lost in this way are difficult to detect even using X-rays. Tissue destruction at the site of bites indicates that the venom also contains certain enzymes that play a role in digestion.

Gila venom is classified as sublethal, since there have been relatively few human deaths from it. Exhaustive studies have concluded that only eight to 10 people have ever died from beaded lizard bites. (It is interesting to note that all of them had consumed varying quantities of alcohol.) In the mid 1990s, as a result of studies on beaded lizard venom, pharmaceutical companies began experimenting with new treatments for diabetics based on elements of the venom. Even more recently the venom was found to have memory-enhancing properties, but more research will need to be done on this. Had the Gila monsters not been given protection, such medical advances would not have been possible.

A flaccid tail is an indication of poor condition in a Gila monster. As with other desert creatures, most of the moisture it needs is obtained from its food.

Reproduction

In the mating season Gila monsters have a structured social system in which dominance is established by male-to-male combat. Having spent much of the cooler months hibernating in burrows, they feed voraciously to regain body weight as soon as they emerge. Males become highly territorial in April, and wrestling matches take place. They frequently bite each other but are immune to the venom. Mating occurs in late spring and early summer. In late summer

females lay three to 12 elongated, leathery eggs, which they bury in a sunny spot near a stream at a depth of about 5 to 6 inches (13–15 cm). The eggs overwinter and hatch out about 10 months later.

Endangered Gila Monsters

Gila monsters live in small groups each with a home range of several acres. Although slow moving, they can travel several hundred yards a day. Much of their habitat has been reduced by human encroachment or destroyed by agriculture and industry. Deliberate killing through fear, superstition, or ignorance has depleted numbers further. Many Gila monsters have been collected for the reptile trade, and some have gone to institutions and serious herpetologists for captive breeding programs.

These lizards have enlarged lungs, which means that they need extra biotin (part of the vitamin B complex) to turn oxygen into carbon dioxide. In the wild this presents no problems, since fertilized eggs containing biotin form part of their diet; but in captivity many have been fed solely on unfertilized hens' eggs that lack biotin, with disastrous results.

Gila monster enjoy a degree of protection. In Arizona it is forbidden to keep them, but the law is not always enforced. They are listed in CITES Appendix II, and pressure is being applied to upgrade the listing to CITES Appendix I to further restrict the trade.

⬆ Gila monsters grip their prey very tightly in their jaws. Since most of their prey is small and defenseless, venom is not usually needed. Here a Gila monster feeds on a young rodent.

Common name Mexican beaded lizard

Scientific name *Heloderma horridum*

Family Helodermatidae

Suborder Sauria

Order Squamata

Size Up to 35 in (89 cm)

Key features Head rounded; nose blunt; neck quite long; body heavily built; limbs short with long claws on ends of digits; tail long; scales beadlike; eyelids movable; color variable according to subspecies, usually some shade of brown with yellow or cream markings; adults of one subspecies totally black

Habits Diurnal and nocturnal depending on the weather; also climbs trees; during hot weather spends much of daytime in rocky crevices and self-dug or preexisting burrows

Breeding Female lays 1 clutch of 7–10 eggs that hatch after 6 months

Diet Eggs of reptiles and birds, nestlings, small mammals, occasionally lizards

Habitat Edges of desert, thorn scrub, deciduous woodland

Distribution Western Mexico and Guatemala

Status Vulnerable (IUCN); listed in CITES Appendix II; also protected locally

Similar species *Heloderma suspectum*

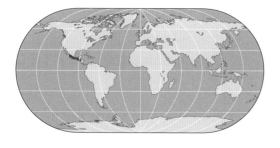

Mexican Beaded Lizard

Heloderma horridum

The Latin name for the Mexican beaded lizard means literally "horrible studded lizard." Its body is studded with beadlike scales, each containing a tiny piece of bone that gives it armor-plated skin.

ALTHOUGH THE MEXICAN BEADED LIZARD belongs to the same genus as the Gila monster, *Heloderma suspectum*, there are some differences between the two species. The Mexican beaded lizard is about 13 inches (33 cm) longer and lacks the two elongated cloacal scales. Coloration is also more subdued in the Mexican beaded lizard, and the patch of light-colored scales on the head is absent. Also its tail is longer and more tapering than that of the Gila monster.

The Mexican beaded lizard is more likely than the Gila monster to climb trees to hunt for birds and raid nests for eggs and nestlings. Its tail, which is not prehensile, is used as a counterbalance during hunting. If the tail is lost to a predator, it will not regenerate.

Strong Jaws

The main enemies of the Mexican beaded lizard are coyotes, a few raptorial birds, and humans. Its jaws are strong enough to crush prey, most of which is slow moving, so it is thought that its

⊕ *The Mexican beaded lizard is typically found in dry, open forest areas with plenty of rocks and sparse vegetation. It burrows to avoid the midday heat.*

Names and Legends

It is often thought that the Mexican beaded lizard's scientific name, *Heloderma horridum*, was given partly based on its appearance and partly as a result of its reputation for being venomous. It has been called "one of the most repulsive lizards known to man" and "the terrible one with the studded skin." In Spanish the Mexican beaded lizard is known as El Escorpion. The name comes from a Mexican legend that tells of a beautiful but dangerous creature capable of inflicting its sting on the leg of a human.

venom is used primarily for defense. As with the Gila monster, it gives the impression of being slow moving but is capable of "turning and snapping with the agility of an angry dog" (Ditmars—American naturalist and author).

Humans are responsible for the destruction and fragmentation of considerable tracts of habitat for slash-and-burn agriculture. In the process many Mexican beaded lizards are suffocated in their burrows. Despite protection by CITES and the Mexican government, the creatures still suffer from overcollection for a lucrative, illegal trade. Their venom is no defense against these enemies.

Reproduction

In some parts of its range the Mexican beaded lizard may undergo a short hibernation period; in other parts it remains fairly active during the winter. Mating takes place in early spring. Two months later seven to 10 elongated eggs are laid in a burrow about 5 inches (13 cm) deep. Unlike those of the Gila monster, the embryos are more developed at the time of laying and so do not overwinter. About 6 months later the hatchlings emerge.

Identifying the Subspecies

Taxonomists claim that there are four subspecies of the Mexican beaded lizard, although not all are recognized as valid, since the characteristics used to identify them overlap considerably. In 2000, in an attempt to solve the dilemma, a program of genetic analysis using DNA of both captive and wild Mexican beaded lizards was started. The four subspecies have been identified as:

Heloderma horridum horridum—has a wide range in Mexico from Sonora through Oaxaca; coloration is lightish brown with pale yellow or cream markings; the head is darker brown to black

Heloderma horridum exasperatum—ranging widely through southern Sonora and northern Sinaloa in subhumid tropics as well as arid areas; specimens of this subspecies have more yellow than *H. h. horridum*

Heloderma horridum alvarezi—has a restricted range in northern Chiapas and was named after a Mexican botanist; it is smaller than the other subspecies, and although young specimens have the familiar yellow markings, adults lose them and acquire a totally black coloration

Heloderma horridum charlesbogerti—inhabits a relatively small area in the Rio Montagua drainage system; it has larger yellow markings that end at the armpits

American Sunbeam Snake

Loxocemus bicolor

Loxocemus bicolor is a muscular snake with smooth, iridescent scales. It is reminiscent of the Asian sunbeam snake, among others, and over the years it has been placed in a number of different families, including the pythons.

Common name American sunbeam snake (American burrowing snake, burrowing python)

Scientific name *Loxocemus bicolor*

Family Loxocemidae

Suborder Serpentes

Order Squamata

Length From 39 in (100 cm) to 4.3 ft (1.3 m)

Key features Body cylindrical with small, shiny scales; head barely wider than its neck; snout pointed; appears iridescent; dark gray or brown in color with strange, irregular white spots over body; some individuals have large white areas, giving them an almost piebald appearance; pelvic girdles present as well as vestigial hind limbs in the form of small spurs

Habits Probably a burrower but also active on the surface; nocturnal

Breeding Egg layer, with small clutches of 2–5 eggs; eggs hatch after about 65 days

Diet Other reptiles, including their eggs, and rodents

Habitat Tropical forests, including dry deciduous forests

Distribution Central America from western Mexico to Costa Rica

Status Common

Similar species None in the region; superficially similar to the Asian sunbeam snakes, *Xenopeltis* species, with which it used to be classified

THE AMERICAN SUNBEAM SNAKE bears a superficial resemblance to snakes in several other families. This is coincidental, however, and the snake is not closely related to any of them. In fact, it has no close relatives and is placed in a family of its own, the Loxocemidae. It has a combination of primitive and advanced characteristics.

American sunbeam snakes are uncommon or hard to find, or both, and so little is known about their habits in the wild. Most herpetologists (people who study reptiles and amphibians) agree that they are nocturnal and spend the day in burrows or hidden in thick vegetation. They live in forest habitats.

The unusually pointed snout is often interpreted as a sign that American sunbeam snakes are burrowers, but that has not been confirmed. It seems more likely that they use their snout to grub through sand and soil in search of food, especially reptile eggs.

Eggs of the green iguana, *Iguana iguana*, are particular favorites, and the snakes feed heavily on them at certain times of the year. During the height of the iguana breeding season they may feed exclusively on these eggs. Since the eggs are buried about 12 inches (30 cm) down in the soil, the snakes must have some means of detecting them—presumably smell—and of reaching them. Where their habitat fringes on the coast, the snakes eat turtle eggs, which also have to be dug up.

Varied Markings

American sunbeam snakes have unusual markings in the form of randomly scattered

⤒ *The American sunbeam snake can be found in leaf litter, among piles of rocks, under logs, and along roadsides at night. It is a secretive snake whose habits are not fully known.*

patches of white scales. Some individuals have hardly any patches, while others are liberally speckled with them.

The hatchlings are uniform dark brown in color with an iridescent sheen. As they grow, white flecks appear on their bodies. These flecks may get progressively larger each time the snake sheds its skin, making the body almost completely white. As far as anybody knows, there are no other snakes with a similar pattern change (although many undergo a gradual transition in color or markings as they mature), and there is no obvious explanation for this unique characteristic.

Males use their spurs during courtship; and since they are razor sharp, they sometimes injure females, causing deep wounds on their backs. The female lays two to five elongated eggs but does not coil around them. They hatch after about 65 days.

Eggs on the Menu

Although American sunbeam snakes eat other prey apart from reptile eggs, their pointed snouts may be adaptations for digging eggs out of the ground. Evidence for this comes from other species of snakes that are well-known reptile-egg eaters and that have similar-shaped snouts.

They include the kukri snakes, *Oligodon,* that come from Southeast Asia, and of which there are almost 70 species. They all have slightly upturned snouts with which they root through the soil in search of food (although, like the American sunbeam snake, they also eat other prey). They get their common name from the shape of their enlarged sharp-edged teeth, which are supposed to resemble the curved kukri knives used by Nepalese Gurkha troops, and which they use to slit through the leathery shells of reptile eggs. *Oligodon* is paralleled in Africa by the shovel-snouted snake, *Prosymna*, which also has an upturned snout and feeds largely on reptile eggs. In the United States its counterpart is the leaf-nosed snake, *Phyllorhynchus*, which also has a tendency to eat reptile eggs, especially those of the banded gecko, *Coleonyx variegatus*.

Common name Texas thread snake (plains slender blind snake)

Scientific name *Leptotyphlops dulcis*

Family Leptotyphlopidae

Suborder Serpentes

Order Squamata

Length About 12 in (30 cm)

Key features Pinkish with smooth, shiny scales; body very slender; tail bears inconspicuous horny spike; eyes are darker patches

Habits Burrower, rarely coming onto the surface and only at night

Breeding Egg layer, with clutches of up to 8 eggs

Diet Larvae and pupae of ants and termites, as well as other soft-bodied invertebrates

Habitat Prairies, lightly wooded places, and bare, rocky hillsides, but usually where there is some moisture in the soil

Distribution Southeastern United States west to Arizona and adjacent parts of northeastern Mexico

Status Common in suitable habitat, although rarely seen

Subspecies *Leptotyphlops dulcis dulcis*, the plains thread snake, and *L. d. dissectus*, the New Mexico thread snake

Similar species Western thread snake, *Leptotyphlops humilis*

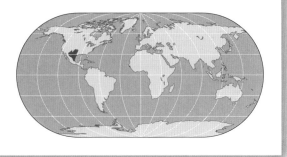

Texas Thread Snake

Leptotyphlops dulcis

The smallest snake in the United States, the Texas thread snake is frequently overlooked. Since it spends most of its life underground, some aspects of its lifestyle remain a mystery.

TEXAS THREAD SNAKES look more like earthworms than snakes and no doubt are often mistaken for them. On picking the snakes up, however, the differences are quite clear: The skin of the thread snakes feels hard and shiny, and the body is muscular and nowhere near as flexible as that of a worm. Close examination reveals the features that identify them as snakes. They are slender, cylindrical, and of uniform thickness from the head to the tip of the tail, which has a short horny spine that is more easily felt than seen. They probably use the spine to gain purchase on the ground when crawling or burrowing. The body is covered in smooth, shiny silvery-pink scales, and the eyes are reduced to dark spots under the scales. The snout is blunt, and the head is covered with large scales similar to those on the rest of the body. In common with all members of the family Leptotyphlopidae, they lack the normal wide belly scales associated with other snakes.

Shy but Sociable

The habits and social behavior of the Texas thread snakes are still largely a mystery—a smallish snake that spends most of its time underground is hard to study. We know that they prefer moist, crumbly soil and are most commonly seen in the spring. Later in the year, when the surface becomes baked hard by the sun, they go deeper or find moisture beneath partly buried logs and boulders.

There they often live together in loosely associated groups, having apparently found each other by following scent trails. Chemical communication is important in their social life

⊕ **Leptotyphlops dulcis**, *the Texas thread snake. As its name suggests, it is a very slender snake with an indistinct head. Its body can range from pink to gray to tan, and it usually has a metallic sheen.*

and, apparently, in finding prey. They often turn up in ant or termite nests.

Because they are small, defenseless, and look like earthworms, thread snakes are on the menu of a wide range of predators, including small mammals such as skunks and armadillos, birds, and other snakes. Although they have little defense against attack, some individuals pretend to be dead when they are picked up. They also use their tail spines to press against the predator's skin, but it is hard to imagine that this has any significant effect.

A similar species, the western thread snake, *Leptotyphlops humilis*, occurs farther west, and in western Texas the ranges of the two species overlap. They have similar lifestyles and can be distinguished only after close examination: The Texas thread snakes have a cluster of three small scales on the crown of the head between the eyes, while the western thread snakes have only one scale in that position.

A Curious Partnership

One predator of the Texas thread snake is the eastern screech owl, *Otus asio*, with which the snake has a strange association. Adult owls bring thread snakes to their nests, presumably to feed their young. Some of the snakes wriggle free, however, and set up home among the twigs and debris of the owls' nests.

In one study 18 percent of nests contained live Texas thread snakes. Here they live off the larvae of flies and other parasitic insects that are attracted to the owls' nests. Researchers found that young owls living in nests where thread snakes occurred grew more quickly than those in nests without thread snakes (presumably because they carried fewer parasites, since the snakes had eaten many of them).

It seems unlikely, however, that the snakes benefit greatly from the association with the owls. Once the young owls leave their nest, the snakes' food source runs out, and their chances of surviving for more than a few months would be slim unless they simply drop to the ground and crawl away.

Common name Common boa (boa constrictor)

Scientific name *Boa constrictor*

Family Boidae

Suborder Serpentes

Order Squamata

Length Up to 13 ft (4 m) but often much smaller; island forms rarely more than 6.5 ft (2 m)

Key features Head wedge shaped; a dark line runs through each eye, widening toward the angle of the mouth; background color gray, brown, tan, or pink, with a series of large rounded saddles in maroon or dark brown down the back; tail saddles may be reddish

Habits Arboreal or terrestrial; often enters the water and is a good swimmer

Breeding Bears up to 60 live young but more commonly 10–15

Diet Small mammals; birds

Habitat Very adaptable; rain forests, deciduous forests, dry scrub, and even beaches; often common around human settlements

Distribution From northwestern Mexico through Central America and into South America as far as northern Argentina; also found on some West Indian islands (St. Lucia and Dominica)

Status Generally common, but some subspecies (e.g., Argentine boa, *B. c. occidentalis*) are Endangered (CITES Appendices)

Similar species None

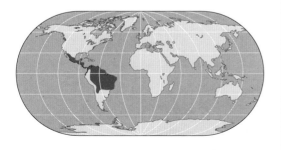

Common Boa

Boa constrictor

The common boa, or "boa constrictor," suffers greatly from its deadly reputation and is often persecuted by people. However, it is not dangerous to humans.

ALTHOUGH THE COMMON BOA is a massive snake by any standards, it is actually only the sixth biggest. Until quite recently its maximum size was thought to be 18.5 feet (5.6 m), from a specimen killed in Trinidad during World War II by a malaria control party. In recent years, however, doubt has been cast not so much on the size of that specimen but on its identity. It seems that the gigantic "boa constrictor" was, in fact, an anaconda.

Leaving aside this dubious record, the largest common boa came from Brazil and measured 14.8 feet (4.5 m). Common boas are also quite heavy bodied, so any snake over 10 feet (3 m) in length would be capable of eating a large dog, for instance. However, it is highly unlikely that they would take human prey.

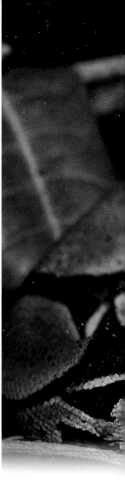

⬆ *The characteristic dark line running through each eye toward the mouth is obvious on this common boa from northern Brazil.*

⬅ *A 19th-century engraving showing South American hunters stringing up a common boa from a tree in order to skin it. Boas are still hunted for their skins.*

➡ *The pelvic spurs of this male common boa can be clearly seen. The spurs are used in mating.*

Spurs

All boas, pythons, and most other primitive snakes have "spurs" in the form of small thornlike structures on either side of their cloaca. They are the remains of their limbs and are attached to the pelvic girdle that is present in these species. But what use are they?

Although the spurs are largely vestigial—they are the remains of structures that have become redundant through evolution and are in the process of disappearing altogether—males use them in courtship. When the male approaches a female, he crawls along her back. More advanced snakes often make regular twitching movements at this stage, but male boas and pythons use their spurs to scratch the

female's skin. When the spurs are moved backward and forward, they seem to stimulate the female into raising her tail so that mating can take place. In species that have them, the spurs of males are nearly always significantly longer than those of the females, whose spurs may be so small that they are difficult to see. In a few species of dwarf boas females lack spurs altogether, although males have them.

Characteristics

The species is distinctive and difficult to mistake for any other snake because of its size. Young common boas, however, may be confused with several other species, including venomous pit vipers, and are often killed in the belief that they are dangerous. The basic color of a typical common boa is silvery gray with about 25 large saddles (blotches) of dark brown or reddish brown. The saddles near the tail tend to be of a richer color than those on the front end of the body. Variations in color depend to some extent on where the specimen comes from.

Up to 10 subspecies have been named, but not all of them are recognized by everyone. A common feature found on all forms of boa constrictor is the pair of wedge-shaped lines that start at the snake's snout and lead backward, through each eye, becoming broader as they reach the angle of the mouth. Another thin line starts just behind the snout and runs back along the top of the head, continuing as far as the nape of the neck. The markings on the head, body, and tail serve to break up the

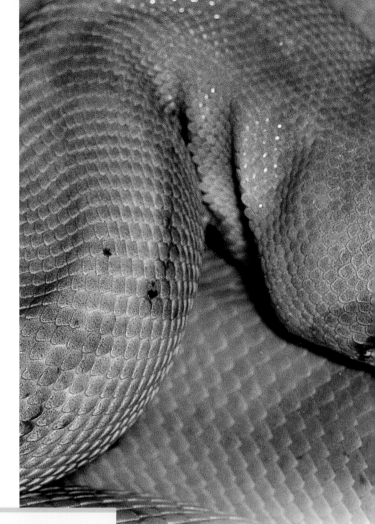

snake's shape and are a good example of disruptive coloration. Common boas' scales are small, and the skin has a silky texture. There is a pair of large scales, or spurs, on either side of the cloaca.

Variations

Boas living in cooler conditions tend to be darker, and the Argentine form, *Boa constrictor occidentalis*, has an overall filigree pattern in black obscuring its markings. Other forms have tan or pinkish background colors, and the colors of the saddles may be especially bright in specimens from Peru, Guyana, and Surinam, for example. They are the so-called "red-tailed" boas that are simply color forms (meaning they are the same in all other respects but color).

The form from Dominica in the West Indies is known as the clouded boa, *B. c. nebulosa*. It is darker in color than mainland forms, and the blotches on its back may be completely obscured in older snakes. The St. Lucia form, *B. c. orophias,* also has poorly defined blotches down its back, and their shape may be less regular than the blotches on typical boas. Boas from small islands off the coast of Honduras are often paler and much more pink than those from the mainland. They can change color to a limited degree, becoming lighter at night.

Habitat and Distribution

Taken as a whole, the various forms of boa constrictor have a huge range. In the north the snake occurs up the west coast of Mexico as far as Guaymas in Sinaloa, while in the south it reaches northern Argentina and Paraguay. As the habitat varies within this area, so the boa constrictor has adapted to a wide range of situations and climates. It is usually considered to be a snake of the rain forest, where it climbs into trees in search of prey such as roosting birds. It hides itself away in hollow tree trunks, caves, or crevices during the day and becomes

Boa Distribution

At first glance it seems unlikely that the common boa, *Boa constrictor*, and the three Madagascan boas, such as Dumeril's boa, *B. dumerili*, are closely related, since they come from opposite sides of the world. Continental drift, however, provides the explanation. About 100 million years ago, at a time when the early snakes were beginning to diversify, South America, Africa, and Madagascar were joined together as a Southern Hemisphere landmass known as Gondwanaland. As it broke apart and the separate pieces drifted away from each other, numbers of a boa ancestor were presumably trapped on each of the new landmasses. In South America it evolved into the common boa, and on Madagascar it evolved into three separate species. In Africa it died out, possibly due to competition with pythons. Apart from the boas, Madagascar shares a number of other animal families with South America, such as iguanas, which are also absent from the African mainland.

sometimes at the cost of some domestic poultry. However, they are often persecuted in the belief that they are dangerous.

They also live in arid, scrubby habitats in coastal Mexico and in the more open countryside of Argentina and Paraguay, where they have few opportunities to climb at all. Climatic conditions may dictate that they become dormant for several months of the year in some places, while they are continually active in others. Those in tropical lowlands may be more active during the day, even basking in exposed places in order to raise their body temperatures.

Common boas eat lizards, mammals, and birds. Newborn young are large enough to tackle prey up to the size of mice or small rats. As they grow, the range of prey they take increases. A 3-foot (1-m) long boa will easily take prey up to the size of a domestic chicken, and adults can handle medium- to large-sized mammals. They regularly eat white-tailed deer where they occur.

Their method of hunting is typical "sit-and-wait." They often coil just inside the entrance to a hollow tree or a mammal burrow and wait for prey to come within range. At other times they home in on places where numbers of possible prey are likely to congregate, such as fruiting forest trees.

Although common boas do not have the heat-sensitive pits that characterize some other members of the family, they do have temperature-sensitive nerve endings in the scales of the head. They help them locate and pinpoint warm-blooded prey even in darkness. When suitable prey has been located and identified, the boa lunges forward at great speed with its mouth agape, ready to grasp the prey with its backward-pointing teeth. As soon as contact is made, it immediately throws several coils of its body around the victim. Constriction may take some time, during which the snake progressively tightens its coils each time the prey takes a breath, until it becomes

On Hog Island (Cayo de los Cochinos), Honduras, a lighter-colored form of the common boa is found. It reaches about 5 feet (1.5 m) long and is often pinkish gray, although it can change color and be milky white, orange, or lemon depending on the time of day.

active at night or in the evening and early morning.

Large boas are not fast-moving snakes and often travel in a straight line (using rectilinear locomotion) when they are moving across the ground. When climbing, they do so slowly and deliberately, often using concertina locomotion to make their way up tree trunks and along branches.

Due to their great bulk adult common boas are limited to climbing large limbs of trees and often rest in the fork of two thick branches. Unlike more specialized tree boas, they are not able to span large distances between branches. Although not especially aquatic, common boas are good swimmers.

Rat Catchers

Common boas are often found around human settlements, where they perform a useful service in keeping down rat populations,

unable to fill its lungs. When the snake senses the prey is dead, it slowly releases its coils. Swallowing starts with the head and for large prey items may take an hour or more.

Breeding

The breeding habits of common boas are hardly known in the wild, but they are widely bred in captivity. Information from both sources shows that those from tropical populations prefer to mate during the cooler parts of the year, but year-round matings have been recorded. However, populations from regions with a well-defined cold season, such as northern Argentina, probably mate in spring (but there are no field observations to confirm this).

The gestation period lasts about six months, and a litter consists of 6 to 60 young, with the older and larger females producing the largest litters. A typical medium-sized boa of about 6 feet (1.5 m) in length will usually give birth to about 10 to 15 young.

Human Adversaries

Common boas have a number of enemies, including birds of prey and carnivorous mammals. As they grow, the number of animals that can harm them diminishes, and they may even be able to turn the tables on some of them—a captured adult boa has been seen to eat an ocelot. By the time they are 6.5 feet (2 m) long, they probably have few natural enemies apart from humans. Boas are hunted for food and for their skins, and are killed by traffic. Boas are also collected for the pet trade, although most of the demand in recent years has been met by captive breeding—wild common boas are protected internationally by CITES regulations. Their main means of defense is to retreat into a hole or crevice; but if cornered, they defend themselves vigorously by hissing loudly and lunging repeatedly. A bite from a large boa can cause serious injury.

⊖ *A newborn common boa emerging frm its egg sac. Each newborn snake measures 18 to 24 inches (50 to 75 cm) in length.*

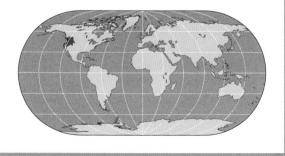

Rubber Boa

Charina bottae

There could hardly be a greater contrast than that between the gigantic anaconda and the diminutive and inoffensive rubber boa—yet they both belong to the same family of snakes.

ALTHOUGH THE RUBBER BOA is several orders of magnitude smaller than its giant relatives, it is also a powerful constrictor and has many other aspects of behavior, form, and structure in common with them. It is a member of the Erycinae, the subfamily of boas that is found mainly in Africa and the Far East, with just two species (the rubber boa, *Charina bottae*, and the rosy boa, *Charina trivirgata*) occurring in the New World.

Like the other members of the subfamily, the rubber boas are primarily burrowing snakes. Their cylindrical body, small shiny scales, and blunt snout are all indicators of this lifestyle. They do not burrow through packed soil, however, but push their way through more loosely packed substrates such as leaf litter and carpets of pine needles. Despite that, they are also good climbers and may enter birds' nests in low bushes and shrubs in order to eat the nestlings. They also swim well.

Nest Invaders

Young rodents are the most common prey for rubber boas, however. They often enter a nest and eat all the young in a litter, consuming their own body weight in a single meal. Rubber boas are slow moving and do not expend much energy, so they eat very infrequently—a good meal can last several weeks.

When feeding in rodent nests, rubber boas must frequently come under attack from parents defending their young. Furthermore, being small and superficially wormlike in appearance, they are potential prey for a wide range of insectivorous birds and small mammals. Their strategy under these circumstances is to hide their head in the

Common name Rubber boa

Scientific name *Charina bottae*

Family Boidae

Suborder Serpentes

Order Squamata

Length Up to 31 in (79 cm); usually 12 in (30 cm)

Key features Looks and feels "rubbery"; brown, olive, or tan in color; body stocky and cylindrical; tail and head blunt in shape; top of head covered with large scales; eyes small; no heat pits; body scales are tiny, adding to the smooth, silky feel; small spurs on either side of cloaca, larger in males than in females

Habits Remains hidden during the day under bark or logs or in the burrows of small mammals; active at night even in quite low temperatures, when it hunts by poking around in crevices and entering rodent nests

Breeding Bears live young; litters of 2–8 young

Diet Small mammals, birds (especially nestlings), salamanders, lizards, and snakes

Habitat Grassland, scrub, light woodland, and conifer forests in mountains

Distribution Western North America from British Columbia, Canada, to southern California and inland to central Wyoming; distribution patchy, only occurring where there is suitable habitat

Status Protected (CITES Appendix II) and nationally; probably not rare, but suffers from habitat destruction and collecting for the pet trade

Similar species None in the area; at least 3 subspecies recognized, but differences between them are slight, and they are not easily told apart

middle of their coils and raise their tail. Because the tail is blunt and similar in shape to the head, it takes the brunt of pecks and bites while the real head is protected. Adult rubber boas frequently have scars on their tails as evidence of these bouts.

A closely related snake is the Calabar ground boa, *Charina reinhardtii* from West Africa, which behaves in an identical way. In many ways it is a larger counterpart of the rubber boa, with the important exception that it lays eggs instead of bearing live young.

Rubber boas are more tolerant of cold than other members of their family and are frequently found in areas that have temperatures well below freezing in winter. In the Lagunas Mountains of southern California, for example, their habitat may be covered in snow well into March or even April.

Breeding

Under such conditions rubber boas have a short season of activity. Mating takes place in the spring, and the young are born three to four months later. The most common litter size is three or four, but litters of two to eight have been recorded. The young boas are threadlike and lighter in color than their parents, but they are capable of constricting and swallowing newborn mice. They probably reach breeding size in three to four years.

Although populations of rubber boas in the wild have been poorly studied, other species with similar habits and lifestyle have been observed in captivity. It is thought that female rubber boas only breed every two or three years. They need the years in between to recoup the body weight they have lost and regain breeding condition.

⊕ *An accomplished burrower, the rubber boa remains hidden during the day. However, if discovered, it is docile and curls into a ball when picked up.*

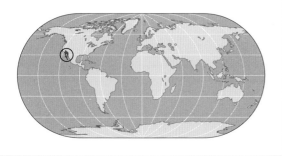

Common name Rosy boa

Scientific name *Charina trivirgata*

Family Boidae

Suborder Serpentes

Order Squamata

Length From 24 in (60 cm) to 39 in (100 cm)

Key features Body stout, with a thick neck so that the narrow head is not distinct from the body; head covered with many small scales; eyes small; no heat pits; various colors, usually arranged in 3 longitudinal stripes on a lighter background

Habits Active at night and in the evening; mainly terrestrial but climbs well among rocks

Breeding Bears live young with litters of up to 12, although 4–6 is more typical

Diet Small mammals and birds

Habitat Rocky deserts and scrub, often along dried watercourses and near oases

Distribution Southwestern North America from southern California and Arizona throughout the length of the Baja California peninsula and into western Sonora (Mexico)

Status Common in suitable habitat; large numbers are killed on the road; also collected for the pet trade despite being protected (CITES Appendix II)

Similar species None in the region; the young of some forms could be mistaken for rubber boa, *Charina bottae*, which favors a different habitat

Rosy Boa
Charina trivirgata

The rosy boa is a delicate-looking snake that hardly seems capable of making its living in some of the most inhospitable regions of the American Southwest and neighboring parts of Mexico. Along with the Gila monster, chuckwalla, and desert tortoise, the rosy boa is a characteristic reptile of the Southwestern deserts.

ROSY BOAS ARE QUITE SPECIFIC in their habitat preferences. They occur from sea level to about 5,000 feet (1,500 m), but their main requirement is for rocky places. They are found on well-drained mountain slopes and foothills and also along the bottoms of canyons and gullies where water collects at least occasionally. They appear not to need water themselves, however, and are probably attracted to such places because their preferred prey species are more numerous there.

The jumbled volcanic landscapes of Baja California, with its scattered rock outcrops, boojum trees, and elephant trees, and the high deserts of southern California and Arizona—dotted with numerous cactus and agave plants—are typical places in which to find them, even though they are rarely seen.

Warm Nights

During the spring and summer they are almost entirely nocturnal, although they may become active in the late afternoon in early spring, when nighttime temperatures are too cold for them. The rocky outcrops among which they live provide plenty of hiding places when they are resting. By going deeper into crevices, they can also escape the extremes of the weather. Ideal conditions for rosy boas are warm nights, ideally above 82°F (28°C), when they will venture out in search of food.

The rosy boa shares many physical characteristics with the other members of the subfamily (which are burrowing snakes), such as a short tail, smooth scales, and a cylindrical body. However, they do not have the flattened head and the shovel-shaped snout of the sand boas, for example. Also, they are rarely able to burrow in the packed, gravelly soil that covers much of their range. Neither they fast moving—they crawl slowly between boulders and in crevices looking for small mammals and ground-nesting birds.

They climb well and will scale vertical rock faces while foraging. Individuals living near roads may cross them in the course of their activities, and large numbers are killed by traffic—sometimes accidentally, but often deliberately. If rosy boas feel threatened, they often freeze, hoping to escape notice, a perilous strategy when vehicles approach.

When handled, rosy boas rarely attempt to bite but will often crawl gently between the fingers, seemingly unconcerned. If they are treated roughly, however, they coil into a ball with their head in the center. Should the rough treatment persist, they may secrete a foul-smelling fluid from their cloaca and attempt to smear it over their tormentor. This is designed to encourage predators to drop them.

Squashed to Death

Like the rest of the Boidae, rosy boas are constrictors but will often kill their prey by squeezing it against a hard surface rather than coiling around it. This may be an adaptation to feeding in burrows, where there is little room to form coils. Rosy boas are reluctant to take very large prey and seem to prefer meals consisting of several small items rather than one large one. Again, this may be associated with their

⊕ *A rosy boa eating a mouse. Rosy boas prefer to feed on a number of smaller prey items rather than tackle a larger victim.*

habit of feeding in mammal burrows or birds' nests, where they will usually eat the complete litter or brood. Their close relative the rubber boa, *Charina bottae*, has almost the same feeding habits.

Male rosy boas have prominent spurs, while those of females are small and hard to see. There is little information about courtship in rosy boas, but it is likely that males locate females by chemical trails that they lay down when they are in breeding condition. They mate in the early summer after a rather unexciting courtship in which the male scratches the female's back with his spurs to stimulate her.

Females that have mated stop feeding shortly after mating. The gestation period lasts for 14 to 20 weeks depending on temperature. The young, measuring about 8 inches (20 cm), are born from September to November. Depending on the location, rosy boas (including the young) may become inactive during the winter months. The young reach sexual maturity at three to four years of age and can live for 18 years or more in captivity.

⊕ *The central Baja rosy boa—subspecies* **C. t. saslowi,** *is the most colorful of the rosy boa subspecies. Its orange stripes stand out well against its paler background color.*

Naming and Classification

The rosy boa has only recently been added to the genus *Charina* along with the rubber boa and the Calabar ground boa, *Charina reinhardtii.* Prior to this it was placed in a genus of its own, *Lichanura,* and is still listed as such in many older publications. The old name comes from the Greek words *lichanos,* meaning "forefinger," and *oura,* which means "tail." The name is very apt because its tail does indeed look like a human forefinger, being thick, blunt, and of about the same length. It has a stout cylindrical body that is not very muscular. Its skin is soft and supple owing to the covering of small scales, and its similarity to the rubber boa, the only other North American member of the Erycinae, is quite obvious.

Variations

Although there is only one species of rosy boa, it is divided into four subspecies that are color variations of the same theme. The pattern

C. t. myriolepis, is from southwestern Arizona and parts of southern California. Its stripes are orange-brown and have ragged edges, while the background color may be cream or gray. Finally, the central Baja rosy boa, *C. t. saslowi,* is the most colorful of the subspecies. Its orange stripes are straight and well defined, and the background is buff.

Where the ranges of two subspecies meet, snakes may have intermediate markings, and there are also several isolated populations that have quite distinctive markings. An additional subspecies, *C. t. bostici*, was described from Cedros Island, off Baja California, but most herpetologists think that this is not valid and that it is, in fact, *C. t. trivirgata*.

Of the four subspecies the coastal form, *C. t. roseofusca,* is the most distinctive. It lives in a less barren habitat and grows larger than the others: All the largest specimens belong to this form. Perhaps because of its size it also has the largest litters of young—up to 12—while the others rarely have more than four or five.

consists of three wide stripes starting on the snake's neck and running the length of its body and onto its tail.

In the Mexican rosy boa, *C. t. trivirgata*, the stripes are deep chocolate-brown or black, and the background is pale beige. The coastal rosy boa, *C. t. roseofusca* from the border region, has stripes that are brown but poorly defined because they differ little from the slaty-gray background, and some older individuals are uniform in color. The desert rosy boa,

Rosy Boas and the Pet Trade

The different color forms of the rosy boas, together with their gentle nature and adaptability, have made them popular with collectors and amateur snake breeders. In the past large numbers were taken from the wild. Rosy boas are easily picked out in car headlights; and because they are slow moving and docile, they are easily caught. Collection from the wild and international trade in these snakes are strictly regulated (the boas are listed in CITES Appendix II and come under federal and state protection).

Many populations of rosy boas live in national parks and monuments, notably Organ Pipe Cactus National Park in Arizona and Joshua Tree National Park and the Anza-Borrego Desert Conservation Area in California. Unfortunately, unscrupulous collectors poach rosy boas from the wild and sell them, claiming that they are bred in captivity—there are no restrictions on the trade in captive-bred rosy boas. In addition, traffic kills, urban development, and the resulting fragmentation of the snake's habitat are also affecting populations. Numbers also decline during periods of drought, which seem to be occurring more frequently in the part of the world in which they live.

Common name Western shovel-nosed snake

Scientific name *Chionactis occipitalis*

Subfamily Colubrinae

Family Colubridae

Suborder Serpentes

Order Squamata

Length 10 in (25 cm) to 17 in (43 cm)

Key features Small snake with shiny scales; pattern
consists of black bars across a cream-colored
background; snakes from some areas have
secondary bars of red between the black
ones; lower jaw deeply inset, and snout is
flattened like a shovel

Habits Burrowing, active on the surface at night

Breeding Egg layer with 2–4 eggs laid in summer

Diet Invertebrates

Habitat Deserts

Distribution Southwestern North America

Status Common in suitable habitat

Similar species The Sonoran shovel-nosed snake,
C. palarostris, has wider red bars, and the
banded sand snake, *Chilomeniscus cinctus*,
has a darker ground color and fewer rows of
scales around its midbody; banded forms of
the ground snake, *Sonora semiannulata*, lack
the flattened head and shovel-shaped snout

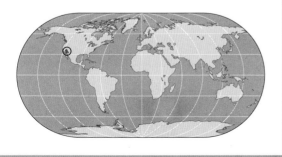

Western Shovel-Nosed Snake *Chionactis occipitalis*

*Shovel-nosed snakes are "sand swimmers"—species
that live in loose sand and force their way through it
by wriggling rapidly from side to side as though they
were swimming.*

DUE TO THE NATURE of the layer in which shovel-nosed snakes live, they do not form permanent
tunnel systems because the sand collapses
behind them. To stop the sand from clogging
their nostrils, they have valves to keep them
closed when they are moving; for a similar
reason the lower jaws are underslung. The head
is flattened, and the upper jaws have a wedge-shaped profile that meets with little resistance
as the snake moves through the sand.

Desert Trails

Their method of locomotion makes their choice
of habitat rather limited. In the Lower Colorado
River Valley they can be found in areas where
sand has accumulated between the
characteristic vegetation of the region: creosote
bushes, mesquite, cholla cacti, and agaves. In
places there are quite large expanses of suitable
habitat, such as dune systems or smaller
pockets such as gulleys and shallow basins
between rocks and outcrops, and river washes
where finer material has collected. During the
day the snakes remain under the surface and
may prefer to stay among the roots of desert
plants. At night, however, they emerge to hunt
on the surface, and shovel-nosed snakes can
sometimes be seen crossing roads at night.
Their presence can often be established by
looking for their tracks; as they cross open areas
of sand between bushes, they leave
characteristic wavy trails.

They feed on arthropods such as spiders,
scorpions, centipedes, insects and their larvae,
and the buried pupae (chrysalids) of moths.
Night-active insects such as crickets and
cockroaches tend to figure most heavily in their

Other Sand Swimmers

Although there are snakes in other parts of the world that swim through sand and soil, most of the reptiles in this category are lizards. They include a number of skinks whose smooth, shiny scales help them slide through the particles of sand. Many species have reduced limbs that they lay alongside their bodies when they are moving rapidly, including the well-named sandfish, *Scincus scincus,* while some have lost their limbs altogether. They include a whole subfamily of African legless skinks, the Acontinae, with 18 species.

diet. In captivity shovel-nosed snakes emerge from the sand in the early evening regardless of whether there is a light on in their cage or not. If crickets are placed in the cage, however, they will often come up out of the sand at any time.

A closely related species, the organ pipe shovel-nosed snake, *Chionactis palarostris,* also occurs in the American Southwest. The two snakes avoid competition

⊕ *Western shovel-nosed snakes from the south of the species' range have secondary bars of red between the black ones. Their pattern may have evolved to mimic that of dangerous coral snakes.*

with each other by using slightly different habitats. *C. palarostris* lives in the upper rocky deserts of southern Arizona and northern Sonora, Mexico, among the saguaro cactus and the palo verde trees. In the United States it is only found in and just outside the Organ Pipe Cactus National Monument in Arizona. The ground in this region is rockier and more irregular, and the little snake presumably adapts its methods of locomotion to suit the terrain. It is more brightly colored than *C. occipitalis* with wider and brighter red bands between the black ones. Since its range is entirely within that of the Arizona coral snake, *Micruroides euryxanthus,* it may be mimicking this venomous species. The western shovel-nosed snake's range, however, is mostly outside that of the coral snake.

The third sand swimmer in the region is the banded sand snake, *Chilomeniscus cinctus*. It lives in loose sand and usually moves around just below the surface. When the sand collapses behind it, it leaves distinctive furrows, which may be the only clue that the species is there.

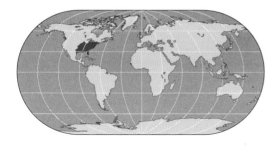

**Black ratsnake
(Elaphe obsoleta obsoleta)**

Common name American
ratsnake (black, Everglades, gray, Texas,
or yellow ratsnake)

Scientific name *Elaphe obsoleta*

Subfamily Colubrinae

Family Colubridae

Suborder Serpentes

Order Squamata

Length From 39 in (1 m) to 8.1 ft (2.5 m)

Key features Long, muscular body; color varies
depending on subspecies; juveniles marked
differently than adults except in the gray
ratsnake; scales weakly keeled on the back
but smooth on the sides; distinct ridge along
either side of the belly, which helps them
climb

Habits Terrestrial and arboreal; black ratsnake swims
well

Breeding Egg layer with clutches of 10–20 eggs,
exceptionally up to 40 or more; eggs hatch
after about 70 days

Diet Small mammals and birds

Habitat Varied but usually in places with trees; forest
edges, thinly wooded hillsides, and
hammocks

Distribution Throughout the eastern half of the United
States

Status Common

Similar species Black form, *E. obsoleta obsoleta*, may be
mistaken for the black racer, *Coluber
constrictor*, but that species has smooth
scales and is fast moving

American Ratsnake

Elaphe obsoleta

*The American ratsnake is a powerful, impressive snake
that manages to live in almost any situation owing to
its great adaptability. In its various forms it is found
throughout the eastern half of North America.*

THERE ARE FIVE FORMS OF AMERICAN ratsnake. In the
north the black form, *Elaphe obsoleta obsoleta*,
lives on rocky, timbered hillsides and forest
edges. Farther south the yellow and Everglades
ratsnakes (*E. o. quadrivittata* and *E. o.
rossalleni*) live in coastal and inland swamps of
the Carolinas and Florida, where they forage on
drier ground among the cypress trees and live
oaks. The other two forms, the gray and Texas
ratsnakes (*E. o. spiloide and E. o. lindheimeri*),
live in a range of intermediate habitats. All
ratsnakes seem partial to abandoned buildings,
which are the easiest places to find them.

Ratsnakes usually stop moving when
disturbed, in the hope that they will escape
notice. They sometimes draw their body up into
a series of bends, perhaps to form a less regular
shape and blend into the background better or
perhaps to be ready for "flight or fight."

Pretend Rattlesnakes

If they think they have been discovered, they
often raise the front third of the body and draw
back their head, forming an "s"-shaped curve
with the neck. At the same time, they open the
mouth slightly and make a loud, prolonged hiss
and vibrate their tail rapidly. If they happen to
be resting among dead leaves, they produce a
sound not unlike that of a rattlesnake, designed
to intimidate their enemies. If all else fails, they
lunge out, often so forcefully that they almost
leave the ground. However, there seems to be a
difference in temperament between the
subspecies, with the Texas form having the
reputation for being the most aggressive, and
the gray ratsnake usually being relatively calm.

⊕ **Elaphe obsoleta
rossalleni**, *the Everglades
ratsnake, with jaws
agape in a display of
aggression. The true,
nearly patternless
Everglades ratsnakes
have a very small
distribution. They
intergrade with the
yellow ratsnake where
the ranges of the two
subspecies meet.*

Yellow ratsnakes, **Elaphe obsoleta quadrivittata,** *occur in the coastal regions of the Carolinas, central Georgia, and Florida. They are often found in citrus groves, pasture lands, and abandoned buildings.*

All American ratsnakes are great climbers. They use ridges at the edges of their ventral scales to hook onto irregularities in tree bark and wind slowly upward by concertina locomotion. They feed on arboreal mammals such as squirrels and nestling birds. They are efficient nest raiders and are frequently mobbed by the parents of the nestlings and other nearby birds. They often rest in tree hollows and return to the same place time and again.

Adult black ratsnakes patrol a well-defined home range. They use different parts of it at different times of the year according to whether they are actively feeding, looking for a mate, or hibernating. In places they switch from hunting for arboreal birds' nests to those of bank swallows, *Riparia riparia.* The birds live in colonies that provide the snakes with the opportunity to eat well for very little effort. Apart from climbing, they also swim well and can stay underwater for up to an hour.

American ratsnakes are active mainly in the day, with peaks of activity in the early morning and late afternoon. In midsummer they may become more active later in the evening to avoid the heat of the day. In Canada they may hibernate for up to seven months, secreting themselves in hollow trees, caves, or old buildings. Several individuals may use the same hibernaculum, and it is not unusual to find them sharing with other species of snakes. Farther south the period of hibernation gradually reduces: In Florida, for example, they can be active all year long, sheltering for a few days at a time if the weather turns cold.

Mating Rivalry

In populations that hibernate, breeding activity typically begins immediately after the snakes emerge (in April or May), once they have shed their skin. Males are very competitive and engage in vigorous combat. They raise the front half of their bodies, intertwining them, and trying to force their opponent to the ground. Mating takes place after these bouts, and the female lays her eggs about

40 days later. Rotting tree stumps or piles of dead leaves are favorite places. A typical clutch contains 10 to 20 eggs, although much larger clutches have been recorded—the record was 44. As in all snakes, larger females lay larger clutches. The pure white, slightly oval eggs are tacky when laid so that they stick together and form a large single cluster. Sometimes several females lay their clutches in the same place—a communal nest of 76 eggs was once recorded.

The eggs hatch about 70 days after they have been laid, and the young snakes measure about 10 to 12 inches (25 to 30 cm) in length. Their first food is usually nestling mice, but they may also take small lizards and frogs. They reach maturity in about two to four years depending on where they live. Snakes in the northern part of the range that hibernate for up to half of each year grow more slowly than those from the south, which feed more or less throughout the year. Southern snakes also have an extended breeding season and may even lay more than one clutch of eggs in a single year.

Changing Colors

American ratsnakes undergo a dramatic color change (known as ontogenetic color change). Hatchlings are pale gray with darker blotches along their back. As they grow, the background color changes gradually, and the blotches fade (except in the gray ratsnake, which does not have a color change). In the black ratsnake the overall color darkens until it is nearly uniform black by the time it is about two years of age.

The Texas ratsnake goes through a similar change, but its blotches never disappear completely. In the yellow and Everglades ratsnakes the background color slowly changes from light gray to pale yellow or orange respectively as the blotches fade. Traces of four longitudinal stripes gradually become apparent. By the time they are adult, there is no sign of the blotches, but the stripes are well defined.

⊙ *A young Texas ratsnake,* Elaphe obsoleta lindheimeri. *The opaque cast on its eye indicates that it is ready to shed its skin.*

American Ratsnake Subspecies

There are five subspecies of *Elaphe obsoleta*. From north to south of their range the first is *E. obsoleta obsoleta,* the black ratsnake. Adults are totally black or black with traces of lighter markings. Next is *E. o. spiloide,* the gray ratsnake or oak snake. It is light- to medium-gray with dark brown or gray blotches along its back. It is the only form of *Elaphe obsoleta* in which adults and juveniles look the same.

The third subspecies is *E. o. lindheimeri*, the Texas ratsnake. It is a blotched form, with an indistinct pattern. It often has reddish areas between its scales. *E. o. quadrivittata,* the yellow ratsnake or chicken snake, is the fourth subspecies. It is yellow or pale brown with four well-defined dark lines running from its neck to its tail. Finally, there is *E. o. rossalleni,* the Everglades ratsnake. It is similar to the yellow ratsnake, but with an orange background color. This form was named after Ross Allen, a snake expert from Florida.

Other American Ratsnakes

There are several other separate species of American ratsnake, including Baird's ratsnake, *Elaphe bairdi* from southern Texas and adjacent parts of Mexico. It is gray, and each of its dorsal scales has an orange base. It sometimes has four dusky lines down its back. Juveniles are gray with darker blotches. *Elaphe vulpina,* the fox snake, is from the north-central United States and adjacent parts of southern Canada. It is a thickset species with rich brown blotches on a yellowish to light-brown background.

Elaphe guttata, the corn snake or red ratsnake from eastern North America, is a distinctive snake with red or orange blotches on a background that may be yellow or gray. Its underside is checkered black and white. The Central American ratsnake, *Elaphe flavirufa*, has large reddish-brown blotches on a dirty yellow or gray background and occurs from southeastern Mexico, including the Yucatán Peninsula, to Honduras.

Three other ratsnakes, formerly included in *Elaphe* but now in different genera, are the trans-pecos ratsnake, *Bogertophis subocularis,* the Baja ratsnake, *B. rosaliae,* and the green ratsnake, *Senticolis triaspis.*

Corn Snake

Elaphe guttata

Common name Corn snake (red ratsnake)

Scientific name *Elaphe guttata*

Subfamily Colubrinae

Family Colubridae

Suborder Serpentes

Order Squamata

Length From 43 in (110 cm) to 5.8 ft (1.8 m)

Key features Slender but muscular snake; head narrow; scales weakly keeled; eyes moderately large; pupils round; pattern consists of black-edged, deep-red to orange saddles on a background of gray, silver, or yellow; there is nearly always an arrow-shaped marking between the eyes; underneath it is black and white, often arranged in a checkered pattern

Habits Basically terrestrial but climbs well and may also spend time below ground

Breeding Egg layer with clutches of 5–25 eggs; eggs hatch after about 65 days

Diet Mostly small mammals (including bats) and occasional birds, but it sometimes takes frogs and lizards when young

Habitat Open woods, hillsides, clearings in forests, and forest edges; often attracted to human settlements, especially farm buildings

Distribution Eastern United States to southern and northern Mexico

Status Common

Similar species Some milksnakes, such as the eastern milksnake, *Lampropeltis triangulum triangulum*, are similar but have smooth scales; young ratsnakes, *Elaphe obsoleta*, are blotched but lack the arrowhead mark

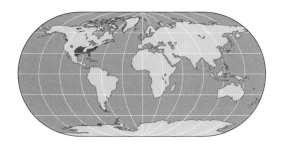

The corn snake is bred in greater numbers than any other species. It is undoubtedly among the most familiar snakes to pet keepers over much of North America and Europe.

THE CORN SNAKE'S GREAT popularity among breeders is due to its (usually) docile nature and its adaptability. Corn snakes thrive under the sometimes inappropriate conditions provided by well-meaning but inexperienced reptile keepers. In their natural habitat corn snakes live in a wide range of habitats and frequently turn up in the vicinity of houses and barns—no doubt in search of mice and rats attracted by discarded and stored foodstuffs. (This habit has earned them the alternative common name of red ratsnakes.) They are powerful constrictors, and adults tackle prey up to the size of full-grown rats. They also raid birds' nests, including those inside bird boxes.

False Rattlers

Corn snakes are active at night during the summer, but in early morning and late evening when the weather is cooler. They are rather slow, deliberate crawlers and will often "freeze" if discovered in the open, relying on their disruptive markings to help them melt into the background. If approached, they often vibrate the tip of their tail rapidly. If they happen to be resting among dead leaves, this can cause a rustling or buzzing noise similar to that made by some rattlesnakes.

They hibernate from October to March in northern parts, but in the south they may be active throughout the year, emerging from their retreats on warm days. They mate in spring, and the female lays her eggs, which can number up to 30, in June, July, or August. Northern forms tend to lay fewer, larger eggs. The hatchlings typically measure 8 to 12 inches (20 to 30 cm), but those of the northern subspecies are larger. Males reach breeding size in two years, but females usually take three.

Selective breeding has resulted in an amelanistic form of the corn snake, in which all traces of black pigment are missing.

The corn snake's natural coloration varies depending on location. The most colorful examples are those from South Carolina, where a typical example will have rich red saddles with wide black borders on a straw-colored background. Farther south in parts of Florida the background color is often silvery gray, and the saddles are paler red, sometimes orange, with no black borders. In the Florida Keys the subspecies *E. g. rosacea* has little or no black pigment, and the whole snake has a reddish-orange wash. The population farther west, known as the Great Plains ratsnake, however, has no red on it but has brown blotches on a grayish background.

⬆ *Snow corn snakes have no black or colored pigmentation and only a hint of a pattern. The pinkish coloration comes from their blood.*

Designer Snakes

The number of naturally occurring color forms, or subspecies, is nothing compared with the array of "sports" produced by selective breeding in captivity. Because the corn snake is such a prolific and easy animal to breed, it was inevitable that occasional mutations would occur sooner or later.

The first was a form in which all the black pigment (melanin) was missing. These amelanistic corn snakes have all the red markings in the right places but no other markings, and their eyes are pink. The next mutation to be produced was the opposite—snakes in which all the black areas were present as normal, but in which the red pigment was absent. These are anerythristic corn snakes, not as colorful as the wild type or the amelanistic form, but interesting in their own right. More importantly, they represent a step toward producing corn snakes without any pigment at all by crossing them with amelanistic individuals. The resulting form, which takes two generations to create, was the first man-made corn snake variety and is called the snow corn snake.

Other slight variations appear from time to time among breeders' "crops," such as specimens in which the blotches are replaced with a single straight or zigzag stripe down the back. They have been propagated by selective breeding, and some dealers list a dozen or more corn snake "sports," often with fanciful names, no doubt created simply to enhance their desirability among snake-keepers.

Common name Common king snake (each subspecies
has its own name, such as California king
snake, black king snake, etc.)

Scientific name *Lampropeltis getula*

Subfamily Colubrinae

Family Colubridae

Suborder Serpentes

Order Squamata

Length 35 in (90 cm) to 5.8 ft (1.8 m)

Key features Muscular snake with an almost cylindrical
body; small head hardly wider than neck;
pupils round; smooth, glossy scales; markings
variable but nearly always consist of a
contrasting pattern of black (or dark brown)
and white (or cream) in various
arrangements; the Mexican subspecies is
uniformly black

Habits Nocturnal; mainly terrestrial

Breeding Egg layer with clutches of up to 24 (but
typically 6–12); eggs hatch after about 70
days

Diet Small mammals, lizards, and other snakes

Habitat Varied from lowland swamps to deserts

Distribution Southern half of the U.S. and adjacent parts
of northern Mexico

Status Common in places

Similar species None in the area

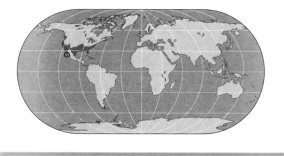

Common King Snake

Lampropeltis getula

*The king snake probably gets its common name from
its habit of killing and eating other snakes, including
venomous ones. Snakes, however, form only part of its
diet. A powerful constrictor, it tracks down small
mammals and reptiles before squeezing them to death.*

KING SNAKES HUNT AT NIGHT, covering the ground
methodically as they search for prey in burrows
or rock crevices. Their roughly cylindrical shape
helps them enter small spaces and burrow
through loose soil, sand, or leaf litter. When
they locate their prey, they throw several coils of
their body around it and squeeze tightly. When
it stops breathing, they swallow it. If the prey is
a venomous snake, such as a rattlesnake, the
king snakes bite it behind the head and coil
around its upper body. In this way they
immobilize it; but if they do get bitten, they are
immune to the venom and can retain their
vicelike grip. King snakes have been found with
rattlesnakes equal to their own length inside
their stomach, packed in like a concertina.

Pit vipers identify king snakes by smell and
react by immediately taking up a defensive
posture: They raise the thickest part of their
body off the ground in an arc. They then thrust
it toward the king snake while trying to make
themselves look as large as possible. They may
even use the raised part of their body to club
the king snake.

*The king snake,
Lampropeltis getula,
devours a black-headed
snake,* Tantilla *species.*

Egg Thieves
Less ambitious items on the king snakes' menu
include birds' eggs (especially those of ground-
nesting species) and reptile eggs, including
those of freshwater turtles. They find the latter
by smell and dig them up using their snout. In
places where turtles nest regularly, king snakes
may travel some distance to the breeding sites
at the appropriate time of year, showing that
they have good memories. They also eat young

turtles on occasion. In short, king snakes are "general purpose" snakes.

Because of their southerly distribution king snakes may be active all through the year. But populations living at high elevations, such as the desert king snakes, *L. g. splendida* from Arizona, and animals from the northern states, may undergo a period of prolonged hibernation in winter. Otherwise, their activity period depends on local conditions, and they may simply become inactive during cold snaps.

Either way they mate in the spring, and males fight for dominance, intertwining their bodies while lying on the ground and testing each other's strength. The female lays her eggs in the summer, about six to eight weeks after mating. She chooses a place that will retain

some moisture. The eggs usually stick together to form a single clump, and they take about 70 days to hatch. The young measure 10 to 12 inches (25 to 30 cm) in length.

Variation

Across their geographical range king snakes have remarkable color variations. In the southeastern United States, for example, each scale is yellow or cream with black edges. Some

↧ *As its common name implies, the variable king snake,* Lampropeltis mexicana thayeri *from Mexico, occurs in different color phases. Its background color can be light gray, peach, silver, or buff.*

scales have more yellow on them than others, and may be arranged into a faint pattern of bars or blotches. The speckled king snake, *L. g. holbrooki*, is the most evenly marked of this type, with each scale having a small yellow spot at its base. Moving farther west, the markings have progressively more contrast, until on the West Coast the California king snake, *L. g. californiae*, may have one of two different but equally bold patterns. They are either black or brown with wide white or cream bands encircling the body, or they are brown or black with a single white stripe running right along the back. Interestingly, both forms can hatch from a single clutch of eggs, but the striped form only occurs in part of the subspecies' range (mainly in San Diego County, where about 30 percent of king snakes are striped). One subspecies, the black king snake, *L. g. nigritus* from Sonora, Mexico, is jet black in color without any traces of paler markings.

In the West desert forms tend to be black and white, whereas forms from farmland, woodland, swamps, and coastal marshes tend to be less contrasting. They are often brown and cream or even yellow.

Night Hunters

Although they are basically nocturnal, common king snakes may be active in early morning and late afternoon in the spring and fall. However, in midsummer they rarely emerge before sunset, especially in the warmer parts of their range (such as California, Arizona, and Mexico). Their shiny skin reflects car headlights, and they are often seen crossing roads at night. During the day they hide in rotting stumps, under debris (including human trash), among rocks, and in rodent burrows. In the American Southwest they sometimes shelter at the base of old agave bushes.

The common king snake is popular among snake keepers and breeders in all its forms

⊙ **Lampropeltis getula brooksi,** *the southern Florida king snake, lays a clutch of eggs. She will leave shortly after finishing, and the eggs will develop independently.*

because it adapts well to captivity and is usually placid and pleasant to handle. It breeds well in captivity—some king snakes can reach sexual maturity in just 18 months—and several color forms, such as albinos, have become commonly available through selective breeding.

Because they eat other snakes, however, common king snakes must be kept separately. Even introducing males to females at breeding times can be nerve-racking (for the male snake as well as its owner, presumably). They rarely eat each other, but an overeager female may grab a newly introduced male if she thinks she is about to be fed.

Polymorphism

Most species of snakes have fairly constant colors and patterns. Some species, however, exist side by side in two or more distinct forms. This is known as polymorphism. (To be exact, if they occur in just two forms, it should be known as dimorphism.) It is important to distinguish between regional variations, sometimes classified as subspecies, and polymorphism.

In polymorphism two or more forms occur together in the same region; and in the case of many snakes they may even hatch from the same clutch of eggs. Snakes can be polymorphic in color or in pattern. The eyelash viper, *Bothriechis schlegelii*, for example, may be colored green and brown, like lichen, or plain orange.

Other examples are the American mangrove water snake, *Nerodia fasciata compressicauda*, which can be greenish with dark blotches or plain dull orange, and the Asian crab-eating snake, *Fordonia leucobalia*, which can be plain yellow, orange, or black in color. It may even be mottled with a combination of these colors.

California king snakes provide a good example of pattern polymorphism. In most parts of their range they are black with white bands, but in some areas a proportion of them are black with a white line down the center of their back (sometimes the combinations are brown and cream, but the patterns are still the same). Other snakes with polymorphic patterns are the Sonoran ground snake, *Sonora semiannulata*, which can be plain,

striped, or banded, and the leopard snake, *Elaphe situla*, which can be spotted or striped. Male boomslangs, *Dispholidus typus*, are not only different than the females (this is called sexual dimorphism) but are also highly variable themselves both in color and in pattern—a very complicated situation.

The purpose of polymorphic patterns is thought to be defense. To be successful, polymorphism relies on the principle that predators build up a mental picture or "search image" of their preferred prey species. Animals that do not match this image are often ignored, even though they may be equally good to eat. If a predator builds up an image of a striped snake, for example, the banded individuals may be overlooked. As a rule, predators would be expected to maintain a search image of whichever form was most common in the region, and the less common form would benefit by being overlooked. After a while the latter may become the most common form because of this, and predators in the area may switch their attention accordingly.

In the long term polymorphism is maintained in the population, and both forms would be expected to occur in roughly similar numbers, all other things being equal. (In the California king snake, however, the proportions are slightly skewed in favor of the banded form, so it appears that other factors may also have a bearing on the frequency of the two forms.)

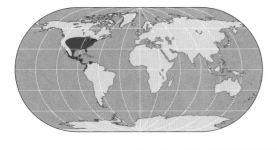

**Red milksnake
(*Lampropeltis
triangulum syspila*)**

Common name Milksnake (different
subspecies have different
common names)

Scientific name *Lampropeltis triangulum*

Subfamily Colubrinae

Family Colubridae

Suborder Serpentes

Order Squamata

Length From 20 in (50 cm) to 6.5 ft (2 m)

Key features Cylindrical snake with glossy scales; head
quite small with no distinct neck; eyes also
small and pupils round; body usually marked
with a combination of red, black, and white
(or yellow), but some forms are brown and
gray, while others become uniform black as
adults

Habits Mostly nocturnal, although sometimes active
in the late evening and early morning
depending on locality; secretive

Breeding Egg layer with clutches of 4–15 eggs; eggs
hatch after 40 to 60 days

Diet Small mammals, lizards, and other snakes

Habitat Extremely varied; found in almost every
habitat within its wide range except the most
arid deserts

Distribution From Canada in the north through Central
America and south to Ecuador

Status Common in most places

Similar species At least 3 other members of the genus
Lampropeltis with red, black, and white
bands (triads) around their bodies, but they
tend to be restricted to montane habitats

Milksnake   *Lampropeltis triangulum*

*With many different forms or subspecies,
the milksnake has one of the largest
ranges of any terrestrial snake. It is
found from Canada in the north to
Ecuador, south of the equator.*

IN THE UNITED STATES milksnakes occur across all
the central and eastern states as far west as
Utah and Arizona. Farther south they are found
along both coasts of Mexico but are missing
from the highland areas in the north-central
region. They occur throughout Central America
and south into Colombia, Venezuela, and
Ecuador. Within this huge north–south range,
covering 3,600 miles (5,800 km), the milksnakes
occupy a variety of habitats and are absent only
from the driest deserts and the highest
mountains. Only the European adder, *Vipera
berus*, covers a larger area, while the American
vine snake, *Oxybelis aeneus*, and the indigo
snake, *Drymarchon corais*, are the milksnakes'
nearest rivals in the New World. Neither of
those species occurs as far north, but their
range extends farther south into Argentina.

Adaptability

Milksnakes differ from the other wide-ranging
species by the way in which they have adapted
to a wide range of conditions and habitats.
They live on beaches at the edge of the sea in
Maine, in bog forests in the American
Northeast, in semidesert regions in south Texas
and northeastern Mexico, in tropical rain forests
in Central America, and as high as 8,850 feet
(2,700 m) in the Andes of Colombia.

They are equally adaptable in their choice
of microhabitat. In the American Northeast they
are common in woods, meadows, prairies, and
around towns and timber buildings. (The name
milksnake refers to the belief that they steal
milk from cows because they are often found in
barns searching for mice.) In the Southeast,
however, they are strongly associated with pine

⤒ *An eastern
milksnake,* Lampropeltis
triangulum triangulum,
*rests on dead leaves with
its head slightly raised.
This subspecies relies on
camouflage rather than
warning coloration.*

The Subspecies Problem

The concept of different subspecies within a species is not universally accepted among biologists. When it is used, it describes a geographically isolated population within a species' range that is distinct in size, shape, or color. The most obvious form of isolation in reptiles is when populations are confined to islands, mountain tops, or some other place surrounded by a "sea" of unsuitable habitat that prevents them from spreading. (Or, more importantly, it prevents gene flow from one population to another.) It is not the same as polymorphism, in which two or more distinct forms occur within a single population.

The 25 or so subspecies of milksnake are not isolated in this way, however. Their variation is gradual from one population to another, and it is difficult to see where one subspecies ends and another one starts. For this reason some experts argue that the milksnake should not be divided into subspecies at all.

However, if subspecies were not used, some other way of differentiating between the various forms would be needed. For example, the gray and brown eastern milksnake from the Northeast needs to be differentiated from the spectacularly colored Sinaloan milksnake from the Mexican West Coast. And at just 20 inches (50 cm) the diminutive scarlet king snake from Florida is quite different from the relatively gigantic Ecuadorian milksnake that measures over 6 feet (1.8 m).

King Snakes

Apart from the milksnake, there are seven other species in the genus *Lampropeltis*. They are known as king snakes. They all have smooth, glossy scales (the name *Lampropeltis* means "bright shields," referring to its scales). Several are tricolored snakes with alternating rings of red, black, and white.

Lampropeltis alterna, the gray-banded king snake, occurs in a multitude of patterns and lives in southern Texas, extending down into Central Mexico. Then there is *L. calligaster,* a species that consists of two different forms, the prairie king snake and the mole snake. They are gray or brown with darker blotches.

The third species is *L. getula,* the common king snake. It lives mainly in the United States and is a black-and-white or brown-and-cream species with several geographic races. *L. mexicana,* the Mexican king snake, is the fourth species. It is also a snake of many forms, some of which have red blotches on a gray, cream, or buff background. Others have rings of red or dark gray around the body.

Next, there is *L. pyromelana,* the Sonoran mountain king snake. It is a beautiful tricolored king snake with bands of red, white, and black and a white snout. It lives in the rocky outcrops of mountain ranges in Arizona, Nevada, Utah, and New Mexico, and in northern Mexico. The sixth species is *L. ruthveni,* the Querétaro king snake. It is another tricolor found in the Mexican states of Michoacán, Querétaro, and Jalisco. At one time it was classified as a milksnake.

Finally comes *L. zonata,* the California mountain king snake. It is similar to the Sonoran mountain king snake, but its snout is black. Isolated populations occur in California, Oregon, and Baja California, Mexico.

Sonoran mountain king snakes, **Lampropeltis pyromelana,** *are mainly terrestrial but can be seen climbing trees and hunting in low bushes. They usually live in mountains or rock piles.*

forests. They favor rotting stumps in which they hibernate and lay their eggs. Other populations hide under flat pieces of rock, and many have been collected so infrequently that it is not possible to build up a picture of their lifestyle.

Seasonal Habits

Milksnakes from tropical regions of Central and South America are probably active throughout the year. Even in the southern states they may hibernate halfheartedly, emerging for short spells whenever the weather is warm. Populations from the northern parts of the species' range, however, hibernate from October to April every year.

The eastern milksnake, *L. t. triangulum*, is thought to hibernate communally because several individuals—as many as 28—have been found in close proximity to each other in the fall. Similarly, gravid females (ones that are full of eggs) of this subspecies may congregate in certain places prior to laying their eggs.

Studies have also shown that eastern milksnakes may move seasonally to drier upland sites in the fall when looking for somewhere to hibernate and to moister lowland sites in the spring and summer during feeding and mating. Such migratory behavior has already been shown for a few other species, such as the northern adder, *Vipera berus*, in the United Kingdom and the carpet python, *Morelia spilota*, in Australia. There is every reason to suspect that this milksnake, which lives in similar situations, has similar adaptive behavior.

Living in a temperate climate, the eastern milksnake and another northeastern form often lay their eggs in piles of rotting sawdust, manure heaps, and decomposing vegetation. The heat produced by rotting material speeds up the development of the eggs, just as in the case of the European grass snake, *Natrix natrix*, which also lives in a cool climate.

Smaller in the North

The appearance of the milksnake also changes over the two continents on which it occurs. Some changes are minor and of interest only to

taxonomists, but others are more dramatic. They concern the species' size, color, and pattern. Its total length can vary from about 20 inches (50 cm) in the southeastern states to over 6.5 feet (2 m) in South America. The difference in weight between the two forms is, of course, even greater. In many snakes that occur over a wide range of latitude (and in snakes in general), the largest individuals are found in the warmer tropical regions.

That is broadly true of the milksnakes: The largest forms live nearest the equator (*L. t. micropholis* in Ecuador and Venezuela), and they become smaller farther north toward Mexico and the United States.

⊕ *Pueblan milksnakes,* **Lampropeltis triangulum campbelli** *from Mexico, usually lay six to eight eggs in a clutch. The eggs take about 60 days to hatch.*

Carbon Copies?

Why does the milksnake vary so much from one part of its range to another? There are a number of different explanations as to why it differs in aspects such as size and color. One that is particularly attractive revolves around its mimicry of the venomous coral snakes of the region.

In order for mimicry to be effective, the mimicking species must be a good copy of the model. The coral snakes, however, tend to have small ranges. That means that in one place the milksnake shares its range with one species, while a few hundred miles away it may share it with a completely different coral snake. But coral snakes are not all the same; although they are mostly red, black, and white, their bands are often spaced differently. It is possible that natural selection has enabled each population of milksnake to copy the pattern of the particular coral snake with which it shares its range.

⤒ *A Mexican milksnake,* L. t. annulata, *hatches out. Except for the eastern milksnake, young of all subspecies start life as red snakes with black-and-white bands.*

⤳ *In Pennsylvania a juvenile milksnake basks on a leaf. The eastern milksnake,* L. t. triangulum, *is the most northerly subspecies.*

There is a blip in this trend, however. In the United States itself the largest form is found in the Northeast (the eastern milksnake), but the smallest is in Florida. (This is *L. t. elapsoides*, the scarlet king snake. Despite its common name, it is a form of milksnake.) The discrepancy can probably be explained by the burrowing habits of the scarlet king snake. It lives most of its life coiled inside decaying tree stumps, which would be difficult to do if it were a large snake.

Red, Black, and White Bands

Color variations can take many forms. The eastern milksnake is unusual, being gray with chestnut-colored saddles, or blotches, down its back. All the other milksnakes start life as red snakes with black-and-white bands, or triads, in the sequence red-black-white-black-red. However, many forms change color as they grow, and most get darker. The darkening occurs as black pigment infuses the tips of the white-and-red scales and gradually spreads. In most forms the red-and-white bands become darker but are still clearly visible.

In one form, the black milksnake from the Andes of Colombia, the black continues to spread until by the time the snake is fully grown, it is totally black save for a small dusky-white area on its chin. A common theory for this is that snakes in cooler climates (including higher altitudes) are darker because black pigment absorbs heat more efficiently. So why aren't they black from the start? Probably because tricolored milksnakes mimic venomous snakes from the area. While they are small, that is more important than their ability to absorb heat. When they grow up, they are larger than the venomous snakes they were mimicking, so changing color is no disadvantage.

Another color variation is found in forms such as the Mexican milksnake, *L. t. annulata*, the Pueblan milksnake, *L. t. campbelli*, and the Honduran milksnake, *L. t. hondurensis*, in which the pale bands are cream or even orange instead of white. This could simply be a case of chance mutation; and because it has neither advantages or disadvantages, the variation remains in the population by default.

How Many Bands?

Pattern variation concerns the number of bands, or triads, around the snake's body. The number can vary from 10 to 54, the largest score coming from the eastern milksnake and the smallest from a Mexican subspecies, the Sinaloan milksnake, *L. t. sinaloae*. The latter has wide red interspaces between its black-and-white bands, but other forms are more regularly banded. There is great variation within all the forms, and even snakes from the same litter can have different numbers of bands.

However, all these variations—in size, color, patterns, and numbers of bands—coupled with other factors such as scale counts, have been used to describe 25 different subspecies of milksnake in total. Although there is clearly a need to differentiate between the separate populations of such a highly variable species, some experts doubt the usefulness of describing such a large number of forms, and many even question the subspecies concept altogether.

Common name Rough green snake

Scientific name *Opheodrys aestivus*

Subfamily Colubrinae

Family Colubridae

Suborder Serpentes

Order Squamata

Length From 22 in (56 cm) to 32 in (81 cm)

Key features Slender snake with an elongated head; scales keeled; color uniform light green; when dead, it quickly turns blue-gray; juveniles are also grayish-green

Habits Arboreal, lives among the leaves of trees and bushes; rarely descends to the ground except when moving to its egg-laying sites

Breeding Egg layer with clutches averaging 6 eggs; eggs hatch after 30–90 days

Diet Insects, mainly caterpillars, crickets, and grasshoppers

Habitat Dense stands of trees and shrubs, often those overhanging streams or the edges of lakes

Distribution North America; most of the eastern half of the United States, extending over the border into northeastern Mexico

Status Very common in suitable habitats

Similar species The smooth green snake, *Liochlorophis vernalis,* is similar but smaller with smooth scales

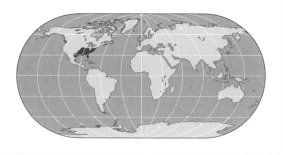

Rough Green Snake
Opheodrys aestivus

The rough green snake is dainty and inoffensive. Owing to its excellent camouflage colors, it is often overlooked, even in places where it is abundant.

THE ROUGH GREEN SNAKE has taken the art of camouflage to the extreme. Not only is it uniformly grass-green in color, but it remains motionless for long periods of time, perfectly hidden among the foliage and stems of the trees and bushes where it lives. When it hunts, it only moves if there is a slight breeze to disturb the branches, and it swings its head from side to side as it goes. Its movements are reminiscent of the movements of other cryptically colored species such as chameleons, walkingsticks (phasmids), and praying mantids.

The rough green snake moves in order to hunt the small invertebrates on which it feeds. It hunts during the day and probably relies heavily on sight. Its eyes are relatively large with round pupils. Favorite prey items are crickets and the larvae of butterflies and moths, which it simply approaches stealthily, grasps in its mouth, and swallows.

Colonial Living

Colonies of rough green snakes tend to be concentrated in the trees and bushes, such as alders, that grow alongside streams or that surround small lakes and ponds. When conditions are good, population densities are estimated to be about 200 per acre (429 per ha.). Assuming the habitat is a row of trees or shrubs—which it often is—this is equivalent to one snake every 9 feet (2.7 m).

Within its home range each snake moves on average about 10 feet (3 m) per day, but females that are looking for somewhere to lay their eggs travel an average of just over 100

Smooth Green Snake

The other small, plain green snake from North America is *Liochlorophis vernalis*. It is similar to the rough green snake, but it is slightly smaller and has smooth scales, so it is called the smooth green snake. This species has a slightly more northerly distribution, even extending into Canada, although the two species overlap in places. It lives in meadows and marshes, and is not so dependent on the water's edge as the rough green snake. It is also active during the day but spends most of its time on the ground searching for spiders and insects. It sometimes hibernates communally, as do other snakes from the cooler northeastern states.

feet (30 m) each day. They leave the water's edge and move inland, which often forces them down to the ground. They make for a hollow tree, and there is evidence that females return to a favorite tree where they or other females have laid previously, even if it means crawling past other equally suitable hollow trees. At this time they are extremely vulnerable. Almost half may be eaten by predators, especially king snakes, *Lampropeltis getula*, and racers, *Coluber constrictor*. Birds such as blue jays also eat the rough green snakes.

⊕ **The rough green snake is frequently found in woody vegetation growing alongside or overhanging water, sometimes up to 20 feet (6 m) above the ground.**

Nevertheless, females outnumber males slightly in most populations. With such large population densities, enough females must lay their clutches successfully to keep the numbers up (even if they get eaten on the way back to the waterside). Interestingly, male rough green snakes display to females in the spring with an exaggerated version of the swaying movements they use when stalking their prey.

The average clutch size is just over 6 eggs, which hatch into tiny snakes measuring about 8 inches (20 cm) long. They are grayish-green and do not attain the bright-green color of the adults until their second summer.

Common name Ground snake (Prairie ground snake, Sonoran ground snake)

Scientific name *Sonora semiannulata*

Subfamily Colubrinae

Family Colubridae

Suborder Serpentes

Order Squamata

Length From 8 in (20 cm) to 19 in (48 cm)

Key features Small, slender snake with a narrow head no wider than its neck; eyes small; scales smooth; colors and markings highly variable

Habits Secretive; nocturnal and rarely seen

Breeding Egg layer with clutches of 4–6 eggs laid from June to August; eggs hatch after 50–70 days

Diet Invertebrates, especially spiders, scorpions, centipedes, crickets, and insect larvae

Habitat Dry places, including gravelly or sandy hollows and hillsides, preferring places where some loose material has collected

Distribution North America from southern Idaho to the tip of Baja California, Mexico, and from eastern California to central Texas, north to southern Kansas and Missouri

Status Common, although becoming rare in some places due to habitat destruction

Similar species The various color forms all seem to have lookalike species, including the young of venomous coral snakes

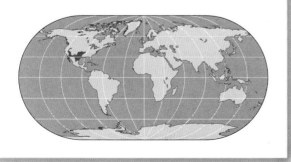

Ground Snake

Sonora semiannulata

The ground snake is a small, secretive snake that is not often seen on the surface without some careful searching. Most are caught on desert roads at night or, more often, by turning over rocks during the day.

THE DAINTY LITTLE GROUND snake lives in some of the harshest habitats in North America. It occurs up to 6,000 feet (1,800 m) in elevation, where the days can be blistering hot and the nights freezing cold. As far as anyone can tell, it spends the days sheltering under rocks and other debris or perhaps buried in sand and gravel, although it has no obvious adaptations for burrowing.

Its eyes are small, however, indicating a nocturnal lifestyle. It ventures out mainly when most of its prey are active. Prey items consist of venomous invertebrates such as centipedes and scorpions, as well as insects and their larvae. When hunting, ground snakes simply grasp their prey and chew on it. Their rear teeth have shallow grooves on the outside edges, so they probably produce venom to help subdue the prey. These snakes are, however, obviously too small to be dangerous to humans.

Their variable coloration presents a problem because the various forms can sometimes be found together in a small area, and some of them can be easily confused with other species. In other places a single form predominates, and there are even populations where only one form is found.

In the west the most common pattern is a wide reddish-brown or orange stripe down the back, interrupted at regular intervals by black cross bands. This form can look very similar to the shovel-nosed snakes, *Chionactis*, from the same region, and both species may be mimics of venomous coral snakes, *Micrurus* and *Micruroides*. At other times ground snakes may be cream with black crossbars or have just a single cross-band behind the head. Less commonly, they may be plain red or brown.

Common Ancestors

The genus *Sonora* is named for the region of Mexico where the snakes were first discovered. Apart from *S. semiannulata,* there are two other species, *S. aemula* from northern Mexico and *S. michoacanensis* from north-central Mexico. The latter species is a brightly marked "false coral" snake with peculiar spiny scales on its tail, thought to help in burrowing. Both the Mexican species are thought to have lifestyles similar to the more northern species. A fourth species, *S. episcopa*, is now combined with *S. semiannulata*.

Along with *Sonora* there are several other genera from the same part of the world that seem to have arisen from the same ancestor. They have several things in common: They are all small, they prefer dry rocky or sandy places, and they eat invertebrates, often venomous ones. First, there are the shovel-nosed snakes, *Chionactis,* the sand snakes, *Chilomeniscus,* and three genera of hook-nosed snakes (*Ficimia, Gyalopion*, and *Pseudoficimia*), all of which eat spiders. Next, there are over 50 species of black-headed snakes, *Tantilla*, that feed mainly on centipedes. Then there are six species of *Conopsis* from Mexico, which eat caterpillars and other insect larvae, and finally a tropical genus, *Stenorrhina*, whose two members eat scorpions and the large hairy spiders commonly known as tarantulas. All these snakes have successfully exploited a niche that allows them to live in otherwise inhospitable places. They are sometimes placed together in a loose taxonomic unit (a tribe)—called the Sonorini.

⊕ *A plain brown example of a ground snake,* Sonora semiannulata, *from the mountains of central Baja California.*

Banded water snake
(Nerodia fasciata
fasciata)

Common name Southern water snake

Scientific name Nerodia fasciata

Subfamily Natricinae

Family Colubridae

Suborder Serpentes

Order Squamata

Length 39 in (1 m) to 5.25 ft (1.6 m)

Key features Body thick; head broad; snout oval; eyes large with round pupils; scales heavily keeled; usually brown with darker crossbands but may also be red, orange, or olive-green; in the wild often caked with mud, and markings can be hard to define; large individuals, especially females, sometimes become totally black

Habits Semiaquatic; can be very bad tempered and will hiss, strike, and bite, although it tends to be less aggressive than other water snakes

Breeding Bears live young with litters of up to 50; gestation period about 70–80 days

Diet Fish and amphibians

Habitat Freshwater ponds, lakes, and swamps; sometimes in brackish waters near the coast (e.g.,the Mississippi Delta); related species also occur in brackish and salt water along the Gulf Coast of Texas

Distribution Southeastern North America

Status Very common

Similar species Other water snakes are found in the region, but the species most likely to cause confusion is the venomous cottonmouth, *Agkistrodon piscivorus*, which shares the water snake's habitat and is equally pugnacious

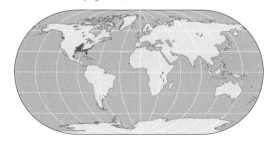

Southern Water Snake

Nerodia fasciata

American water snakes have a reputation for being dull colored, bad tempered, and foul smelling. However, the southern water snake is more attractive than most.

THE VARIOUS FORMS AND SUBSPECIES of southern water snake are usually banded, with the width of the bands and the background colors varying greatly. The southern water snake is less likely to strike and bite than the other species of water snakes. Instead, it uses the pungent contents of its anal gland as a defense.

Although this species is less likely to be confused with the venomous cottonmouth, *Agkistrodon piscivorus*, than some other water snakes, they all lack facial pits. However, the cottonmouth is often reluctant to move off, preferring to stand its ground with its mouth agape; but the water snakes are much more likely to dive into the water and swim away.

Lifestyles and Threats

All water snakes are mainly nocturnal in the southern parts of North America, hiding away in the daytime in bankside burrows and under dead vegetation. In cooler weather, however, they may bask—several snakes often lie out together on logs and branches that stick out of the water. This position allows them to make a quick getaway if danger threatens, by dropping into the water below.

Overall the southern water snake uses a wide range of habitats, from swamps and weed-choked ditches and waterways to open drainage canals and rice fields. Because of their habitat, water snakes tend to be spread out along a line such as a creek or the shore of a lake rather than being scattered over a wide area. They can occur at high densities—one snake every three or four yards (3–4 m). Although on average they may move over

⊕ In North Carolina a banded water snake, Nerodia fasciata fasciata, basks on a log, ready to make a quick getaway into the water if threatened.

140 yards (128 m) each year, many hardly move at all because they have plenty of available food without having to search too hard. Despite that, they do not appear to have a well-defined home range. They are tolerant of each other and may live in close proximity at times when food is heavily concentrated, for example, when frogs and toads congregate to breed. Coastal species may migrate inland to freshwater habitats when frogs and toads are breeding.

Along the coast the southern water snake tolerates brackish water, living in coastal marshes and tidal flats. In particular, the Gulf salt marsh water snake, *N. f. clarki,* favors this habitat and even swims out to sea to recolonize low islets and sand bars that have been temporarily inundated during hurricanes or spells of stormy weather. This subspecies often uses the burrows of crayfish and fiddler crabs, and may occur in large numbers in suitable situations. However, its numbers have been reduced recently

The *Nerodia fasciata* Complex

There are several recognized races or subspecies of the southern water snake, but the situation is confused, and changes will probably be made.

Banded water snake, *N. f. fasciata:* red, brown, or black crossbands. Coastal plain, northern Carolina to Florida panhandle and west to southwestern Alabama.

Broad-banded water snake, *N. f. confluens:* broad dark crossbands with yellow between. Western Alabama to eastern Texas and along Mississippi River as far as southern Illinois.

Florida water snake, *N. f. pictiventris:* dark spots on side, red or black marking on underside. Peninsular Florida.

The following are often regarded as subspecies of a separate species, *Nerodia clarki,* but are included here because they have formed part of the *N. fasciata* complex for many years.

Gulf salt marsh water snake, *N. f. clarki:* yellowish with dark longitudinal stripes. Gulf Coast from southeastern Texas to northwestern Florida. (Regarded as a separate species, *N. clarki,* by some experts even though it interbreeds freely with forms of the southern water snake where their ranges meet.) If treated as a separate species, it would include the following subspecies:

Mangrove water snake, *N. f. compressicauda:* greenish with dark blotches or crossbands, or plain red or reddish orange. Coastal Florida from Miami south through the Keys, north to Tampa Bay. Also northern Cuba.

Atlantic salt marsh, *N. f. taeniata:* Endangered. Stripes on forepart of body, the rest light with dark blotches. Coastal Florida from Daytona Beach to Vero Beach.

due to drainage and to pollution from chemical and sewage effluent that has seriously damaged the ecology of the area. Other coastal populations, especially those of *N. f. taeniata*, are threatened by urban development along the popular Florida coast.

All populations of water snakes are affected to a greater or lesser degree by exposure to insecticides, including residual DDT that was used to control mosquitoes in the past. A third coastal form is the mangrove water snake, *N. f. compressicauda,* which occurs in two forms—a blotched olive-brown or plain orange. As its name suggests, it lives in brackish mangrove swamps.

Diverse Diet

The southern water snake eats a wide range of food species, including frogs, toads, mullet, killifish, crayfish, and shrimp, but the picture is

far from straightforward. First, there is a difference between the diets of juveniles and adults, with juveniles preferring fish, and adults preferring frogs and toads.

The changeover comes when the young snakes are eight or nine months of age and measure about 20 inches (50 cm) in length. From this point on, females grow more quickly than males and eventually reach a greater size. That not only allows them to eat larger individual fish but also to exploit different species of fish. They may also live in different habitats that influence their prey choices.

Southern water snakes often live in communities with other species of water snake. They appear to "split up" the resources and therefore avoid competition by using different prey species, hunting at different times of the day, and living in subtly different habitats or microhabitats. This has been well studied in some regions and explains why several similar and closely related species can coexist.

Reproduction

Like all members of the genus *Nerodia* (but unlike their close relatives *Natrix* in Europe and Asia), southern water snakes bear live young. Females are significantly larger than males, and males differ from females in having an area of heavily keeled scales on the back just in front of their vents. They also have a number of small tubercles on the chin. The roughened dorsal scales are thought to help during the mating process, and the tubercles may help females recognize males of the correct species as they rub their chin over the male's back. This prevents similar species from hybridizing.

⊕ *Basking on a branch overhanging water in Florida, the brown water snake,* Nerodia taxispilota, *remains fairly inconspicuous.*

Salt Balance

The Gulf salt marsh water snake, *N. f. clarki*, is one of a few colubrids to enter seawater, but it also lives alongside brackish water in the inlets and creeks of the Texas Gulf Coast. Seawater is saltier than the body fluids of snakes; so if it enters the snake's body, osmotic pressure will suck water out of its tissues, and the snake will eventually die of dehydration.

Reptile skin acts as a barrier to salty water, but the snake is still at risk if it drinks salt water or ingests it with its food. Sea snakes (*Pelamis* species) and file snakes (Acrochordidae) have specialized salt glands to help rid them of excess salt and so reduce the osmotic pull, but the Gulf salt marsh water snake has no such organs. Instead, it simply does not drink salt water.

Experiments have shown that when freshwater species of water snake are placed in seawater, they begin to drink, become dehydrated due to excess salt, and die. Estuarine species, however, are programmed not to drink salt water, and so they do not become dehydrated. When they feed in salt water, they choose food that is less salty than the surrounding water.

⟵ **Nerodia cyclopion floridana,** *the Florida green water snake, ranges from South Carolina through Florida to southern Alabama.*

Males do not engage in combat during the breeding season but scramble for matings with receptive females. This takes place on land in April. The gestation period is about 70 to 80 days, and the newborn young measure about 8 to 9 inches (22–23 cm) in length. A typical litter consists of about 10 young, although up to 50 are possible in the case of very large females.

The young are more boldly marked than the adults. Related species, notably the northern water snake, *Nerodia sipedon,* can have much larger litters—up to 100. Needless to say, the majority of the young perish long before they reach adulthood, victims of a host of potential predators, including large frogs and toads, small carnivorous mammals such as raccoons and rats, and many birds.

Other Water Snakes

The genus *Nerodia* consists of eight to 10 species altogether, depending on how they are classified. They are all North American and range from Canada to Mexico, mostly on the floodplains of the eastern part of the continent. Most have wide ranges, but Harter's water snake, *N. harteri,* is very restricted in two river systems of Texas—those of the Brazos River and the Concho and Colorado Rivers. The latter populations are sometimes regarded as a separate species, *N. paucimaculata.*

A complete list of the species of water snakes (including recently separated species) consists of the following:

Gulf salt marsh water snake, *N. clarki;* green water snake, *N. cyclopion;* plain-bellied water snake, *N. erythrogaster;* southern water snake, *N. fasciata;* Florida water snake, *N. floridana;* Harter's water snake, *N. harteri;* Concho water snake, *N. paucimaculata;* diamondback water snake, *N. rhombifera;* northern water snake, *N. sipedon;* brown water snake, *N. taxispilota.*

Eastern garter snake
(*Thamnophis sirtalis
sirtalis*)

Common name Common garter snake

Scientific name *Thamnophis sirtalis*

Subfamily Natricinae

Family Colubridae

Suborder Serpentes

Order Squamata

Length From 18 in (45 cm) to 4.25 ft (1.3 m)

Key features Body slender; head well separated from neck; large eyes with round pupils; keeled scales; pattern consists of several longitudinal stripes from neck to tail, but width and color of stripes depend on locality

Habits Semiaquatic in most places; diurnal and very alert, taking off at the slightest disturbance

Breeding Bears live young, with litters of up to 24; gestation period 60–90 days

Diet Amphibians, fish, and invertebrates such as worms

Habitat Ditches and ponds, streams in dry regions, damp meadows, marshes, parks, and gardens; from sea level to 8,000 ft (2,450 m)

Distribution North America (Atlantic to Pacific coasts and Canada to the Southwest and Southeast); absent from deserts

Status Common in most places, but some forms are rare: The San Francisco garter snake, *T. sirtalis tetrataenia,* is one of North America's rarest snakes

Similar species Garter snakes in general can be difficult to identify since most of them are striped

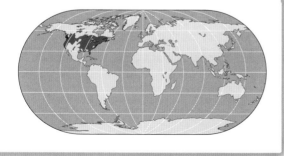

Common Garter Snake

Thamnophis sirtalis

The common garter snake is an easy species to study since it is active in the day. They are also numerous and fairly predictable in their comings and goings.

SEVERAL IMPORTANT STUDIES on snake biology have used the common garter snake as their subject, including investigations into hibernation, chemical communication, and feeding strategies. Some results are specific to garter snakes, but many have helped us understand snakes as a whole.

Because common garter snakes have a large north–south range, their behavior differs from place to place. In southern states such as Texas and Florida, for example, they are active all year around, although they may take cover for a few days at a time during cold snaps.

Suspended Animation
However, in the north, especially in parts of Canada, common garter snakes hibernate for several months every year and undergo dramatic body changes that allow them to survive temperatures close to freezing. The red-sided garter snake, *Thamnophis sirtalis parietalis*, lives in a region that has winter temperatures as low as -40°F (-40°C), with snow on the ground from September to May. During hibernation their body temperature plummets, and they live in a state approaching suspended animation, moving only rarely and extremely slowly. Their blood thickens as it begins to freeze.

Their hibernation dens can become flooded with water, and the snakes are totally submerged. If this occurs, they slow down their system and use less oxygen than usual, obtaining what little they need from the water by absorbing it through the skin. Once spring arrives, they begin to emerge, often while snow is still on the ground.

⊕ *This eastern garter snake,* Thamnophis sirtalis sirtalis *from Canada, has distinctive red stripes down its sides.*

Breeding Patterns

Common garter snakes from different regions have different breeding systems. Those in the far north (such as the red-sided garter snake) are the most studied. Their breeding season is concentrated into a few weeks or less, and competition between males is intense. Males emerge first and wait around the den site for females to emerge. They bask by day but return to the den at night to avoid the cold.

Females emerge gradually over a period of about a month. As each female emerges, she secretes pheromones that stimulate the males. These airborne scent molecules are specific to each species of garter snake, so that where several species occur close together, males do not waste their time and energy pursuing females of the wrong species.

Life in the Freezer

Animals that live in subzero temperatures have to develop behavioral or physiological means of protecting themselves from freezing. Birds and mammals manage by producing metabolic heat internally. They can maintain their body temperatures at a safe level regardless of the environment. Cold-blooded animals do not have this option, however, and have to evolve an alternative strategy. Two such strategies have been explored by reptiles. The first is "supercooling," in which the body fluids can fall below their normal freezing point because they contain substances known as cryoprotectants that act as antifreeze to prevent the formation of ice inside the animal cell.

Garter snakes have cryoprotectants, but only in small amounts, mainly in their liver and heart. They mainly rely on another system known as freezing tolerance. As the temperature drops, ice begins to form in their body fluids, and their blood thickens as it begins to freeze. In experiments garter snakes were able to survive temperatures as low as -58° F (-50°C) for up to three hours in the fall, during which the blood contained up to 40 percent ice. After 10 hours the ice content rose to 50 percent, and only about half the snakes survived. After 24 hours it rose to 70 percent, and none survived. In practice what this means is that garter snakes can survive sudden temperature drops in the fall when they are still above ground. By midwinter they are safely tucked away in their underground chambers and are unlikely to experience such severe temperature fluctuations. As would be expected, their tolerance of freezing temperatures at that time of the year is lower. Despite these "tricks," winter mortality rates among garter snakes can be high—34 to 50 percent in harsh winters.

The male detects the scent with his forked tongue and rubs his snout along her back.

Dozens of males mob each female, forming huge mating balls with the larger female at the center. Each male rubs his chin along the female's back and tries to wrap his tail under hers to copulate. Eventually one male succeeds, and the others abandon the female in search of others. Mating lasts about 15 to 20 minutes. After mating, the successful male leaves a "copulation plug" in the female's vent. This waxy gelatinous plug forms a physical barrier to other males trying to mate with the female and may also contain pheromones that inhibit other males. The successful male is free to pursue other females, safe in the knowledge that his sperm cannot be displaced by a second male.

Summer Migrations

Females leave the den site as soon as they have mated and migrate to their summer feeding sites. Males do not leave until all the females have dispersed. It seems likely that some males mate with several females, but most of them do not mate at all.

The best feeding grounds can be quite a distance from the best hibernation sites, and common garter snakes travel up to 11 miles (18 km) to reach them. They are thought to navigate by the sun, but other factors including pheromone trails can deflect them. Some individuals' travels apparently take the form of a loop that begins and ends at the hibernation den rather than retracing their route in the fall.

Developing Young

Males are free to feed throughout the summer and build up reserves for the next period of hibernation, but females stop feeding when their developing young begin to take up space in their bodies. Garter snakes are truly viviparous: The developing young obtain nourishment from their mother through her blood, which also transports embryonic waste products away from them.

The gestation period is about 60 to 90 days, and the young are born toward the end of summer. Bearing live young has huge benefits in cold climates, where females can bask in the sun to raise their body temperatures

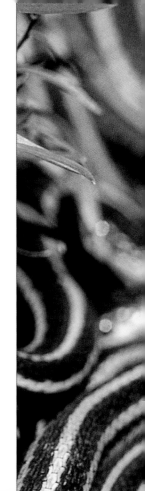

Large Congregations

Garter snakes from northern climes come together to hibernate in underground limestone cavities where frost cannot reach them. Some dens have an estimated 8,000 to 10,000 snakes in them, although populations fluctuate. Farther south, in Michigan for example, winter aggregations are smaller, with up to 150 individuals, while in the far south garter snakes do not congregate at all.

They do not always use underground crevices—abandoned ant mounds are widely used. In a two-year survey in the 1960s 11 ant nests yielded 2,019 red-bellied snakes, *Storeria occipitomaculata*, 276 smooth green snakes, *Liochlorophis vernalis*, and 131 common garter snakes. The highest number from a single mound was 299 snakes, including all three of the above species.

Snakes congregate during hibernation for three main reasons. First, there is often a shortage of good hibernation sites; this is increasingly important in areas where temperatures drop dramatically, because only the deepest crevices will provide adequate protection from the cold. Second, by clumping together, the snakes may gain an additional advantage in reduction of heat loss. Third, they can use each other for mutual insulation and reduce water loss by exposing less of their surface to the atmosphere. The last reason is especially important for small snakes, including several north American species such as the brown snake, *Storeria dekayi*, and the closely related red-bellied snake, Butler's garter snake, *Thamnophis butleri*, and common garter snakes.

A group of red-sided garter snakes, Thamnophis sirtalis parietalis, emerge from hibernation at the same time. Large numbers aggregate in favored places and hibernate for many months of the year.

and therefore those of the developing young. On the other hand, females that have carried their young throughout the spring and early summer have little time to build up their fat reserves. It is likely that in the north they breed every second year, but in the south they have a longer season and breed every year.

Litter sizes vary greatly in garter snakes. Most forms give birth to six to 12 young, but much larger litters are possible, and litters of up to 80 have been recorded.

Varied Diet

All garter snakes eat a variety of food items, including earthworms, leeches, fish, and amphibians. Different populations have different preferences, probably depending on availability. Some populations enter tidal pools to hunt for small marine fish, while others prey extensively on toxin-bearing California newts, which individuals from other populations avoid altogether. Scientists think that where newts are an important food source, the young snakes obtain immunity to toxins from their parents.

Garter snakes are diurnal and hunt initially by sight, but they need the stimulation of smell before they will attack their prey. Once food has been identified as edible, it is simply grabbed and swallowed. Garter snakes eat mostly food that cannot fight back, so there is no rush to subdue it before swallowing. It is not unknown for prey that has been swallowed to be found still alive if it is disgorged later. A few of the larger garter snakes, especially those from drier habitats, occasionally eat small mammals and nestling birds.

Different Forms

Because of its large range, the common garter snake shows considerable variation in form, and several subspecies are recognized. Many bear little resemblance to one another and can be difficult to identify.

The most distinctive form is the San Francisco garter snake, *T. s. tetrataenia*, a highly endangered subspecies that lives only in four small sites within San Mateo County, California.

⬆ **Thamnophis sirtalis concinnus**, *the red-spotted garter snake, is a beautifully colored subspecies found along the coasts of Oregon and California.*

This beautiful snake has a red head. A pair of bright-red, black-edged stripes runs along its back on either side of the white central stripe that is common to most members of the species. Since it lives in a built-up part of California, the species' best hope of survival is through the captive-breeding programs in North American and European zoos.

Neighboring subspecies, including the California red-sided garter snake, *T. s. infernalis*, and the Oregon red-spotted garter snake, *T. s. concinnus*, also have extensive areas of red in their patterns; while others, such as the northern red-sided garter snake, *T. s. parietalis*, have red spaces between their black scales, which only show when their skin is distended, either after they have eaten a large meal or when they flatten themselves in response

➡ **A San Francisco garter snake,** Thamnophis sirtalis tetrataenia, *takes to the water in California. These beautiful snakes are highly endangered.*

The Relatives

There are 26 species of garter snakes altogether and another two species of *Thamnophis* that are popularly known as ribbon snakes, making 28 in all. Of these, 16 occur in the United States, including three that enter Canada and five that enter Mexico. Another 12 live in Mexico (but not the United States), and they include three that extend down into Central America. Two species, the checkered garter snake, *T. marcianus,* and the western ribbon snake, *T. proximus*, extend from the United States in the north to Costa Rica in the south, while one species, *Thamnophis valida*, only occurs in Baja California, Mexico.

to a possible predator. Some herpetologists think that this show of red may be a form of warning coloration.

Common garter snakes in the central and eastern states are less likely to have red in their pattern, but one subspecies from Florida, *T. s. similis*, has an overall bluish wash. It is also among the largest of the common garter snake subspecies. Melanistic (all-black) individuals have been found in several populations but are especially frequent in coastal areas, including those of the Great Lakes, and on islands. George Island, in Halifax harbor, Canada, has a particularly high incidence of melanistic common garter snakes as well as a number of other unusual color forms.

Ringneck Snake

Diadophis punctatus

Common name Ringneck snake

Scientific name *Diadophis punctatus*

Subfamily Uncertain, possibly Xenodontinae

Family Colubridae

Suborder Serpentes

Order Squamata

Length From 8 in (20 cm) to 30 in (76 cm)

Key features Body black, blue-black, dark- or olive-brown with a red or yellow underside and a collar of similar color just behind the head; scales smooth; head is small and hardly distinct from the neck; eyes also small

Habits Secretive, hides during the day; active at night or after rain in the early morning and evening

Breeding Egg layer with clutches of 2–10 eggs (usually 2–6) in June or July; eggs hatch after 28–42 days

Diet Invertebrates such as earthworms, small amphibians, lizards, and snakes

Habitat Damp places such as wood and forest edges, fields, farms, and gardens; in drier regions restricted to the areas around ponds and watercourses

Distribution Much of North America from coast to coast, including southern parts of Canada, extending to northern and north-central Mexico; possibly introduced to the Cayman Islands, West Indies

Status Very common to rare depending on locality

Similar species In Florida the red-bellied swamp snake, *Seminatrix pygaea,* or the worm snake, *Carphophis amoenus,* but they lack the red or yellow collar

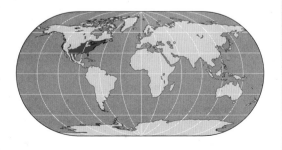

The secretive little ringneck snake is very fond of hiding and often goes unnoticed, even though it is one of the most numerous species in many parts of its range. It can occur in greater numbers than any other snake species.

THE RINGNECK SNAKE IS extremely prolific. In parts of Kansas ringneck snakes occur at the rate of 290 to 749 snakes per acre (719 to 1,849 per hectare). This is the greatest density of any known snake species.

Yet how can so many snakes go unnoticed? Apart from the fact that they are small, ringneck snakes spend most of the day hidden under flat rocks or in rotting logs and stumps. They also use human detritus in the form of discarded slates, tiles, and pieces of corrugated tin: 279 snakes were once found under just 24 pieces of tin. In an experiment 40 ringneck snakes were released into an area with 12 identical slates on the ground, but all the snakes grouped themselves under just four slates, leaving eight unoccupied. This suggests that they gain some advantage by clustering together, but nobody knows what that might be. However, it seems that they track each other down by smell. Ringneck snakes have a distinctive smell even to the poorly equipped human olfactory system.

Damp Habitats

The most favorable conditions for ringneck snakes, and therefore the places where they are most common, are moist fields, woods, and gardens. Where they live in dry regions, they can only live in damp microhabitats, such as around the edges of pools in seasonal rivers and streams, or underground in rocky crevices and among moisture-retaining roots of cacti and shrubs. They emerge only at night, especially after rain. In the dry season they are

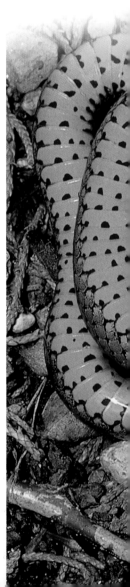

not active on the surface at all. In parts of the southwestern United States they are absent over large areas because it is too dry, and many populations have become isolated from the rest of the species because of unsuitable conditions.

Foul-Smelling Substance

As well as using scent to communicate with each other, ringneck snakes use a strong-smelling secretion produced in their anal glands to deter predators, in common with several other species of snakes. They have a second line of defense, however, in the form of a dramatic display. If they are annoyed, they will coil up their tail like a corkscrew and show off their bright red, orange, or yellow underside. Apart from startling predators, the

bright coloration is thought to deflect the predator's attention away from the snake's head, which remains hidden among its coils. If the predator attacks the snake's tail, it gets smeared with the foul-smelling anal secretion; and after attacking a few ringneck snakes, the predator may learn to leave them alone. If the tail display fails to produce the desired effect, the snakes may turn over onto their back completely, showing the bright underside of their body, and pretend to be dead.

Not all populations go through this sequence, however. Ringnecks from most of the eastern states have yellow bellies and do not display their tails, whereas those from the western states and Florida have red undersides and do display.

⊕ *This regal ringneck snake from Arizona demonstrates its effective warning display by coiling its tail into a corkscrew and revealing its bright-red underside.*

Although an accurate explanation for this is hard to find, scientists have noticed that scrub jays, *Amphelocoma coerulescens*, are common in places where ringnecks are most likely to display, but not in places where they do not. Scrub jays specialize in picking through leaf litter in search of food and could be expected to turn up ringneck snakes occasionally. It is possible that the tail display behavior has evolved in response to scrub jays or similar predators hunting in this way. In Kansas, where the snakes have been well studied, about two-thirds of juveniles coiled their tails when handled, compared with fewer than one-third of adults, so it seems that their behavior changes with age as well as with location.

Unusual Biology

The ringneck is unique. There are no other species in the genus, and it does not seem to be very closely related to any other snakes. It is sometimes placed in the subfamily Xenodontinae ("strange-toothed snakes"), but scientists are not quite sure where it fits into the bigger picture.

Some aspects of its biology are quite unusual too. Despite its small size, it is very successful. Females take three years to reach breeding size. They lay small clutches of two to 10 eggs, but more usually two to six, and they only breed once each year. Even so, studies have shown that on average about 34 percent of newborn ringneck snakes survive their first year; and once they reach adult size, the survival rate goes up to 74 percent per year. That figure is very high compared to other snakes. Ringneck snakes probably live for 15 years, longer than many far larger snakes such as garter snakes, for example, which only live seven or eight years on average.

Female ringneck snakes lay their eggs in crevices, under flat rocks, in cracks in old buildings, and in abandoned small mammal and cicada holes. Several females may choose the same place to lay their eggs. Each egg is elongated like a sausage, and the shell is very thin and translucent. The embryo is quite well

Separate Identities

All subspecies of the ringneck snake intergrade with neighboring subspecies where their ranges come into contact, as is normal with subspecies. The regal ringneck, *D.p. regalis*, and the prairie ringneck, *D. p. arnyi*, interbreed over a wide area in Texas, for example, giving rise to a wide range of intermediate sizes (the prairie ringneck being significantly smaller than the regal ringneck).

In the Guadaloupe Mountains on the Texas–New Mexico border, however, they live side by side and do not appear to interbreed: Both subspecies maintain their identities, and the larger regal ringneck as well as the smaller prairie ringneck can be found in the same area with no intermediates. It seems that two populations were once separated by unsuitable habitat and evolved different characteristics, including size and, presumably, breeding behavior. When the populations came into contact again due to habitat change, they were different enough to prevent interbreeding. Interestingly, they did not evolve away from each other so much that they see each other as potential prey—the regal ringneck snake preys heavily on other snakes but does not appear to eat prairie ringnecks.

advanced when the female lays it, and it hatches after only four to six weeks.

The tiny young measure 3.5 to 5 inches (9–13 cm) long, and there are usually more males than females. Females are larger than males at hatching. This is unusual: In most snake species in which there is a difference in size between the sexes, both sexes start out the same size but grow at different rates. Male and female ringneck snakes, however, are different sizes from birth.

The young snakes probably eat small invertebrates. As they grow, their choice of food widens; and adults eat earthworms, salamanders, frogs, lizards, and other snakes. Their rear teeth do not have grooves but are enlarged. They produce venom that is not dangerous to humans. They subdue their prey by constricting it loosely while chewing on it, waiting for the venom to take effect. In this way they can overcome prey that is relatively large, especially if it is elongated, and ringnecks can eat snakes that are longer than themselves. They eat on average 27 meals in a season, and the combined weight of their meals is about three times their own body weight. (Most other snakes eat more than this.)

In places where the summers are dry, such as Texas, ringneck snakes estivate (meaning that they remain inactive underground to avoid unfavorable conditions). They do this partly because the worms and amphibians that make up most of their diet are hard to find in dry weather. They spend the time hidden away in cracks in dried-out clay, under rocks, or in old rodent and insect burrows.

Variations

Generally speaking, ringneck snakes are aptly named. There are populations that have no collar, or only a very faint one, although they are still called ringnecks. One such population, the Key ringneck, *Diadophis punctatus acrirus*, lives on the Florida Keys, particularly on Big Pine Key and the Torch Keys, where its numbers have been reduced by commercial development. Fortunately, this area is also home

to the endangered Key deer, *Odocoileus virginianus clavium*. A protected area has been set aside for the deer. By chance this may save the Florida ringneck snake as well.

Other variants are divided into about 13 or 14 subspecies. One that is very distinct is the regal ringneck snake, *Diadophis punctatus regalis* from some of the central and western states, including Arizona and Texas, and down into north-central Mexico.

This snake is much larger than the other subspecies, growing to 30 inches (76 cm) in places. It is steel gray in color and feeds almost entirely on other snakes. Its larger size may have evolved as a response to the dry environment in which it lives, since large snakes tend to retain moisture more efficiently than small ones (because they have a smaller surface-to-mass ratio). Its size may also enable it to eat larger prey since its preferred prey elsewhere (such as earthworms) is not found in dry places.

⊙ *The ringneck snake employs partial constriction to subdue its prey. This regal ringneck from Arizona has enveloped a snake in its coils and is waiting for its venom to take effect.*

241

Dipsas indica

Common name American snail-eaters

Scientific name *Dipsas* sp.

Subfamily Dipsadinae

Family Colubridae

Suborder Serpentes

Order Squamata

Length From about 18 in (45 cm) to 30 in (75 cm)

Key features Very slender with short, wide head and narrow neck; snout blunt; eyes large and protruding with vertical pupils; body compressed from side to side, producing a ridge along the backbone; scales are large and show a range of colors and markings depending on species

Habits Arboreal; nocturnal

Breeding Egg layers with small clutches of 2–4 eggs, but details of where they lay them in the wild are not known

Diet Slugs and snails

Habitat Rain forests, living in the forest canopy; rarely seen on or near the ground

Distribution From western Mexico and the Yucatán Peninsula down through Central America into northern South America as far as extreme northern Argentina

Status Probably very common but hard to find and therefore underrecorded

Similar species Some of the 31 species in the genus are superficially similar; other thin, arboreal snakes in the region

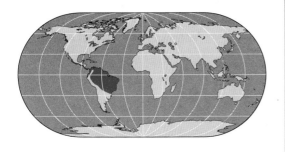

American Snail-Eaters

Dipsas sp.

Living secretive lives in the rain-forest canopy and being active only at night mean that the snail-eating snakes of the American tropics rarely come into contact with humans.

SNAIL-EATERS ARE HARD TO FIND. Following their behavior is even harder, which is why most of our knowledge comes from museum specimens and observation of captive specimens. Their most notable feature is their ability to eat snails. To do this, they have evolved a jaw arrangement that is completely different from that of other snakes (apart from another group of snail-eaters that live in Southeast Asia).

In *Dipsas* species the upper teeth point inward toward the midline of the mouth, not backward as in most other snakes, and the teeth in the lower jaws are long and needle-like. They have an extra joint in the lower jaw so that the front part can move independently of the more rigid rear part. This allows the snake to push each side of its lower jaw forward alternately.

Expert Technique

The snake locates a snail by following its slime trail, using its tongue to pick up a scent. It bites into the snail close to its shell. The snail reacts by withdrawing its body into the shell, dragging the snake's lower jaw with it. The upper jaw slides over the outside of the shell, preventing the snail from withdrawing completely. As this happens, the bones holding the snake's upper rows of teeth bend inward so that the teeth are not damaged. The snake then begins the extraction process by bracing its upper jaw on the snail's shell. Using specialized abductor muscles, it pulls on each lower jawbone alternately. Withdrawing the snail from its shell is the hardest part of the procedure; but once it is out, the snake still has to cope with holding

⬆ *A banded snail-eater, Dipsas bicolor, on a leaf in rain forest in Costa Rica. Snail-eaters rarely come down to the ground, since the rain-forest canopy is an ideal place for finding snails and slugs. For the same reason they are also more active during or after rain.*

and swallowing a wriggling, slippery animal. Its jaw modifications help with this.

Other behavioral aspects of *Dipsas* are not as well known. A female *Dipsas articulata* laid clutches of two and three eggs, one of which hatched in 85 days. This species, together with others that live in tropical regions where the seasons are not well defined, may well breed throughout the year when conditions are suitable. Nothing is known about the egg-laying sites, but it seems unlikely that the snakes come down to the ground. Tropical trees are festooned with epiphytic plants such as orchids, bromeliads, and ferns that accumulate forest debris and moss around them. These aerial compost heaps probably provide the right conditions for the developing eggs.

When captured, snail-eaters do not attempt to bite, but they obtain protection from some predators by resembling venomous snakes. Some species are brightly banded like coral snakes, and others are very good likenesses of arboreal pit vipers that live in the same parts of the world.

Other American Snail-Eaters

The subfamily to which the *Dipsas* species belong, the Dipsadinae, includes many snakes that do not eat mollusks but have more generalized feeding habits. Many of them eat lizards, for instance. The most closely related genus is *Sibynomorphus*, which shares many of the jaw modifications with *Dipsas* and probably feeds in the same way. Two other genera, *Sibon* and *Tropidodipsas*, also eat slugs (and possibly snails) but have to make do without the specialized toolkit of the other species.

Western Hognose Snake

Heterodon nasicus

The western hognose snake is a chunky little snake that has some unusual physiological and behavioral characteristics. It is one of the more interesting North American snakes.

THE HOGNOSE SNAKES are best known for their defensive routine. When it is first discovered, a hognose snake often puts on a show of aggression, inflating its body and flattening its neck, at the same time hissing and striking vigorously. It strikes with its mouth closed, however, and can hardly ever be induced to bite. If its bravado does not have the desired effect, it writhes and contorts its body, eventually rolling over onto its back in a coiled or partially coiled posture. It will often void the pungent contents of its anal gland at the same time, smearing it over much of its body. At this point it may allow its mouth to gape open and its tongue to hang out. It remains motionless for several minutes at a time, until it thinks the coast is clear, when it slowly rights itself. If it senses the enemy is still watching, it may suddenly flip back over and continue to feign death. Indeed, if it is righted by hand, it will immediately turn belly-up again, which sort of gives the game away!

Playing Dead

Scientists have long speculated on the purpose of this defense strategy, which is also practiced by a number of other snakes, notably the European grass snake, *Natrix natrix*, and the African rinkhals, or spitting cobra, *Hemachatus haemachatus*. It is pretty clear that the snake is playing dead, but what is the advantage of this given the fact that many of its predators are happy to eat dead prey? Several theories have been put forward, but the most plausible seems to be that if the predator thinks the prey is already dead, it will be tricked into not killing it. The stratagem is not much use if the predator

Common name Western hognose snake (puff adder—a local name, not to be confused with the venomous African viper of the same name)

Scientific name *Heterodon nasicus*

Subfamily Xenodontinae

Family Colubridae

Suborder Serpentes

Order Squamata

Length 16 in (40 cm) to 35 in (90 cm)

Key features Pointed, sharply upturned snout; stout body and thick neck with heavily keeled scales; usually brown but can be yellowish with well-defined blotches down its back

Habits Diurnal; terrestrial and semiburrowing

Breeding Egg layer with clutches of 4–23 eggs; eggs hatch after 50–62 days

Diet Toads and frogs; also lizards, snakes, reptile eggs, small rodents, and birds

Habitat Well-drained shortgrass prairie, rocky semidesert, fields and wood edges, chaparral, and deserts; also found around human dwellings

Distribution North America (central states) extending into southern Canada and northern Mexico

Status Common and widespread but becoming scarce due to habitat destruction in places

Similar species Eastern hognose snake, *Heterodon platyrhinos*, but that species has a less upturned snout, and blotches on its body are more squarish

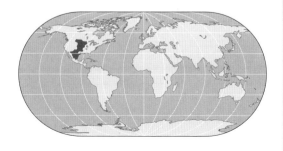

intends to eat the snake right away, but it may decide to hide it before eating it or carry it to its young. That may provide the snake with an opportunity to crawl away later.

The three snakes that adopt such a stratagem all feed heavily on toads. Some herpetologists have speculated that these snakes may accumulate the potent toxins from toads' skins and void them along with the contents of their anal gland (the stuff that smells bad) and so deter predators this way.

Unusual Teeth

Another peculiarity of hognose snakes is the arrangement of their teeth. The name *Heterodon*

⊙ *A western hognose snake feigns death. It is one of a number of snakes that employ this method to fool predators.*

means "different teeth" and refers to the combination of a normal set of teeth along the front part of the upper jaw with enlarged teeth on the jawbone, which is highly movable. Each maxilla houses about five conventional teeth and two or three elongated teeth at the end farthest from the snout. These teeth point directly backward toward the snake's throat. To bring these teeth into play, the snake swings its maxilla forward by about 80 degrees. Even then, the teeth are so far back in the mouth that they are of no use until the prey is well on its way down the snake's throat.

The main purpose of the movable fangs is probably to help push the snake's prey—which is often still alive when swallowing begins— down its throat and to prevent it from backing out. At the same time, they puncture its skin

The Relatives

There are three subspecies of the western hognose snake. The plains hognose snake, *Heterodon nasicus nasicus*, is the typical (nominate) form of the species. It is the northernmost subspecies, extending from Canada through the central states as far as northern Texas and most of New Mexico. The dusty hognose snake, *H. n. gloydi*, has less distinct markings than the nominate form and fewer dorsal blotches. Most of its range is in Texas. The Mexican hognose snake, *H. n. kennerlyi*, is from southern Texas, New Mexico, and northern Mexico. Its dorsal blotches are even less sharp-edged than those of the dusty hognose, and it has a different arrangement of small scales on top of its head.

Closley related to the western hognose snake is the eastern hognose snake, *Heterodon platyrhinos*. It has a more easterly distribution over most of the eastern and southeastern states. It overlaps the western hognose in some central areas. It has a less upturned snout and variable colors and markings. All-black individuals are common in places. The eastern hognose is more inclined to play dead than the western hognose.

The southern hognose snake, *Heterodon simus*, occurs mostly in Florida and in coastal parts of North and South Carolina, Georgia, Louisiana, and Mississippi. It is the smallest species, paler in color than the other two, and a burrower in sandy soil.

and allow toxins from the Duvernoy's glands to run into the wounds. The venom is not used to restrain the prey before swallowing, as it is in most venomous snakes, but it may help stop it struggling while it is in the process of being swallowed. Earlier accounts that the snakes used their movable fangs to puncture the inflated bodies of toads are incorrect, since the fangs are not long enough to penetrate through to the toads' lungs, and they cannot be used until swallowing is well under way.

Hognose snake venom is thick and opaque and not especially powerful. In humans, assuming the snake can be made to bite, it

⬆ Young hognoses hatch in the summer. The young are very similar in appearance to the adults but measure about one-third of their eventual adult size.

⬅ Heterodon nasicus, the western hognose snake, gets its common name from the enlarged upturned scale on its snout that is said to give it a "hoglike" appearance.

causes some pain and swelling around the bite but no dizziness or nausea. The tenderness may last a day or two but then disappears.

Diet

Apart from toads, which figure highly in their diet, western hognose snakes also eat a variety of other vertebrates, including other snakes, lizards, birds, and small mammals. They also eat reptile eggs and have on occasion been known to eat their own eggs in captivity. They may use a section of their body to pin their prey to the ground, but swallowing usually occurs very quickly, even with relatively large prey. They are among the few snakes that seem equally prepared to swallow animals backward, and when eating rodents, they may even grasp them in the middle and fold them in half as they engulf them.

Most of their prey is probably found by smell, and they specialize in catching prey that is hidden underground, either in tunnels or in loose soil. They use their sharp-edged, upturned snout to root out their prey. Hognose snakes, in the wild as well as in captivity, are willing to take food that has been dead for some time, and their acute sense of smell probably helps them locate carrion.

Lifestyle and Breeding

Hognose snakes are solitary, active mostly in the spring and fall, and hibernate singly through the winter. Females breed every second year, using alternate years to replace body weight lost during egg laying. Males, which are considerably smaller than females, move around in the spring in search of mates. They will also mate in the fall, in which case females store the sperm until the following spring. About 40 days after a spring mating the female lays a clutch of six to 12 eggs (exceptionally up to 23 eggs) under dead vegetation or in a chamber in the soil. They take 50 to 62 days to hatch, and the young are about 6 to 7 inches (15–17 cm) long. They are often more inclined to play dead than the adults. Although they are all the same size at hatching, females grow more quickly than males because they have heartier appetites, reaching breeding size in fewer than two years. Adult females average 20 inches (51 cm) in length, whereas males average 16.5 inches (42 cm). On average, males weigh less than half as much as females.

Hognose snakes also use their snouts to burrow beneath the surface to escape hot weather. The desert form, *H. n. kennerlyi*, has a more pronounced snout than the other subspecies, probably because it lives in places where the soil is baked hard by the sun. Unlike most other snakes, hognose snakes rarely crawl under rocks or other objects to hide.

Ants in the Eggs

Conservationists are concerned that in some southern U.S. states certain snakes, including the western hognose snake, are being reduced in number by invading fire ants, *Solenopsis invicta*, which prey on their eggs and newly hatched young. The evidence is based on reduced numbers of egg-laying species in areas into which the ants have spread, compared with numbers of snakes that give birth to live young, which appear not to be declining.

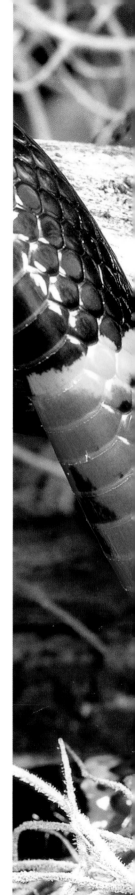

Sonoran coral snake
(*Micruroides
euryxanthus*)

Common name Coral snakes

Scientific names *Micrurus* sp. and *Micruroides euryxanthus*

Subfamily Elapinae

Family Elapidae

Suborder Serpentes

Order Squamata

Number of species 54

Length From 10.5 in (27 cm) to 5 ft (1.5 m) depending on species

Key features Cylindrical snakes; usually slender, but a few species are stocky; head small and a little wider than the neck; tail short; eyes small and black; scales smooth and shiny; typically brightly colored in rings of red, black, and yellow (or white), but there is some variation

Habits Mostly burrowing and secretive, although they can be seen on the surface at least occasionally; 1 species is semiaquatic

Breeding Egg layers, but details of breeding behavior are lacking for most species

Diet Snakes, burrowing lizards, and worm lizards; *Micrurus surinamensis* eats eels

Habitat Varied; from deserts to rain forests

Distribution North America (2 species) through Central America (many species) and into South America as far south as central Argentina

Status Common in places, but some species are known from only a few specimens

Similar species Many, all of which may be mimics

Venom Dangerously neurotoxic; bites may be life threatening unless treated

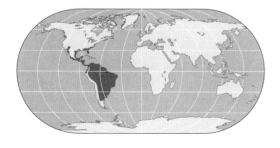

American Coral Snakes

Micrurus and *Micruroides*

"Red and yellow kill a fellow, red and black venom lack." The rhyme reminds us how coral snakes in North America can be distinguished from nonvenomous snakes by the colored rings around their bodies—if red touches yellow, the snake is usually venomous.

CORAL SNAKES HAVE MUCH the same lifestyles as many other secretive species of snakes. They are most often associated with rain forests, but some species live in deserts, scrub, or dry deciduous and thorn forests.

They may be active by day or by night; and in places where there are distinct seasonal differences (such as Arizona and parts of northern Mexico), their activity pattern may change. It may go from day-active in spring and fall to nocturnal in summer.

Forest Foragers

Coral snakes forage through leaf litter, looking for smaller snakes to eat, although one has been seen several feet up in a tree eating a ratsnake. Many Central and South American species eat burrowing reptiles, especially worm lizards, which they follow through their tunnels.

Coral snakes typically bite their prey and then hang on until the venom begins to take effect. They then manipulate the prey in their mouth to swallow it headfirst, using the direction of their prey's scales to find the head.

One coral snake species, *Micrurus surinamensis*, is semiaquatic and eats eels. It is one of the largest coral snakes, reported as reaching up to 6 feet (1.8 m) in length and regularly growing to 5 feet (1.5 m).

An eastern coral snake, *Micrurus fulvius fulvius*, *in Florida. The color sequence reveals it as a true, venomous coral snake (because the yellow and red bands are touching each other).*

Other large species that also grow to 5 feet (1.5 m) include the regal coral snake, *M. ancoralis* from Colombia and Ecuador, and the Venezuelan coral snake, *M. isozonus* also from Colombia. The smallest species may be the Colombian coral snake, *M. spurrelli,* at 10.5 inches (27 cm); but since the species is only known from three specimens, it is possible that it grows larger. A number of other species are rare and known from just a handful of species with a limited distribution. However, Spix's coral snake, *Micrurus spixi*, has a huge range that covers the whole of the Amazon Basin. Others are also widespread.

Little is known about courtship in coral snakes, but all species lay eggs. One relatively well-studied species, *Micrurus fulvius* from southeastern North America, has clutches of between three and eight eggs. The hatchlings are colored in the same way as the adults.

Venom

Although they do not attack humans very often, coral snakes have powerful venom that affects the nervous system. Often there are no

Mimicry in Animals

Mimicry in animals was first described by the English naturalist and explorer Henry Bates in a paper in 1861, although his subject was Amazonian butterflies. He noticed that edible species often had colors and markings almost identical to distasteful ones. He theorized that the predators avoided the edible butterflies after bad experiences with the nasty ones. Since Bates's time many other examples of mimicry have been described, including a species of African swallowtail butterfly, *Papilio dardanus*, in which the females mimic any one of five different distasteful species, beetles that mimic wasps, lizards that mimic beetles, and caterpillars that mimic snakes.

Nelson's milksnake, Lampropeltis triangulum nelsoni *from Mexico, is a nonvenomous mimic of the coral snakes.*

immediate effects in humans, but symptoms begin after two to six hours, and sometimes up to 48 hours, later. The first symptom is double vision followed by general muscle weakness. In the most serious cases the symptoms can lead to respiratory arrest and death. Bites containing venom may prove fatal in about 20 percent of all cases.

Color Mimicry

Many snakes (and other reptiles and amphibians for that matter) use color to increase their survival prospects. There is a theory that some harmless snakes gain protection from predators by mimicking the dangerous coral snake species. (They are sometimes called "false coral snakes.") Predators that have had a bad experience with a venomous coral snake are reluctant to attack

The coral snake Micrurus frontifasciatus *lives in the Andean Desert of Bolivia at 10,000 feet (3,300 m) in altitude and is a very rare species.*

Innate Aversion

In a series of experiments in the 1970s a researcher named Susan Smith showed how birds bred in captivity avoided wooden rods painted with black, yellow, and red rings. However, the birds were indifferent to other rods painted in different color schemes. She called this "innate aversion." In other words, the birds (which had never experienced the real thing in nature) had an inbuilt sense that objects with this coloration were best avoided. Humans are the same: We use similar color patterns (often red) on signs that warn of danger. Having an instantly recognizable signal is important because predators often need to make immediate decisions whether to attack or retreat when they uncover potential prey.

any snake that resembles it. Ever since the theory was first put forward, there have been a number of objections to it; but what is not in doubt is that coral snakes have vivid colors and markings to protect themselves in some way.

Of the 50 or so species most have bands arranged into groups of three, or triads, with the sequence red-yellow-black-yellow-red. There are other arrangements, but they are in the minority. A few species, for example, have only two colors, such as yellow and red or black with white rings.

The bright colors probably work to the snake's advantage in several ways. First, despite their bright colors, coral snakes are not always easy to see in the broken light of a rain forest.

The "Other" Coral Snakes

Of the 54 species of American coral snakes 53 are in the genus *Micrurus,* and the remaining one is the only species in the genus *Micruroides*. It is the Sonoran coral snake, *M. euryxanthus,* which lives in the southwestern United States (mostly in Arizona but also in a small part of New Mexico) and in northwestern Mexico, mainly in the state of Sonora. It is a small species, growing to about 18 inches (46 cm) in length. Its black, red, and yellow or white bands are of roughly equal width.

The Sonoran coral snake has several mimics, including the shovel-nosed snake, *Chilomeniscus palarostris*, and the long-nosed snake, *Rhinocheilus lecontei*. It lives in dry areas, often semidesert habitats, and is active mainly at dusk. It eats small snakes, including quite a high proportion of *Leptotyphlops* species thread snakes. The venom of *M. euryxanthus* is not very potent and usually affects only the area around the bite. There have been no recorded fatalities.

It is important not to confuse the American coral snakes with other coral snakes from around the world, which include the Malaysian species in the genera *Maticora* and *Calliophis*, the South African *Aspidelaps lubricus*, and the Australian *Simoselaps australis*, all of which are also called coral snakes.

Next, there is the startle element: A predator picking through the leaf litter will be surprised when it uncovers a brightly colored coral snake and may hesitate before attacking it, giving the snake time to escape. Third, when a coral snake moves quickly through leaves or vegetation, the colored bands flicker as they pass before the eyes, creating a kind of optical illusion. An observer can still be trying to make out the shape of the snake and figure out which direction it is going when it is suddenly gone.

If an attacker persists, coral snakes all have similar display behaviors. They raise their tail, coiling and uncoiling it repeatedly to divert attention away from the head, which they often hide under their body (the Latinized name

⊕ *A Sonoran coral snake,* Micruroides euryxanthus *from Arizona. The Sonoran species is the only member of its genus.*

Micrurus means flickering or flashing tail). In the final stages of the display they writhe around erratically, thrashing their head from side to side, and snapping at anything they touch. The bright alternating colors enhance this display and may intimidate predators.

Once the snake has convinced a predator that it is dangerous, the snake needs to make sure that the predator recognizes it again in the future, hence the distinctive markings.

Types of Mimicry

Taking this one stage farther, if there are several species of coral snakes in an area and they are all similar in appearance, they will all benefit from each other's signals. This is known as Müllerian mimicry after the German naturalist Fritz Müller, who first described it in 1879.

False Pretenses

But if harmless snakes also look like the venomous ones, they can also benefit under false pretenses. This is known as Batesian mimicry. Many of the coral snake mimics, such as the milksnake, *Lampropeltis triangulum*, also thrash around if they are disturbed, adding to the similarity. The sequence of colored rings on some of the false coral snakes is different from that of real coral snakes—but predators would be unable to analyze such detailed information. (In Batesian mimicry the mimicking snake is known as the mimic, and the snake it is mimicking is called the model.)

There are some objections to the mimicry theory. The first is that coral snakes are so venomous that predators would be killed in their first encounter, so the lesson would be wasted. In the past some scientists argued that the real models were not coral snakes at all but mildly venomous rear-fanged species—such as *Erythrolamprus* from Central and South America. In fact, the explanation is probably simpler than this.

It seems that predators have an "innate aversion" to coral snakes and all other brightly colored animals. In other words, they avoid them whether they have seen them before or not. Perhaps they learned their lesson from brightly colored caterpillars that are distasteful but not deadly, or perhaps they are genetically programed to avoid brightly colored animals. That may be because in previous generations the individuals that did not avoid them were killed and were therefore unable to pass on their genes. The theory of innate aversion has been established scientifically in a number of different experiments.

Other scientists have objected because some of the brightly colored mimics, such as the California mountain king snake, *Lampropeltis zonata*, live in places where there are no coral snakes. Even so, they may have lived side by side in the past. In any case, their predators will include migratory birds that move from place to place and therefore may have seen coral snakes elsewhere.

The final objection is that coral snakes are nocturnal, and predators would never see their bright colors anyway. That is simply wrong. Coral snakes are just as likely to be on the surface during the day as at night. They are especially active in the evening, on overcast days, or during rainstorms.

If brightly colored harmless snakes existed by chance (rather than because they were coral snake mimics), they would be expected to occur randomly in parts of the world far from true coral snakes, such as Europe, Asia, and Africa—but they do not. False coral snakes have been identified in 35 genera of harmless or mildly venomous snakes, all confined (broadly speaking) to the southwestern parts of the United Sates, Mexico, and Central and South America, where coral snakes also live.

Changing Colors

An even more convincing argument points out that if a number of different coral snakes live within the range of a single harmless mimic, the mimic's markings will alter from place to place so that it looks almost exactly like the species with which it is found. The opposite is also true: A single coral snake species that varies from place to place may have different mimics that resemble its various forms. Three false coral snakes belonging to the genus *Pliocercus*, for example, all resemble the widespread *Micrurus diastema* from Central America, but each *Pliocercus* species resembles the particular color form of *M. diastema* with which it is found.

To sum up, coral snakes avoid predation by a variety of different methods. They may startle predators, intimidate them, create optical illusions that make it hard to be handled, or they may play on the innate aversion that most animals have for brightly colored animals. In fact, they probably do all these things.

⊙ *In a Costa Rican rain forest* Micrurus mipartitus *raises its tail in a defensive posture. It is hoping that the predator will attack its tail end rather than its head, which is hidden under one of its coils.*

Common name Copperhead

Scientific name *Agkistrodon contortrix*

Subfamily Crotalinae

Family Viperidae

Suborder Serpentes

Order Squamata

Length From 24 in (61 cm) to 4 ft (1.2 m)

Key features Head triangular with large scales covering
the top and a prominent facial pit; a number
of broad, rich reddish-brown, chestnut, or
coppery bars cross the body and become
narrower toward the midline, like a bow tie,
but the two sides often fail to meet perfectly,
so they are staggered; background color is
tan, and despite its name, the head is also
tan color

Habits Terrestrial; nocturnal or diurnal according to
season

Breeding Live-bearer with litters of 4–14; gestation
period about 83–150 days

Diet Small mammals, lizards, amphibians, and
invertebrates

Habitat Well-drained, lightly wooded places, including
rocky hillsides and gardens, often near
streams and ponds

Distribution Southeastern United States and adjacent
parts of northeastern Mexico

Status Common

Similar species Some water snakes in the region are
superficially similar, but their habitat is
different, and they lack the facial pit

Venom Mildly dangerous; copperheads are placid and
do not bite unless provoked

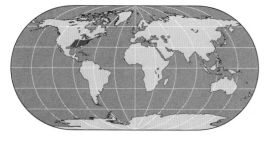

Copperhead

Agkistrodon contortrix

*The copperhead is a common snake of the forested
hills of the American Southeast, but because of its
excellent camouflage coloring it is often overlooked.*

COPPERHEADS PREFER WOODLANDS with clearings in
which to bask and rock outcrops in which to
hide and hibernate. In the northern parts of
their range the outcrops are even more
important because the snakes may hibernate
for up to six months of the year. Their other
requirement is for water or a damp area nearby
and open fields or meadows in which to hunt.
In the absence of natural outcrops copperheads
will live around drystone walls, woodpiles, and
tumbledown buildings. In some places the
woods may become inundated with water, and
they tolerate swampy conditions.

They are also found throughout southern
Texas in scrub and among the yucca and
mesquite bushes of the Chihuahan desert in
northern Mexico, but usually along river courses
or near springs. Much of this region has been
extensively settled with subsequent habitat
change. Copperheads may remain near human
settlements provided some natural areas are
left. They may be nature reserves, neglected
farmland, or narrow gorges that are unsuitable
for development. If such places are not
available, the snakes become isolated into small
colonies that eventually die out.

Perfect Camouflage

It says a lot for their camouflage that although
they are often numerous along the edges of
human habitations and can come into contact
with people in parks and even gardens, they are
rarely noticed. Their markings, which appear so
bold when seen against an unnatural
background, blend beautifully in color and
shape when they are resting among the dead
leaves of their natural habitat. The disruptive
coloration makes it very difficult to pick out the
complete form of the snake. It only works,

however, because the snakes tend to stay motionless. Even if they are suddenly exposed, they remain in a flat coil unless they are provoked. Even then they will turn and crawl away, avoiding confrontation.

The Human "Copperheads"

During the American Civil War (1861–65) southern sympathizers living in the north were called "Copperheads." The name was a play on words because not only was the South the place where copperhead snakes were most common, but there was also a suggestion of hidden danger, even treachery, in the name. Groups of Copperheads called themselves "Sons of Liberty" or "Knights of the Golden Circle" and identified themselves to each other by surreptitiously showing a copper coin with the head uppermost. Toward the end of the war, when events started to swing against the South, the Copperheads gradually melted away.

The only time they are likely to bite is if they are accidentally stepped on or deliberately molested. Then they will vibrate their tail rapidly, often rustling the dead leaves among which they are resting, and strike ferociously. Copperhead venom is typical of vipers, acting on blood corpuscles and blood vessels, causing hemorrhaging, pain and swelling to the bitten area. Yet bites are rarely serious, and effects usually disappear after a day or two.

Unusual Prey

Copperheads are unusual among pit vipers in taking cold-blooded as well as warm-blooded prey. Alongside the list of predictable prey items such as rodents, birds, lizards, and small snakes are surprise items such as frogs, salamanders, and insects and their larvae. They are surprising because they are cold-blooded, and the copperhead's heat pits have evolved to detect warm prey. Cicadas figure highly in the diet of some populations, both as larvae and as newly emerged

⊖ *Like other pit vipers, the copperhead has heat-sensitive facial pits between its nostrils and eyes to help seek out its prey.*

adults. In short, copperheads are not fussy eaters.

Juveniles are about 8 inches (20 cm) long at birth and probably eat mainly frogs and lizards at first. The tip of their tail is yellow or yellowish green. When they sense a likely meal nearby, they raise it above their coils and wave it slowly back and forth to attract the victim's attention and lure it within striking range. The tail loses its conspicuous color as the snake grows and switches its diet mainly to mice—it is no longer needed as a lure.

Shared Dens

Hibernation is an important part of the copperheads' annual cycle, especially in the northern part of their range. They need a suitable place to escape the worst of the cold and, ideally, a basking place nearby where they can benefit from the last warm days of the year and take advantage of early spring sunshine the following year.

Rock outcrops with deep fissures and south-facing ledges are perfect, and large numbers may gravitate there in the fall. They are often shared with other species of snakes, notably timber rattlesnakes, *Crotalus horridus*, but also with black ratsnakes, *Elaphe o. obsoleta*, and milksnakes, *Lampropeltis triangulum*. Mild spring days may bring groups of two or more species to the surface to "lie out" or bask together. Once the danger of frosts has passed, the snakes disperse, probably returning to home ranges with which they are familiar.

There are folktales of copperheads and black ratsnakes warning rattlesnakes that

enemies are approaching. In some places copperheads are sometimes even called "rattlesnake pilots" (and the black ratsnake is sometimes called the pilot black snake). These small, alert species sense danger before the large, heavy-bodied rattlers and take cover first, with the rattlesnakes moving away afterward.

Mating Rituals

Copperheads give birth to live young. They mate in the spring shortly after they emerge from hibernation. Males go through a combat ritual before mating, and females sometimes

⬆ Young cottonmouths, Agkistrodon piscivorus, open their mouths in a threatening behavior. The behavior shows the white interior of the mouth that gives them their common name.

initiate mock combats with males, presumably to judge their fitness as a good mating partner. If the male does not respond, they break off and move away.

Females that have mated are likely to mate again with one or more additional males, and the young in a single litter may have several fathers. This system is probably widespread in snakes, including the adders, but it has not been studied in more than a handful of species.

The young are born in August, September, or later depending to some extent on the weather. Litters range from one to 20 young, but between four and seven are more usual. There are regional variations, with females from northern populations on average having larger litters than those from the south. The markings of the young are rather dull.

After giving birth, the female remains with her young until they have shed their skins, which usually takes place when they are about one week old. Again, such parental care is not often reported for live-bearing snakes but may be more widespread than has been assumed.

The Relatives

The genus *Agkistrodon* used to include a number of Asian species until fairly recently, when they were placed in a new genus, *Gloydius. Agkistrodon* now contains three species, all from North America. The copperheads themselves are divided into five geographical races, or subspecies, all of which differ slightly in their markings, but which have areas where they intergrade (merge gradually) with each other.

The other members of the genus is the cottonmouth, *A. piscivorus*, and the cantil, *A. bilineatus*, from northern Mexico south into Central America. Of these the cantil is the closest relative to the copperheads and has much more in common with them than the cottonmouth does. Distribution of the cantil follows the coast on both the Pacific and Atlantic sides. It lives in dry deciduous forests, grasslands, and scrub but is not found in the more humid, rain-forested interior of the region. It has a reputation for

being aggressive and irascible, striking repeatedly. Like the copperhead, it is banded but much darker overall. Four striking white lines radiate from the tip of the snout, two follow the ridges along the top of the head, and the other two follow the jawline. Juveniles have a yellow tip to their tail like those of the copperheads.

The cottonmouth, also called the water moccasin, is a semiaquatic species from much the same area as the copperheads, but including Florida. Its habitats are low-lying swamps, wetlands, and lake edges. It often basks on emergent logs or stumps and can be reluctant to move away when disturbed. Instead, it opens its mouth widely and gapes, displaying the white interior that gives it its common name.

Cottonmouths are remarkable for their diet: In addition to mammals, birds, frogs, and lizards it may include young alligators, freshwater turtles, and carrion.

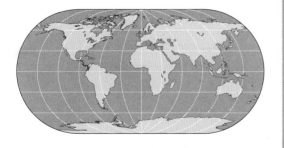

Eyelash Viper

Bothriechis schlegelii

The eyelash viper is a beautiful, dainty, but dangerous snake that ambushes its prey from a coiled position on a branch, leaf, or flower. Its common name refers to the distinctive cluster of raised scales above each eye.

Common name Eyelash viper (eyelash pit viper and many other local names)

Scientific name *Bothriechis schlegelii*

Subfamily Crotalinae

Family Viperidae

Suborder Serpentes

Order Squamata

Length From 20 in (50 cm) to 30 in (76 cm)

Key features Cluster of raised scales above each eye; body fairly slender for a viper; tail prehensile; color highly variable but basically gray-green or golden yellow; color of pupil matches that of body

Habits Tree dwelling, although it sometimes descends to the ground

Breeding Live-bearer with litters of 6– 24 small young; gestation period about 140–168 days

Diet Frogs, lizards, birds, and small mammals

Habitat Rain forests; in Central America it is a lowland and foothill species living to about 4,500 ft (1,400 m), but in South America it is found at higher elevations up to 8,000 ft (2,400 m)

Distribution Central America and northern South America

Status Common in suitable habitats

Similar species Other tree pit vipers in the region, but none have the raised scales above the eyes

Venom Bites quite common, and a small proportion are fatal

EYELASH VIPERS ARE OFTEN found at about 3 to 5 feet (1–1.5 m) above the ground. At that height there is a danger of them biting the human face, upper body, or hands. In Costa Rica about 100 people are bitten by the species each year; and although their venom is not as strong as that of some other pit vipers, its effects can be disfiguring, and a significant number of bites result in fatalities.

Leaf Ambush

The prey of eyelash vipers includes small mammals such as opossums, birds, lizards, and tree frogs. Some of them visit forest flowers, such as lobster claws, *Heliconia* species, for nectar, and the vipers may coil nearby waiting for their next meal to arrive. Even though the vipers are normally nocturnal, they strike opportunistically at hummingbirds that visit the flowers at frequent intervals throughout the day. The young eyelash vipers, which are very

Other Family Members

The genus *Bothriechis* contains seven species. Four of them— *B. aurifer*, *B. bicolor*, *B. marchi*, and *B. rowleyi*—have fairly limited ranges in Central America. The other three (*B. lateralis*, *B. nigroviridis*, and *B. schlegelii*) are more widespread. All are attractive, mostly green in color, and arboreal (tree dwelling). However, the young of *B. lateralis* are dull brown in color and spend the first six months of their lives on the forest floor, eating small lizards and frogs that live in leaf litter. As they grow, their color gradually changes until by the time they are two years old, they are bright bluish green. The local name for this colorful species is *lora*, the Spanish word for "parrot."

small, have pale tips to their tails, which they use as lures to attract frogs and small lizards.

Despite its venomous nature, the image of the eyelash viper (especially the golden form) has become something of a symbol in Costa Rica today, when ecotourism and a welcome reevaluation of biodiversity are a growing force throughout the world. The image is used to epitomize the rain forest or "jungle" in the same way as the toucan and the red-eyed leaf frog have been exploited.

⊕ *A female eyelash viper with newborn young. The young include several color forms.*

⊖ *The golden-yellow form of the eyelash viper,* Bothriechis schlegelii. *The raised scales above its eye can be clearly seen.*

Multicolored Young

Eyelash vipers occur in two basic color forms—gray-green and golden yellow—but both of them are subject to a great deal of variation. The mottled green form often has two rows of reddish spots along its back interspersed with smaller beige or pink ones. Specimens from South America are often suffused in black speckles, while those from Ecuador may have a continuous white line along their flanks. Snakes with any of these variations are well camouflaged when they are resting among lichen-covered branches.

The golden form is the other extreme. It is called the *oropel*, which is Spanish for tinsel (literally "gold skin"). It may also be uniform pale pinkish-brown, salmon, or deep yellow in color. The purpose of this coloration is hard to imagine, but there are several parallels: Young emerald tree boas, *Corallus caninus*, and green tree pythons, *Morelia viridis*, may be yellow or orange, as may tree vipers, *Trimeresurus* species from the Philippines, and bush vipers, *Atheris* species from Africa. Some scientists think that the bright colors may enable the snakes to mimic fruits or flowers and so escape notice (or possibly attract prey). The plain yellow color form is probably controlled by a simple recessive gene, and young of both types may be present in a single litter depending on the genetic makeup of the parents. The large eyes are always the same color as the body.

Common name Terciopelo (fer-de-lance, lancehead, tommygoff, and many other local names)

Scientific name *Bothrops asper*

Subfamily Crotalinae

Family Viperidae

Suborder Serpentes

Order Squamata

Length From 4 ft (1.2 m) to 8 ft (2.5 m)

Key features Body large and stocky; head triangular; snout pointed; color variable but usually tan or brown with pale-bordered triangles down each flank meeting across the back or alternating with each other

Habits Nocturnal; terrestrial, although juveniles may be partially arboreal

Breeding Live-bearer with large litters

Diet Mammals, birds, lizards, mice, and invertebrates

Habitat Rain forests, clearings, banana plantations, and fields

Distribution Central and northern South America from the Atlantic coast of Mexico through the Yucatán Peninsula and Central America and into western Venezuela and northern Ecuador

Status Very common (and probably becoming more common)

Similar species Other terrestrial pit vipers, notably the common lancehead, *Bothrops atrox*

Venom A potent and deadly hemotoxin

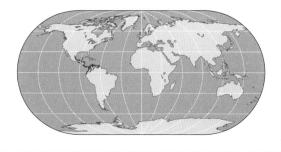

Terciopelo

Bothrops asper

Terciopelos, together with a close relative, the common lancehead, are the most dangerous snakes in the Central and South American tropics. They kill hundreds of people each year, and both species are known by the common name of fer-de-lance.

A NUMBER OF FACTORS combine to make the terciopelo dangerous. First, it is very common in areas where there is a high human population. It adapts well to human activity and disturbed habitats. Its numbers often increase once land is cleared and used for crops of banana and sugarcane, for example, and it is commonly seen around villages and farms, attracted by an abundance of rats and mice. Second, it has long fangs and is not afraid to use them.

Terciopelos have a justifiable reputation for being quick tempered and ready to defend themselves, and they can strike a long distance from a coiled position without warning. Even snakes that appear to be making off can turn and double back on their attacker, injecting large quantities of venom into their victims.

The incidence of snakebite mortalities, especially in the better-developed Central American countries, has greatly decreased since medical facilities have been improved. Another important factor in the decrease is the availability of decent footwear. Even so, in a relatively small country such as Costa Rica about 30 fatal bites are recorded each year, mostly from terciopelos.

⊙ *A juvenile terciopelo, Bothrops asper, in Mexico. This one is on the ground, although juveniles do climb in search of food.*

Close Relations

The terciopelo is closely related to another pit viper, *Bothrops atrox*, the common lancehead, which occurs farther east and south, in northern South America. The two species used to be regarded as one, and the easiest way to tell them apart is by their distribution.

Much of the information about terciopelos applies to both species. They both prefer lowland forest habitats but move up to mountain foothills in places such as the island of Trinidad. Humidity is important; and where they are found in dry places, they usually live along river courses or near other permanent sources of water. Since river courses are often routes that are easy to travel through in dense tropical forests, the habit also brings them into contact with humans. They often coil close to a fallen log or some other cover. Camouflaged against a bed of dead leaves, they are easily stepped on and present a very real danger. Where habitats have been altered, to create banana plantations, for example, they thrive. In such places mice and rats become common, while competing snakes often disappear.

Reproduction

Terciopelos give birth to live young and are among the most prolific snakes. They are seasonal breeders, but their timing varies from place to place. In Central America terciopelos living on the Pacific side of the region's mountainous backbone mate from September through to November and give birth from April to June. Those living on the Atlantic side mate in March and give birth from September to November. Birth is usually timed to coincide with the beginning of the rainy season, which varies from coast to coast.

There are also differences in litter size between the two populations: On the Pacific side litters consist on average of about 18 young, while on the Atlantic side an average litter contains 41. The juveniles eat a wider range of food than the adults, including invertebrates, frogs, and lizards, luring them with their pale-yellow tails. They may climb into low bushes in search of food. However, once they mature at about 36 inches (91 cm) long, they are strictly terrestrial, feeding almost exclusively on mammals such as rodents and opossums, and their tails become darker.

Confusing Names

The terciopelo gets its common name from the texture of its scales: *Terciopelo* is Spanish for "velvet." An alternative name for the snake is *fer-de-lance,* meaning "lancehead." However, that name has French origins and is never used by locals. Confusingly, *fer-de-lance* is also sometimes used for the common lancehead, *Bothrops atrox*. It is more properly applied to another pit viper, *B. lanceolatus*, that lives on the French-speaking West Indian island of Martinique.

Lachesis muta

Common name Bushmasters (matabueys)

Scientific name *Lachesis* sp.

Subfamily Crotalinae

Family Viperidae

Suborder Serpentes

Order Squamata

Number of species 3

Length Up to 10 ft (3 m), exceptionally to over 11 ft (3. 3 m)

Key features Massive vipers; body with heavily keeled scales giving it a knobby appearance; backbone forms a prominent ridge; head large and rounded; distinct facial pits between nostrils and eyes; color usually yellow, tan, or pinkish with sooty black, roughly diamond-shaped marking down the back; some variation in marking between the 3 species

Habits Terrestrial; nocturnal

Breeding Egg layers, with clutches of 5–18 eggs; eggs hatch after about 60 days

Diet Mammals, especially spiny rats when available

Habitat Rain forests

Distribution Central and South America, with gaps between populations

Status Common to rare; population on the southeastern Brazilian coast, *Lachesis muta rhombeata,* is endangered

Similar species The 3 species are similar to each other but unlike any other snakes

Venom Extremely toxic; 75 percent of bite victims die even with medical attention

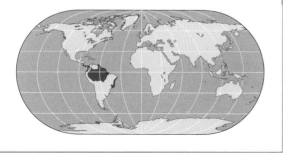

Bushmasters *Lachesis* sp.

Bushmasters are incredible snakes. They are the largest venomous snakes in the Americas and the longest vipers to be found anywhere.

BUSHMASTERS LIVE IN undisturbed rain forests and quickly disappear from areas that have been developed for agriculture. However, individuals may linger on for some time, presenting a danger to workers. Many such bushmasters meet their end at the hands of machete-wielding farmers. There are three species of bushmasters, *Lachesis melanocephala, L. muta, and L. stenophrys.*

Collectively, bushmasters occur from eastern Nicaragua through Central America to Bolivia and southeastern Brazil. However, there is a large break in the distribution between the Amazon Basin population, *L. muta muta,* and the populations from the Brazilian coastal forests, *L. m. rhombeata*. This particular bushmaster is very rare, since forests along the Brazilian coast are being cleared to provide agricultural land for a rapidly expanding human population. Several other rare snakes are found in the same region.

The Three Species

The black-headed bushmaster, *Lachesis melanocephala*, lives in southwestern Costa Rica in a fairly small region with a high level of rainfall. The top of its head is black, and it is more aggressive than the other two species. Differences between the other two species are based largely on scale counts. Both have calmer dispositions, but individuals can be quick to strike and put on a dramatic show that includes inflating the neck, hissing, and vibrating the tail. The latter gives bushmasters one of their many Latin American names of *cascabela muda*, meaning "mute rattlesnake." In some places the snake is called *matabuey* ("bullock killer"), a reference to the potency of its venom.

Bushmasters are lethargic snakes, moving rarely and feeding infrequently. Their hunting method is to find a place where rodents are likely to visit, such as the forest floor beneath a fruiting tree. They probably do this by identifying their prey's scent trails.

Sit and Wait

Once they have found the right place, they take up a strategic position and form a coil, with their head in the center and their neck bent into an "s"-shape. Then they simply wait for a meal to come within striking range. Observations of the snakes in the wild have shown that this occurs very rarely, and a bushmaster may have to stake out a patch of forest floor for several days or even weeks before it is successful. If it has caught nothing after a week or two, it will move 5 to 20 yards (4–18 m) away to try its luck at a new ambush spot. Its meals tend to be large ones, however, weighing 50 to 70 percent of the bushmaster's own weight.

Once it has fed, it moves to a hidden place in which to digest its meal. Because it uses so little energy, a bushmaster may be able to survive on six to ten meals each year. Breeding females, however, need to eat more often than males because their bodies divert a sizable proportion of their food to produce eggs.

Reproduction

The three bushmaster species are unique in being the only American pit vipers to lay eggs (although several Old World species do so). They lay between five and 18 eggs that hatch after about 60 days. The newly hatched bushmasters feed on mammals right from the beginning and are among the few venomous snakes that eat only mammals throughout their lives—the other three being the taipans and the black mamba.

⊖ Lachesis stenophrys *blends in perfectly among leaf litter on a rain-forest floor in Costa Rica. If disturbed, it will strike or vibrate its tail in a warning display.*

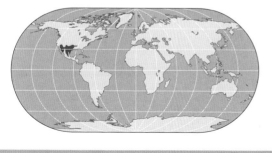

Common name
Western diamondback rattlesnake

Scientific name *Crotalus atrox*

Subfamily Crotalinae

Family Viperidae

Suborder Serpentes

Order Squamata

Length From 30 in (76 cm) to 7 ft (2.1 m)

Key features Body has large diamond-shaped markings along the back, each outlined with lighter scales; background color gray to brown, may be reddish brown or pink; head large and rounded with a wide dark stripe from the eye to the angle of the jaws; tail conspicuously banded in black and white, ending in a large rattle (series of horny segments made of keratin)

Habits Nocturnal in summer but active in late afternoon and early morning in the spring and fall; terrestrial

Breeding Live-bearer with litters of 4–25

Diet Small mammals up to the size of young prairie dogs and rabbits

Habitat Desert, semidesert, arid scrub, and dry grassland

Distribution North America almost from coast to coast; ranges from southeastern California and the Gulf of California to the Gulf Coast of Texas and south into Mexico

Status Very common in places

Similar species The Mojave rattlesnake, *C. scutulatus*, is very similar, and its range overlaps in places

Venom A potent hemotoxin leading to severe symptoms and possibly death unless treated

Western Diamondback Rattlesnake

Crotalus atrox

The western diamondback rattlesnake is at the top of the food chain. It is also an important element in the ecosystem of the desert and semidesert regions of the American Southwest.

THE WESTERN DIAMONDBACK rattlesnake is a large snake that preys on mammals up to the size of weaned jackrabbits, young prairie dogs, and adult ground squirrels.

While most snakes are fairly inconspicuous and have little effect on the ecosystem, this is not true of the western diamondback. It is common to see one crossing a quiet desert road at night in summer. In fact, it is not unusual to see six or more during a 100-mile (160-km) drive across southern Arizona or western Texas. There will be at least the same number of roadkill diamondbacks. Many are deliberately run over by misguided individuals who think they are acting in the best interests of humans. If numbers of this and other large rattlesnakes drop significantly, rodent and rabbit populations may increase with fewer predators to control them. This will have an effect on vegetation, for example, and may have repercussions for the whole ecosystem.

Sensitive to Change

Population densities are thought to be about 75 snakes per square mile (2.5 sq. km) over much of their huge range. The snakes prefer dry habitats but are not restricted to deserts. They also live among scrub, in grassland, and on rocky hillsides. Although they are in many respects generalists, subtle alterations in their environment can cause dramatic population changes. Grazing by livestock, for example, often leads to a reduction in the number of plant species in an area and creates open

→ *A western diamondback,* Crotalus atrox, *strikes a defensive posture with its head raised, its body in an "s"-shaped coil, and its rattle in the upright position.*

patches of soil. That in turn may adversely affect the numbers of small mammals (the main food of diamondbacks). The same changes may favor lizards, and that allows Mojave rattlesnakes, *C. scutulatus*, which eat lizards, to move into the area. These changes can be quite abrupt. Within a few miles diamondbacks can go from being numerous to nonexistent and replaced by Mojave rattlesnakes.

Western diamondbacks also occur on rocky and gravelly hillsides, but only if there is sufficient vegetation to support a healthy population of rodents, rabbits, or prairie dogs. Where the soil is thin and the

vegetation sparse, other species (notably the tiger rattlesnake, *Crotalus tigris*, and the speckled rattlesnake, *C. mitchelli*) replace western diamondbacks. They are more adept than the western diamondback at hunting among rocks and probably include a high proportion of lizards in their diet.

In the higher montane habitats that dot the landscape in this part of the world there are yet more species, such as the rock rattlesnake,

⊕ *Hidden among bark in the Huachuca Mountains in Arizona, a banded rock rattlesnake,* Crotalus lepidus, *basks after eating a large lizard.*

Rattlesnake Roundups

Rattlesnake roundups date back to the 17th century. They began as organized hunts to clear good grazing land of venomous snakes that might endanger settlers, their children, and their livestock. Because rattlesnakes tend to be concentrated around their dens early in the year, killing large numbers in a single day was relatively easy. At a single hunt in Iowa in 1849, for instance, two men killed 90 rattlesnakes in one and a half hours. By the 19th century the roundups had begun to develop a carnival atmosphere, with individuals competing with each other to see who could catch and kill the most snakes. People took picnics, and charities and civic authorities often sponsored the events to raise money. Snake handlers demonstrated their expertise; and the snakes were later killed, and their skins and flesh were sold.

In recent years, when the risk of being bitten by a wild rattlesnake is almost nonexistent, roundups are still held but purely for entertainment and profit. The event in Sweetwater, Texas, for example, was responsible for the slaughter of 70,773 rattlesnakes—mostly western diamondbacks—over a 16-year period. At the Morris snake hunt, Pennsylvania, 751 timber rattlesnakes (an increasingly rare species) were killed in nine years, while the Keystone reptile hunt in the same state accounted for 3,205 deaths in 17 years.

In the beginning, roundups were timed to catch the snakes in the open, after they had emerged from their dens. Nowadays the snakes are targeted while still underground, using dynamite and gasoline fumes to drive them out. Many snakes die in the dens, along with other wildlife, including harmless snakes, tortoises, and small mammals.

A Jaycee (member of the Junior Chamber of Commerce) displays a diamondback rattlesnake at the Sweetwater Rattlesnake Roundup, Texas, in 1995.

C. lepidus, and a host of small, specialized rattlers. The western diamondback is, therefore, a generalist species found over a wide geographical range and that adapts to a variety of different conditions. However, it is ousted in certain smaller patches of the environment where more specialized rattlesnakes prosper.

Reproduction

Western diamondbacks mate in the spring, and males find females by following pheromone trails. Several males may follow the same female, leading to contests between them, as in many vipers. Because combat is a means of natural selection, there is pressure on males to become bigger. Male diamondbacks are 10 to 15 percent larger than the females.

Females give birth at the end of the summer, four to six months after mating. The young are born without a rattle and remain with their mother for up to 16 days until they shed their skin for the first time. Some herpetologists think that the interactions of the young shortly after birth, when they constantly flicker their tongues over each other and over their mother, may help them recognize each other in later life—a skill that could be used when following adults to hibernation dens in the fall and in identifying potential mates.

The Rattle

Early Spanish and Portuguese explorers were the first to remark on the snakes' rattle. One explorer likened it to the sound of little bells (he can never have actually heard a rattler sounding off in anger). Thomas Morton, writing in 1637, says: "There is one creeping beast...that hath a rattle in his tayle, that doth discover his age; for so many years hath he lived, so many joynts are in that rattle, which soundeth (when it is in motion) like pease in a bladder, and this beast is called a rattlesnake." A more modern description of the sound made by one of the larger rattlesnakes is like a pair of castanets knocked together very rapidly, and Morton was slightly wide of the mark about telling the age of the snake from the number of segments

→ *The rattle is a series of connected tail segments. Each time the snake molts, the last scale loosens but does not fall off, and a new segment is formed.*

← *In the Southwest a western diamondback rattlesnake sticks out its tongue and raises its black-and-white banded tail rattle.*

("joynts"). In fact, the number of rattle segments is related to the snake's age, but they do not produce one segment each year.

The Latin name *Crotalus* is from *crotalum* and actually means "rattle" or "castanet." The rattle is unique to the 30 or so species of rattlesnakes, *Crotalus*, and three species of pigmy rattlesnakes, *Sistrurus*. It is made up of a series of horny segments that fit loosely inside each other. They are made of keratin, the material that forms animal hair, horns, claws, and nails. Each segment originates from the scale covering the tip of the rattlesnake's tail. In other snakes the scale is conical, and the horny epidermis covering it slips off with the rest of the shed skin; but in rattlers the tip of the tail has a constriction around it, preventing the horny covering from coming off with the rest of the skin. The skin breaks around the edge of this dumbbell-shaped scale, which is retained as a new segment.

The segments interlock and are quite complicated. They are not symmetrical but are shaped so that they move against each other more when the rattle is shaken up and down than when it is shaken from side to side. This gives the snake more control over its rattle and keeps it from rattling when it is trying to stalk prey. Furthermore, the shape of the segments and the way in which they interconnect allow the rattle to curve upward but not downward. That keeps it from dragging along the ground when the snake moves. When a rattler "sounds off," it raises its tail to a vertical position and shakes it back and forth.

Over a period of time the rattle loses its end segments due to wear and tear. The number of segments in a wild rattlesnake rarely exceeds 12, and five to 10 are more usual. The record appears to be 23, but this is exceptional. Captive snakes are not subject to the same rough-and-tumble as wild ones, and their rattles are on average longer—the record being 29 segments. Because a new segment is added each time the snake sheds its skin, this can amount to four segments or more each year in fast-growing juveniles, rather more than Thomas Morton's assertion suggests.

Newborn rattlesnakes start life without a rattle. All they have is a slightly swollen tip to their tail, called the prebutton, which they lose the first time they shed their skin. The prebutton is replaced with a button, which has a shallow groove around it about halfway along. Because the snake grows quickly during its first year or so, each segment is increasingly larger than the one before, so the rattle becomes tapered, with the smallest segments toward the end. As the snake's growth rate slows with age, each segment becomes roughly the same size as the one before; and because the earlier segments have been lost, the sides of the rattle become almost parallel.

Warning Sound

The purpose of the rattle is defense. Rattlesnakes do not rattle to confuse or mesmerize their prey, nor to "serenade" lady rattlesnakes as earlier writers claimed. Living in a land where the plains were populated with huge herds of hoofed animals—the bison and its ancestors—the main concern of a well-camouflaged rattlesnake was to avoid being trampled. The rattle may have developed to prevent this from happening.

Many snakes, including other pit vipers as well as colubrids, vibrate their tails when they are alarmed. If they happen to be resting among dead leaves, that can create a loud enough noise to attract attention. In a way the rattle is an extension of that behavior and may have evolved from it. Although other snakes do

Close Relatives

The western diamondback rattlesnake has a number of close relatives. The Tortuga Island rattlesnake, *Crotalus tortugensis*, found only on the island of the same name in the Gulf of California, is almost indistinguishable from the western diamondback. Other island forms are at present still classified as *C. atrox* but may be separated at some time in the future.

On the mainland the red diamond rattlesnake, *C. ruber*, also has many characteristics in common with the western diamondback, including a diamond pattern down its back. It is thought to have evolved when an original population of rattlesnakes was divided into two when what is now the Gulf of California extended much farther north along the Colorado Valley. The two populations evolved along different lines for so long that when they were joined again (as the gulf retreated), they were incapable of interbreeding. *Crotalus ruber* is also found on several islands in the Gulf of California, including San Lorenzo, where the population, known as *C. ruber lorenzoensis*, seems to be evolving toward the loss of its rattle. Another close relative living on the island of Santa Catalina has lost it completely and is classified as a separate species, *C. catalinensis*.

not have rattles, they may also use warning sounds such as hissing or rubbing rough scales together, for example, the carpet (saw-scaled) vipers, *Echis* species, and the Sahara horned viper, *Cerastes cerasstes*.

Potent Venom

The western diamondback is the main cause of serious snakebite incidents in the area in which it lives. Only the eastern diamondback, *Crotalus adamanteus*, is equally dangerous, but it has a smaller range and is relatively rare. These two species are the most dangerous because of their size, the potency of their venom, the amount they inject, and their attitude. Both are more than willing to stand their ground. An aroused individual is an impressive sight as it raises its head well off the ground and forms a deep "s"-shape with the forepart of its body. At the same time, it lifts its tail and rattles continuously.

It often flicks out its tongue and may lay it back over the top of its head. At other times diamondbacks can be placid. Considering their numbers, there would be far more snakebite victims if these snakes were as aggressive as their reputation would have us believe.

Each western diamondback produces a yield of 75 to 1,000 milligrams (dry weight) of venom per milking, with an average of 400 milligrams. (The venom is used in the production of antivenom.) The wide disparity is due to the different sizes of the snakes, how often they are milked, and the expertise of the person milking them. A full-blooded bite is serious, and if untreated, it can result in death.

The Mojave rattlesnakes, *C. scutulatus*, are also dangerous because some populations produce a neurotoxic venom that acts faster than the normal hemotoxic venoms produced by most rattlesnakes.

⬇ *The red diamond rattlesnake,* Crotalus ruber, *occurs only in California and Baja California, Mexico. Like the western diamondback, it has a black-and-white banded tail.*

Common name Sidewinder (horned rattlesnake)

Scientific name *Crotalus cerastes*

Subfamily Crotalinae

Family Viperidae

Suborder Serpentes

Order Squamata

Length From 24 in (61 cm) to 30 in (76 cm)

Key features Body smaller and more slender than other rattlesnakes; head flat with raised scales over the eyes, giving the appearance of horns; pattern consists of large blotches of various colors interspersed with dark speckles; background coloration varies with the soil type and may be yellow, beige, pink, or gray

Habits Terrestrial; semiburrowing by shuffling its body down into loose sand; active at night; moves in a sideways looping motion

Breeding Live-bearer with litters of 5–18; gestation period 150 days or more

Diet Mainly lizards, especially whiptails; also small rodents

Habitat Deserts, especially where there are extensive dunes of loose, wind-blown sand

Distribution Southwestern North America

Status Common

Similar species The speckled rattlesnake, *Crotalus mitchelli*, has a larger rattle, but it lives mostly among rocks and does not sidewind

Venom Not very potent, causing pain and swelling around the site of the wound

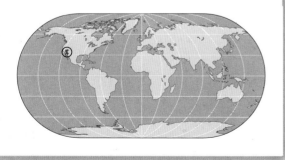

Sidewinder

Crotalus cerastes

The common name for the sidewinder refers to its method of locomotion. It moves quickly over loose sand with a characteristic sideways looping technique.

WHEN SNAKES ARE PLACED on a very smooth or a yielding surface such as sand on which it is difficult to gain a hold, many of them use a sidewinding locomotion in their attempts to move. This is also true of the sidewinder, which has developed it into an efficient and rapid way of covering loose ground.

Other desert species that sidewind include the carpet, or saw-scaled, vipers, *Echis* species from Africa and Asia, Peringuey's adder, *Bitis peringueyi* from southern Africa, the Sahara horned viper, *Cerastes cerastes* from North Africa, and the Patagonian lancehead, *Bothrops ammodytoides*. Another type of sidewinder is the bockadam or dog-faced water snake, *Cerberus rynchops*, from Southeast Asia and northern Australia, which sidewinds across the tidal mudflats on which it lives.

Desert Nomads

Sidewinders are unusual among snakes (especially rattlesnakes) in having no home range. They appear to wander randomly across the desert, covering several hundred yards each night in search of prey, probably looking for sleeping lizards in their burrows. In the morning the sidewinders' distinctive tracks often indicate the route they have taken. By daybreak they shuffle down into the sand to escape the heat, often choosing a patch at the base of a shrub where the sand is cooler. The next evening they emerge to continue their wanderings.

If the opportunity arises, they will ambush prey from their daytime resting position, striking up out of the thin layer of sand that covers them and holding on until their venom takes effect. This avoids the need to venture out in order to locate their dead prey later. If they had to leave their cover and move onto an open patch of sand, they would be very conspicuous.

The sidewinder, Crotalus cerastes, has horn-shaped scales bulging out above the eyes, earning it the nickname of "horned rattlesnake" in some places.

Diet of Lizards

They mainly eat desert lizards, especially whiptails, *Cnemidophorus*, which are almost unbelievably fast moving during the day when they are warm but easy to catch at night when they are cold and therefore not very energetic. Other prey species include side-blotched lizards, *Uta stansburiana*, and fringe-toed lizards, *Uma notata*. One captive sidewinder was seen eating a desert horned lizard, *Phrynosoma platyrhinos*, without any apparent ill effects; but on the other hand, a wild one was found dead with one of these spiky lizards lodged in its throat. Immature sidewinders apparently use their tails as lures for small lizards, moving them slowly across the ground so that the segments look like those of a crawling insect.

Apart from lizards sidewinders occasionally eat small desert rodents and birds, although opportunities to eat the latter must be very limited since they are hard to catch. Sidewinders have been

found swallowing small rodents, apparently killed by traffic in which rigor mortis had set in. Vipers in general, including many rattlesnakes, will take advantage of food that they did not kill themselves.

Some Like It Hot—but Not the Sidewinder

Sidewinders come from the hottest parts of the American Southwest, including Death Valley, California, which has the highest-ever recorded temperature on earth. You might think that would make them more tolerant of higher temperatures than other snakes, but that is not so.

Sidewinders avoid the extremes of heat by being strictly nocturnal. If they are exposed to daytime temperatures, they soon die. Their somewhat flattened body shape enables them to gain and lose heat quickly from the soil or other surface because more of their body is in contact with the surface. As the temperature falls at night, they form a flattened coil on a warm surface (for example, on tarred roads) to absorb heat quickly and remain active. During the day they shuffle down into cool sand and lose the heat.

A sidewinder moves across the sand in the Anza-Borrego Desert, California. The sideways looping technique keeps much of its body off the ground, enabling it to move efficiently across shifting surfaces.

Common name Massasauga

Scientific name Sistrurus catenatus

Subfamily Crotalinae

Family Viperidae

Suborder Serpentes

Order Squamata

Length From 30 in (76 cm) to 36 in (91 cm)

Key features Small with a tiny rattle; head has large plates on top, distinguishing all *Sistrurus* species from *Crotalus*; body has row of large round dark-brown blotches down its back; flanks have smaller spots; background color grayish or brown; some individuals from northern parts may be suffused with black

Habits Terrestrial; diurnal in cool places, becoming more nocturnal in the south

Breeding Live-bearer with litters of 2–19; gestation period 71–115 days

Diet Small lizards, mice, and invertebrates

Habitat Desert grassland, bogs, and forest edges

Distribution Central North America from southeastern Arizona and northern Mexico to New York State

Status Rare

Similar species Once the rattle has been seen or heard, it cannot be mistaken for any other snake; some snakes, such as the western hognose, *Heterodon nasicus*, are similar in size, color, and markings

Venom Very toxic, but yields are small; symptoms include local swelling, intense pain, and nausea

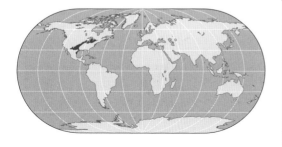

Massasauga $\quad$ *Sistrurus catenatus*

The small rattlesnake commonly known as the massasauga has suffered greatly as a result of agricultural development and urbanization. Today it is becoming rare over much of its range.

MASSASAUGAS TYPICALLY REST IN tussocks of grass, where they are well camouflaged. Their background color varies according to the color of the soil on which they live. Melanistic (with black pigmentation) individuals are relatively common in the northern states. Northern populations also tend to consist of larger snakes that eat frogs and mice. Southern populations, on the other hand, eat invertebrates such as centipedes as well as small lizards and rodents. Although they mate in the spring, as in most other temperate snakes, their main breeding season is in the fall. After mating, females store sperm that fertilizes their eggs the following year. An average of seven or eight young are born from late July to early September. Northern populations have larger litters and larger individual young.

Depending on where they live, massasaugas are active from around April to late October. During spring and fall they are on the move in the daytime but mostly in the afternoon up until about four o'clock. In the summer, however, they are active in the early evening and at night. In the hot dry southern states their daytime activity is restricted to early morning and early evening, but during the latter they are active for much longer.

⊕ *The subspecies S.c. tergeminus is from the southern part of the species' range and is often paler in color than other massasauga subspecies.*

Threatened Populations
The northern populations of the massasauga (subspecies *Sistrurus c. catenatus*) spend the winter and early parts of the spring in swamps, bogs, and damp meadows. They hibernate in crayfish burrows, which often become flooded in winter. They rest with their head raised above the water's surface, while their body is

submerged. After emerging from hibernation, they slowly disperse to drier situations to feed, mate, and give birth. The snakes are becoming threatenened, and such habits makes their conservation difficult, since a variety of different habitats as well as the corridors between them need to be preserved. In addition, crayfish also need to be conserved because their burrows are important in massasauga ecology. The northeastern form, *S. c. catenatus*, is one of only two venomous snakes in Canada. It used to be common, but it has suffered through the drainage of prairie marshes for agriculture. In Illinois, for example, it once occurred in 24 locations, but it is now found in only six or eight. In Wisconsin populations have fallen by 90 percent or more, and colonies are now so small that there is a good chance that the species will disappear from the state altogether. Part of the cause was a bounty of $5 per tail that was paid by the state on rattlesnakes, which until 1975 were considered to be a pest species. In that year the bounty was lifted, and the massasauga was placed on the Wisconsin Endangered and Threatened Species List.

The desert massasauga, *S. c. edwardsi*, lives in a grassland habitat in southern Arizona. Again, the land has been brought under agriculture, and the plant community has been altered. Desertification has occurred due to overgrazing, and the massasauga populations have declined dramatically. Although it has always been a dry habitat, summer rains once provided the necessary seasonal moisture for massasaugas (rain promotes plant growth, which boosts rodent populations). At present only rodent burrows give the snakes access to the moist microhabitat that they need.

Conservation Backfires

One of the massasauga sites in Missouri happens to be on a wildlife reserve. That should be good news for the snakes, but, unfortunately, management practices that suit the other inhabitants of these reserves—mainly wetland birds—work against the massasaugas. Surrounding prairie is burned regularly to encourage new growth, and people in cars have unrestricted access so that they can look at the birds. Much of the human activity takes place in the spring and fall when massasaugas are moving from their hibernation sites to their summer foraging areas. Many of them are inadvertently caught up in the controlled burns that take place, and others are killed on the roads and tracks.

Common name American alligator

Scientific name *Alligator mississippiensis*

Subfamily Alligatorinae

Family Crocodylidae

Order Crocodylia

Size Large specimens measure up to 13 ft (4 m); reports of individuals up to 20 ft (6 m) long are unsubstantiated

Weight Can exceed 550 lb (249 kg)

Key features Body almost black; snout relatively long, wide, and rounded; front feet have 5 toes on each; hind feet have 4; when the mouth is closed, only upper teeth visible (which distinguishes alligators from crocodiles)

Habits Active during the summer; may hibernate during the winter, especially in northern areas; semiaquatic, emerging to bask on land; can move quite fast on land and will search for new habitat when pools dry up

Breeding Female lays clutches of 30–70 eggs; hatchlings emerge after about 2 months

Diet Carnivorous; feeds on prey ranging from crustaceans to much larger aquatic life, including fish, turtles, and wading birds, as well as mammals

Habitat Rivers, marshland, and swamps; sometimes in brackish water; rarely seen at sea

Distribution Southeastern United States from Texas to Florida and north through the Carolinas

Status Delisted from being an endangered species in 1985, having been the subject of a successful recovery program; listed on CITES Appendix II

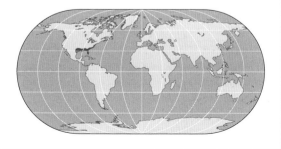

American Alligator

Alligator mississippiensis

Once on the verge of extinction, the American alligator has made a real comeback. Trade in its skin and meat is now strictly controlled, and the alligator has been reinstated as a vital part of the entire ecosystem.

THE AMERICAN ALLIGATOR USED TO range over a much wider area. About half a million years ago it reached as far north as the present-day state of Maryland. Then climatic changes occurred, and its range started to contract. However, when European settlers reached the southeastern area of the country, they found that these reptiles were still very common. Habitat modifications and hunting pressures subsequently reduced their range even more, and American alligators disappeared from the southeastern parts of Virginia and Oklahoma. Today their range includes Mississippi, Arkansas, eastern Texas, the Carolinas, and Alabama, although the species' main strongholds are southern Georgia, Louisiana, and Florida.

The relatively large size of these reptiles has given them a critical role in maintaining the entire ecosystem in which they occur because they dig so-called "gator holes" using their tail and snout. These provide temporary reservoirs of water and therefore maintain suitable aquatic habitats for various other animal and plant life. Vegetation around "gator holes" always tends to be lush thanks to the silt that the alligators deposit on the banks. The movements of alligators on regular paths can also create additional channels that enable water to run into marshlands more easily during periods of heavy rain.

Disguised as Logs

These reptiles often spend long periods floating motionless on the surface of the water, where they resemble partially submerged logs. They lie with their nostrils above the water's surface so that they can breathe easily. This behavior allows them to spot and ambush prey and also helps them maintain their body temperature, since they can warm themselves up from the sun without leaving the water. This is achieved by means of the osteoderms, or bone swellings, along the back that are linked with blood vessels. Heat is absorbed into the body there, helped by the alligators' dark coloration, and then circulated through the bloodstream.

A similar method is used by many other crocodilians, but it is especially important in this species because of the relatively temperate areas in which the alligators are found. During the winter they become sluggish. They retreat to the bottom of the waterway or burrow into a riverbank below the waterline and only emerge when the weather is warm. At this time their heart rate can reduce to just one beat per minute. The heart has a complex four-chambered structure more like that of a mammal than a reptile. American alligators can also survive being trapped in ice, provided that their nostrils are not submerged. It has even

⊖ *Almost black in color, the American alligator has prominent eyes and nostrils and coarse scales all over its body. Its upper teeth are visible along the top jaw.*

It Just Takes Two

The only other species of alligator is the smaller Chinese alligator, *A. sinensis*, which reaches a maximum size of approximately 7 feet (2.13 m). It has a very limited area of distribution today in China's Yangtze Valley and is highly endangered, with an overall population of only about 300 individuals. Captive-breeding programs in China and overseas, particularly in the United States, are underway with the aim of creating a more viable population. In terms of its habits this species appears to have a lifestyle similar to that of the American alligator, hibernating in burrows over the winter. The young mature slightly earlier, however, typically at about four years old.

been known for them to recover after over eight hours frozen beneath the water's surface without breathing thanks to their low oxygen requirement under these conditions. Alligators lose their appetite dramatically in the winter, and they are likely to stop eating altogether simply because their slow metabolism does not allow them to digest food at this stage.

Their relatively wide snout allows them to tackle a variety of prey, and the mouth itself contains about 80 teeth. They are constantly replaced throughout the alligator's life as they become worn or even broken, but the rate of growth slows markedly in old age. As a result, older alligators may have difficulty catching prey to the point of facing starvation. Older individuals are more likely to resort to attacking people for this reason, since they often represent a relatively easy target.

Encounters with Humans

With the ability to swim and run over very short distances at speeds of up to 30 mph (48 kph)—significantly faster than a human—American alligators will take a wide variety of prey. Generally they do not pose a major threat to humans. But as they have increased in numbers again over recent years and development has encroached farther into the swamps of Florida, for example, greater conflicts have arisen. They often take the form of an alligator emerging onto the green of a golf course or roaming into a backyard area rather than actual attacks. Unfortunately, chain-link fencing is not an effective barrier, since these alligators can climb fences up to 6 feet (1.8 m) tall without a problem. Those that threaten or harm the public are caught under a nuisance alligator program and may be moved elsewhere.

When attacks on people occur, they are often the result of the reptile being threatened or caught unawares. Feeding alligators is

Mutant Alligators

Two very rare color mutations of the American alligator have been documented. There is a pure albino form, characterized by its reddish eyes and white body. There is also a separate leucistic variant, in which the alligators have an attractive pale yellow body color. They can be further distinguished from the albino form by their blue eyes.

There are an estimated 70 albinos, and many of them are exhibited in zoological collections or breeding farms that are open to the public. This is because their coloration makes them so conspicuous that they would be extremely vulnerable to predators in the wild. Leucistic alligators are even rarer, known from a clutch of just 17 individuals that were discovered in Savoy, Louisiana, in 1987. A single female was then found at a site 100 miles (160 km) away in 1994. Both these mutant forms are also vulnerable to skin cancer because of the lack of protective melanin pigment in their bodies, and so they need to be kept in shaded surroundings.

⊕ *Albino American alligators are quite rare. Most of them, including this individual from Los Angeles, are kept in captivity because they would be unable to survive in the wild.*

⊖ *American alligators will eat anything they can catch. In the Florida Everglades a raccoon is this alligator's next meal.*

especially dangerous, since they soon come to associate people with being a source of food. Children are more vulnerable to attack than adults because of their smaller size, but dogs are especially at risk. Alligators appear to have a particular dislike for them, possibly because they regard their barking as a threat.

American alligators communicate with each other by letting out a roar that can be heard over 1 mile (1.6 km) away. They also make a noise by slapping down their jaw on the water's surface. In addition, they keep in touch with each other by means of vibrations transmitted through the water using their throat and stomach. These sounds are made more frequently in the spring—males call to attract females in their territories, which may extend over an area of up to 10 square miles (26 sq km). They also track each other by means of special scent glands located in the cloaca and on each side of the jaw.

Dry Nesting Sites

The mating period is influenced by locality but typically lasts from March to May, with egg laying occurring a month later. The female will seek out a spot that is unlikely to flood but that is nevertheless located close to the water and often partially concealed among trees and other vegetation. The eggs will not survive in flooded ground and will be ruined if they are immersed for more than 12 hours. The female constructs a nest for her eggs by piling plant matter up to a height of 36 inches (90 cm). As the vegetation rots, it emits heat and warms the eggs, which measure about 3 inches (7.5 cm).

The incubation temperature is critical in determining the gender of the hatchlings. At temperatures below 85°F (29.5°C) the majority of hatchlings will be female, whereas above that figure males will predominate. It will be about two months before the young

⊕ *Although as adults they are among the largest reptiles and can grow up to 13 feet (4 m) long, American alligators are only about 9 inches (23 cm) in length when they hatch.*

alligators emerge from the nest. Their mother hears them uttering their distinctive "yipping" calls and helps them out. She carries them to the water in her mouth, with her tongue serving as a pouch.

The young alligators measure about 9 inches (23 cm) long when they hatch and are much more brightly colored than the adults, with a black-and-yellow banded patterning on their body. They stay together as a group (known as a pod) in close proximity to the female until they are two years old. During this time the mother will try to protect them. A number will be lost, however, sometimes even to large males. Other potential predators include wading birds, gars, and other large fish. By the time they are six years old, the young alligators are likely to have reached about 6.8 feet (2.1 m) in length, after which their growth rate slows significantly.

Alligator Recovery Programs

In the first half of the 20th century American alligators were killed in large numbers. Some estimates suggest that more than 10 million of these reptiles were hunted and killed for their skins between 1870 and 1970. Since that time, however, their numbers have increased dramatically thanks to effective conservation measures based partly on an acknowledgement of the commercial value of the alligators.

There are now over 150 alligator farms in various states, including Louisiana, Florida, and Texas. In the early days especially they helped restore wild populations. Farmers were permitted to remove a percentage of eggs from the nests of wild alligators, which they could hatch artificially, but a significant percentage of the resulting offspring had to be returned to the wild to repopulate areas where the species had disappeared or become very scarce.

An incidental but important benefit of these recovery programs has been our increased knowledge of the biology of the alligators. In turn this has helped develop effective management plans for wild populations. In Florida, for example, it has been shown that the

alligators' reproductive potential is such that eggs could be taken from half of all nests with no adverse effects on the overall population.

Because of better habitat management larger areas are available to alligators and the other creatures living alongside them. There are some new concerns, however, notably about the rising level of mercury in certain alligator populations as a result of industrial pollution. Since the alligators are at the top of the food chain, this contaminant accumulates in their bodies from their prey. Its long-term effects are as yet unclear because, once they have survived the vulnerable stage as hatchlings, alligators can live for at least 50 years and possibly closer to a century in some cases.

↑ *This eight-week-old hatchling in the Florida Everglades is vulnerable to predation by larger aquatic animals. Juveniles usually stay in small groups close to their mother for the first two years.*

Skin Tagging

Careful monitoring by means of tagging ensures that skins of illegally killed alligators cannot be traded. The success of this program has been shown by the fact that the alligator population in Louisiana has grown today to just below that of a century ago in spite of the massive development that has occurred during this period.

Although the skins are the most valuable items and are exported worldwide (especially to markets in Europe, such as Italy, as well as to Japan), alligator meat has also acquired something of a gourmet reputation and can be found on the menus of fashionable restaurants in many cities. Even the teeth of these reptiles are in demand and are made into jewelry or simply sold as curios.

⊝ *American alligators often live in close proximity to humans and are an important attraction on the itinerary of many tourists visiting the southeastern states.*

Glossary

Words in SMALL CAPITALS refer to other entries in the glossary.

Acrodont (teeth) teeth attached to the upper edge of the jaw, as opposed to the inside surface (PLEURODONT) or in sockets (THECODONT)

Adaptation a characteristic shape, behavior, or physiological process that equips an organism (or group of related organisms) for its way of life and habitat

Advanced relatively recently evolved (opposite of "primitive")

Albino an animal that has no color pigment in its body and has red eyes

Amniotic egg an egg with a fluid-filled sac within a membrane that encloses the embryo of reptiles, birds, and mammals. Animals that produce amniotic eggs are known as amniotes

Amplexus the position adopted during mating in most frogs and many salamanders, in which the male clasps the female with one or both pairs of limbs. See AXILLARY AMPLEXUS and INGUINAL AMPLEXUS

Annuli the growth rings often visible on the shell of CHELONIANS

Anterior the front part or head and shoulders of an animal

Aposematic coloration bright coloration serving to warn a potential predator that an animal is distasteful or poisonous

Arboreal living in trees or shrubs

Autotomy self-amputation of part of the body. Some lizards practice CAUDAL autotomy: They discard all or part of their tail

Axillary amplexus mating position in frogs in which the male grasps the female behind her front limbs. See INGUINAL AMPLEXUS

Barbel a small, elongated "feeler," or sensory process, on the head, usually of aquatic animals, e.g., some pipid frogs

Binocular vision the ability to focus both eyes on a single subject. The eyes must point forward (not sideways as in most reptiles and amphibians). Binocular vision enables animals, including humans, to judge distances

Bridges the sides of a turtle's shell, attaching to the CARAPACE above and the PLASTRON below

Brille the transparent covering over the eyes of snakes and some lizards, such as geckos

Bromeliad member of a family of plants restricted to the New World. Many live attached to trees, including "urn plants" in which ARBOREAL frogs sometimes breed

Calcareous containing calcium carbonate

Carapace the upper part of the shell of turtles and tortoises, the other parts being the PLASTRON and the BRIDGES. Also used to describe the hard structure covering part of any animal's body

Caudal relating to the tail, as in subcaudal scales beneath a snake's tail and caudal (tail) fin

Chelonian a member of the ORDER Chelonia, containing all reptiles variously known as terrapins, turtles, and tortoises

Chromatophore a specialized cell containing pigment, usually located in the outer layers of the skin

Chromosome a thread-shaped structure consisting largely of genetic material (DNA), found in the nucleus of cells

Cirrus (pl. cirri) a slender, usually flexible appendage on an animal

CITES an international conservation organization: Convention on International Trade in Endangered Species

Class a TAXONOMIC category ranking below PHYLUM, containing a number of ORDERS

Cloaca the common chamber into which the urinary, digestive, and reproductive systems discharge their contents, and which opens to the exterior; from Latin meaning "sewer" or "drain"

Clutch the eggs laid by a female at one time

Continuous breeder an animal that may breed at any time of year

Convergent evolution the effect of unrelated animals looking like each other because they have adapted to similar conditions in similar ways

Coprophagy the practice of eating excrement

Costal relating to the ribs

Costal grooves grooves or folds along the flanks of caecilians and some salamanders that correspond to the position of the ribs

Crocodilian a member of the order Crocodylia, including alligators, caimans, crocodiles, and gharials

Cryptic having the ability to remain hidden, usually by means of camouflage, e.g., cryptic coloration

Cutaneous respiration breathing that takes place across the skin's surface, especially important in amphibians

Cycloid disklike, resembling a circle

Denticle toothlike scale

Dermis layer of skin immediately below the EPIDERMIS

Dewlap flap or fold of skin under an animal's throat. Sometimes used in displays, e.g., in anole lizards

Dimorphism the existence of two distinct forms within a SPECIES, which is then said to be dimorphic. In species in which there are more than two forms, they are polymorphic. See SEXUAL DIMORPHISM

Direct development transition from egg to the adult form in amphibians without passing through a free-living LARVAL stage

Dorsal relating to the back or upper surface of the body or one of its parts

Ectotherm (adj. ectothermic) an animal that relies on external heat sources, such as the sun, to raise its body temperature. Reptiles and amphibians are ectotherms. See ENDOTHERM

Eft juvenile, TERRESTRIAL phase in the life cycle of a newt. The red eft is the terrestrial juvenile form of the eastern newt, *Notophthalmus viridescens*

Egg tooth small toothlike scale that some amphibians and reptiles have on the tip of the snout to assist in breaking through their eggshell

Endemic SPECIES, GENERA, or FAMILIES that are restricted to a particular geographical region

Endotherm (adj. endothermic) an animal that can sustain a high body temperature by means of heat generated within the body by the metabolism. See ECTOTHERM

Epidermis surface layer of the skin of a vertebrate

Epiphyte plant growing on another plant but not a parasite. Includes many orchids and BROMELIADS and some mosses and ferns

Estivation a state of inactivity during prolonged periods of drought or high temperature. During estivation the animal often buries itself in soil or mud. See HIBERNATION

Estuarine living in the lower part of a river (estuary) where fresh water meets and mixes with seawater

Explosive breeder a SPECIES in which the breeding season is very short, resulting in large numbers of animals mating at the same time

External fertilization fusing of eggs and sperm outside the female's body, as in nearly all frogs and toads. See INTERNAL FERTILIZATION

Family TAXONOMIC category ranking below ORDER, containing GENERA that are more closely related to one another than any other grouping of genera

Farming hatching and rearing of young CHELONIANS and CROCODILIANS from a captive-breeding population. See RANCHING

Fauna the animal life of a locality or region

Femoral gland gland situated on an animal's thigh

Femoral pores row of pores along an animal's thighs. Most obvious in many lizards

Fertilization union of an egg and a sperm

Gamete OVUM or sperm

Genus (pl. genera) taxonomic category ranking below FAMILY; a group of SPECIES all more closely related to one another than to any other group of species

Gestation carrying the developing young within the body. Gestation period is the length of time that this occurs

Gill respiratory structure in aquatic animals through which gas exchange takes place

Gill slits slits in which GILLS are situated and present in some amphibians and their LARVAE

Granular (scale) small grainlike scales covering the body, as in some geckos and in the file snakes, *Acrochordus*

Gravid carrying eggs or young

Gular pouch area of expandable skin in the throat region

Hedonic glands glands in a male salamander that stimulate a female when they are rubbed against her body

Heliotherm an animal that basks to regulate body temperature

Hemipenis (pl. hemipenes) one of two grooved copulatory structures present in the males of some reptiles

Herbivore animal that eats plants

Heterogeneous (scales) scales that differ in shape or size. See HOMOGENEOUS (SCALES)

Hibernation a period of inactivity, often spent underground, to avoid extremes of cold. See ESTIVATION

Hinge a means by which the PLASTRON of some CHELONIANS can be pulled up, giving the reptile more protection against a would-be predator

Home range an area in which an animal lives except for MIGRATIONS or rare excursions

Homogeneous (scales) scales that are all the same shape and size. See HETEROGENEOUS (SCALES)

Hyoid "u"-shaped bone at the base of the tongue to which the larynx is attached

Inguinal pertaining to the groin

Inguinal amplexus a mating position in which a male frog or salamander clasps a female around the lower abdomen. See AXILLARY AMPLEXUS

Intergular scute a single plate, or SCUTE, lying between the paired gular scutes on the PLASTRON of side-necked turtles

Internal fertilization fusing of eggs and sperm inside the female's body, as in reptiles and most salamanders. See EXTERNAL FERTILIZATION

Interstitial the thin skin between the scales of reptiles. Sometimes called "interscalar" skin

Introduced species brought from lands where it occurs naturally to lands where it has not previously occurred

IUCN International Union for the Conservation of Nature, responsible for assigning animals and plants to internationally agreed categories of rarity. See table below

Jacobson's organ (or vomeronasal organ) one of a pair of grooves extending from the nasal cavity and opening into the mouth cavity in some mammals and reptiles. Molecules collected on the tongue are sampled by this organ, which supplements the sense of smell

Juvenile young animal, not sexually mature

Karst a porous form of limestone

Keeled scales a ridge on the DORSAL scales of some snakes

Keratophagy the practice of eating molted skin

Lamella (pl. lamellae) thin transverse plates across the undersides of the toes of some lizards, especially geckos

Larva (pl. larvae) early stage in the development of an animal (including amphibians) after hatching from the egg

Lateral line organ sense organ embedded in the skin of some aquatic animals, including LARVAL salamanders and some frogs, which responds to waterborne vibrations. Usually arranged in a row along the animal's side

Leucistic an animal that lacks all pigment except that in its eyes. Partially leucistic animals have patches of white over an otherwise normally pigmented skin. See ALBINO

Life cycle complete life history of an organism from one stage to the recurrence of that stage, e.g., egg to egg

Life history history of a single individual organism from the fertilization of the egg until its death

Lifestyle general mode of life of an animal, e.g., NOCTURNAL predator, aquatic HERBIVORE, parasite

Live-bearing giving birth to young that have developed beyond the egg stage. Live-bearers may be VIVIPAROUS or OVOVIVIPAROUS

Lure (noun) part of the body, such as the tail, that is used to entice prey closer

Mental gland gland on the chin of some newts and salamanders that appears to stimulate the female during courtship; one of the HEDONIC GLANDS

Metabolism chemical or energy changes occurring within a living organism that are involved in various life activities

Metamorphosis transformation of an animal from one stage of its life history to another, e.g., from LARVA to adult

Microenvironment local conditions that immediately surround an organism

Migration movement of animals from one place to another, often in large numbers and often for breeding purposes

Milt sperm-containing fluid produced by a male frog during egg laying to fertilize the eggs

Mimic an animal that resembles an animal belonging to another SPECIES, usually a distasteful or venomous one, or some inedible object

Montane pertaining to mountains or SPECIES that live in mountains

Morph form or phase of an animal

Morphological relating to the form and structure of an organism

Nasolabial groove a groove running from the nostril to the upper lip in male plethodontid salamanders

Neonate the newborn young of a live-bearer

Neoteny condition in which a LARVA fails to METAMORPHOSE and retains its larval features as an adult. Species with this condition are said to be neotenic. The axolotl is the best-known example. See PEDOMORPHOSIS

Neotropics the tropical part of the New World, including northern South America, Central America, part of Mexico, and the West Indies

Newt amphibious salamanders of the genera *Triturus, Taricha,* and *Notophthalmus*

Niche the role played by a SPECIES in its particular community. It is determined by its food and temperature preferences; each species' niche within a community is unique

Nocturnal active at night

Nuptial pad an area of dark, rough skin that develops in male amphibians on the hands, arms, or chest of some SPECIES prior to the breeding season. Its purpose is to allow the male to grip the female in AMPLEXUS

Occipital lobe the pyramid-shaped area at the back of the brain that helps an animal interpret vision

Ocular of the eye

Olfactory relating to the sense of smell

Omnivore an animal that eats both animal and plant material

Order taxonomic category ranking below CLASS and above FAMILY

Osteoderm small bone in the skin of some reptiles; lies under the scales

Ovary female gonad or reproductive organ that produces the OVUM

Overwinter survive the winter

Oviduct the duct in females that carries the OVUM from the ovary to the CLOACA

Oviparous reproducing by eggs that hatch outside the female's body

IUCN CATEGORIES

EX **Extinct,** when there is no reasonable doubt that the last individual of the species has died.

EW **Extinct in the Wild,** when a species is known only to survive in captivity or as a naturalized population well outside the past range.

CR **Critically Endangered,** when a species is facing an extremely high risk of extinction in the wild in the immediate future.

EN **Endangered,** when a species is facing a very high risk of extinction in the wild in the near future.

VU **Vulnerable,** when a species is facing a high risk of extinction in the wild in the medium-term future.

LR **Lower Risk,** when a species has been evaluated and does not satisfy the criteria for CR, EN, or VU.

DD **Data Deficient,** when there is not enough information about a species to assess the risk of extinction.

NE **Not Evaluated,** species that have not been assessed by the IUCN criteria.

Ovoviviparous reproducing by eggs that the female retains within her body until they hatch; the developing eggs contain a yolk sac but receive no nourishment from the mother through a placenta or similar structure

Ovum (pl. ova) female germ cell or GAMETE; an egg cell or egg

Papilla (pl. papillae) aised projection(s) of soft tissue often seen on the head and neck of aquatic CHELONIANS

Parietal eye a VESTIGIAL eye situated in the top of the head of tuataras and some lizards, sometimes known as the "third eye"

Parietals pairs of bones forming the rear of the roof of the brain case

Parotid glands pair of large glands on the shoulder, neck, or behind the eye in some salamanders and toads

Parthenogenesis a form of asexual reproduction in which the OVUM develops without being fertilized. Such SPECIES are said to be parthenogenetic

Parturition the process of giving birth to live young

Pectoral girdle the skeleton supporting the forelimbs of a land vertebrate

Pedogenesis form of reproduction by an animal still showing LARVAL characteristics

Pedomorphosis the retention of immature or LARVAL characteristics, such as GILLS, by animals that are sexually mature. See NEOTENY

Permeable property of a substance, such as skin, allowing another substance, such as water, to pass through it

Pheromone a substance released by an organism to induce a response in another individual of the same SPECIES, such as sexual attraction

Phylum taxonomic category ranking above CLASS and below kingdom

Pigment a substance that gives color to part or all of an organism's body

Plastron the ventral portion, or underside, of the shell of a turtle

Pleurodont teeth teeth that are attached to the inside surface of the jaw, as opposed to the upper edge (ACRODONT) or in sockets (THECODONT)

Pond-type larva salamander LARVA with high fins and a deep body, adapted to living in still water. See STREAM-TYPE LARVA

Preanal pores chemical- or pheromone-secreting pores in front of the CLOACA, usually in lizards

Prehensile adapted for grasping or clasping, especially by wrapping around, such as the tail of chameleons

Preocular relating to the front of the eye

Ranching artificial incubation of eggs collected from the wild followed by captive-rearing of the young. A method used with both CHELONIANS and CROCODILIANS to increase population numbers, carried out in an environment free from predators

Rectilinear locomotion a form of movement used by heavy-bodied snakes in which the body progresses in a straight line

Riffle agitated water flowing over rocks or gravel in shallow streams or rivers

Rostral processes extensions to the snout, including horns and other ornamentation

Salt glands glands located in the vicinity of the eye that allow marine turtles and some CROCODILIANS to excrete excessive salt from their bodies, helping prevent them from becoming dehydrated in the marine environment

Satellite male a male frog that does not call but sits near a calling male and intercepts females attracted to the calling male

Savanna open grasslands with scattered trees and bushes, usually in warm areas

Scute enlarged scale on a reptile, including the colorful scales that cover the shell of turtles; divided into different groups, such as the vertebral scutes that run above the VERTEBRAL COLUMN

Sexual dimorphism the existence of marked morphological differences between males and females

Species taxonomic category ranking below GENUS; a group of organisms with common attributes capable of interbreeding and producing healthy fertile offspring

Spermatheca a pouch or sac in the female reproductive tract in which sperm are stored

Spermatophore a structure containing sperm that is passed from the male to the female in some animals, such as in many salamanders

Stream-type larva streamlined LARVA with low fins and elongated body, adapted for living in flowing water. See POND-TYPE LARVA

Subcaudal beneath the tail, as in "subcaudal" scales. See CAUDAL

Subocular usually refers to scales below the eye. See PREOCULAR

Subspecies a locally distinct group of animals that differ slightly from the normal appearance of the SPECIES; often called a race

Substrate the solid material on which an organism lives, e.g., sand, mud, etc.

Suture the zigzag patterning formed beneath the SCUTES where the bones of a CHELONIAN's shell fuse together

Tadpole LARVAL stage of a frog or toad

Talus slopes slopes covered with loose rocks and slabs. Also known as scree

Taxonomy the science of classification: the arrangement of animals and plants into groups based on their natural relationships

Temporal relating to the area between the eye and ear

Terrestrial living on land

Territorial defending an area so as to exclude other members of the same SPECIES

Territory an area that one or more animals defends against other members of the same SPECIES

Thecodont teeth growing in sockets. See ACRODONT

Thermoregulate to expose to or move away from a heat source in order to maintain desired body temperature

Thermoregulation control of body temperature by behavioral or physiological means, so that it maintains a constant or near-constant value

Thyroid gland a gland lying in the neck that produces the hormone THYROXINE

Thyroxine a hormone containing iodine that is involved in a variety of physiological processes, including METAMORPHOSIS in amphibians

Toad any stout-bodied, warty-skinned frog, especially one living away from water. The term has no TAXONOMIC basis, although members of the FAMILY Bufonidae are often called toads

Tongue-flicking constant use of the tongue by snakes and some lizards when exploring their surroundings. Used in conjunction with JACOBSON'S ORGAN

Tubercle a small, knoblike projection

Turtle any shelled reptile, including tortoises and terrapins

Tympanum (pl. tympana) eardrum

Unisexual species a SPECIES consisting only of females, in which reproduction is by PARTHENOGENESIS

Unken reflex a defensive posture shown by some amphibians when attacked, in which the body is arched inward with the head and tail lifted upward. Its purpose is to display a brightly colored underside

Uterine milk a uterine secretion that provides developing embryos with nourishment

Vent the CLOACAL opening of the body. Measurements of reptiles and amphibians are often given as "snout-vent" lengths or simply "s-v" lengths

Ventral describing the lower surface of the body or one of its parts

Vertebral column the spinal skeleton, or backbone, consisting of a series of vertebrae extending from the skull to the tip of the tail

Vertebrate a member of the subphylum Vertebrata, comprising all animals with a VERTEBRAL COLUMN, including fish, amphibians, reptiles, birds, and mammals

Vestigial smaller and of more simple structure than in an evolutionary ancestor. In reptiles and amphibians often used to describe limbs that have become reduced in size through the evolutionary process

Viviparous giving birth to living young that develop within and are nourished by the mother. Often used incorrectly, however, to describe any live-bearing species. See also OVOVIVIPAROUS

Volar pores pores on the underside of the feet

Webbing folds of skin present between the toes of both CROCODILIANS and aquatic CHELONIANS

Xeric adapted to life in an extremely dry habitat

Yolk sac a large sac containing stored nutrients, present in the embryos of fish, amphibians, reptiles, and birds

Further Reading

Alderton, D., ***Crocodiles and Alligators of the World.*** New York: Facts On File, 2004.

————. ***Turtles & Tortoises of the World***. New York: Facts On File, 2003.

Behler, J. L., and King, F. W., ***The Audubon Society Field Guide to North American Reptiles and Amphibians.*** New York: Alfred A. Knopf, 1979.

Bogert, C. M., and del Campo, R. M., ***The Gila Monster and its Allies.*** New York: Bulletin of the American Museum of Natural History, Volume 109, 1956.

Campbell, J. A., and Brodie, E. D. (eds.), ***Biology of the Pitvipers.*** Tyler, TX: Selva, 1992.

Dodd, C. K., ***North American Box Turtles: A Natural History.*** Norman, OK: University of Oklahoma Press, 2001.

Duellman, W. E., and Trueb, L., ***Biology of Amphibians.*** Baltimore, MA: Johns Hopkins University Press,1994.

Ernst, C. H., and Ernst, E. M., ***Snakes of the United States and Canada.*** Washington, DC: Smithsonian Books, 2003.

Halliday, T., and Adler, C. (eds.), ***The New Encyclopedia of Reptiles and Amphibians.*** New York and Toronto: Firefly Books, 2002; Oxford: Oxford University Press, 2002.

Henkel, F. W., and Schmidt, W., ***Geckos.*** Malabar, FL: Krieger Publishing Company, 1995.

Klauber, L. M., ***Rattlesnakes: Their Habits, Life Histories and Influence on Mankind.*** Berkeley, CA: University of California Press, 1997.

Klemens, M. W. (ed.), ***Turtle Conservation.*** Washington, DC: Smithsonian Institution Press, 2000.

Mattison, C., ***The Encyclopedia of Snakes.*** London: Blandford Press, 2002.

————. ***Frogs and Toads of the World.*** London: Blandford Press, 1998.

————. ***Rattler: a Natural History of Rattlesnakes.*** London: Blandford Press, 1998.

Nickerson, M. A., and Mays, C. E., ***The Hellbenders.*** Milwaukee, WI: Milwaukee Public Museum, 1972.

Parsons, H., ***The Nature of Frogs.*** Vancouver, Toronto, and New York: Greystone Books, 2000.

Petranka, J. W. ***Salamanders of the United States and Canada.*** Washington, DC and London: Smithsonian Institution Press, 1998.

Pianka, E. R., and Vitt, L. J., ***Lizards: Windows to the Evolution of Diversity.*** Berkeley, CA: University of California Press, 2003.

Rossman, D. A., Ford, N. B., and Seigel, R. A., ***The Garter Snakes: Evolution and Ecology.*** Norman, OK: University of Oklahoma Press, 1996.

Sherbrooke, W. C., ***Introduction to Horned Lizards of North America.*** Berkeley, CA: University of California Press, 2003.

Smith, H. M., ***Handbook of Lizards.*** Ithaca, NY: Cornell University Press, 1995.

Williams, K. L., ***Systematics and Natural History of the American Milksnake***, Lampropeltis triangulum. Milwaukee, WI: Milwaukee Public Museum, 1988.

Wright, A. H., and Wright, A. A., ***Handbook of Snakes of the United States and Canada.*** (2 vols.). Ithaca, NY: Cornell University Press, 1994.

Useful Websites

Frost, Darrel R. 2004. Amphibian Species of the World: an Online Reference. Version 3.0 (22 August, 2004). Electronic Database accessible at: **http://research.amnh.org/herpetology/ amphibia/index.php**
American Museum of Natural History, New York, USA

Myers, P. 2001. "Vertebrata" (Online), Animal Diversity. Accessible at: **http://animaldiversity.ummz.umich.edu/site/accounts/informati on/Amphibia.html**

http://www.anapsid.org/gartcare.html Devoted to the natural history and care in captivity of garter snakes

http://www.caudata.org/ An extensive website with information about caudates (newts and salamanders) throughout the world

http://www.chelonia.org/ Plenty of information and many links about tortoises and freshwater turtles

http://elib.cs.berkeley.edu/aw/index.html AmphibiaWeb, a site inspired by global amphibian declines, is an online system that allows free access to information on amphibian biology and conservation. Lists all known species of amphibians and gives species accounts, photographs, and distribution maps to some. New material is added constantly

http://www.embl-heidelberg.de/~uetz/LivingReptiles.html The University of Heidelberg reptile database. List of species with bibliographies and links to important references

http://www.flmnh.ufl.edu/natsci/herpetology/brittoncrocs/csp_ amis.htm Information on the American alligator and other crocodilians of the world

http://www.gekkota.com/ The website of the Global Gecko Association, with photos, caresheets, and links

http://www.greenigsociety.org/ Website of the Green Iguana Society provides information on iguana care as well as details of current iguana adoption and rescues throughout the United States and Canada

http://hellbenders.sanwalddesigns.com/index.shtml The hellbender home page, dedicated to the conservation of North American giant salamanders

http://www.kingsnake.com Many pages about reptiles and amphibians, especially their care in captivity, and links to other organizations

http://www.open.ac.uk/daptf/index.htm A website that records and documents information concerning endangered frogs and toads and the possible causes of their decline

http://www.rattlesnakes.com Web page of the American International Rattlesnake Museum, Albuquerque, New Mexico

http://research.amnh.org/herpetology/amphibia/index.html "Amphibian Species of the World." A catalogue of all amphibian species with synonyms and additional information, accessed with a good search engine

http://www.seaturtle.org/ A useful and active sea turtle conservation site

http://www.si.edu/resource/faq/nmnh/zoology.htm#vz General information about reptiles and amphibians and links to many educational sites

Index

Picture credits